THE COMMUNITY OF KENT AND THE GREAT REBELLION 1640–60

THE COMMUNITY OF KENT AND THE GREAT REBELLION 1640–60

by

ALAN EVERITT M.A., Ph.D., F.R.Hist.S.

Hatton Professor of English Local History
in the University of Leicester

LEICESTER UNIVERSITY PRESS

1973

FIRST PUBLISHED IN 1966 BY
LEICESTER UNIVERSITY PRESS

SECOND IMPRESSION 1973

PRINTED AND BOUND IN GREAT BRITAIN BY
UNWIN BROTHERS LIMITED
OLD WOKING, SURREY

ISBN 0 7185 1121 2

CONTENTS

MAPS

PREFACE

THIS BOOK is based principally on research undertaken between 1952 and 1957 for a doctoral thesis of the University of London. Since then it has been entirely rewritten in the light of further work on other counties—Suffolk, Leicestershire, and Northamptonshire—and upon Kentish society in other periods. In turning to different parts of the country, one quickly realizes one's good fortune in Kent, in the extraordinary wealth of manuscript material for the seventeenth century. The survival of so many family collections, particularly those of the Oxindens, Twysdens, Derings, and Peytons, enables one to sense with peculiar certainty the *genius* of that local environment in which Stuart politics took shape. One also realizes how well one has been served by county historians and local genealogists, whose work alone makes it possible to reconstruct the pattern of Kentish family life in this period.

I am under many obligations both to scholars and to archivists and librarians in London, Oxford, and Kent. Mr R. C. Latham of Royal Holloway College first kindled my interest in the subject, and his encouragement and criticism have been throughout invaluable. I am also indebted to the late Professor R. H. Tawney and to Professor S. T. Bindoff for advice on several chapters in their original form; to Professor David Underdown for his comments on the last two chapters; to Miss Veronica Wedgwood, who generously read and commented on the whole book; and to Professor H. P. R. Finberg and Professor Jack Simmons, without whose patient assistance it would not have been published. I should like to thank also the staffs of the Public Record Office, the British Museum, the Bodleian Library, the Institute of Historical Research, the University of London Library, the Kent County Archives Office, the Dean and Chapter Library at Canterbury, and the Maidstone Museum, for much courteous and unfailing help. I must also thank the Carnegie Trust for awarding me the scholarship which enabled me to complete my research and write this volume. The greater part of two chapters has already appeared in print, and I am grateful to the Leicester University Press and the Society of Genealogists for permission to reprint them: Chapter V was published in 1957 as No. 9 in the series of Occasional Papers issued by the Department of English Local History in the University of Leicester; most of Chapter II appeared as 'The Community of Kent in 1640' in *The Genealogists' Magazine*, XIV, viii, 1963. Finally, I am indebted to more fellow-students than I can name, in this country and in America, for drawing my attention to sources, for information on many points of detail, and for that quickening interchange of ideas without which this book would not have been written. For any imperfections and shortcomings I alone, of course, am responsible.

A.M.E.

University of Leicester

LIST OF ABBREVIATIONS

AC	*Archæologia Cantiana.*
BL	Bodleian Library.
BM	British Museum.
CAC	Canterbury Accounts Committee.
Carter	M[atthew] C[arter], *A most True and Exact Relation of that as Honourable as Unfortunate Expedition of Kent, Essex, and Colchester*, 1650.
CCAM	*Calendar of the Proceedings of the Committee for Advance of Money, 1642–1656* . . ., ed. M. A. E Green, 1888.
CCC	*Calendar of the Proceedings of the Committee for Compounding, etc., 1643–1660* . . ., ed. M. A. E. Green, 1889–92.
CCSP	*Calendar of the Clarendon State Papers preserved in the Bodleian Library*, I, ed. O. Ogle and W. H. Bliss, 1872, II and III, ed. W. D. Macray, 1869 and 1876.
CDB	Day Book of the Canterbury Accounts Committee.
CJ	*Journals of the House of Commons.*
Clarke Papers	*The Clarke Papers*, I–IV, ed. C. H. Firth, Camden Society, N.S., XLIX, 1891, LIV, 1894, LXI, 1899, LXII, 1901.
CSPD	*Calendar of State Papers, Domestic Series.*
CSPV	*Calendar of State Papers and Manuscripts, relating to English Affairs, existing in the Archives and Collections of Venice.*
DNB	*Dictionary of National Biography.*

E	Thomason Tracts, British Museum. (For brevity's sake each tract is cited by its reference number, as listed in the *Catalogue of the Pamphlets, Newspapers, and Manuscripts . . . collected by George Thomason, 1640–1661*, 1908.)
EcHR	*The Economic History Review.*
EHR	*The English Historical Review.*
F and R	*Acts and Ordinances of the Interregnum, 1642–1660*, ed. C. H. Firth and R. S. Rait, 1911.
Hasted	Edward Hasted, *The History and Topographical Survey of the County of Kent*, 2nd edn, I–XII, 1797–1801.
HMC	Historical Manuscripts Commission, *Reports.*
KCA	Kent County Archives Office, County Hall, Maidstone.
LAC	Central Accounts Committee, London.
L'Estrange his Vindication	Sir Roger L'Estrange, *L'Estrange his Vindication to Kent. And the Justification of Kent to the World . . .*, 1649, n.p.
LJ	*Journals of the House of Lords.*
Mordaunt LB	*The Letter Book of John Viscount Mordaunt, 1648–1660*, ed. Mary Coate, Camden Society, 3rd Ser., LXIX, 1945.
Nicholas Papers	*The Nicholas Papers*, I–IV, ed. G. F. Warner, Camden Society, N.S., XL, 1886, L, 1892, LVII, 1897, 3rd Ser., XXXI, 1920.
Proc. in K.	*Proceedings, principally in the County of Kent . . .*, ed. L. B. Larking, Camden Society, 1st Ser., LXXX, 1862.
PRO	Public Record Office.
RAC	Rochester Accounts Committee.
Rushworth	John Rushworth, *Historical Collections*, I–VII, 1721–22.

Sandwich Muniments	Muniments of the Corporation of Sandwich, formerly in Sandwich Guildhall, now in the Kent County Archives Office, County Hall, Maidstone.
SP	State Papers, Public Record Office.
Thurloe	*A Collection of the State Papers of John Thurloe, Esq.*, I–VII, ed. Thomas Birch, 1742.
TRHS	*Transactions of the Royal Historical Society.*
True and Exact Relation	*True and Exact Relation of the whole Proceedings of the Parliament's Force that went out under the Command of Colonel Brown . . .*, July 1643.
Twysden's Journal	'Sir Roger Twysden's Journal. From the Roydon Hall MSS', *Archæologia Cantiana*, I, 1858, II, 1860, III, 1859, IV, 1861.
Weller Papers	'Papers relating to Proceedings in the County of Kent, A.D. 1642–A.D. 1646', ed. R. Almack, *Camden Miscellany*, III, 1854 [Papers of Thomas Weller, an official of the County Committee of Kent].
Whitelock	Bulstrode Whitelock, *Memorials of the English Affairs*, 2nd edn, I–IV, 1853.

NOTE ON TRANSCRIPTION

In quoting from contemporary documents and tracts, and in citing titles of books and pamphlets, I have modernized spelling, punctuation, and capitalization, and extended abbreviations, except in a few instances where the original form is significant.

I

INTRODUCTORY

PERHAPS NO EVENT in English history tore aside the veil concealing the innermost secrets of society quite so ruthlessly as the Great Rebellion. During that momentous event the springs of human activity were opened up with a suddenness and completeness that terrified contemporaries and has fascinated historians ever since. The complexity of the revelation, the abundance of the source-material, and the variety of historical interpretations of the period are indeed bewildering. What justification is there for the approach to the problem adopted in this book: for isolating one single county and its gentry from the rest of England, and studying it on its own? The justification is a simple one. In many respects, despite its ancient centralized government, the England of 1640 resembled a union of partially independent county-states or communities, each with its own distinct ethos and loyalty. Of course, not all were equally independent; but the history and social structure of counties like Kent, Suffolk, Leicestershire, Staffordshire, Cumberland, and Cornwall were surprisingly dissimilar. One important aspect of the history of the Great Rebellion is certainly the gradual merging or submerging of these communities, under the stress of revolution, in the national community of the New Model Army and the Protectorate. Perhaps we have tended too much to look at the period through the eyes of the government, and especially of parliament. The social and political life of the vast majority of Englishmen, even among the gentry, was lived almost wholly within the confines of their county—their 'country' as they significantly called it. One of the principal reasons, I believe, for the growing unpopularity of parliament between 1640 and 1648, in many areas, was that an institution which most people, apart from politicians, regarded as an *extraordinary* means of government, to be summoned only in an emergency such as occurred in 1640, became the *normal* governmental institution, invading and controlling many spheres of life hitherto relatively independent. The county community, in other words, was compelled at last to give way to the community of the realm. Under the pressure of military and political forces, it was driven to sink its intense localism in the larger loyalties of the nation-state. The Great Rebellion, of course, neither began nor ended this historical phenomenon; but it marked perhaps one of the most decisive stages in its lengthy story.

This book attempts to trace the history of an English county in which both the political pressure of the central government and the independent attitude of the community to the state were exceptionally, and in some ways surprisingly, powerful. Kent was not a 'typical' county. The pressure was peculiarly intense because on the whole Kent was more in sympathy with the king than with parliament and yet, because of its isolation from other royalist shires, it never succeeded in escaping from the vice-like grip of parliamentary control. The grip was vice-like because of the strategic situation of the county, and because parliament simply could not afford to countenance rebellion so close at hand: more than once in past centuries—under men like Cade and Wat Tyler—the men of Kent had made the city of London tremble. The localism of the community was intense for many deep-seated and complex reasons peculiar to the society of the county. The secret of this localism historically is traced in the opening chapter of the book describing the story of the Kentish landscape and the history of the Kentish gentry. Contrary to what has usually been supposed, the gentry of Kent were not in general of mercantile or legal extraction. They were, in fact, unusually deeply-rooted in their native soil, temperamentally conservative, and excessively inbred. The county developed, in consequence, an individuality of its own in marked contrast to that of its sister-counties and London. "I speak of Kent intentionally," writes a modern author of his adopted county, "as a distinct personality, for one has only to live within its borders to think of it in that way . . ."[1] If his remark was true in 1963, it was far more so in 1640, and in particular among the gentry who formed the backbone of its patriarchal society.

[1] Richard Church reviewing D. P. Capper, *Moat Defensive*, in *Country Life*, 1963, p. 642.

By 1640, the local loyalties and the conservatism of the community of Kent had united the county, like most others, in opposition to the political autocracy and religious novelties (as most people regarded them) of Strafford and Laud. This unity of outlook lasted, despite a good deal of family rivalry, until 1642, when, under the pressure of national political events two small cliques of genuine royalists and ultra-parliamentarians emerged on either wing of the Kentish community, which at heart wished to remain neutral. Both cliques strove earnestly to secure the support of the community as a whole; but owing principally to the proximity of parliament, the Cavaliers were defeated, and the Roundheads succeeded in gaining control of the county and setting up a committee of the gentry to govern it. This situation produced a kind of concealed schizophrenia in the mentality of Kent. The sympathies of the bulk of the gentry veered mildly towards the king, because it was parliament that was now the innovator and autocrat; but circumstances forced them either to remain aloof from politics or to support the parliamentarian County Committee in the interests of local order. The king was aware of their latent sympathies and endeavoured on several occasions to force a way into the county and blockade London. A number of local risings took place in his favour; but the county was completely cut off from other royalist shires, and these rebellions were quickly crushed.

In these circumstances, the personal character of the parliamentarian leader of the county, Sir Anthony Weldon, was of vital importance. Though an able administrator, a man devoted to Kentish interests, and no friend to parliamentary autocracy, Weldon was personally detestable. His violence, spleen, and dictatorial methods gradually antagonized almost everyone in the county. Outwardly the Committee remained united; but inwardly it became increasingly antipathetic to parliament. The intense inbreeding and family feeling of the county made it possible for the leaven of opposition to work in secret, unrealized either by parliament or by Weldon himself, until by 1647 the whole community, outside Weldon's own immediate circle, was at heart virtually united against parliamentarian tyranny. It was the return of the Cavaliers from Oxford to

Kent, after the defeat of the king, that sparked off this explosive situation in the astonishing Rebellion of 1648. Contemporaries were amazed that a county apparently loyal to parliament should within a few days suddenly rise as one man against it. In part, the phenomenon was due to the excitable and temperamental Kentish character—the 'Kentish fire' of the old saying. But it is clear that deeper causes were also at work.

The story of this Rebellion illustrates how quickly a county movement could be organized in a society where ties of kinship counted for so much as in Kent. Essentially, the rising was a local and family affair. From the king's point of view, it was too much a local and family affair; for it was organized without reckoning either on royalist activity elsewhere or on the victorious power of the national New Model Army. The hard-won victory of Fairfax at Maidstone in 1648, and the consequent collapse of the reviving royalist hopes, in fact represented the victory of the nation-state of England over the 'county-state' of Kent: just as the formation of the New Model Army in 1645 had represented the victory of the same nation-state in East Anglia over powerful county communities such as that of Suffolk, which had hitherto strenuously opposed it.[1] In Kent, as a result of Fairfax's victory, the true political sentiments of the county once again went underground. The old County Committee had been destroyed in the Rebellion and there was now no institution of any kind through which those sentiments could express themselves. The greater county gentry and the galaxies of minor gentry dependent upon them remained neutral, and endeavoured to repair the injuries done to their estates by six years of warfare, sequestration, and composition fines.

In his efforts to govern the county in the 'fifties, Cromwell was thus compelled to rely, not on the natural leaders of the shire, but on a small clique of newer families who, unlike the older gentry, were intensely puritanical and politically minded. Essentially, these new conditions in the county were not different in kind from those in most other parts of the country;

[1] Cf. Alan Everitt, *Suffolk and the Great Rebellion, 1640–1660* (Suffolk Records Society, III), 1960, pp. 28–34.

but the contrast with the political and social conditions which had obtained in Kent in the 'forties was more pronounced than elsewhere because the revolution of 1648 had been more violent in Kent than in other counties. Unfortunately, Cromwell's attempts to win the sympathy of the community were even less successful than those of Charles I and parliament before him: ultimately his failure was due to precisely the same cause—the absence of support among the leading gentry of the county. The far-reaching power of these indigenous Kentish clans still worked, if in a hidden and half-conscious way, through countless secret channels against him. Such families had no special love for the Stuarts, but the way of life to which they were accustomed could not survive without a more stable form of government than that of the Protectorate. They longed to return to the old days before the war, which seemed in retrospect, however mistakenly, so placid and secure: days when there had been no army, no major-generals, no restless plotting, no sectarian experimentation, and no incessant spying upon those quiet manor-houses whose unquestioned dominion and ordered, tranquil life was the only kind of existence they could understand. The profound spiritual insights that accompanied the vagaries of some of the sects, and the demand of an expanding mercantile class for greater independence, were as far beyond their mental horizon as the cravings of the Cavaliers to escape from the fetters of puritan repression and rural tradition.

It was the paradox of Cromwell's régime that in one sense its very measure of success was the cause of its own downfall. If it was based upon the victory of the nation-state over the county community, it also, in the end, created that longing apparent in all parts of the country to return to older forms of society and government whose genius was essentially provincial and local. Much of the secret of the success of General Monck in restoring Charles II depended on the fact that in so many county communities, separately and independently, the gentry united to present their own *local* petitions in favour of a restored parliament and a more stable government. How far the counties were successful in achieving their desire to return to the older and more local forms of life is a question whose complex answer would take us far beyond the year 1660 and the bounds set for this study. In many ways it was inevitable that the diversities in provincial life should become assimilated to a national pattern of existence; certainly that pattern came increasingly to be expressed in the kind of social life that centred round Westminster, and the commercial life of the port and city of London. Yet it is safe to say that the power of the county gentry in ordering the life of the community of Kent after 1660 was not less than it had been before 1640. The monarchy was restored and for the time being the Cavaliers were to all appearance pre-eminent. The outward fashions of rural society changed with the changing fashions of the nation. Here and there rich businessmen like the Bankses and Furneses bought up country estates and married into the ancient families of the county.[1] But for another century or more, the community of Kent as a whole remained as insular and as inbred as ever. Its intractability had survived the onslaught of Charles I's conciliar government and the autocracy of Oliver Cromwell. Its eventual submission to the all-pervasive authority of the state, in the nineteenth century, was brought about rather by the gradual processes of social and economic change, both within and without the shire, than by the edicts of Westminster or Whitehall.[2]

[1] For the influx of new wealth after 1660, see D. C. Coleman, *Sir John Banks: Baronet and Businessman*, 1963, and 'London Scriveners and the Estate Market in the Later Seventeenth Century', EcHR, 2nd Ser., IV, 1951–2, pp. 221–30. It is noteworthy, however, that most of the families whom Dr Coleman mentions in the latter article as selling or mortgaging their property were either relative newcomers to Kent or heirs to reckless Cavaliers; they rarely represented the major native gentry of 1640–60.

[2] A useful popular outline of events in Kent during the Great Rebellion is contained in H. F. Abell, *Kent and the Great Civil War*, 1901. In the following chapters I have only occasionally relied on Abell's statements, however, since they are rarely supported by exact references, apart from a few obvious sources such as Twysden's Journal and Carter's *True Relation*.

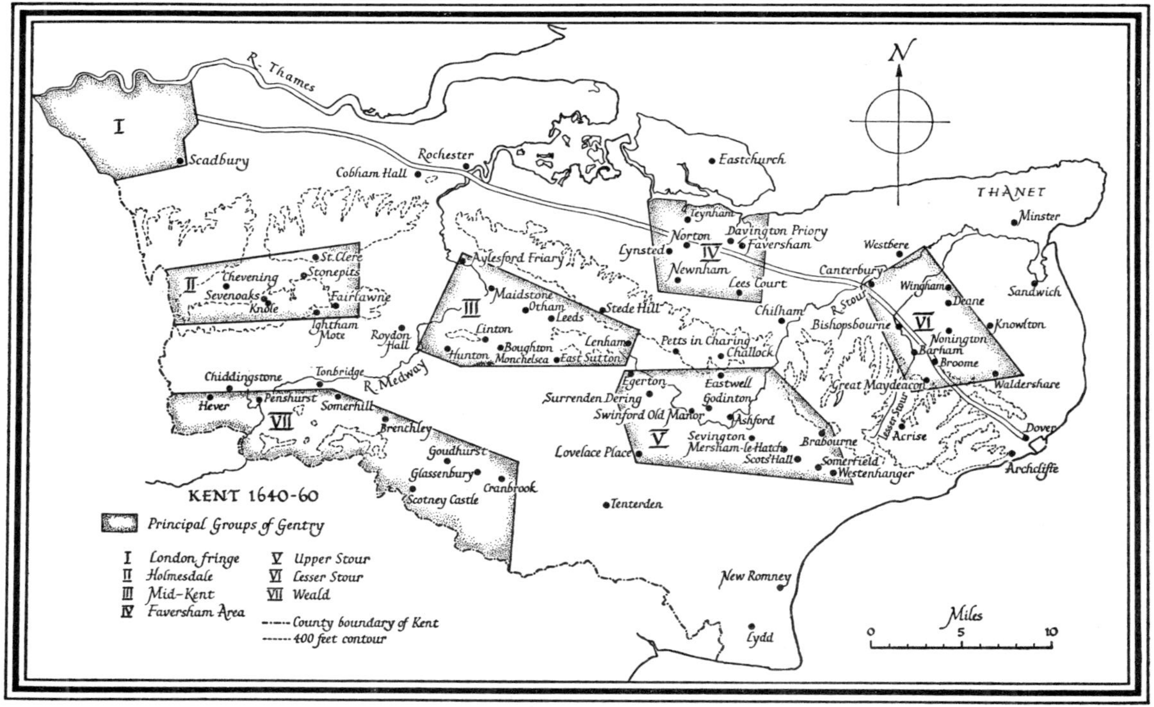

The map does not indicate all gentle-family seats but only those mentioned in the text of Chapter II.

II

THE COMMUNITY OF KENT IN 1640

(i) *The Kentish Landscape*

IF THE TRAVELLER today looks out from Ide Hill, down the steep oak-clad escarpment, southward and eastward over miles of tiny fields, the endless network of Wealden boundaries and lanes stretching away towards Hever and Penshurst, he sees broadly the same maze of fields and woods and villages that travellers saw in 1640:

> "Meadow and orchard, garden of fruit and hops,
> A green, wet country on a bed of clay,
> From Edenbridge to Appledore and Lympne
> Drained by the Medway and the Rother stream,
> With forest oaks still hearty in the copse,
> Sylva Anderida to Romans. Here
> Stretched Andredsweald, and joined the wood of Blean,
> Forest and warren, cropped by herds of deer."[1]

The rural scenery of modern Kent has not changed so much as the scenery of the Midland counties. The prospect from Ide Hill and many another eminence in the county is substantially the same as it was in 1640, and it was then already ancient. Antiquity, indeed, was perhaps the salient fact in the seventeenth-century history of the county: antiquity shot through with vivid threads of change and revolution.

There were, and still are, six Kents, covering a million acres and stretching 70 miles east and west, and of each area this theme was broadly true: of the Marshland from the Thames past the Swale to Thanet Minster; of the Downland with its southern scarp and winding northward valleys; of the wooded ragstone hills and Holmesdale; of the Low Weald with its many 'dens'; of the High Weald with its ridge of 'hurst' villages; or again of the Marsh from Stone to New Romney.

[1] The quotation is from Victoria Sackville-West's poem *The Land*.

The towns themselves were then largely rural. Sandwich, with three ancient churches, a receding river, and many aliens, was declining. Maidstone, the market town of Wealden yeomen and the youthful metropolis of West Kent, was expanding. Its single parish church, though the largest in the county, could not hold its 3,000 or so inhabitants, and on the Sabbath puritan townsmen attended outlying villages like Otham. Episcopal Rochester, with the expanding town of Chatham, looked out on the king's ships in the Medway; and royal Dover and its castle looked nervously towards France. There were a dozen little market towns, mostly with under 1,000 inhabitants, like Tenterden, Ashford, and Cranbrook in the Weald, or Lydd and New Romney in the Marsh, or Faversham next the levels by the Swale; with another score of market villages scattered in all parts of the county. But the most important town was Canterbury, with twenty parishes, 6,000 inhabitants, the ruins of half-a-dozen monasteries, a circuit of medieval walls, and a dominating cathedral. Few of its townsmen but clothworkers were conscious in 1640 of its impending decline. Many gentry gathered about it, and its churches are still full of their monuments: Haleses and Harfleetes and Culpepers; Lovelaces, Wottons, Hardreses, and Boyses. But Canterbury, which supplied but 2 per cent of the county's revenue in the sixteen-forties, scarcely dominated the county as Exeter dominated Devon.[1] Few Kentish towns were important industrially; primarily they were markets for the produce of Kentish fields.

It seems to be a commonly accepted view that the society of the south-eastern counties in the seventeenth century was largely an offshoot of London; that compared with Devon or Yorkshire a county like Kent had little individuality; that its members were lawyers or merchants transplanted a generation or two since and often retaining their London connexions. Lambarde himself is often cited in evidence of this thesis:

[1] D. C. Coleman, *The Economy of Kent under the later Stuarts* (London Ph.D. thesis), 1951, chapters I, V, pp. 186–96; V. E. Morant, *The Historical Geography of Maidstone* (London M.A. thesis), 1948, chapter V; SP. 28: 130, Charles Bowles's Receiver General Account Books; Alan Everitt, chapter on 'Marketing' in forthcoming *Agrarian History of England*, IV, ed. Joan Thirsk.

"The gentlemen be not here (throughout) of so ancient stocks as elsewhere, especially in the parts nearer to London, from which city (as it were from a certain rich and wealthy seedplot) courtiers, lawyers, and marchants be continually translated and do become new plants amongst them."

Sir Keith Feiling speaks of the county's "innumerable homes of the legal, professional, and crown-service families," and describes its royalism as "peculiarly metropolitan and trimmer." Mr Peter Laslett, in his admirable article on 'The Gentry of Kent in 1640,' has even suggested that "the home counties . . . had a far greater unity with each other than each had within itself."[1] It is obvious that the nearer a county lay to the capital the more powerful metropolitan influence was likely to be. But the curious fact about the Great Rebellion, so far as the southern counties are concerned, is how little sense of solidarity there was between them as compared, for example, with the counties of the Eastern Association. It is safe to say that a gentleman of Kent had no more sense of community with one of Hertfordshire or Hampshire than with one of Devon or Lincolnshire. In the particular case of Kent, moreover, the extent of the county and the careful qualifications implicit in the remarks of Lambarde need to be taken into account.[2] Kent is a peninsula; Canterbury is in fact further from London than Cambridge, and Sandwich as far as Market Harborough. Apart from Watling Street, the roads of the county were notoriously bad, and many villages were completely isolated in winter months. In visiting Kent in the mid-eighteenth century, Horace Walpole remarked that about Lamberhurst "the roads grew bad beyond all badness, the night dark beyond all darkness, and

[1] William Lambarde, *A Perambulation of Kent*, 1826 edn, p. 6; K. Feiling, *A History of the Tory Party, 1640–1714*, 1924, p. 16; T. P. R. Laslett, 'The Gentry of Kent in 1640', *Camb. Hist. Jnl*, IX, ii, 1948, pp. 152, 163. I owe much in this chapter to Mr Laslett's illuminating study. Dr D. C. Coleman has recently supported Sir Keith Feiling's view in his study *Sir John Banks: Baronet and Businessman*, 1963, pp. 97, 170. But although Banks represented a social phenomenon of increasing importance in the county, he was far from typical of post-restoration society in Kent as a whole.

[2] The operative word, in this connexion, is "throughout:" in Lambarde's own area, near London, the gentry were not for the most part of ancient stock; elsewhere, as the following pages show, they were.

our guide frightened beyond all frightfulness."[1] Even within the orbit of London the ancient ways still lingered surprisingly. Caxton had averred that the dialect of his native Weald was "as broad and rude English as [in] any place in England;" and in Holmesdale the wild red deer still roamed at will, within 25 miles of St Paul's. In fact the most striking political feature of Kent during 1640–60 was precisely its insularity. Both the elections of 1640 and the petition of 1642 were primarily expressions of county sentiment, and the insurrections of 1643 and 1648 appealed, if bombastically, to the legend of the unconquered county. "Bravely resolved, great hearts," one would-be poet addressed his countrymen,

> "I see some good
> Is still remaining, and that daring blood
> Of your unconquered ancestors curvetts
> In your quick veins where mounting honour sits . . ."[2]

No doubt such remarks were mere sentiment; but it does not need the seventeenth century to tell the twentieth that the political nation is as much moved by sentimentality as common sense. During the reign of the county committees between 1642 and 1660, moreover, no body of gentry wielded more power than those of Kent.[3] Such independence is difficult to reconcile with a society whose connexions lay primarily with London. What kind of families were in fact comprised in the history of the gentry? What were the roots of the Kentish economy?

As in much of the West and North of England, it was centuries since the open-field system, so far as it ever existed, had given place to enclosure and the typical Kentish landscape of today: with its isolated manors and denes, its scattered settlement, its small estates, and irregular fields. The whole property of Henry Oxinden, a gentleman of East Kent, probably covered little more than 600 acres. In Marden in the Weald the farms were "in general small, the houses of them ancient well-

[1] Quoted in Thomas Burke, *Travel in England*, 1942, p. 71.

[2] BM, Harl. MS 6918, f. 34; cf. *Halesiados: a Message from the Normans to the General of the Kentish Forces*, 1648.

[3] See Chapter v, *infra*.

timbered buildings, standing dispersed at wide distances, many of them on the different greens or forstals throughout the parish." About Edenbridge the farmhouses were "old-fashioned timber buildings, standing single and much dispersed. . . ." Northwards from the River Eden the country was

"very much covered with woods, among them are situated Sharp's Place, Boar Place, and . . . Boar's Hill . . . which names, among many others of the like import hereabouts, certainly took their origin from the wild boars formerly in plenty in these parts. . . . There are many greens and small hamlets in different parts of it as Wickhurst Green, Bough Beech, Hill Hoath, Carey's Cross, Ranesley Heath, and others."

The same dispersal and slow organic growth was found in the hamlets of the Downland, with their small and lonely churches, flint-strewn fields, and woods of yew and whitebeam. There had been few lost villages and no widespread Tudor enclosure in Kent, as in the Midlands, to sweep away county landmarks; there were few overmighty landlords or absentees, and the transition from medieval to modern, if in some ways more complete than elsewhere, had been comparatively gradual.[1] The wide diffusion of landownership did not offer the large opportunities so desirable in the eyes of Midland graziers and the greater *nouveaux-riches*. In this important respect an estate in Kent was a less attractive proposition to wealthy courtiers and metropolitan businessmen than one in an open field county offering the prospect of widespread enclosure, such as Northamptonshire. And in fact Stuart Northamptonshire was certainly more dominated by its new magnates than Stuart Kent; just as the textile regions of Suffolk and the West Country were more dominated by clothing magnates than the Weald.[2] In many ways the history of Kentish lathes and parishes had been one of relative continuity and conservatism.

[1] H. L. Gray, *English Field Systems*, 1915, pp. 415–18; C.S. and C.S. Orwin, *The Open Fields*, 1938, pp. 59, 64; Hasted, VII, p. 53, III, pp. 180, 211; M. W. Beresford, *The Lost Villages of England*, 1954, pp. 358–9.

[2] In Defoe's time Wiltshire clothiers were often worth £10,000 to £40,000: a different order of wealth from those in Stuart Kent.—*A Tour through England and Wales*, Everyman edn, I, p. 281.

Within this conservative framework, it is true, there had been a remarkable increase in wealth. Gradually, from its midway place in the subsidies of the Hundred Years' War, Kent had risen in wealth to second or third place among English counties by 1640–50. During the past century fruit farming had begun to bring prosperity within a pattern of small farms like the celebrated Teynham Newgardens:[1]

"... Rich Teynham undertakes thy closets to suffice
With cherries, which, we say, the summer in doth bring ...
Whose golden gardens seem th' Hesperides to mock:
Nor there the damson wants, nor dainty apricock ...
The pearmain, which to France long ere to us was known,
Which careful fruiterers now have denizen'd our own ..."[2]

Some metropolitan fruiterers were already buying up the prospective crop of Kentish orchards in the rich lands alongside Watling Street; a few seem to have purchased orchards themselves. Factors bought hops for London brewers, chiefly from the populous Canterbury area, where there seems to have been a rudimentary hop-exchange. Wheat was sent in large quantities to the capital from the ports of the northern seaboard, and some Thanet gentry exported their barley harvest from convenient little harbours like Margate.[3] "It is one of the best cultivated counties of any in England," said a traveller from Berkshire after the Restoration,

"and great part of my way that I went [to Dover] being through delicious orchards of cherries, pears, and apples, and great hop-gardens. In husbandry affairs they are very neat, binding up all sorts of grain in sheaves; they give the best wages to labourers of any in England, in harvest giving 4 and 5 shillings for an acre of wheat and 2*s.* a day meat and drink, which doth invite many stout workmen hither from the neighbouring country to get in their harvest."[4]

[1] Cf. pp. 158–9 *infra*; Morant, *op. cit.*, pp. 196–7.

[2] Michael Drayton, *Poly-Olbion*.

[3] PRO, Req. 2. 34/38, 35/92, 61/39, 97/55; C. 2. James I. H. 13. 24; SP. 14: 112, No. 12. i; cf. F. J. Fisher, 'The Development of the London Food Market, 1540–1640', EcHR, v, ii, 1935, pp. 46–64.

[4] HMC, XIII, ii, p. 280. The writer is Thomas Baskerville.

It would be a mistake, however, to suppose that fruit and hops were generally cultivated for the market by any but the larger farmers. Their culture struck contemporary travellers because the Dover road passed through the principal fruit and hop-growing area of the county; elsewhere, on the Downs and in the Weald and Marshland, orchards and hop-gardens were a rarity. For the majority of Kentishmen the dominant interests were still sheep and cattle farming in the Weald, arable husbandry on the Downs, and pasture with some grazing in the Marshlands. In the Isle of Harty, for example, Mr Samuel Thornhill pastured over 1,300 sheep on the 490-acre meadows and salts of Longhouse Farm. A minor gentleman of Tenterden, Edward Austen, left a personal estate of nearly £1,000, including 96 sheep, ten oxen, 33 other cattle, and £50 worth of corn. A large Downland farmer, Arthur Seath of Rodmersham, kept nearly 200 acres under crops, including 108 acres of wheat. Stephen Hulkes of Newnham, an unusually wealthy yeoman, owned 894 sheep and 49 cattle pastured in summer time in Romney Marsh, where there was a lodge and an "old removable house," and in winter time on the Downs: an ancient custom of transhumance which survives in places to the present day. One of the greater Downland gentry, Sir George Sondes of Lees Court, records that besides flax and hops he

"had at least one hundred head of great cattle, half a hundred horses, . . . some of them being worth forty or fifty pounds apiece . . . five hundred sheep, besides other stock: about a thousand quarters of wheat and malt in granaries, and ten barns (none of the least) all full of good corn. . . ."[1]

It was mainly East Kent that shared in this agricultural prosperity. There had always been a marked difference between the seaward East and the landward West: "a remarkable combination of advanced civilization on the one hand, which prevailed along Roman roads . . . and on the other of the very primitive conditions natural to fen and deep wood." It was

[1] PRO, E. 178. 1158 (a case of 37 Eliz. I; cp. E. 178. 1105); KCA, PRC, 28/5, f. 9; PRC, 10/35, f. 428; PRC, 28/9, f. 270; Harleian Miscellany, x, *Sir George Sondes his Plain Narrative . . .*, 1655, p. 65.

rarely the elegant 'gentlemen's seats' of a later age, set in the countryside, but not truly of it. Each was a genuine farmhouse as well as a manorial hall, the centre of its parish or community, a microcosm of rural society. Their fields came up to the garden quickfriths and the barns adjoined their courtyards. At Boughton Monchelsea Place, in addition to the great barn and stables, there were a court room, milkhouse, stillinghouse, wheat loft, brewhouse, fish-house, boultinghouse, bakehouse, workhouse chamber, 'seller,' and buttery surrounding the yard; the dining room, parlour, gallery, great hall, nursery, wardrobe, kitchens, chambers, and garrets looked into the court and down the steep hillside to the fishponds; across the lawn lay the church, and beyond it the Weald stretched many miles away towards Romney Marsh. In the house of a junior branch of the Dering family at Egerton, in addition to gallery, 'dormy chamber,' wainscot chamber, 'fair ceiled parlour,' and hall, there were a wheat loft, 'buntinghouse,' milkhouse, brewhouse, malthouse, outhouses, and a chamber for their men.[1]

Few such houses were entirely new, and none except Cobham could rival the Jacobean palaces of the Midlands like Burghley, Wollaton, or Hardwick. Hexagonal Chilham and its oriels was a modest fantasy of the Diggeses, set beside their Norman keep. Scots' Hall and Penshurst were essentially medieval houses, added to by each succeeding generation. Cobham Hall, which was said to have cost Lord Cobham £60,000, was the most palatial Kentish mansion, and its park was "a place which will feast the spectator's eyes with delightful objects. Fair lawns bedecked with flourishing groves of yew, oak, teal, and hawthorn trees, under which the nimble deer and coneys do sport the time away."[2] A small but notable group of houses followed the new Palladian manner of the Carolean court: Chevening Place, Lees Court, Norton Court, and St Clere. But these all occupied the old site and often incorporated part of the original building and foundations; few houses were like Somerhill, quite newly built by an Irish

[1] MSS of Michael Winch, Esq., Boughton Monchelsea Place, Inventory of Belknap Rudstone; KCA, PRC, 28/8, f. 101.

[2] HMC, XIII, ii, p. 281 (teal = teil, i.e. linden or lime tree).

peer on a windy hilltop.[1] The typical pattern of domestic architecture in Kent consisted of a Saxon or Norman site, a medieval building, with Tudor accretions, and Jacobean embellishments. Such settlements were founded in hundreds in Kent in the two centuries following the Norman Conquest, carved by freemen out of the Wealden forest or the woods on the ragstone charts and chalk downlands. Many, like Outridge, surviving today as a stone cottage in a remote valley near Westerham, were destined to remain farmhouses for the rest of their existence; others, like Knole a few miles to the east, developed from farms to manor-houses and manors to palaces or castles in successive generations. The history of each one was unique, although the origins of so many of them were similar. Between the fourteenth-century towers of Scotney Castle, set on an island in a lake in the Weald, the Darells had built a Tudor manor-house, and on the site of the great hall they added a suite of Palladian chambers. When the county committeemen rode their horses through the Green Court of Knole and met in the Poets' Parlour, it was not simply a Jacobean palace but Archbishop Bourchier's building they were entering: parts of it probably of the thirteenth century, in plan medieval, and as early as 1469 described as the 'great house' of the archbishops.[2] Many families, like the Culpepers at Leeds, still lived in medieval castles, and probably more than a hundred in moated and fortified manor-houses of the later middle ages, like the Selbys at Ightham Mote, and a branch of the Fanes at Hunton Court. The majority inhabited the fourteenth-to-sixteenth century 'hall houses' still so numerous in Kent, of which some were large, like Brenchley Palace or Finchden, and many, like Nizel's Hoath, little more than yeomen's houses. Edward Austen's home at Tenterden consisted of a hall, buttery, two parlours, four chambers, and the garrets above them; that of the Boyses of Challock on the Downs was still smaller—a hall, kitchen, closet, milkhouse, cheesehouse, and two chambers.[3] In the sixteenth century these houses were

[1] *Country Life*, 1920, pp. 512–18, 1922, pp. 178–80, 211–15, 310–16.

[2] V. Sackville-West, *Knole and the Sackvilles*, 1958 edn, p. 22; F. R. H. Du Boulay, 'A Note on the Rebuilding of Knole by Archbishop Bourgchier', AC, LXIII, pp. 135–9.

[3] KCA, PRC, 28/5, ff. 9, 73.

often much altered, the central halls divided and their end-chambers extended and multiplied. Some, like Godinton, were quite transformed: with its mullions and Dutch gables it appears a large Elizabethan manor-house, but its brick front screens the splendid fourteenth-century roof of a timber hall-house which the Tokes, long seated at neighbouring Swinford Old Manor, acquired about 1480 by marrying the heiress of the Goldwells, who themselves originated at neighbouring Goldwell. Such conservatism was natural when a house descended from heir to heir of the family as each generation added and altered, and there were many such families in Kent. By 1640 the Belkes had been at Coperham Sole for at least four centuries. The Robertses, or Rookhersts, had been at Rookehurst for 274 years when they married the neighbouring heiress of the "fair sumptuous house" in "the valley of Glassenbury," where by 1640 they had lived a further 250 years. Or if houses passed from hand to hand, it was generally through Kentish hands that they passed: as the inheritance of the Aldrindens of Aldrinden passed to the Selbrittendens, and from the Selbrittendens to the Twysdens—all families, as their names suggest, of Wealden origin.[1]

Such houses were always built of local materials; there were no Kentish mansions of imported stone like Audley End in Essex. Knole was built from stone dug principally in small quarries in the park: such 'petts' or pits often survive near ragstone manor-houses today, and they often influenced both siting and name, as at Petts in Charing and Stonepits in Seal. Towards Sussex the soft bright sandstone of Penshurst and Hever was used; on the Downs, flints and clunch, as at Davington Priory; in the Weald and other parts, oak timbers cut green and unseasoned; or perhaps, as when the Boyses built Boys Hall, the 'old frame' of a neighbouring house like Sevington Mote was re-used. In larger manor-houses, such as Surrenden Dering and Roydon Hall, the new small red bricks were popular, and a man like Sir Edward Dering or Sir Roger Twysden would have his own brick-kiln. When Basil Dixwell

[1] *Country Life*, 1962, pp. 1396 sqq.; John Harris, *History of Kent*, 1719, p. 280; W. Tarbutt, *Annals of Cranbrook Church*, 1873, II, p. 34, and monuments in Cranbrook church; Hasted, VII, p. 161.

built Broome, "there were used about the house, outhouses, and walling twenty and seven thousand bricks which he made." Much care was spent in embellishing these buildings. The palatial additions of the Sackvilles at Knole were not exceptional, but typical of those of many far humbler men, like Henry Oxinden of Great Maydeacon, who in "1640 . . . wainscotted my great parlour, wainscotted, birthed and ceiled the withdrawing room, made the door going into the garden, birthed the room over it, and made the two windores out of them next the garden." On another occasion Oxinden "new builded the well house, and made the well. . . ." In 1633 he "new builded the brewhouse, and milkhouse, and that part of the entry belongs to them with the rooms over them: paved the said brewhouse and milkhouse, new hung and new mended the copper and brewing vessels." Altogether he spent £1,420 between 1629 and 1649 in improving the little manor-house of his grandfather.[1] In most houses the original features were preserved, and in particular many medieval chapels. Sometimes a new chapel was added, as at St Clere in 1633, or prayer closets like that at Knole, where books of private devotion, sometimes compiled by the family itself, were kept. At Godinton, the profits of seventy years' farming by Nicholas Toke were lavished in ornamenting hall and solar, where a remarkable carved frieze depicts the exercising of the Kentish militia, of which Toke was a captain.

Gardens and outbuildings received similar attention. In 1640 Henry Oxinden "made my brick gate, as it now stands, with part of the wall before the house, and the oaken gates to it, set up rails before it, paved the way from it with Purbeck stone and built and leaded the porch." In his garden he

"walled in forty six rods of stone wall at £2 10*s*. the rod . . . making and levelling my flower garden and artichoke garden, carrying out all the rubbage, and bringing in mould, levelling of it, quick-setting it, planting it, making the summer houses, and setting up the frame for the vines, making the pear garden and the terrace walk in it."

[1] Hasted, VII, p. 567; BM, Add. MS 34162, *passim*; Loan 18, Capel Cure MSS, Henry Oxinden's Diary and Memorandum Book; KCA, U. 47. 3. E 1. 'Birth' is a Kentish word for laying a floor.

In 1635 Oxinden planted "my cherry gardens . . . there being thereof ten acres, cost then £100," and in 1638 the hop-garden and kitchen garden next it. In 1645 he planted "the 2 yew trees in my well house court and the hithermost holly tree . . . cleaned the pond in my place . . . planted the yew tree next the pigeon house in the garden at South Barham." Such new planting gave occasion for a little convivial ceremony at which Henry's son Thomas, or cousin Henry Oxinden of Deane planted an oak tree, pear, or cob. At the same time, Oxinden's neighbour Basil Dixwell of Broome was planting apples and ash friths in Coles Dane, and "his orchard against his back door against the hall." His widow later planted an "hundred walnut trees about the house . . . in the base court," and his brother John Dixwell, one of the Cromwellian regicides, built the dovehouse.[1]

No doubt there was idyllicism in Ben Jonson's well-known lines on Penshurst, a manor-house which cast a spell over other poets than he; but Sir Edward Dering was not unique when, returning from Oxford in 1644, he described the air of his native county as "the sweetest air in the land. . . ."[2] These men unaffectedly loved their county—their 'country' as they called it. The care of an estate like Dering's involved unremitting labour, but for such a man it was a labour of love. During the puritan revolution there were many thousands in Kent and other counties who thought little of abstract liberty who yet cared much for the freedom to enjoy their birthright, as they would have described it, and for whom their native shire was a little kingdom worth fighting for—something unique, and independent, and their own.

(ii) *The Kentish Gentry*

The number of gentry in Kent in 1640 was exceptionally large, at least 800 and possibly more than 1,000:[3] a figure that may

[1] BM, Loan 18, Capel Cure MSS, Henry Oxinden's Memorandum Book.

[2] Sir Edward Dering, *A Discourse of Proper Sacrifice . . .*, 1644.

[3] The following account is based upon the history of the 170 families (of these 800–1,000 gentry) who formed the dominant group in county government between 1640 and 1660, on both the parliamentarian and royalist sides,

seem surprising but resembles that of other counties of comparable size or economy, like Somerset or Suffolk. Many parts of England still predominantly unenclosed or under the rule of a great lord usually supported fewer armigerous families. Wiltshire, with an acreage four-fifths that of Kent, probably had under one-third the number of gentry. In Leicestershire, a county slightly more than half the size of Kent, there were about 350.[1] The Kentish figure is less surprising when it is remembered that at least three-quarters of these families probably possessed only one or two manors. Their sphere was the parish rather than the county, and, as the monuments in Kentish churches show, many parishes contained half-a-dozen such men as Henry Oxinden of Great Maydeacon, with his 600 acres or so. Such parochial gentry would very rarely aspire to parliament, and few of them ever sat on the Bench of Justices. They shone instead as lesser stars ranged in the larger constellations of *county* gentry, like the

---

including all the peers (10) and baronets (31) and most of the knights (50) in the county. If it had been possible to study the remaining (mostly minor) gentry, the picture would probably be even more conservative than it is. By 1660 the establishment of a few new families had increased this total of 170 to 179. The principal sources used include Hasted; W. Berry, *Pedigrees of the Families in the County of Kent*, 1830; G. E. Cockayne, *Complete Baronetage* and *Complete Peerage*; Burke, *Landed Gentry*, 1937 edn; MS collections relating to various families in the BM and KCA; and many genealogical articles in *Archaeologia Cantiana*, genealogical journals, and family and parish histories. Genealogically, Kent has been far better served by historians and antiquarians than many counties. For the number of gentry, the Heralds' Visitations of 1619 and 1663–8 cannot be relied on: they list only about 300, and include only one-third of the 170 principal gentry in the county. A contemporary estimate of 600–700 gentry in Kent (*Letter from a Gentleman in Kent*, 1648) is also an underestimate. Approximately 275 Kentish gentry at some time sat on the parliamentarian County Committee, 500 compounded as royalist 'delinquents,' and many remained neutral.

[1] The figure for Somerset is based on information kindly supplied by Dr T. G. Barnes; for Suffolk cf. Alan Everitt, *Suffolk and the Great Rebellion, 1640–1660* (Suffolk Records Society, III), 1960, p. 26; for Wiltshire see *Vict. County Hist.*, *Wiltshire*, V, p. 122, where Professor Bindoff suggests a figure of 285 families in the county in 1623; in Yorkshire, about 1642, there were 679 identifiable landed gentry (*Past and Present*, XXVIII, July 1964, p. 64); the figure for Leicestershire is based on information collected for my forthcoming study on *Leicestershire and the Great Rebellion*.

Oxindens of Deane, whose estates extended over several parishes.

Socially and politically, most English counties were dominated either by a single great family, like the Derbys in Lancashire, or by two or three rivals as in Leicestershire and Somerset, or by a knot of closely related families of comparable standing. Kent was among these last. It was not a county of lordly magnates, like Georgian Northamptonshire. Of the peers, only the earl of Thanet was of much weight locally. With an income apparently of £10,000, his family was the wealthiest in the county; but much of his property lay in Sussex and his influence was confined to the area between Ashford and Maidstone.[1] Of the remaining peers, the duke of Lennox and the earls of Dorset and Leicester concerned themselves with national rather than county affairs; the earl of Winchilsea and Viscount Strangford were minors, and Lords Teynham and Abergavenny recusants. The ancient dominance of the Cobhams had been destroyed by James I, and no one had yet replaced them. The real leaders of Kentish society were composed, besides Thanet, of twenty or thirty related 'county' families such as the Derings, Haleses, Twysdens, Scotts, Diggeses, and Oxindens of Deane as a *group*. Most of these families comprised several separately established branches and they were not usually in origin distinct from the lesser or 'parochial' gentry, who were often drawn from their junior scions. Thus the Boyses numbered two knightly and eight untitled or parochial families, the Finches one peer, one knight, and seven minor men. The existence of such 'clans,' with many separately established branches, was not a phenomenon peculiar to Kent; but, probably through the influence of gavelkind tenure, it was a far more striking feature of Kentish society than of counties like Suffolk, Leicestershire, or Northamptonshire. By 1640, in each case, one branch of the family, in general the eldest, had extended the ancestral patrimony beyond the parish borders and attained a place among the natural leaders of the county community. Their connexions spread far and wide and united the whole body of the gentry. The eldest sons of the Boys clan had within a few generations

[1] CCC, p. 839. But his £9,000 fine may suggest only £4,500 p.a.

married into nearly fifty different Kentish families, including Ropers, Knatchbulls, Derings, Guldefords, Honywoods, and Finches. When Mary Honywood died in her ninety-fourth year in 1620 there can have been few Kentish gentry unrelated to her 367 descendants.[1] It was no mere illusion when the gentry appealed to the 'whole community of Kent' to support their 'liberties' in 1642 or 1648, but a solid fact, however vague they may have been about what those supposed liberties were.

Such a corporate sense was of course shared by many counties. But contemporaries agreed that it was particularly marked in Kent, and modern research confirms their impression. The origins of the gentry help to explain it. Despite the proximity of London, only one-eighth of the gentry were complete newcomers to the county, arriving since Queen Elizabath's reign; a proportion that may be compared with that for Suffolk of at least 36 per cent. A further eighth had entered the county under the Tudors. but almost three-quarters were indigenous (in comparison with a mere third in Suffolk).[2] Virtually all the leading families—Culpepers, Derings, Oxindens, Sondeses, Scotts, and Twysdens, for example—and nearly three-quarters of the knights and four-fifths of the peers were drawn from these indigenous gentry. Moreover, though many parochial gentry stemmed from Tudor yeomen, between 80 and 90 per cent of the gentry as a whole, including virtually all the 'county' families, were reckoned gentle well before the Tudor period. Families like the Culpepers, Sondeses, Haleses, and Walsinghams had been appointed to the commission of the peace since before the Reformation. So deeply rooted a society could trade with good effect upon the anxiety of newcomers, such as the Barnhams of Boughton Monchelsea, to intermarry with them, and could assimilate such new wealth without impairing their own power. For, as Mr Laslett excellently puts it, "in marrying into a landed family, the heir of a city merchant, whether daughter or son, was submitting to an

[1] *DNB*, s.v. Mary Honywood. The 170 families upon which the study is based comprised 81 different stocks (i.e. family patronymics).

[2] For the Suffolk comparison see Alan Everitt, *Suffolk and the Great Rebellion, 1640–1660* (Suffolk Records Society, III), 1960, pp. 20–1.

authoritarian system and entering into a set of relationships which would inevitably involve all the descendants of the marriage."[1]

Equally significant is the distribution of the gentry through the various regions of the county, separated as they were by the North Downs and the Vale of Kent. In north-west Kent, where the influence of London was strong, nearly half the gentry had settled in the county since 1603, and less than a third were indigenous. (This was the part from which Lambarde came and to which, as his qualifications imply, he was primarily referring.) About Sevenoaks, half the gentry were pre-Tudor, nearly half were Tudor, and only one-fifth were newcomers. Round Maidstone, the proportions were roughly the same as for the county as a whole, more than half the gentry in this area being of Kentish origin. In the three galaxies of gentry centred around Canterbury, Ashford, and Faversham, where they were seated between 45 and 75 miles from London, 85 per cent were indigenous, and only 3 per cent had come into the county since 1603. In the isolated dens and hursts of the Weald, all the gentry came of original Kentish stock. Thus in east and central Kent virtually all were indigenous, and it was in these parts, not in the metropolitan fringe, that political movements in Kent arose: just as much of the county's wealth and its cities and corporate boroughs were also situated there. Except the Walsinghams at Scadbury in Chislehurst, not one important county family lived near the capital.

The origin of these Kentish families sheds some light, if obliquely, on the controversy concerning the 'rise of the gentry.' A full study of their early history would be a major undertaking, but the ample evidence accessible in print suggests a marked similarity to that of their counterparts in Devon. In general, the Kentish gentry began to emerge in the thirteenth or early fourteenth century, as small freeholders, often taking their name from the land they held. The Twysdens' first recorded representative, Adam de Twysden, held

[1] *Camb. Hist. Jnl*, IX, ii, 1948, p. 150. All the peerages and two-thirds of the baronetcies created between 1642 and 1685 in Kent were also conferred on the indigenous gentry (of pre-Tudor origin).

the dene of that name in the Weald by the end of the thirteenth century, and the earliest period of the Honywoods, Sedleys, Oxindens, and Hardreses, amongst others, was similar.[1] The end of the fifteenth century marked the conclusion of a long period of slow consolidation and the commencement of a more rapid rise. In 1530, the gentry already owned some 815 out of 1,350 manorial estates in the county; but by 1640 much of the property of the monasteries, the crown, and the older nobility had also passed into their hands, and they were possessed of some 1,100 of these manors.[2] But very rapid expansion in the fortunes of the gentry was rare. Families who played for high political or financial stakes, like the Fanes and Vanes, were exceptional: such a course was in fact more often ruinous than rewarding. The norm was the gradual, painstaking, and sometimes fluctuating increase gained over a century and a half, under Tudors and Stuarts, by families such as the Boyses, Derings, Honywoods, Oxindens, Twysdens, and their kind. Of the five factors in the rise of the gentry—land, law, trade, office, marriage—the first thus seems generally to have been the most important. Even among new arrivals it eventually came to provide the basis of prosperity. Families from other counties, like the Botelers and Twistletons, acquired a footing in the county only by marrying a Kentish heiress; a merchant like Martin Barnham established his position by intermarriage with the Rudstones of Boughton Monchelsea, and by wedding his children to sons and daughters of long-founded local families.[3] The pattern was typical: the drift of wealth and interest, once built up, was invariably from London to the land.

Careful marriages were not the monopoly of merchants, of course: they had been a more important factor than either trade or the law in the rise of most of the Kentish county families of 1640.[4] Prudent matrimony was the natural hand-

[1] Cf. W. G. Hoskins, *Devon*, 1954, pp. 75–9; W. G. Hoskins and H. P. R. Finberg, *Devonshire Studies*, 1952, pp. 81–2; Sir J. R. Twisden, *The Family of Twysden and Twisden*, 1939, pp. 17–24.

[2] I am much indebted to Mr C. W. Chalklin for this information.

[3] *The Ancestor*, IX, 1904, pp. 191 sqq.

[4] Cf. Hoskins and Finberg, *op. cit.*, *passim*, for the same phenomenon in Devon.

maid of prudent estate management. Almost every Kentish family owed much to it, and often it laid their foundation. It led to the establishment of many junior branches of county gentry, like the Oxindens of Great Maydeacon. Nevilles, Lennards, Finches, and Fanes owed titles as well as wealth to a well-dowered heiress. The Sackvilles were saved from ruin by marrying the daughters of Sir George Curzon and the earl of Middlesex; the Sidneys were enriched by the heiress of the Gamages; and the Finches acquired, over a period of two centuries, much of the patrimony of the Sewards of Lynsted, the Elyses of Otham, the Passendens of Passenden, the Twysdens of Wye, the Moyles of Eastwell, the Kempes of Olantighe, the Belknaps, the Maycotts, the Pepleshams, the Cralles, the Thwaites, the Heneages, and a wealthy city widow, Mrs Bennett. Most of this wealth accrued to the senior branch, created in 1628 earls of Winchilsea: the pedigrees of junior branches are more obscure or the list would no doubt be longer. That all but two or three of the thirteen Finch heiresses came of native families is an illustration of the fact that, of the great number of gentry whose male line became extinct between 1440 and 1640, the bulk of the estates passed to rising families, less by rapacity and extortion from those in difficulty, though of course that also occurred, than by the peaceful, natural process of marrying their heiresses. Successive waves of gentry thus inherited their predecessors' wealth. One of the most striking features of the Tudor and Stuart period in Kent is the gradual reduction in this way in the number of freeholders and the concentration of land in an ever-narrowing circle of proprietors. The tendency may not have gone so far as in some parts, such as Northamptonshire, and the Kentish gentry of 1640 were not an irresponsible aristocracy wholly divorced from the soil. But it was a trend fraught with problems for the future: the remarkable fall in the numbers of minor gentry in Devon in the eighteenth century, noted by Baring-Gould, was also evident in Kent.[1]

The influence of mercantile wealth in Kent was less widespread than might be expected. One family in six owed some-

[1] Cf. S. Baring-Gould, *Old Country Life*, 1890, p. 9. It was also apparent in Northamptonshire, more so indeed than in Kent.

thing in its rise to commerce or manufacture, but in many cases it arose from modest activities in Canterbury or Maidstone: or perhaps from trade at Dover, as in the case of the Hugessens of Lynsted; from ironworking, as with the Streatfeilds of Chiddingstone; or from the cloth industry, as with the Austens, the obscure Wealden ancestors of Jane Austen. Only rarely was commerce a major factor in gentle fortunes, and in only two instances—Styles and Barnhams—were major families permanently established by commerce. The scintillation of men like Sir Peter Richaut of Aylesford Friary was meteoric, but usually unenduring. In the course of the war Richaut sacrificed his wealth for the king and his name eventually vanished from the county. By means of the law, probably less than one family in twenty rose to any considerable extent; and although well-known names like Filmer and Sedley were among them, few gentry were established solely by the law. More widespread was the wealth of office-holders and grantees. Such obvious instances as Fanes and Vanes, St Legers, Sackvilles, and Sidneys scarcely need to be mentioned. With some families, such as the Marshams, office augmented trade. With a few, like the Percivalls of Archcliffe, positions so lucrative as the customership of Dover provided the main source of wealth. But with many of the 52 families (out of 170) who at some period in their history held office or obtained reward it is difficult to be certain how much benefit accrued. Some gained little, and some, like the Walsinghams, Twysdens, and Derings, appear to have found office an embarrassment.[1] Few major families except the Sidneys built up their fortunes primarily on the spoliation of abbeys and chantries, though many profited ultimately from the Dissolution. The Sackvilles had squandered their monastic property early in the seventeenth century, and the senior branch of the Haleses, long since surpassed in wealth by the third branch who had received no such grant, was now extinct. Other monastic grantees, like the Cheyneys of Shurland, had also fallen into decreptitude or extinction, and their land had passed—though by purchase, not gift—into a variety of hands. The Hamonds of Nonington

[1] Cf. Sir J. R. Twisden, *op. cit.*, pp. 118, 137 sqq.; E. A. Webb, etc., *op. cit.*, pp. 149 sqq. *et passim.*

bought the lands of St Albans Abbey, of which they had been tenants, and in 1640 they were still reaping their profit. The immediate recipients of monastic grants of over £200 p.a. included none of the leading Kentish families of 1640.[1] The Dissolution of the monasteries enriched many already well established gentry, but it did not revolutionize the structure of society or introduce overmighty magnates like the Russells in Devon and the Spencers in the Midlands.

A glance at the wealth of Kentish families in 1640–60 also demonstrates this as yet unchallengeable dominance of the older gentry. The 135 families whose income is discoverable in this period received a total of £88,578 p.a. Of this sum, the indigenous gentry, with an average of £719 p.a. each, received 72 per cent; families of Tudor origin, with an average of £602, 14 per cent; and Stuart families, with an average of £683, only 11 per cent. Peers, averaging £4,089, received 28 per cent of the total; baronets, £1,405 and 20 per cent; knights, £873 and 24 per cent; and untitled gentry, £270 and 28 per cent.[2] In emphasizing the wealth of the Kentish gentry as compared with those of the north or west of England, it is important to remember that the great majority were quite modest men, and hundreds had an income of under £250 per annum.

The insularity of the Kentish gentry also appears in their social links with neighbouring counties. Only four families—Lennard, Culpeper, Sackville, and Palmer of Wingham—were connected in the male line with Sussex gentry; only two with Surrey; and, despite the connexion which has sometimes been alleged between the gentry of the two counties in the rebellion of 1648, only three or four with Essex. In London, junior branches of six Kentish families registered their pedigrees at the Heralds' Visitation of 1633–35, and many younger sons entered the law or were set up in trade with a few hundred pounds by their fathers. But new sprigs like Robert Dering, a London draper, and a distant cousin of Sir Edward of Surrenden Dering, relatively rarely reset themselves in Kent and scarcely ever surpassed their parent stock in status: most are not heard

[1] H. A. L. Fisher, *The History of England . . . 1485–1547*, 1919, p. 500.

[2] See Appendix, Table III. Assuming a total of 840 gentry, peers would receive 12 per cent of total income, untitled families 61 per cent.

of again. The vast majority of Kentish families in fact were entirely confined to the county: the ten branches of the Boyses, the nine of the Finches, the seven of the Tokes, the six of the Haleses, the five of the Godfreys and Masters, the four of the Robertses, the three of the Twysdens, Harfleetes, and Sedleys—and there are scores of other examples—were restricted to Kent and had apparently never had branches settled elsewhere.

It is less easy to show that a family held no property in other shires. Several of the peers, like the Lennards Lords Dacre, held lands in half-a-dozen counties or more.[1] But scrutiny of the records of the Committees for Compounding and Advance of Money, supplemented by Hasted, *Archæologia Cantiana*, and parish and family histories, shows that the estates of the vast majority (perhaps four-fifths) of those major gentry who formed the backbone of Kentish society were confined, not only to the one county, but to a few parishes within it. The same feature was also characteristic of other counties, but there is reason to think that Kent was again to some degree exceptional. The owners in 1652 of over half the estates in a list of twenty Cambridgeshire Catholics and delinquents resided in other counties. In a sample of 114 Suffolk landowners about 1645, two-fifths also held land elsewhere in the Eastern Association and at least a further quarter—mainly the leading families—in counties further afield.[2]

Kentish marriage connexions were hardly less insular.[3] In the county as a whole over two-thirds of the gentry married among their neighbours. As might be expected, the peers, with their widely scattered estates and more national outlook, together with recusant families like the Nevilles and Ropers, went furthest afield in seeking their wives, and only one in three of them married within the county. Among the minor gentry, by contrast, more than four-fifths married locally: occasionally they wedded the daughters of local yeomen or clothiers, for the Kentish gentry had not yet become the rigid

[1] T. Barrett-Lennard, *An account of the Families of Lennard and Barrett*, 1908, *passim*.

[2] CCC, p. 539 *et passim*; CCAM, *passim*.

[3] See Appendix, Tables I and II.

caste of the Georgian era, although they were certainly tending in that direction.[1] Equally interesting were the regional differences in the marriage connexions of the gentry. In the environs of London only one-sixth of them married into Kentish families; along the Upper Stour, where nearly one quarter of all the gentry were seated, 72 per cent; and in East Kent, where more than a further quarter lived, 85 per cent. It was in these latter regions, it will be remembered, that political movements in the county took their rise. The irrigating effects of metropolitan wealth in Kentish marriages were more restricted than might be thought: even in parishes adjoining the Thames less than one-third of the gentry married Londoners.

A more direct link with the capital lay in the possession of a London house, a practice already common in noble families and not infrequent in those of baronets, though among lesser gentry at this date very unusual.[2] After the civil war began, the importance of such a connexion was circumscribed by the flight of some families to Oxford, the confinement of 'suspected persons' to their estates, and the imprisonment of Kentish 'delinquents' in Leeds Castle or Westenhanger. The intimate life of one such family with metropolitan links is portrayed in the Oxinden correspondence in the British Museum. The senior branch had a town house, two branches had younger sons or brothers in London, one had a sister married to a London merchant, and another eventually secured a seat in the House of Commons. These connexions were significant and they were made use of. But the interests and riches of the family remained rooted in the soil of Deane and Maydeacon in East Kent, in Canterbury a few miles to the north, and in the county committee at Maidstone on the other side of the Downs.[3] The great majority of the gentry spent their lives

[1] The tendency for city magnates to mingle with gentry became more marked with the eighteenth century; but recruitment from the ranks of local yeomen became more strictly barred. The evidence for this is given in my unpublished paper 'Social Mobility in Early Modern England', for the Past and Present Society Conference, 1965.

[2] For examples of those with London houses cf. Sir J. R. Twisden, *op. cit.*, p. 155; BM, Stowe MS 184, f. 71; CJ, II, p. 550; Harleian Society, XLII, *The Visitation of Kent . . ., 1619–1621*, 1898, p. 224; CSPD, 1638–9, p. 568; AC, III, p. 193.

[3] BM, Add. MSS 28000–28005, *passim*.

within a few miles of their manor houses in a circle almost as narrow as that of their tenants. If they ever visited the capital, it was usually to attend some wearisome lawsuit. When Henry Oxinden of Great Maydeacon was forced to spend some weeks there, his solitary visit, in making good his rights against a neighbour, he wrote to his wife:

". . . I will make all the haste I can to thee, taking no more pleasure in being at London than in being amongst my enemies" . . . "I wish my business at an end that I might come home and see after my harvest, fearing I may receive prejudice by my absence" . . . "I am fain to trudge up and down all day from morning to night" . . . "If I can once get clear of it [London], I never desire to come again to it" . . . "Dear Heart, this is only to let thee know how infinitely I long to be with thee. . . ."[1]

It was natural that such devotion to his native fields and family should characterize a man like Henry Oxinden, because it also characterized all his cousins and neighbours. And men of wider interests than he, like Sir Edward Dering and Sir Roger Twysden, were equally prone to it. A casual eye cast over English society in 1640 naturally tends to alight on celebrated names of national importance like Sackville and Sidney. But far more numerous, and in county affairs more important, were those like the Oxindens and Derings, families of ancient standing, local outlook, and moderate fortune. Quite two-thirds of the Kentish community was composed of such families, who as far as we can tell usually owed in their rise little or nothing to trade or office, and whose connexions were confined to the circle of neighbours and cousins whom they met in their manor-houses day by day.

In the generations following the Restoration, it is true, a number of important families whose wealth had been acquired in the capital began to appear in Kent. Sir John Banks, originally of Maidstone, purchased Aylesford Friary; the Papillons settled at Acrise Place; and the Furneses succeeded the ancient family of Monins at Waldershare Park. Although, as we have seen, this influx of mercantile wealth was not an altogether

[1] BM, Add. MS 28002, ff. 174, 306, 311, 317, 320, 342.

novel phenomenon, it certainly became more pronounced with the expansion of London after 1660, and it lends some colour to Sir Keith Feiling's description of Kentish royalism as "peculiarly metropolitan." But even in the eighteenth century it would be a mistake to regard such families as typical of the Kentish scene. Despite the decline or disappearance of some of the older gentry, moreover, such as the Walsinghams of Scadbury, the Lovelaces of Lovelace Place, and the Heymans of Somerfield, the phalanx of solidly local families like the Oxindens, Derings, and Twysdens continued to hold their own in the county until the eighteenth and indeed the nineteenth centuries.[1]

(iii) *Kentish Ideals*

It is not surprising that such a community as the one we have described should develop an ethos of its own, and a deep devotion both to its own past and to its present fortunes. Ideals are not confined by county boundaries, and many of the leaders of the county naturally did not confine their interests to Kent. The work of men like Sir Edward Dering of Surrenden Dering was already well known among scholars elsewhere.[2] But seventeenth-century society was still intensely local, and the appeals to county loyalty in the Kentish Rebellion of 1648 had their natural counterpart in the intellectual activities of the gentry. Many of these men shared the preoccupation of their age with the genealogy of county families, their studies ranging from the notes jotted in diaries by Oxindens and Peytons to the elaborate family trees compiled by Sir Edward Dering, the large collections of pedigrees of Samson Lennard of Chevening, Bluemantle Pursuivant, and the Heraldic Visitations of John Philipot, Somerset Herald. The earliest essay of the gentry in county history, Lambarde's *Perambulation*, had by 1660 been followed by Dering's *Historical Account of the Weald of Kent*, his neighbour William Darell's *Castra in Campo Cantiano*, his cousin Sir Roger Twysden's *Discourse concerning the Weald*, the two Philipots' *Villare Cantianum*, and William

[1] See Appendix, Table VI, and pp. 323 sqq.

[2] KCA, U. 350; BL, Gough Kent MS 18; *DNB*, s.v. Sir Edward Dering.

Somner's history of Canterbury and *Treatise of the Roman Ports and Forts in Kent*. That such books were published at all indicates a wide interest in county history among Kentish families, and other works are known to have circulated in their manor-houses in manuscript. White Kennett's list of "friends to learning and good letters" who supported Somner's undertakings gives the names of many men, like Sir Henry Heyman of Somerfield, whose intellectual pursuits we should not otherwise have suspected.[1]

It would be a mistake, however, to suppose these interests were merely antiquarian or snobbish. Their basis was often practical. Genealogy was a matter of some importance in difficult questions of descent, and a natural pursuit in a clannish community where bonds of society and government were still personal. Disputes about tithes gave rise to the treatises on the Weald, where woodland was claimed to be tithe-free. The lathal subdivisions of the county and the detached Wealden parts of upland hundreds still reflected the customs of the Jutish kingdom, and found a necessary place in works of county history. Gavelkind itself, although not peculiar to Kent—it was found in other areas of scattered settlement like Wales, the Cheviots, and the Pennines—was there especially widespread, so that works like Somner's *Treatise of Gavelkind, both Name and Thing* touched a vital issue.[2] The influence of partible inheritance, the chief point of gavelkind, had been important in the history of many Kentish families. Probably it helps to explain the early enclosure of the county from which they benefited, and also the modest size of their estates, as well as the existence of far-spreading clans like the Boyses and Finches, and the unusual number of ancient minor gentry. No doubt the presence of many yeomen and tenants alongside such families (for instance around the Ropers at Lynsted and the Haleses in the Weald) bearing the same

[1] *DNB*, under names cited in text; Hasted, III, p. 108; White Kennett, *The Life of Mr Somner* (prefixed to William Somner, *A Treatise of the Roman Ports and Forts in Kent*, 1693), pp. 113–17. For the exuberant intellectual interests of the Kentish gentry in general, see T. P. R. Laslett, 'The Gentry of Kent in 1640', *Camb. Hist. Jnl*, IX, ii, 1948, pp. 148–64.

[2] Cf. PRO, E. 134. 18 James I. E. 13 and M. 2; John Earle's character of 'A younger brother' in his *Microcosmography*, 1899 edn, p. 17.

patronymic as their landlord, has a similar origin.[1] These features were of course not absent from other counties—they were found, for example, in Suffolk—but once again they seem to have been particularly characteristic of Kent.

During the century preceding 1640, it is true, partibility had been giving way to primogeniture. Some hundreds of gavelkind cases in the Court of Requests suggest that, although partible inheritance was still common, it was under widespread attack. Though the tradition of founding separate establishments for younger sons like the Oxindens of Great Maydeacon lingered, the tendency to convert gavelkind into primogeniture, at least among the gentry, was rapidly becoming universal. Nevertheless, both kinds of tenure contributed to the intense corporate feeling of Kentish families, and to their patriarchalism. As Mr Laslett has described it, the family head governed not only wife and children but also brothers, sisters, grandchildren, nephews, brothers-in-law, cousins, servants, and tenants.[2] Henry Oxinden of Great Maydeacon received marked deference from his younger brothers, sisters, and brothers-in-law, and in the little support he afforded parliament in the war he followed the lead of the more ardent senior branch of the family, headed by his uncle Sir James of Deane. When Sir Edward Dering referred to his 'family,' he thought not only of his relatives but his servants and labourers. It was natural to do so when many farms and manor-houses lay isolated in Wealden woods or upland valleys, and master and labourer shared the same roof. Kentish probate inventories like that of Edward Bathurst of Goudhurst often refer to the 'folks' chambers' or 'menservants' chambers,' where the labourers slept, and not infrequently servants were their master's kinsmen. The Lennards of Chevening employed a Henry, Thomas, and apparently an Alexander Lennard; Sir George Sondes of Lees Court his brother Nicholas; William Stede of Stede Hill

[1] Cf. C. I. Elton, *The Tenures of Kent*, 1867, pp. 50 sqq.; Lodge, *op. cit.*, pp. xvi sq.; G. C. Homans, 'The rural Sociology of Medieval England', *Past and Present*, IV; C. S. and C. S. Orwin, *op. cit.*, p. 64; KCA, West Kent Sessions Order Book, 1625–51, f. 141; Elizabeth Selby, *Teynham Manor and Hundred*, n.d., pp. 47 sqq.

[2] Lambarde, *op. cit.*, pp. 531–3; T. P. R. Laslett, ed., *Patriarcha and other Political Works of Sir Robert Filmer*, 1949, p. 24 *et passim*.

his cousins John and Francis Stede; and the Tokes of Godinton sons and daughters of branches of the family at Otham, Lenham, and Westbere.[1]

In noting the prevalence of class rivalry in the seventeenth century, it is well not to overlook the sense of responsibility to dependants which social conditions of this kind tended to foster. It was a typical move of Henry Oxinden, when Goodwife Gilnot of Barham was accused by her neighbours of witchcraft, to give her a letter to his brother-in-law Bargrave, who was a justice of the peace. After relating the case at length, he adds:

"Sir, my earnest request unto you is that you will not lightly believe such false and malicious reports as you hear, or may hear, alleged against this woman, whom I believe to be religiously disposed. . . . And for so much as the neighbours healp [*sic*] themselves together, and the poor woman's cry, though it reach to heaven, is scarce heard here upon earth, I thought I was bound in conscience to speak in her behalf. . . ."[2]

Similarly, when "certain rich men who had great stock of cattle did go about to break the . . . custom" of Braborne Leaze, Sir Thomas Scott of Scots' Hall, on behalf of the poor,

"being then lord of the said manor of Braborne . . . caused the court rolls of the said manor to be produced and read unto divers and sundry of the said tenants, wherein the said custom, usage, and by-law was written and set down, and thereupon, and upon his command therein, the said greedy tenants did desisse from their said oppression and surcharge of the said common. . . ."[3]

Without this sense of duty to dependants, and the social structure underlying it, the Kentish gentry would not have received the support of their tenantry in times of crisis, and there would have been no county rebellion in 1648.

[1] KCA, PRC, 28/8, f. 52; PRO, SP. 23: G: 158, f. 138; T. Barrett-Lennard, *op. cit.*, pp. 286–8; Harleian Miscellany, *loc. cit.*, *passim*; Lodge, *op. cit.*, pp. xxxix–xl.

[2] Dorothy Gardiner, ed., *The Oxinden Letters, 1607–1642*, 1933, p. 222.

[3] PRO, C. 2. James I. G. 5. 70.

The classical exposition of the political theory of patriarchalism in the works of Sir Robert Filmer thus arose naturally in Kentish society. Filmer's *Patriarcha*, in fact, was not written primarily for the nation at large, but for a circle of cousins and neighbours round East Sutton Place in the middle of Kent. Many other Kentishmen were also scholars and authors in their own right, and their works, like Filmer's, were largely conditioned by their environment, and by its preoccupation with theological and political thought. There was a long tradition of theological interest in families like the Derings, one of whom had been a monk of Christ Church and supporter of the Nun of Kent, another the celebrated Elizabethan divine, whilst the present head of the family was author of a number of controversial religious works. Others, like Sir Thomas Peyton, were students of Hebrew and Greek: "I remember I saw in your mysterious study," he wrote to his brother-in-law Henry Oxinden, "an Hebrew Grammar of Martinius, which . . . I desire to borrow of you."[1]

In the cradle of English Christianity, where clergy and gentry had long been closely linked, this theological preoccupation was to be expected. At least sixty of the reformed cathedral clergy of Canterbury and Rochester, and all but one of the deans of Canterbury, had been drawn from or had founded Kentish families: Cranmers, Boyses, Bargraves, Fotherbys, Wottons, and Darells, for example. Friendships like that of Henry Oxinden with bishop Warner further strengthened these relationships, and many parish ministers in Kent were younger sons of the gentry or were married to their daughters. Coupled with the fact that only three-tenths of Kentish livings were in lay control (a remarkably low percentage compared with that of other counties),[2] such close interconnexion produced a society deeply permeated by anglicanism. The devotional works of Samson Lennard and Sir Richard Baker, the

[1] *Letters and Papers . . . of the Reign of Henry VIII*, VII, p. 28; *DNB*, s.v. Edward and Sir Edward Dering; BM, Add. MS 28001, f. 13.

[2] Cf. Christopher Hill, *Puritanism and Revolution*, 1962 edn, p. 44, where it is stated that by the end of the sixteenth century five out of every six English benefices were in lay patronage, largely in consequence of the Dissolution and redistribution of monastic property.

treatises of Sir Francis Wyatt and Sir Norton Knatchbull, the prayers of Henry Oxinden of Maydeacon, the letters of Sir Thomas Peyton and Robert Abbot, Sir Roger Twysden's *Historical Vindication of the Church of England*, and the lives of saintly women like Lady Peyton, all display the spirit of charity and reasonableness which came to be associated with the name of Richard Hooker. The appeal of Hooker's *Ecclesiastical Polity* —in part written when rector among them at Bishopsbourne— to history, law, and reason as well as the literal teaching of the Bible powerfully attracted men of the antiquarian cast of Dering and Twysden. The ordered life, the daily watches, prayers, and reading from devotional works and Scriptures that marked Little Gidding and Bemerton also characterized such Kentish manor-houses as Roydon Hall and Knowlton Court. Dr Fell's vignettes of Penshurst under Henry Hammond and his patron the earl of Leicester may well be idyllicized, and no doubt such piety was far from universal: but the ideal was influential, and the facts need not be altogether discounted.[1]

An intimate picture of such a household is presented in a series of remarkable tracts occasioned by Freeman Sondes's notorious murder of his elder brother in 1655. This terrible family tragedy impressed the whole county, and "the earnest supplications of many thousands [were] sent up to heaven in his [Freeman's] behalf," many gentlemen attending him to the place of execution. The attacks of certain puritan ministers, and his son's confessions to those attending him in prison, drew from the "silly pen" of Sir George Sondes, the father, a *Plain Narrative* of his own life at Lees Court. "It is the master's part," he says of his household,

"to see them perform the outward duties of God's service, as prayer and going to church, and to shew them the way by his own godly example; this I was always mindful of, frequenting the church on the Lord's day, both forenoon and afternoon, . . . and calling upon my servants to do the same. And all the week after, it was my constant course to pray with my

[1] Cf. Sir Roger Twysden, *Certain Considerations upon the Government of England*, Camden Society, XLV, 1849, ed. J. M. Kemble, p. xxiii; Life of Henry Hammond, prefixed to J. Fell, ed., *The Miscellaneous Theological Works of Henry Hammond*, 3rd edn, 1847–50, *passim*.

family once, if not twice every day; and if I had not a Levite in my house, I performed the office myself. It is true, though in my own private devotions, morning and evening, I used constantly, without failing, my own conceived ejaculations to heaven; yet, to my family, after reading some part of the scripture, I commonly used the set forms of prayers of the church, or of some other godly men: which in public meetings . . . I conceive to be very fitting. . . ."

During Freeman's imprisonment he composed a prayer which "was used in my family for my son, morning and evening, as long as he lived, and recommended to the churches about me." Such a view of his position as the family head involved Sir George Sondes in a strict code of duty. His estate, he said, he managed "as near as I can to the best," for "sure there is good warrant, both from reason and scripture, that every man should labour and endeavour in that way God hath placed him. . . ." But he would not put his money "out to use, but pleasured friends with it. I have paid many a thousand pound for the use of money, but never in all my life received one hundred for all the money I ever lent." To "the poor I have ever been charitable . . . as the members of my Saviour Christ. My other neighbours, of what quality soever, I have treated as brethren." As for hospitality,

"I am sure no man's house in the country is more open to poor and rich than mine; . . . there are twenty poor people at least weekly relieved, and that more than once. My lowest proportion in my house, whether I be there or not, is every week a bullock, of about fifty stone, a quarter of wheat, and a quarter of malt for drink, which makes about a barrel a day for my household. . . . And for setting poor people to work (which I take to be as good a deed as most) I think few have exceeded me. I am sure for well nigh thirty years . . . I have expended on labourers and workmen, at least a thousand pounds a year."

As for his tenants, "I confess," he says,

"as . . . leases expired, I took no fines to renew . . . but let out my farms at improved rents, both the tenant and myself better liking of it. But I do not know that I let a farm to any tenant for more than . . . I would have given for it myself. . . . I never arrested or imprisoned any tenant for his rent. . . . I have scarce demanded my rents of late, because of the cheapness of corn, . . . and spared my tenants, that they might not be forced to put off their corn at too mean rates."

Concerning his relatives, Sondes says that to his aunt he allowed £50 a year and diet, and to his brother and eldest half-brother £100 a year. Another half-brother was apprenticed to his father-in-law, "who loved him dearly, and would have done much for him;" four others were also provided for, and to his half-sister he gave £40 a year and promised a dowry of £500. ". . . For my part," he concludes, "as long as I live I will endeavour honestly . . . in all my actions, and as much as in me lies labour to have peace with all men."[1]

Clearly such ideals had political repercussions also. If it was but a slight exaggeration for the Kentish gentry to regard their community as a single family, and if its bonds were sealed, as it seemed to them, by the teachings of Christianity, any attempt to encourage parties in the state must be antichristian. If society was a living organism, how could division be justified? So they argued—not insincerely, if naïvely. Christians, as a friend of Sir George Sondes defined them, were those who "live soberly and honestly, with repute in their several callings; whose compass (by which they steer their lives) is faith, not faction; whose profession, too, is not to side with parties, but to serve the Lord Jesus." This was the essence of the quarrel of the Kentish gentry with both Archbishop Laud and the more extreme puritans: militant idealists, it seemed to many Kentishmen, who did not take due account of practical difficulties. Countrymen like Dering and Twysden knew well how easily the latent lawlessness of their parishes broke out, and how much tact was needed to preserve the "well-ordered chain of government" whose "several golden links" stretched from the king at Whitehall through Council, gentry, ministers, yeomen, and constables "even to the protection of the poorest creature that now lives among us."[2] High wages might amelior-

[1] Harleian Miscellany, *loc. cit.*, pp. 51, 57, 49, 64, 50, 54, 65.

[2] *Ibid.*, p. 38; *A Collection of Speeches made by Sir Edward Dering . . . in matter of Religion*, 1642, p. 166.

ate class jealousy, but riots easily broke out when in harvest-time "the roads [were] full of troops of workmen with their scythes and sickles, going to the adjacent town to refresh themselves with good liquor and victuals." On one occasion a crowd of parishioners locked 200 people out of Thanet Minster church and next week seven of them, rushing into the building, pulled Richard Culmer the minister from the pulpit, and crushed his body and bent his ribs on a plank till he vomited blood. Such incidents were only too frequent, and violent iconoclastic puritans like Culmer were often ready to incur the disorder. But men like Sir Roger Twysden were unable to see how God was glorified by the disruption of society. Neither, on the other hand, could they approve the imprisonment of humble separatists, like the truggers and woodmen of Egerton, however misguided they might be. Instead, their neighbouring squire invited them to a conference at his manor-house of Surrenden Dering and with his Calvinistic friend John Reading endeavoured to reason them out of their opinions.[1]

Such men, though neither Laudian nor puritan, were evidently not without their ideals, though few would have gone so far as Sir Edward Dering in formulating them. In his plan of reform, "every several shire of England [was] to be a several circuit or diocese" and each bishop, chosen from three elected by the country clergy and confined in his activities to the shire, was "constantly to reside within his diocese [or county], and to keep his especial residence in some one prime . . . city . . . as in particular the bishop of Kent at Canterbury." The revenues of cathedral clergy were to be periodically surveyed "by choice commissioners in every several county," while the "parochial ministers [were] to be entrusted and endued with more power than formerly," and were to operate through weekly vestries, quarterly ruridecanal meetings, and annual synods; the national synod was to meet only once every three years.[2] Most of the Kentish gentry, however, would have agreed with the localism

[1] HMC, XIII, ii, p. 280; Richard Culmer, jr, *A Parish Looking-Glass for persecuted Ministers*, 1657, pp. 24–5; BM, Stowe MS 184, f. 27; W. Scott and J. Bliss, eds., *The Works of the Most Reverend Father in God, William Laud, D.D.*, 1847–60, v, p. 347; KCA, U. 350. C. 2/54.

[2] E. 197. 1, pp. 155–61.

evinced in Dering's scheme, and that the anglican liturgy should remain unaltered, that bishops should "perform all those services and employments trusted unto and expected from the present bishops," and that patience and moderation were imperative if reform was to be achieved without civil confusion. "Make bishops Timothies," said the friend who succeeded Dering in parliament, "by lopping off their temporal . . . employments and by paring away their superfluities. Then will they be more apt to teach . . . [but] God let them be bishops still."[1] Such moderation, of which the aim was to make the church and its episcopate contribute more, not less, fully to the life of the local community, and to unite not divide society, was perhaps more widespread in country parishes than we realize. It appealed to the lingering notion of 'hospitality' which came naturally to an agrarian civilization, and which, as Fuller expressed it, "gave its last groan" in Kent. Moderation, indeed, seems peculiarly characteristic of this southern county as compared, for example, with puritan East Anglia or Northamptonshire. The 'veritable clan' of puritan families in the eastern counties, like the Barringtons and Barnardistons, who shared in the colonizing activities of Pym and Warwick, was quite absent from Kent.[2] In days of laxity and indifferentism like our own, moderation in matters of religion may not be the primary requirement: in the violent animosities and unreasoning prejudices of the Civil War it was not altogether ignoble or unnecessary, and without some understanding of its latent strength the history of seventeenth-century Kent, and indeed of England, can hardly be understood.

Such a social structure as that of Kent involved many political and administrative problems, both for the central government and the local gentry. The fundamental question was one of control. Since the county was the primary unit of taxation, of provincial government, and of parliamentary election, a county leader—whether sheriff, or chairman of the Bench of Justices,

[1] BM, Stowe MS 744, f. 13.

[2] Cf. A. P. Newton, *The Colonizing Activities of the English Puritans*, 1914, p. viii. The Vanes of Fairlawne belonged to this group, but their main interest now centred in national politics and their north-country estates, not in Kent.

or knight of the shire—was imperative. In Lancashire or Wiltshire, counties headed by a single great family, the choice might be obvious. But in a county with a knot of leading families instead of a single head, how was the leader to be selected? The interest of the Great Rebellion, so far as Kent is concerned, lies in the successive attempts of Charles I, of Parliament, of the Commonwealth, and of Cromwell to solve this problem, and the failure of each of them in turn. They all failed because, although the general opinion of the county was moderate, a small group of extremists emerged on either hand upon whose allegiance circumstances forced them to rely. Since these extremists were men of great determination, thinking in terms not of local politics but of national principles, it was not difficult for them to grasp the reins in an emergency. But most of them, like the regicides Sir Michael Livesey and John Dixwell, were drawn from new or comparatively unimportant families in the county, unrelated to the natural leaders of the shire, and unable to render their control permanent. It was not until power returned again to the older gentry, the natural leaders of the county, in 1660, that a permanent settlement of the issues raised in 1640 was possible.

III

THE COMMUNITY IN OPPOSITION, 1640

(i) *The Development of Opposition, 1630–40*

THE INTEREST OF the years before the Civil War, in Kent as in England generally, consists in the way in which all the diverse elements in the community gradually fused together in united opposition to Charles I. In Kent, this unity was as widespread as elsewhere; but it was less solid and enduring than in parliamentarian counties such as Suffolk and Northamptonshire. In certain important respects, it was also different in kind from the opposition in these counties. In the first place, despite strong secular elements, it was more marked by ecclesiastical than political or economic characteristics.[1] Politics pure and simple were not so distinctive an interest of the gentry as in other shires, such as Buckinghamshire and Suffolk, where society was dominated by a striking political personality. None of the Kentish members in the Long Parliament was of much consequence politically. Secondly, this ecclesiastical opposition was essentially moderate. It came to be temporarily linked with certain powerful puritan groups in the county; but its spirit was alien to the puritanism of London, Suffolk, or Northamptonshire. Whoever emerged to lead the county in its mounting discontent against Charles I was thus bound to find a more difficult problem than that confronting the gentry in counties where the issues were relatively simple and clear-cut.

This ecclesiastical discontent of the county came to the fore immediately upon Laud's appointment to the see of Canterbury in 1633. Hitherto restricted to small groups of puritans, it now became general, and it was directed against Laudianism

[1] There seems to have been little economic complaint in Kent save among clothiers, whose grievances were taken up by Sir John Culpeper of Hollingbourne in the Long Parliament (E. 135. 36; HMC, IV, p. 62; LJ, IV, p. 237; E. 196. 8). Nor, amongst the gentry and farmers of a prosperous and old-enclosed county, was there much agrarian opposition.

rather than episcopacy or the anglican liturgy. Neither Laud, who rarely visited his see, nor his henchman Warner of Rochester—so most men felt—understood the problems of the county. There were many abuses requiring reform, as men like Sir Edward Dering or Sir Roger Twysden readily admitted, but the archbishop was too impatient to observe the ideals underlying them. He pulled up the wheat with the tares. ". . . My visitation," he wrote to his chapter as soon as he was appointed, ". . . I think fit should begin at my own seat and diocese . . . I hear that some of that body have been a little too bold with me. . . . If upon enquiry I do find it true, I shall not forget that nine of the twelve prebends," he added with a threatening note, "are in the king's gift. . . ." Their timid objections to his statutes were swept aside; their choir was too meanly furnished; the "peevish" disputes among them must be settled forthwith; the absentee archdeacon, who complained that his house was in disrepair, was told that he "shall not now, after so much wealth gotten in this time, take a better house . . . and leave his that is ruinous to a . . . poorer prebend." The archbishop's finger touched every detail, down to the very lock of the muniment-room door. "I see somewhat amiss in all . . .," he angrily declared; and again, "I shall expect some better success hereafter. . . ."[1] There was much to be said for Laud's reforms. Yet with the learning of Meric Casaubon, the sanctity of Thomas Paske, and in general the respect of corporation, gentry, and Walloons, the chapter of Christ Church was not altogether discreditable.

Laud's next attack was launched against the foreign churches of the county. ". . . The Dutch churches in Canterbury and Sandwich," he told the king, "are great nurseries of inconformity in those parts." An injunction was issued that members born in England should attend English parish churches; but with the support of Secretary Coke and others the 1,450 foreigners in Kent put up a strenuous resistance.[2] Many meet-

[1] W. Scott and J. Bliss, eds., *The Works of the Most Reverend Father in God, William Laud, D.D.*, 1847–60, VII, pp. 56, 257, 258, 349, 350, 362, 363; AC, XLII, pp. 110–13.

[2] Scott and Bliss, *op. cit.*, V, p. 323; E. 285. 6, p. 27; CSPD, 1640–1, p. 526. The foreign congregation of 900 members at Canterbury was the

ings took place at which Laud's officers tried to force the ministers to surrender. Bishop Warner "startled and snuffed, . . . using some discourteous words," and the archbishop

"spake often very harshly and bitterly . . . and in a jeering and scoffing way spake very basely of their communion, said that their churches used irreverence at their communion, sat altogether as if it were in a tavern or alehouse, . . . that they would make a state in a state, . . . that their churches were nests and occasions of schism, that his intention was to hinder the schism in Kent. . . ."

The foreigners and the county had not always been harmoniously disposed, but the attack united them. Justices commended the Walloons' behaviour, and the gentry their support of the poor and employment of many local inhabitants. The chapter of Christ Church praised their orderly carriage "towards God and all the King's Majesty's officers," and wished that English parishioners would follow their example. Dean Bargrave and Prebendary Casaubon, ordered to see the injunction obeyed, summoned the ministers and mildly suggested that "they might go down into the [dean's] garden and there talk and communicate together."[1] Laud's vicar-general spoke

"so much for them that my Lord was awondered and in a manner angry, that he was more for the foreign churches than for his injunction and reformation: he had told his Grace that the ministers were his good friends, religious and peaceable men, and there were divers knights and gentlemen . . . had spoken to him in their behalf. . . ."

Finally, the corporation of Canterbury wrote to Laud, beseeching their patron to reconsider his decision: many trades would fail, many women and children be unemployed, and the burden on the poor rates become insupportable, if the churches were suppressed. But the archbishop angrily answered: "First

---

largest in England outside London, where there were 1,400 French and 840 Dutch. There were 500 in Sandwich and 50 in Maidstone.—E. 285. 6, p. 22.

[1] E. 285. 6, pp. 2, 9, 10, 11, 5. The *DNB*, s.v. Isaac Bargrave, is incorrect in stating that Bargrave pressed for the conformity of the foreign churches and Laud disapproved of "these high-handed orders."

I must let you know that there is not one particular thing mentioned in your letter . . . which the ministers . . . did not formerly represent." Each objection was impatiently brushed aside, and Laud concluded: "My injunctions must be obeyed, and . . . I shall go constantly on with them, and . . . require you, the mayor and governors of that city to second [them]. . . ."[1] Thus "the three foreign [churches] of Kent . . . endured the greatest brunts, stood in the gap, were in the front, received the blows, and bare the reproaches, and did what they could to save and deliver the churches from . . . slavery. . . ."[2] But the injunctions were executed.

Meanwhile, the archbishop turned his attention to the native puritans. Their two leaders, Thomas Wilson of Otham and Richard Culmer of Thanet Minster, were suspended for refusing to read the Book of Sports. Wilson continued to preach in his rectory in secret, and on one occasion, when a pursuivant from the Council suddenly appeared, narrowly escaped arrest by slipping through a doorway in the screen at the back of the hall. Culmer, with a wife and seven children to support, several times petitioned the archbishop for absolution; but Laud was adamant. "If you know not how to obey," he said, "I know not how to grant;" and, when Culmer pleaded for consideration, "in a great rage said 'Consideration! I will take nothing into consideration, and if you conform not all the sooner I'll take a more round course with you'; and so saying he threw Mr Culmer's petition at him violently."[3] Equally impatient was Laud's treatment of the Wealden separatists. ". . . All of the poorer sort," he told the king, "and very simple, so that I am utterly to seek what to do with them." Three of their leaders were successively imprisoned, and the scattered congregation removed their conventicle to the house of "John Fenner the trugger of Egerton." When Fenner was

[1] E. 285. 6, pp. 43, 34–7. There was a long tale of antagonism between Laud and the corporation on other matters: cf. HMC, XIII, ii, p. 279. The corporation probably meant that Laud's injunction would lead to mass emigration of the Walloons: cf. Valerie Morant, 'The Settlement of Protestant Refugees in Maidstone', EcHR, 2nd Ser., IV, 1951–2, pp. 213–14.

[2] E. 285. 6, p. 40.

[3] Richard Culmer, jr, *A Parish Looking-Glass for persecuted Ministers*, 1657, p. 3 *et passim*; CSPD, 1640–41, pp. 453–4, 1644, p. 15.

arrested, one of the leaders escaped, and when recaptured stood silent before the court of High Commission "in such a jeering, scornful manner," said the archbishop, "as I scarce ever saw the like. So in prison he remains."[1] These were the kind of men to whom the New World and the remote Bermudas held out hope: travelling far from the "storms and prelate's rage," several companies of Wealden clothiers, hemp-dressers, and others left Sandwich for New England in the early seventeenth century.[2]

Despite Laud's assertion that there were many such factions, there would have been little to fear from these puritans if he had not also antagonized the moderates of the county. Neither the rigour of Thomas Wilson nor the pathological spleen of Richard Culmer attracted many disciples: Culmer's own writings show how few were his supporters and how severely they were persecuted. But there were many men, like Sir Thomas Peyton of Knowlton, with a genuine dislike of the increasing "pomposities of the clergy."[3] When the Long Parliament met in 1640, their feelings found vent in a spate of petitions to the Committee for Religion, of which their county's representative, Sir Edward Dering, was chairman. Most of these documents were organized by minor local gentry, like William Hales and Robert Edolphe at Hinxhill, or the Rouths and Proudes at Boughton-under-Blean.[4] The story behind one of them will show the kind of social conditions in which these petitions were hatched, and how little some of them represented the genuine sentiments of the countryside. The saintly but pluralist minister of St Mary-at-Hoo, Richard Tray, was accused in one petition of non-residence, of excommunicating parishioners on frivolous charges, vexing them in ecclesiastical

[1] BM, Stowe MS 184, f. 27; Scott and Bliss, *op. cit.*, v, p. 347; KCA, Dering MSS, Dering to Laud, 20 Jan. 1635/36.

[2] W. Boys, *Collections for an History of Sandwich in Kent*, 1892 [i.e., 1792], II, pp. 707, 708, 751, 752; Morant, *loc. cit.*

[3] BM, Add. MS 44846, f. 7.

[4] Proc. in K., pp. 174, 175. Approximately 140 such minor gentry were involved in organizing these petitions. Of these 45 later became committee-men, the majority becoming royalists or remaining neutral, so that it is misleading to regard the movement behind these petitions as essentially puritan.

courts, striking the parish clerk in church, and other enormities. But one of the subscribers later confessed that he had put his mark to the petition only when the local squire, Edward Alchorn, told him that others had already done so: "for which he is very sorry, and thinks he was bewitched, and that if ever the devil had power over him, he had . . . then. . . ." Another confessed that Alchorn

"did oftentimes solicit me at Hartlip alehouse to set my hand to his petition, . . . but I twice or thrice denying, at length, with much importunity, he got my hand thereunto, being much, I confess, overtaken with drink; but I never heard above 2 or 3 lines thereof . . . I am very sorry for so doing; for I never knew nor heard but very well of Mr Tray, having been my minister all my lifetime . . . all, or the most part, of the said petition is false and untrue."

Another subscriber stated that Alchorn came to his house "ten times . . . at least, and inviting me as often to his house, and there feasting me day and night, and giving me overmuch drink, did at last get my hand to his petition. . . ." When one parishioner refused to subscribe, the desperate squire, "told him that if he came any more to fetch any water at his tenant's pond, he would break his pails upon his head, and would pull his house down upon him. . . ."[1]

Nevertheless, unlike the general puritan petitions openly based on copies sent down from London, the evidence of these sixty or so local petitions cannot be altogether discounted. Their complaints on the whole were moderate. Their usual grievance, pluralism, Laud himself had tried to remedy. Only three parishes complained of ministers supporting the new canons and the 'etcetera oath;' only two of prelatical tyranny. None condemned episcopacy as such, and only eighteen objected to 'innovations.' Few showed any interest in puritan theology, and one parish actually complained because "the orthodox [were] vilified with the name of puritanical." Countrymen did not often believe, with orthodox puritanism, that the curate they drank with of an evening at the inn was an emissary of the pope. Their complaint was rather like that of

[1] *Ibid.*, pp. 160–2, 168, 171, 173, 168.

the parishioners of Capel-cum-Tudely, sleepy little Wealden villages, whose minister "says that if he be ever so far from his text, yet if he keep but talking on, it will serve our turn," and "that if ever Scot go to heaven, the devil will go too."[1]

Such were the disparate religious groups, uneasily drifting together in Kent in the 'thirties to form the opposition to Charles I. Their complaints, it is clear, were highly amorphous, and it would have needed a very remarkable man to keep them permanently together. In fact, the only figure who emerged with any real power to unite them was Sir Edward Dering of Surrenden Dering. In some respects Dering was a remarkable man. Contemporaries admitted his intellectual brilliance, even when his politics appeared enigmatic and mercurial. As the great-nephew and namesake of a celebrated puritan divine and the cousin of Dean Bargrave, Dering lived from childhood in an atmosphere of theological disputation; while his natural parts and reputation as an antiquary, his position as head of an ancient Kentish house, and perhaps a strain of restless ambition, by 1640 procured him a kind of popular ascendancy among the gentry of the county.[2] In all its aspects theology fascinated him. The ecclesiastical opponent yet personal friend of the archbishop, the companion at once of catholics and of separatists, the leader of moderates and puritans, he was in touch with every facet of religious life in Kent, and by 1640 Surrenden Dering had become the natural centre of the ecclesiastical opposition in the county. With Robert Abbot, the learned rector of Cranbrook, Dering worked out his own peculiar theological system; while at the same time he corresponded with the archbishop at Lambeth, with Henry Hammond the high church rector of Penshurst, with his moderate cousin Sir Roger Twysden of Roydon Hall, his puritan cousin George Haule of Chillington Manor, and with a motley group of friends about Dover, whom he drew round him when lieutenant of the Castle in the 'thirties. Such a network of friendships obviously brought its own dangers. Dering never supported extreme measures for their own sake; but his academic detachment and impulsive, sympathetic nature laid him open to the eager influence of puritans like Thomas Wilson

[1] *Ibid.*, pp. 101–240, *passim*. [2] E. 197. 1; Proc. in K., *passim*.

at home and Sir Henry Vane and Sir Arthur Hesilrige in the House of Commons.[1] Clearly Dering would be unlikely to form a stable opposition party; but only a man so variously gifted as he could have organized one at all in the peculiar conditions of Kentish society.

Meanwhile, as Sir Edward Dering was coming to lead the ecclesiastical opposition of the county, a number of diverse figures were coming to the fore in the political affairs of the community. These aspects of the opposition ran to much the same general pattern as in other counties. The more determined men began to emerge in Kent in the 1620s. Sir Peter Heyman of Somerfield acquired minor fame for publicly denouncing his cousin Sir John Finch, the notorious Speaker of the Commons, as a disgrace to his county and his name, and for opposing Charles I's forced loans. In consequence, Heyman was sent on foreign missions at his own charge, and was imprisoned for refusing to divulge to the Privy Council what had been said *in camera* in the House of Commons. Equally determined in their political persuasions were Sir Dudley Digges of Chilham Castle, one of the promoters of the Petition of Right; Sir Edward Boys of Fredville Court; and Sir Edwin Sandys, the colonizer, of Northbourne Abbey. Such men were often influenced by family tradition—Boys was grandson of Peter Wentworth, Sandys the son of a puritan archbishop—and their sons often followed in their footsteps. Sir Henry Heyman, son of Sir Peter, and John Boys, son of Sir Edward Boys, both became prominent members of the County Committee in the 'forties; three of the Sandyses became parliamentarian colonels; and Edwyn Sandys played a decisive part in securing the county for parliament in 1642.[2]

What led to the union of the hitherto quiescent moderates with these men was the levy of Ship Money. It is striking that active opposition to Ship Money stemmed mainly from the

[1] BM, Stowe MS 744, f. 13; KCA, Dering MSS, Hammond to Dering 16 May [? 1639]; Dering to Laud, 20 Jan. 1635/36, 23 Jan. 1640/41; Sandwich Muniments, Letter Book, 1295–1753, letters of Dering to Sandwich Corporation, *passim*.

[2] *DNB*, s.v. Sir Peter Heyman and Sir Edwin Sandys; M. F. Keeler, *The Long Parliament, 1640–1641*, 1954, pp. 114, 214.

older families of the county, like the Honywoods of Evington and the Haleses of Woodchurch. Many of Dering's relatives were also involved: his neighbour Sir Robert Darell of Calehill, his cousin Sir Roger Twysden, his brother-in-law the earl of Thanet, and his cousins the Wilsfords of Ileden. Some, like Twysden, at first acquiesced in the levy, but after carefully searching precedents became convinced of its illegality, and were distrained for non-payment. A 'Book of Arguments' against Ship Money, probably in manuscript, was circulating amongst their manor-houses, and Twysden compiled a "note of Extraordinary Charges . . . laid on this County since my being a Justice of Peace." When, in this connexion, the Kentish justices were ordered to carry timber for the ships from Sussex to Kingston-on-Thames in Surrey, they objected that it was "a thing unknown to go out of this county into another to carry timber from thence into a third."[1] It is often supposed that the levy of Ship Money was administered with remarkable equity; but in fact its efficiency depended on the character and convictions of the sheriffs and collectors. When Sir George Sondes was sheriff, he "carried himself . . . with much moderation and temper, neither was there anything you could easily find fault with, if it were not a desire [of] too great contenting all men." But during David Polhill's shrievalty, there was "much repining" because in some hundreds he levied his predecessor's arrears both from those who had paid the levy and from those who had not. "The farmers do bitterly complain," wrote Theophilus Higgons of Hunton to Twysden, discussing the validity of the levy and outlining a more equitable scheme of collection. Yet Higgons found "the more ingenious sort of countrymen do verily conceive that the king, in case of necessity, may impose it, and that he is the most proper judge of the necessity. . . ." What was feared was a regular tax, levied year by year, without the consultation of the community.[2]

[1] HMC, XII, i, p. 274; Sir Roger Twysden, *Certain Considerations upon the Government of England*, Camden Soc., XLV, 1849, ed. J. M. Kemble, pp. xxxvii, 145; BM, Add. MS 44846, f. 3; Add. MS 34176, ff. 70–1; CSPD, 1637–38, pp. 479, 550.

[2] Maidstone Museum, 'MS Papers of Sir Roger Twysden . . . relating chiefly to the Civil Wars . . .', items 38, 41, and Twysden MSS, 'Memorials since my being a J.P.', f. 14; BM, Add. MS 34173, f. 18.

With the events of 1639 the latent antagonism of the county increased, less because of the political issues of the war with Scotland than because 1,200 Kentishmen were sent out of the county into the north. The deputy lieutenants complained bitterly of their "sufferings" in this "troublesome and unfortunate service. . . ." When the bands assembled, many of their muskets had "no touch holes, and some others [were] so large as one might turn one's thumb in them, and the pikes were so rotten as they were shaken, many of them [in the transit to Gravesend], all to pieces; some few of the muskets were reasonably good; the captain commending one of those muskets wished they had been all so good. 'Nay,' saith the musketeer, 'my master sought to have found a worse musket, but he could find none in all the town; if he could, I should have had it.' These ill arms, and the poor undisciplined men [were] hired for £8, £10, and £12, by the trained men to go in their stead. . . ." Everyone tried to avoid sending men or arms, including even the dean and chapter of Canterbury. A more satisfactory contingent was raised in Kent in 1640; but at the rendezvous some would not

"go beyond their colours, others will not go into Scotland, all are yeomen and farmers who say they must be as assuredly undone by going as by refusing. . . . They have thrust out their rugged resolutions in this language, Take one and take all; and then forsaking rank and file they fell into disorder, not to be reduced by the command of their officers."

The billeting of troops from other counties was equally unpopular: "the Sussex men are especially ungovernable," said the inhabitants of Rochester.[1]

Some officers indeed were as independent as the men. Taking his troops into the north in 1639—sixty of them, he said, worthy to be generals—Sir Thomas Wilsford of Ileden came one morning, with "free speech and courtesy" to the king and told him:

"He was come out of Kent . . . and said, 'I pray God send us well to do in this business, but,' said he, 'I like not the

[1] CSPD, 1638–39, p. 514; 1639, pp. 53, 50; 1640, pp. 148, 539–40; BM, Add. MS 27999, f. 310.

beginning . . . because you go the wrong way to work.' The king smiled and asked him which was the right way. He answered, 'If you think to make a war with your own purse, you deceive yourself; the only way to prosper is to go back and call a parliament, and so should you have money enough. . . .' The king replied, 'There were fools in the last parliament.' 'True . . . but there were wise men too, and if you had let them alone the wise men would have been too hard for the fools. For there was myself for Dover, and shall be again whensoever you call a parliament, except your Majesty . . . hinder, which I think your Majesty will not do.' The duke of Lennox . . . said, 'How can you have a parliament, the king being absent?' 'No matter . . ., we shall do our business well enough without him.' "

As Warham and Wolsey had found a century earlier, "some men in Kent think nothing can be done without them."[1] Wilsford was one of that obstinate group of cousins, already mentioned, who included Sir Peter Heyman of Somerfield and Sir Dudley Digges of Chilham Castle.

Underlying the obstinacy of the Kentish gentry and farmers was their constant fear of invasion. The Thirty Years' War was in progress, England was without allies, and the weakness of the Kentish coastline was notorious. "To let you know in what condition the castles are," wrote Sir John Manwood, lieutenant of Dover, to Secretary Windebank,

"I have done it so often that I need not any more do it . . . I have but eleven barrels of powder, and for the other castles, I believe they have scarce one barrel apiece; but to be a suitor for powder before the cannon be mounted and the castles repaired . . . is to no purpose."

There was "daily a great store of Spanish people ashore and some Hollanders" after their battle in the Downs. "I sent to prohibit their landing, . . ." Manwood continued, "for there is neither a guard sufficient to keep the peace nor are the castles in a condition to give assistance." The trained bands

[1] CSPD, 1639, pp. 244–45; *Letters and Papers . . . of the Reign of Henry VIII*, IV, p. 656.

were called out, but the Spaniards—"poor and miserable people as ever I beheld," said the Lord Warden—were robbed and "very rudely used" by the Kentishmen.[1] In parishes bordering the Thames the mere rumour that a recusant widow had laid in a store of arms threw Plumstead village into uproar. "God keep us," wrote Sir Thomas Peyton of Knowlton to his brother-in-law Henry Oxinden, "upon whom the ends of the world are come: for such the state of the age would persuade it to be when the universal frame of nature seems to be thus distracted." ". . . The sword, famine, and other plagues that hang over us are ready to swallow up the wicked age . . . in this fiery declination of the world."[2]

While the storm of discontent at the government of Charles I broke out in the seaboard parishes of the county, Sir Roger Twysden, in his quiet manor-house in the Weald, began writing his well-known treatise, *Certain Considerations upon the Government of England*. His careful analysis of the historical and legal claims of both crown and parliament was remarkable at once for its solidity, its moderation, and its integrity. Twysden was equally opposed to the extreme claims of king and of parliament, and in all probability he expressed the unspoken sentiments of the majority of Kentishmen. Gradually he came unconsciously to assume the political leadership of the county, just as his cousin Sir Edward Dering had come to voice its ecclesiastical grievances. Government, Twysden assumed, existed solely for the benefit of the subject, and tolerant cooperation between king and country was his ideal. But how were the subject's liberties to be preserved when the king's ministers "by flattery teach him to think his power wholly above law," and by steps "win upon the people's liberty?" (He was doubtless thinking of Ship Money and his unpopular ministerial cousin Sir John Finch.) ". . . The ancient proceedings of parliament, well-followed, there is the least likelihood of hurt to ensue to any particular [person], and the most good to the general. . . ." As knight of the shire, Twysden's hopes

[1] CSPD, 1637–38, p. 290; 1639, p. 510 (cf. p. 522); 1639–40, pp. 35, 45; BM, Stowe MS 744, f. 2.

[2] CSPD, 1640, pp. 228, 262; BM, Add. MS 27999, f. 294; Add. MS 28000, f. 16.

therefore ran high at the meeting of the Short Parliament in 1640; and when "most unexpectedly, without doing anything," it was dissolved, he found "great amazement of many understanding men, . . . it having carried itself with such moderation as not to have put to the question anything [that] might displease the king. . . ." On the other hand, parliament itself might infringe liberty. For its claims soon grew to that height that some claimed that, should a member owe money, "I may not at all demand it for fear of interrupting his thoughts;" for "his mind as well as his body is to be free." What could prevent such encroachment? Only the common law: the "Houses are not to meddle with anything triable by the common law," he said. Even Strafford's trial, though Twysden was no advocate of his, was indefensible. An admirer, though not an uncritical one, of Sir Edward Coke, Twysden thus appealed finally to the decision of the common law in the ordinary courts of justice. Royal prerogative and parliamentary privilege were studiously to be observed, but they existed solely for the subject. Carefully listing his cases, he observed that the Commons had always had "strict . . . dependence . . . upon those towns or counties whom they represented. . . ." Little interested in the abstract origin of authority, Twysden always argued from long and weighty precedent, deriving his information primarily from Kentish history. "What is the opinion of these days," he characteristically concluded, "I conceive not greatly material for such as seek the basis or foundation on which this Commonwealth is built, but how former times, before the dispute came, did interpret it. . . ."[1]

It was the deep conservatism of Sir Roger Twysden, coupled with his ancient family connexions, that explained his influence in the county. He lacked the quickness of mind of his colleague and cousin Sir Edward Dering; but there was an oak-like stability about him which Dering did not share, and an integrity his bitterest enemies were compelled to respect. In this way the two cousins represented certain contradictory yet

[1] Twysden, *op. cit.*, pp. 181, 161, 145, 165–6, 89, 129, 154, 128. Twysden's book was not published till 1849, but it circulated in manuscript, like many other works by Kentish authors, in local manor-houses between 1640 and 1660: see Sir J. R. Twisden, *op. cit.*, p. 190.

complementary elements in the personality of the county. Dering displayed the versatile, temperamental strain, the 'Kentish fire' so often noted by contemporaries: Twysden a certain slow-moving, deep-thinking element which, when it was moved, as in 1642 and 1648, could make Westminster itself tremble. In a sense they were rivals; but beneath their curious, ambivalent relationship was a fundamental sympathy which, in time of crisis, more than once united them in defence of their county and against the state.

(ii) *The Elections of 1640*

It was these complex conditions—social, religious, political, and personal—that underlay the Kentish elections to the Short Parliament and Long Parliament in 1640. The broad political principles which moved the nation at large were not absent from the county; but they operated within a self-centred society which transmuted them into something other than pure royalism and parliamentarianism. Depicted as it is in extraordinary detail in the family correspondence of the period, the story of these elections thus tells us more about the secret springs of rural society than about the development of English politics. It shows how Sir Edward Dering and Sir Roger Twysden gradually emerged as the leaders of the county, not because of their connexion with national politics, but because of their family influence and personality.

The Kentish elections of 1640 formed no part of that concerted plan to secure the House of Commons which was noticeable in some counties. There were no links with the parliamentary connexion of Pym or Warwick; there was no dominant family to control the county, and no proper electoral discipline. During the war the social pretensions of one of the rival parliamentary candidates of 1640 were satirized by an enemy:

> "Culpeper he grows hot in the mouth,
> Damns peace as if he meant,
> Rather than not to be a lord,
> Fight to be king of Kent."[1]

[1] *The Sense of the Oxford Junto concerning the Late Treaty* [1645, n.p.].

But though there were five titled branches of the Culpeper family in Kent—at Hollingbourne Manor, Leeds Castle, Preston Hall, Hackington, and Bedgebury—there was no real danger of an ascendancy of Culpepers or of any other single family in the county. The interest of the elections consists in the way in which, in these circumstances, a popular movement in Kent was organized. Essentially, every popular movement of the period was organized in the same manner. The whole social hierarchy of the county was involved in the organization. The family who set out to control the shire must first of all secure the adherence of its group of cousins and friends amongst the greater county gentry, and they on their part that of their kinsmen and neighbours amongst the parochial gentry of the shire; finally, all in turn must obtain the allegiance of their tenants and labourers. In this way, the rival family galaxies which fought the elections of 1640 were gradually built up. The nexus of the whole system was intensely feudal and personal; but if loyalties were unduly strained, fragments of the original connexion tended to break off and re-form under the suzerainty of some rival candidate. Both Twysden and Dering found some of their supporters deserting them on more than one occasion. "I find some . . . especially about Maidstone," wrote Sir John Sedley of St Clere, with characteristic spleen, when canvassing for Dering, "so poisoned with faction, and so full of falsehood and treachery, that I know not how to judge of their integrity, unless I did see their hearts, which it were happy that some of them were anatomized to that purpose."[1]

In the election of knights of the shire for the Short Parliament there were several stages in this formation of family connexions. Initially, in December 1639, neither Dering nor Twysden took part, but supported the claims of Norton Knatchbull of Mersham-le-Hatch, Sir George Sondes of Lees Court, and his friend Sir Thomas Walsingham of Scadbury. For the first seat Knatchbull was firmly supported by many influential cousins and neighbours, in particular the Scotts of Scots' Hall and the Boyses of Fredville. "Mr Knatchbull is an honest gentleman, and I believe will have many voices both

[1] Proc. in K., p. 13.

for his own worth, and Sir Ed[ward] Scott's sake," said Twysden. But the second seat for the county was challenged, not only by Sondes and Walsingham, but by Sir Henry Vane the elder, of Fairlawne, near Tonbridge. At first, Vane endeavoured to secure the support of his neighbour the earl of Dorset at Knole, and his cousin and factotum Sir John Sackville. "Mr Bowles, your chaplain," Sir John Sackville wrote to him, "brought me your commands touching your standing to be knight of the shire. I have . . . procured for you most of the voices of this town [Sevenoaks] . . . I have my Lord of Dorset's bailiff and other agents working for you in the country."[1] Next, Vane obtained the allegiance of his cousin Sir Roger Twysden. Twysden's estates lay eastward from Fairlawne, in East Peckham in the Weald. At this time he regarded his cousin Vane, in spite of his Treasurership, as "a man truly devoted to God and his country's good, and that had persuaded the king to this course," though "truly the common people had been so bitten with Ship Money they were very averse from a courtier." Twysden therefore "dealt with all my neighbours effectually," and induced the modest Sir George Sondes and Sir Thomas Walsingham (now assured of the family seat at Rochester), to stand down and obtain for Vane the support of the gentry of north-east and north-west Kent. "Yet could I not be confident of his being elected," Twysden wrote; for Sir Edward Dering, he heard, who was campaigning on his own behalf at Dover, was suspicious of the king's Treasurer.[2]

The election thus came to turn upon the personal relationship of the two cousins, Dering and Twysden. Approached by the latter for his support, Dering at first suggested that Twysden himself should stand: "I observe a most free alacrity of voices for yourself, if you would own them. You are better beloved than your modesty will suffer you to believe. . . . If you love Mr Treasurer persuade his desistance." But Twysden

[1] *Ibid.*, pp. 3–6; KCA, Dering MSS, Kempe to Dering, 29 Jan. 1639/40; BM, Stowe MS 743, ff. 136, 140; Stowe MS 184, f. 10; KCA, Darell MSS, Sondes to Darell; CSPD, 1639–40, pp. 526–7. Sondes may have been living at Throwley Place, the family's former home, at this date, and not at Lees Court, which was being rebuilt.

[2] Proc. in K., pp. 6–7; cf. BM, Stowe MS 743, f. 136.

was not deceived by the politesse of his cousin, and eventually Sir Edward Dering seemed to offer to support Vane. It was not many days, however, before Sir George Sondes reported rumours that Dering intended to stand for the county himself. "I do verily believe," Edward Kempe of Dover told Dering, "had you stood for the shire you could not have missed." Many of the minor or mayoral families who tended to cluster round Kentish towns were also eager in persuading Dering to offer himself: his brother-in-law Anthony Percivall, captain of the forts and customer of the port of Dover; his two cousins the Braemeses, descendants of a Dover merchant and, like Percivall, landowners in neighbouring parishes; his old boon-companion, Humphrey Mantell, cousin of his neighbour Walter Mantell of Monks' Horton, the political thinker; along with John Reading, the Calvinistic minister of St Mary's, Dover, Thomas Teddeman the mayor of the town, and the Cullens, Knights, Prengles, and Booths, all of whom were members of the corporation.[1]

The assiduity and personal charm of Sir Edward in cultivating these friendships, when lieutenant of Dover Castle in the 'thirties, now began to bear fruit. The final scene in the election to the Short Parliament opened with his offer of himself as knight of the shire during the Easter assizes. His supporters, apart from those at Dover, were led by three influential cousins: Dean Bargrave in the east of the county, the wealthy Sir Edward Hales of Tunstall in the Downland, and Sir John Sedley of St Clere in Holmesdale in the west. Sedley himself secured the support of George Strode of Squerryes Court, near Westerham, Sir Edward Gilbourne of Otford, and the Seyliards of Delaware on the Eden. Along the upper Stour, Dering was supported by his neighbour Sir Robert Darell of Calehill; and when Vane withdrew, in face of rising opposition, Sir George Sondes also joined him. Of these men all save Strode came of old and powerful county families, not excluding the dean of

[1] Proc. in K., pp. 2, 7; KCA, Dering MSS, Kempe to Dering, 29 Jan. 1639/40; Dering to Braemes, 31 Dec. 1639; Dering to Prengle, Booth, Reading, Monins, and Knight, 31 Dec. 1639; Kempe to Dering, 20 March 1640/41; Hasted, IX, p. 288, VIII, pp. 60–1; *DNB*, s.v. John Reading; J. B. Jones, *Annals of Dover*, 1916, pp. 306–7.

Canterbury himself. But when Twysden heard of Dering's resolve, he

"took this so unkindly to see so little respect of that which I took him to have promised . . . [that] I could not refrain myself, but told him of it very plainly, and acquainted Mr Treasurer [Vane], . . . who instantly resolved not to stand himself, but writ to me, with all the rest of his friends hereabouts, to set up myself and oppose Dering. . . . This was a troublesome task; all the gentlemen of Kent were engaged already for Knatchbull. Dering . . . did never lie still, but rid up and down soliciting everybody . . . I could do no more but this, to give out to my friends that if I were chosen I should take it for a great favour, and do the country all service. . . ."[1]

Thus of the six candidates three—Sondes, Walsingham, and Vane—had dropped out; one, Norton Knatchbull, remained secure; and two—Sondes and Vane—added their forces to either of the two remaining contestants, Twysden and Dering.

During the following weeks Twysden's family-supporters exerted all their zeal to secure his election. "I doubt not," wrote Theophilus Higgons, rector of Hunton, that as the county

"shewed their loves to you, so you will shew your care for them; according to that knowledge, judgement, integrity and moderation which are observed in you. . . . I hope, Sir, that yourself, with other worthy discreet gent[lemen], will sweeten all things to your power, and not provoke his Majesty where things may be, by fair treaty and entreaty, reduced to a good and peaceable conclusion."[2]

The opinion of the county thus gradually slid towards the mild Sir Roger, and Dering's followers became alarmed. "Sir Henry Vane," reported Sir John Sedley to Dering,

"useth all the instruments . . . he possible [*sic*] can now to set up Sir Roger Twysden; who . . . hath endeavoured . . . to

[1] KCA, Dering MSS, Kempe to Dering, 29 Jan. 1639/40; BM, Stowe MS 184, f. 10 ("Mr Dean" is Dean Bargrave); Stowe MS 743, ff. 140, 142; KCA, Darell MSS, letter of 6 March 1639/40; Proc. in K., pp. 7–8.

[2] BM, Add. MS 34173, f. 18. Higgons was actually writing after the election; but his letter illustrates the enthusiasm of Twysden's friends.

poison the good opinion the country hath of you by possessing them how diligent and eager a servant you were for the Court in the knighting moneys. This aspersion (wheresoever I have met with it) I have vindicated you from. . . ."

But neither Dering's enthusiasm nor Sedley's somewhat venomous vindications availed. When the poll for the election to the Short Parliament was declared, Norton Knatchbull and Twysden proved to be the successful candidates.[1]

The Kentish boroughs and Cinque Ports, like the county, returned mainly moderate men of old county families; there were but two outsiders.[2] Maidstone had elected a neighbouring Fane of Hunton Court and Barnham of Boughton Monchelsea Place to nearly every parliament since Queen Elizabeth's reign: it now returned Sir Francis Barnham and Sir George Fane. Rochester had returned a Walsingham of Scadbury to most Tudor and Stuart parliaments, and elected Sir Thomas Walsingham for the sixth time. New Romney had returned one of the Godfreys to most Stuart parliaments, and chose Thomas Godfrey of Hodiford in Sellindge (much of whose patrimony lay in the Marsh) and his nephew William Steele.[3] Queenborough once more returned Sir Edward Hales of Tunstall Place, probably much the wealthiest commoner in the county. After a violent battle, incited by the puritan Richard Culmer because the archbishop sought the election of his secretary, Canterbury returned two local men, Sir Edward Master and his son-in-law John Nutt. Ignoring the traditional influence of the Lord Warden and Lord High Admiral, Dover returned the two most determined Kentish opponents of the Court, Sir Edward Boys of Fredville and Sir Peter Heyman of

[1] BM, Stowe MS 743, f. 140. Sedley afterwards accused the sheriff, Sir Edward Master of Langdon Abbey, of "gross partiality" in managing the election.

[2] Sir John Wolstenholme (elected for Queenborough), and John Wandesford (for Hythe).

[3] M. F. Keeler, *op. cit.*, pp. 97, 378; *DNB*, s.v. Sir Edmund and Sir Francis Walsingham. Thomas Godfrey was father of Sir Edmund Berry Godfrey and of Lambarde Godfrey (the solicitor-general of the Kentish Sequestration Committee), and son-in-law of William Lambarde, the Kentish historian.

Somerfield. Hythe had elected Heymans to most parliaments since the reign of Elizabeth, and now returned Sir Peter's eldest son, Henry.[1]

The brief, unhappy history of the Short Parliament need not concern us here. In the little it achieved, the Kentish members played a very insignificant role. It is safe to say that their opposition was more mild than that of most of their colleagues; but it became intensified with the dissolution of parliament, the deepening fear of invasion, and the vulnerable position of the county. During the summer of 1640 more troops and arms were sent to the north of England, and Kentish people felt increasingly defenceless and frustrated. When the writs for a new parliament were sent out in October, county sentiment was far more exacerbated against the government than it had been in the spring.

For Kent, the story of the elections to the Long Parliament is even more fully documented than for the Short Parliament.[2] The correspondence of several of the participants has survived,

[1] M. F. Keeler, *op. cit.*, pp. 200–1, 269, 288; E. 279. 13, p. 28; E. 532. 12, p. 18 [mispaginated, between pp. 23 and 24]; KCA, Dering MSS, Kempe to Dering, 29 Jan. 1639/40; CSPD, 1639–40, p. 400. Mrs Keeler seems to suggest (*op. cit.*, p. 76) that Boys was a nominee of the Lord Warden; but this is hardly credible in view of his family traditions and his subsequent conduct (*ibid.*, p. 114). His home, Fredville Court, was only ten miles from Dover, and though acting constable of the Castle, he opposed the king, and his election was more probably the result of local influence.

[2] In the elections for the boroughs and Cinque Ports there were few changes, save for the replacement of Fanes and Godfreys by Tuftons of Le Mote and Lees of Great Delce (M. F. Keeler, *op. cit.*, pp. 246, 366), and the victory of Sir Thomas Peyton and Sir Edward Partheriche at Sandwich in opposition to the nominees of the Lord Keeper, Lord Warden, and Lord High Admiral (BM, Add. MS 44846, f. 4; Sandwich Muniments, Letter Book S/N. 5, ff. 60–1). Peyton and Partheriche had fought a fierce, but unsuccessful, battle against court nominees in the spring. Only one outsider was returned for a Kentish seat to the Long Parliament (M. F. Keeler, *op. cit.*, p. 206). At least six Kentishmen sat for other constituencies: Sir John Finch (not the former Speaker) for Winchelsea, James Rivers for Lewes, Lord Buckhurst (Dorset's son) for East Grinstead, Sir Henry Vane, senior and junior, for Wilton and Hull, and Sir Peter Wroth for Bridgwater: most of whom had some kind of connexion with the towns they represented (e.g., the original family seat of the earls of Dorset was Buckhurst Place, near East Grinstead, close to the Kentish boundary).

and shows once again how the whole community of the county vibrated with feverish activity. There can have been few manor-houses in Kent in which the election of the new knights of the shire did not for the time eclipse every other topic of conversation. On this occasion no fewer than six candidates offered themselves, though for only three was there any serious chance of success. It was rare in Kent for anyone to stand for the county on two successive occasions, and when Sir Henry Vane found the inhabitants of his native Weald antipathetic to his renewed candidature, he withdrew at once and looked for a safer seat elsewhere. More persistent were Sir Robert Mansell, the admiral, and Richard Spencer, son of Lord Spencer of Wormleighton; but though both were resident in the county, neither of these men were related to the more important Kentish family connexions, and they obtained little support.[1] The three candidates between whom the real contest lay were men of moderate political convictions: Sir John Culpeper of Hollingbourne, his kinsman Sir Edward Dering, and (in consequence of the tacit rule precluding his own re-election) Twysden's own candidate, his cousin Richard Browne of Singleton Manor. Though a scion of the Brownes of Betchworth Castle in Surrey, the wealthy heir of his mother, and the husband of the heiress of Singleton, Browne's influence depended solely upon the powerful family influence of the Twysdens; otherwise his following in the county would have been negligible.

Thus the contest still in fact lay between Sir Roger Twysden and Sir Edward Dering, and once again Dering became the dominant figure in the county. At first Dering tried to regain the support of his cousin Twysden; but the answer he received was short and sharp:

"I told you at Maidstone what barred me of running freely to serve you . . . I do not hear of any but comes singly into the field, and I think it much the better, for I find the county in many parts desirous of their freedom too in placing their voices. You are I hope assured. I wish Sir Edward Dering well. . . ."

[1] BM, Stowe MS 743, ff. 149, 156, 158; Proc. in K., pp. 15, 17.

Rebuffed by his cousin, Dering thereupon determined on a conjunction of forces with Sir John Culpeper. Clarendon's character of Culpeper, as a country knight who never sacrificed to the muses, and as one whose religion was indifferent, was less than just; but hitherto, with interests mainly economic and agrarian, Culpeper had had little to do with Dering, and their present friendship was hardly cordial.[1] They agreed to canvass for one another among their friends and in their own areas, but they made no arrangement as to who should take the coveted first seat. If they played their hands ill, there might be a landslide of votes to Browne, and in consequence their co-operation was hampered by incessant suspicion. Nevertheless, the support for Dering seemed widespread. Old friends like Sir John Sedley of St Clere and those at Dover were full of enthusiasm. "God hath kindled in your breast an ardent love to the house of God," wrote Thomas Wilson, the puritan minister of Maidstone, ejected by Laud. "You do yourself a great deal of right in resuming your pretension," wrote the moderate high churchman, George Strode of Squerryes Court. "You were the son of our county's delight," said Augustine Skynner of East Farleigh Hall, the advocate of reformed episcopacy who succeeded to Dering's seat in 1642: "God . . . put it into your heart to . . . give the first assault . . . on the Goliath of Hierarchical Episcopacy. . . ." The whole world, it was said, began to dote upon Dering's accomplishments.[2]

In this election, there was no social link, no friendship, and no family relationship which Dering and his supporters did not turn to good use. Wives, sons, brothers-in-law, cousins,

[1] BM, Stowe MS 743, ff. 149, 150, 156, 158; Stowe MS 184, ff. 15, 16, 17; KCA, Dering MSS, Peyton to Dering, 25 Oct. 1640; E. 196. 8; cf. Edward Hyde, earl of Clarendon, *The History of the Rebellion* . . ., ed. W. D. Macray, 1888, I, p. 457; *The Life of Edward, Earl of Clarendon*, 3rd edn, 1761, I, pp. 93–4; *DNB*, s.v. Sir John Colepeper. The usual spelling of the family name was Culpeper, as in the text, though Sir John's peerage granted in 1644 was spelt Colepeper.

[2] BM, Stowe MS 743, f. 150; cf. Stowe MS 184, ff. 15–16; KCA, Dering MSS, Player to Dering, 10 Oct. 1640; E. 156. 14 ('Epistle Dedicatory' to Dering); Proc. in K., p. 8; Stowe MS 744, f. 13; E. 135. 43. What Augustine Skynner objected to was not episcopacy as such but an irresponsible archiepiscopate.

ministers, agents, stewards, bailiffs, and friends: all were directed day by day from Surrenden Dering, where Lady Dering managed electoral affairs while her husband travelled all over the county. "This will be a chargeable business," she wrote to him, "but being only assumed for God's glory it is not to be valued. Thus with my heartiest prayers for His blessing . . . I present thee with my heart's love." Dering's cousin Dean Bargrave remained as "earnest and real for you" now as he was in the spring. Sir Thomas Palmer of Wingham was another "material man" whom Lady Dering secured, with William Byng of Deal. "I was zealous formerly," Byng replied, "and my zeal is no whit abated . . . I will be advised by your Ladyship what and how to do. . . ." At Dover, Lady Dering said, "you are beholding to my brother [in-law] Percivall, who is very active and careful for you, both in sending and going himself." Thomas Teddeman, the mayor of Dover, made sure of the support of his jurats and "other your friends in the town," and, though unable to leave the port himself, promised to send his servant to vote for both Dering and Culpeper.[1]

Two of Dering's friends, Edward Kempe of Dover and John Player, vicar of Kennington, in the Stour Valley, voluntarily acted as his 'agents.' Kempe visited Lydd, Hythe, Romney Marsh, and the "somewhat wavering" Weald, and on the 8th October reported that, despite Culpeper's and Twysden's influence, he heard "nothing but Sir Edward in the first place." John Player toured the country north and east of Surrenden Dering, which, through the activity of Dean Bargrave and others, was "as firm for you as a rock." About Maidstone, in the heart of Culpeper country, both Thomas Wilson and his patrons the Swynokes were active for Dering, and elsewhere Culpeper's following was "like rather to decline to a consumption than [receive] any healthy augmentation." A constant watch upon their followers' affections was necessary, but Player felt assured they would secure the coveted first place. Ardently labouring for Dering in East Kent, Sir Thomas Peyton of Knowlton reported that "the general acclamation of the county . . . concur all in one cheerfulness to give you the

[1] KCA, Dering MSS, Lady Dering to Dering, 3 and 23 Oct. 1640; BM, Stowe MS 743, f. 152.

priority." About Fredville, Peyton's activities were seconded by his neighbour Sir Edward Boys, who gave Culpeper a "flat denial" but obtained for Dering, as well as his own tenants' votes, the support of his relatives the Swans of Denton Court.[1] Nearer home, Sir Robert Darell of Calehill obtained the allegiance of Norton Knatchbull's powerful following, including the Scotts of Scots' Hall, the Honywoods of Evington, the Heymans of Somerfield, and their many cousins and brothers-in-law clustering along the upper Stour. "For my sons," Sir Peter Heyman wrote to Dering, "I know not but you may use them as your servants, and myself as your friend and respective neighbour." In the Downland and around Tenterden in the Weald, Dering's cousin Sir Edward Hales of Tunstall was a powerful ally; for by prudent marriages Hales had now united the extensive inheritance and family influence of both the Cromers and the Wottons with his own patrimony. Five miles east of Tunstall, James Hugessen of Provender in Lynsted offered Dering "as many of my tenants as I can procure. . . ." "I received a letter," he added, "from my respected neighbour Sir Edward Hales to stand for Sir John Culpeper and yourself. I conceive that Sir Edward Hales hath requested divers other gentlemen and others to the same effect. . . ." From Lees Court near by, John Craige (probably Sir George Sondes's steward) wrote to Sir Edward Dering:

"I thought it my duty to give you notice what I am doing in your business. Sir George shewed me your letter and told me . . . you might have his assistance . . . in his friends and tenants. My Lord Chamberlain hath sent for them all, I suspect it is to set up a deputy, but it will be too late. I have done what I could at Faversham and Canterbury. . . . I spoke with Mr Greenstrete, who promises to labour the town. I find the yeomen about us wonderfully desirous to choose you."[2]

[1] BM, Stowe MS 743, ff. 150, 153, 159; cf. Stowe MS 184, f. 15; KCA, Dering MSS, Player to Dering, 10 Oct. 1640; Proc. in K., pp. 15–16, 10–11; BM, Add. MS 44846, ff. 4v, 5.

[2] BM, Stowe MS 743, ff. 146, 155; Proc. in K., pp. 9–10, 18–19. Mr Greenstrete was presumably a member of the old though minor family of that name at Greenstreet, near Faversham.

The west of the county seemed less promising. Despite the optimism of Player and Wilson, the enthusiasm of the people of Maidstone gradually cooled off as the election drew near: it was in the heart of Culpeper country. "You must speedily appear in these parts," wrote George Haule of Chillington Manor, "either in person or by letter; . . . they wish they had your letter to publish; you will lose many by it else . . . I doubt Sir John Culpeper's voices in these parts will not be very fast to you." West of Maidstone, Sir John Sedley of St Clere was once again active in Dering's behalf. Though he was now at loggerheads with his neighbours the Vanes of Fairlawne, the Twysdens of Roydon Hall, and the Rayneys of Wrotham, the influence of Sir John Sedley was still widespread, and personally he was devoted to his cousin Dering.[1] Assuring him "of the choicest share in my affections," he had, he said, "before your letter arrived me [*sic*], engaged many of my friends for you, and will do more. . . ." Very zealous in Dering's behalf was Sedley's neighbour and companion, William James of Ightham Court Lodge. Five miles west of St Clere, Sedley secured the support of the Gilbournes, an old and knightly family of Otford and Shoreham, and, in the Downland to the north, that of Sir Stephen Lennard of West Wickham (cousin of the Lennards Lords Dacre of neighbouring Chevening) and Sir Humphrey Style of Langley. In this area Dering was able to exert no direct influence, and Lennard's and Style's promises of at least 100 'voices' was a valuable one. In the Eden valley, Sedley obtained the support of the Seyliards of Seyliards and Delaware, and beyond Tonbridge of the Styles of Wateringbury, cousins of Sir Humphrey of Langley.[2]

Nevertheless, Sedley was not unduly optimistic of the affections of this part of the county. Though allowance must be made for his splenetic language, there was probably some truth beneath his slanderous remark that Maidstone was "poisoned with faction," and that his own hope of election, for the town,

[1] Proc. in K., pp. 11–12. Sir John Rayney described Sedley as a "knight and baronet with one eye, a most malicious neighbour . . . who seeks all occasions, though never so small and frivolous, to vex and trouble [me]."—CSPD, 1636–37, p. 52.

[2] Proc. in K., p. 12; BM, Stowe MS 184, ff. 15–16.

had been frustrated by Sir Francis Barnham of Boughton Monchelsea, "whose malice, were it not in hourly machination busied against one or other, he could not live. . . ." On the 21st October, Sedley sent Sir Edward a long account of the "plots I have discovered to be against you. . . . First, the malevolency of Sir Roger Twysden who turns all the teeth he hath, though but few and those ill, upon you by setting up old Browne . . . [who is] gotten so strong by the support of Twysden and his bangle-eared props out of the dirt. . . . Barnham's faction and all other that can be seduced will turn to Browne. . . ." All the Culpeper clan, Sedley remarked, were conspiring to obtain the first place, which would lose many voices to Browne, although "Sir John [Culpeper] will have excuse enough to say he persuaded seriously, but could not compel." Hearing of these suspicions, Sir John Culpeper offered to discuss election prospects with Sedley, but the latter remained bitterly suspicious and unsatisfied, and imagined yet further plots behind Culpeper's innocent statement that he had "aerated" 800 freeholders for Dering "in the second place." "There will be great hazard in it," Sedley confided to Dering, "we fear it much."[1] A less melancholy account of the state of Dering's party in "the extremity of the west" came from George Strode of Squerryes Court. In the middle of October Strode reported that all Dering's rivals had withdrawn from the field but Culpeper and Browne; for neither Richard Spencer nor Sir Robert Mansell were natives of Kent, and they had found little support amongst the local gentry.[2]

Meanwhile, as the kinsmen of Twysden, Culpeper, and Dering were thus building up their rival connexions in the county, a polite but somewhat cat-like correspondence took place between the two latter rivals. To obtain the first place, Sir John Culpeper relied upon his influence in the countryside around Maidstone, "not one of forty not promising." Dering at once became suspicious, and Culpeper for his part suspected Sir Edward of duplicity with regard to Richard Browne and

[1] Proc. in K., p. 13; BM, Stowe MS 184, ff. 15–16. Sedley was mystified by Culpeper's word "aerated." The earliest instance of it recorded in the *Oxford English Dictionary* dates from 1794.

[2] Proc. in K., pp. 16–17.

the Knatchbull group. "Upon Saturday last," he complained, "in my way to Canterbury I met with the traces of one who crossed the country from Ashford to Faversham who bespoke . . . all the voices he met with for Sir Ed[ward] De[ring] and Mr Browne. . . ." Culpeper hopefully supposed that the treacherous agent was a "volunteer," but the relations between the two men were clearly strained. Sir Edward had agreed to undertake the canvassing in parishes within five miles of Surrenden Dering himself, while Sir John Culpeper took over that within the twenty-three parishes of his own hundred. But Dering's directions for the "second voices" for Culpeper were not being satisfactorily carried out. Sir John therefore sent him the letters he had received from his own twenty-three parishes to convince him of *his* fulfilment of the bargain, and to demand its completion by Dering. His own activities, he said, had secured for Sir Edward

"above 400 householders; there are but three who have not promised me their second voices for you. The like I have done by my friends in every parish in Milton hundred [adjoining his own], whence I have full assurance for you as well as for myself. . . . My request must be that in your neighbourhood you will send to one or two fit men in each parish to make sure for me the second voice of every freeholder; without this particular, you may fail of the success of your intentions in favour of me."[1]

When the day of election drew near, Dering and Culpeper became more friendly, and agreed to entertain their supporters with a tun of sack at the polling booths on Penenden Heath. The whole county was in a state of feverish excitement. Never before had so vast a concourse gathered on the Heath as on the day before the election. The followers of Dering and Culpeper came in from the Weald, of Sedley and Strode from Holmesdale, and of Hales and Sondes from the Downland. The Peytons, Oxindens, and Bargraves came from beyond Canterbury, passing the night on the way with their relatives the Merediths at Leeds Abbey. The walls of the Shire House on the Heath were broken down in the anxiety of electors "to

[1] BM, Stowe MS 743, ff. 149, 157.

put through the names of the freeholders, for their friends to be written down."[1] When the poll was declared, it was found that Twysden's candidate Richard Browne was unsuccessful, and Sir Edward Dering and Sir John Culpeper were returned.

Such was the way in which the opposition to Charles I was organized in Kent in 1640. Historically, it is more important for its revelation of the social organization of the county than for its insight into the politics of the nation. In fact, abstract principle played only a minor part in the electoral activity in Kent, and there was little difference in political or religious conviction between the three principal candidates. Fundamentally, they were much closer to one another than to men like Sir Nathaniel Barnardiston of Suffolk or Sir Arthur Heselrige of Leicestershire, with whom they were for the moment united against Charles I. Their rivalry was essentially a struggle between different family connexions for the control of the county. In a shire with no clearly dominant family, this lengthy struggle for power was unavoidable; the same method of securing control came into operation in each subsequent crisis. First, the knight or baronet who set out to rule the county secured the support of the countryside around his own manor-house. Then his kinsmen among the greater gentry obtained the allegiance of their own labourers, tenants, and neighbours. Finally, each major family secured the adherence of those groups of minor gentry whose social influence depended on their place in these galaxies of greater gentry. In this way, the whole community of the county gradually gathered into a series of rival family connexions. The whole system was reinforced by the tours and reports of the leader's unofficial 'agents,' by his own hasty journeys through the county, and by the canvassing of "one or two fit men" in each parish.

[1] *Ibid.*, f. 156; BM, Add. MS 28000, f. 41; Maidstone Museum, Twysden MSS, 'Memorials since my being a J.P.', f. 15.

IV

THE COMMUNITY DIVIDES, 1640–2

(i) *The Breakdown of Unity, 1640–2*

IF THE HISTORY of Kent before 1640 shows the gradual fusion of the diverse elements in the community in opposition to Charles I, its history between 1640 and 1642 shows the subsequent breakdown in this unity, and the gradual alienation of the county from parliament. For the first few months of the period, political developments in Kent were closely associated with developments in parliament, and more particularly with the activities of Sir Edward Dering and the group of members who represented the county's boroughs and Cinque Ports. The rapid emergence of puritan pressure groups in the county, however, brought to light not only the essential cleavage between the moderates, headed by Sir Edward Dering, and the puritan leaders in the House of Commons, but also the difficulties Sir Edward Dering encountered in retaining his control over the local community. The expulsion of Sir Edward from the Commons early in 1642 brought about the complete alienation of the county from parliament. It was followed by the organization of the famous Kentish Petition in favour of county autonomy and moderate reformation of the church. The subsequent imprisonment of the petitioners delivered Kent into the hands of a clique of hotheaded Cavaliers, who endeavoured to secure the county for the king. Finally, the discovery of a conspiracy organized by these Cavaliers compelled parliament to send a military expedition into the county to suppress opposition, and to establish the County Committee.

Quite clearly, the role which Sir Edward Dering had assumed in 1640 as leader of the county was no easy one. The combination of family influence and personal charm which had won him dominion in Kent soon brought him to the notice of the opposition leaders in the House. His ecclesiastical interests procured him the position of chairman of the Committee for Religion, and on this Committee he was supported by several of his fellow-members from Kent. Neither he nor they were puritans; essentially they were provincials and conservatives rather than radicals. They were mostly middle-aged men, members of old county families, nurtured in the church of Hooker, and deeply versed in the intricacies of local administration. At 42, Sir Edward Dering was much the youngest man among them. Sir Edward Hales and Sir Peter Heyman, who had sat in parliament five times before, were respectively 64 and 60; Sir Francis Barnham, who had sat seven times, and Sir Edward Boys, three times, were also over 60; Sir Thomas Walsingham, who had sat in seven previous parliaments, was 46; and Sir Edward Partheriche, Sir Edward Master, and Sir Humphrey Tufton were at least 50.[1] The chief preoccupation of all these men was ecclesiastical reformation and the restoration of "primitive episcopacy." "Neither Star-Chamber," said Sir Edward Dering, "nor High Commission, nor Ship Money, nor Strafford's death . . . are . . . equivalent to the settling . . . of the Church." In this "settling . . . of the Church" the Kentish members of the Committee for Religion aimed at a severe reformation of Laudian pretensions, but they wished to retain both the liturgy and the bench of bishops.[2]

Whilst the Kentish members of parliament, led by Sir Edward Dering, were thus wrestling with the problem of ecclesiastical reformation, the puritans of the county were forming a powerful pressure group in Kent, and endeavouring to force their demands on the Committee for Religion.[3] So long as the pressure was voiced in local petitions to the Committee for a "most severe reformation" of local grievances and Laudian pretensions, all was well.[4] Sir Edward Dering knew that the archbishop's "crimes were many;" for the complaints, as he admitted, were "fresh with me, and myself . . . as fit as any to strike," being "servitor for that shire . . . where some of his hardship [was] then fresh. . . ." But puritans like Thomas Wilson and Richard Culmer were not content with a revival

[1] CJ, II, *passim*; Keeler, *op. cit.*, pp. 97, 114; *DNB*, s.v. Sir Edmund Walsingham, Sir Francis Barnham, Sir Peter Heyman.

[2] E. 197. 1, p. 67.

[3] Cf. Proc. in K., pp. 80–100. The Kentish members comprised half the active members of the Committee.

[4] For these local petitions, cf. pp. 60–62, *supra*.

of the "primitive episcopacy" which the Kentish members of parliament desired, or the virtually autonomous county churches advocated by Dering. For them the Scottish presbytery and its rigorous discipline, not the vague personal sanctity of a resident bishop, was the only true safeguard against lordly prelacy. Like his Kentish colleagues in the House, Dering did not "dream . . . of extirpation," but he ultimately found that "such of the prelatic party as are in love with present pomp and power will be averse unto me because I pare so deep: the Rooters, the antiprelatic party, declaim against me because I will not take all away."[1]

The first move of the Kentish puritans was to organize a petition in December 1640, and present it to Dering's Committee for Religion. The Committee had already received a number of unimportant petitions complaining of local grievances in a variety of Kentish parishes; but this document purported to voice the views of some 2,500 malcontents in twenty or more Wealden wool villages. In fact, it was not a local petition at all, but was founded upon a copy sent down into the county from London, and it demanded that episcopacy "with all its dependencies, Root and Branch, may be abolished." Dering was greatly perturbed on receiving it, and hastened into Kent to meet its promoters—his friend John Elmeston of Goudhurst among them—and "finding it a parrot . . . by rote calling for Root and Branch, I dealt with the presenters thereof, . . . until . . . I taught it a new and more modest language." His clerical friends like Robert Abbot of Cranbrook and James Wilcocke of Goudhurst, he found, were being bitterly persecuted by these puritans. ". . . I would fain be cleared of blasphemy," complained Wilcocke, and of "leading of souls to hell: I could have borne innumerable other outrages, . . . but God only knows how much my soul hath been overcharged with these imputations," and "others of my brethren, infinitely deserving better, have been engaged as deeply: our backs are daily ploughed upon. . . ."[2] The clauses

[1] E. 197. 1, section 1 and pp. 159, 161, 162; cf. Proc. in K., p. 19.

[2] KCA, Dering MSS, Elmeston to Dering, 1 Dec. 1640; E. 197. 1, pp. 16–17; E. 172. 30. Wilcocke published his sermons to clear himself from these accusations.

in the petition relating to "the pride, the avarice, the ambition, and oppression of our ill-ruling clergy" Dering therefore deleted. For that regarding "Root and Branch" he substituted a clause "that this hierarchical power may be totally abrogated," which preserved episcopacy but was intended to preclude "lordly prelacy." Early in 1641 he presented the puritan petition, thus modified, to the House of Commons.[1]

Foiled in their first attack, the Wealden puritans turned their attention to the celebration of the anglican liturgy in their local parish churches. "That which most toucheth me to the quick . . .," wrote Robert Abbot to Dering, "is the Common Prayer Book. . . . My people . . . fall upon it with much bitterness. . . . Some say it is stinted, compelled worship, some that it is Popery. . . ." Abbot narrated a conference held in his rectory at Cranbrook, and the arguments employed to convince his puritan antagonists; but

"all this will not satisfy them, and keep me from daily vexations . . .; tomorrow will 40 come unto me to persuade me to lay down the Common Prayer Book quite, or else they will not come to the church . . . I do fearfully groan under this burthen. . . . The God of heaven . . . enable you to be assistant, lest I be driven through tumult to leave my station."

Since Abbot refused to give up the use of the Prayer Book established by church and law, his offer to undertake the daily lecture, on which his puritan parishioners insisted, was rejected. "None will please [them]," he wrote, "but one that is for down, down." "I have a pope in my belly," they say, "and [am] unfit for such a work." "To have my conscience, credit, and pains trampled upon by my people after 24 years is an hard task . . . I beseech you feel with me and, if you can, put in an hand to help, or a word of counsel. . . ." But Dering was now no longer able to help; for his own influence in the House of Commons had recently suffered a sudden and violent setback.[2]

[1] E. 197. 1, p. 17; Proc. in K., pp. 28–32; CJ, II, p. 67; W. Notestein, ed., *The Journal of Sir Simonds D'Ewes*, 1923, p. 249.

[2] BM, Stowe MS 184, ff. 43, 44, 47, 23; Stowe MS 744, f. 15; E. 197. 1, p. 93.

As Dering had sat in the House on 21 May 1641, Sir Henry Vane, Sir Arthur Heselrige, and Oliver Cromwell had suddenly thrust into his hand a bill entitled "An Act for the utter abolishing and taking away of all Archbishops," earnestly urgent, he said himself, that he should present it. An impulsive man, spurred on by their enthusiasm, and caught unprepared in a period of despair at the endless obstructions to the "severe reformation" he worked for, Dering rose and spoke. "I never was for *ruin*," he said,

"so long as I could hold any hope of *reforming*. My hopes that way are even almost withered. . . . When this Bill is perfected, I shall give a sad aye unto it. And . . . if my former hopes of a *full reformation* may yet revive and prosper, I will again divide my sense upon this Bill, and . . . *underprop* the primitive, lawful, and just *episcopacy*: yet . . . *root out* all the undue adjuncts to it, and superstructures on it,"

by which Dering signified the overweening prelacy of Archbishop Laud.[1] One month later, however, a presbyterian project for "putting all church government into the hands of commissioners" was added to this otherwise negative bill. Dering at once protested. To the archiepiscopacy of "a *lordly prelate*, . . . who . . . will have no assessors . . ., no senate, no consultation . . ., but elates himself up into usurped titles . . ., assuming a *soleship* both in *orders* and in *censures* . . ., not content with ecclesiastic pride alone" but demanding "offices secular," he was as opposed as anyone. But presbyterianism, "the rule of many," he said, "cannot be without confusion, unless there be one to guide and direct the rest." He desired the election of a president or bishop ("the name of *bishop* disturbs not me"), "chosen out among the rest, and by the rest put into a several *degree* (not into a distinct superior *order*)

[1] *Ibid.*, section I and pp. 64–5. Dering's attitude of mind at this time is shown by his remark "my despairs begin to go above my faith:" Proc. in K., p. 46. He introduced the above bill partly in order to force the hands of the Lords, where the bill for the abolition of the secular jurisdiction of the bishops had long been labouring. It was principally against this *secular* jurisdiction of the bishops, and what Dering and others in Kent and elsewhere regarded as the "lordly prelacy" of the archbishop, that they were opposed They did not object to episcopacy as such or from presbyterian convictions.

above the rest . . . in matters spiritual" only. Having briefly outlined his own idealized system of church government, he moved that the present proposal be "laid by, and that we may proceed to reduce again the old original episcopacy," the pastoral government of the primitive church.[1]

The puritans were furious. One London citizen informed Dering that he had lost "the prayers of many thousands;" other critics, equally charitable, that he had "fallen from grace" and "apostatized;" one, that he had been infected with the poison of Dr Brownrig; another that he had a "pope in [his] belly." It was averred, as a crime, that he had succumbed to the influence of Robert Abbot and John Reading: Abbot had, indeed, recently written to him to insist upon episcopacy as "a divine precept," and it was probably either he or Reading who had sent him "Humble Considerations . . . whether all bishops ought to stand or fall. . . ."[2] But in fact Dering's views had not changed: they had been worked out, in some detail, several years before, although his enemies could not or would not see any alternative to presbyterianism on one hand and Laudianism on the other.

To win a hearing for reformed episcopacy and retention of the liturgy, Dering therefore decided to employ Root and Branch methods himself, and to organize a county petition of his own. Like-minded moderates in other counties, such as Somerset, were adopting precisely the same procedure. The family connexion which had originally supported Dering in Kent was beginning to disintegrate: but old friends who had seceded in 1640, like Sir Roger Twysden, had begun to rejoin him. In the autumn of 1641 Dering therefore arranged a meeting with them, drew up a petition, and circulated copies of it amongst his friends. "Whereas it hath been desired by some," this document ran,

"that there be an utter abolition of all government by bishops, and an abrogation of the public form of Common Prayer, . . . we do earnestly and heartily concur . . . for relief and ease against the many exorbitancies . . . in the

[1] E. 197. 1, pp. 74–5, 71; cf. pp. 65 sqq. Dering especially objected to Laud's desire for a "patriarchate," as he expressed it.

[2] E. 197. 1, pp. 162–4; BM, Stowe MS 184, ff. 39 sqq.

Church and state; but we do withal [as] earnestly . . . as possibly we can beseech and pray this honourable House, both in the Church government and in our present liturgy (if . . . by learned men any errors shall be found in either), to give us a severe reformation, not an absolute innovation. And . . . pray, even for God's sake, . . . that you will either command a free national synod to be forthwith called, . . . or else that you please not to conclude us up unheard, . . . but grant us a solemn, free debate . . . before you, whereupon you may please to settle such resolutions as may deservedly bind all our obedience. . . ."[1]

As in the elections of 1640, Dering's friends once again began to mobilize the parochial gentry and clergy of the county, and to summon their relatives, tenants, and servants to subscribe the petition in their parish churches. At Frittenden in the Weald, three of the Webbe family thus undertook the organization of Dering's petition; at East Langdon four of the Marshes of Martin; around Dover many of Dering's old companions, such as the Percivalls of Archcliffe, the Kempes and Mantells, the Cullens, Moninses, Teddemans, Prengles, and Streatfeilds.[2] Under Dering's leadership, the moderates of the county thus began to diverge in their political loyalty from the puritan leaders of the House of Commons, and to separate themselves more definitely from the small cliques of puritans in the county, with whom they had temporarily aligned in 1640.

[1] BM, Stowe MS 744, f. 13; Add. MS 26785, ff. 49–50; Proc. in K., pp. 60–4, and cf. footnote to p. 61 for the phrase in brackets. For similar moderate petitions of other counties, pleading for continuance of the present church government and liturgy, see John Nalson, *An Impartial Collection of the Great Affairs of State* . . ., 1682–83, II, pp. 720–2 (Hunts.), 726–7 (Somerset). The Somerset petition claimed (no doubt with exaggeration) to be signed by 14,350 people, including 200 gentlemen and 221 divines, who said they did not care whether episcopacy was of divine origin or not, but knew it was ancient, and desired "that the precious may be separated from the vile, that the bad [clergy] may be rejected and the good retained." Such moderate views, though often suppressed or forced underground after 1642, were widespread. They were certainly not peculiar to Kent, Hunts., and Somerset, though in the former county they were unusually prevalent. All three petitions show the same objection to the extremes of both Laudianism and puritanism.

[2] Proc. in K., pp. 62–4.

But was not their divergence too timid? Did not their petition, in calling for a national synod, raise a political issue? Had the lower House, to which it was addressed, the power to summon such an assembly? Was it not rather the "native prerogative of the king?" Thus Robert Abbot characteristically questioned Dering, and the issue turned from religion to the validity of the Commons' orders, and the problem of political sovereignty. At the quarter sessions in the autumn of 1641, Twysden and his fellow-justices interrogated Dering in similar vein, and on 21 October he took the matter up in parliament. He knew he would offend, but he must speak his conscience. No law existed, he said, by which men could be bound to observe the orders of the House, and none could be punished for neglecting them. Perhaps many members of the Commons in their hearts agreed with Sir Edward Dering; but the puritan leaders of the House were once again incensed.[1]

The final breach between Dering and the parliamentarian leaders came in connexion with the Grand Remonstrance in 1642. Sir Edward and his fellow-justices in Kent knew well how easily the "well-ordered chain of government" was broken in their own parishes at home, and they feared deeply the uncontrollable lawlessness which, as they saw it, the Remonstrance would let loose. Dering himself deplored the attack in the Remonstrance upon clerical "luxury," and the demand for parity of ministers; for in his view prospects of promotion provided a much-needed inducement to the provision of a learned ministry, and he was painfully aware of the hardships that many clergy faced, through poverty, in their efforts to pursue their theological studies. Neither would Dering agree that the episcopate had introduced idolatry; for the bishop of Durham, he said, "hath fought in the front against Roman superstition and idolatry," not to mention many other prelates.[2] He was shocked, moreover, that the opposition "should

[1] BM, Add. MS 26785, f. 49; Twysden's Journal, I, pp. 190–1; E. 197. 1, p. 82 and section x; W. H. Coates, ed., *Journal of Sir Simonds D'Ewes*, 1942, pp. 19–20.

[2] BM, Stowe MS 184, ff. 43, 47; E. 197. 1, pp. 112–18; cf. Proc. in K., pp. 169–70 (Dering was behind these two documents regarding Richard Tray). The other prelates Dering specifically referred to were Williams, Hall, Juxon, Curll, Bridgeman, Potter, and Duppa.

remonstrate downward, tell stories to the people, and talk of the king as of a third person." "My heart pities a king so fleeting and so friendless, yet without one noted vice," he confided to his wife when the king left London for Hampton Court. "And why are we told," he asked the Commons,

"that the people are expectant for a declaration? . . . I do here profess that I do not know any one soul of all that country [*sc.*, county] for which I have the honour to serve, who looks for this at your hands. They do humbly and heartily thank you for many good laws and statutes already enacted and pray for more. . . . They do not expect to hear any other stories of what you have done, much less promises of what you will do."[1]

With his fellow-knight Sir John Culpeper, Sir Edward Dering therefore voted against the Grand Remonstrance. He continued to attend the House, but he took no further part in the opposition. He was in fact ill, and he was "almost tired out with swimming against the stream. . . ."[2] Having failed to justify moderate anglicanism to the House, he had determined to make a final attempt to justify it to the world at large, and to vindicate his own consistency, by publishing his parliamentary *Speeches*, annotated with a carefully argued commentary.[3] Significantly enough the demand for this little volume at once became intense. Dering's sister-in-law, a member of the Queen's household, gave a copy of one of the speeches to the king, who swore it witnessed an "honest heart." But on the 2nd February it was debated by the Commons, voted a scandal to the House, and ordered to be burned by the common hangman. Dering was accused of "discovering the secrets of the House," "disgracing the acts of the House," and "naming members of the House to their disgrace." He was disabled from sitting, and, with "hundreds of boys and girls at his heels . . . crying out, 'Which is Sir Edward Dering?' " he was sent to

[1] E. 197. 1, pp. 108–9; Proc. in K., p. 67.

[2] E. 197. 1, p. 119; Proc. in K., pp. xliii, xlix. The disease of which he died in 1644 already afflicted him.

[3] E. 197. 1. The Thomason Tract *Catalogue* gives the date of publication of this volume as November 1641, but in fact it did not appear till January 1642.—Proc. in K., pp. xliii, xliv.

the Tower. Such was the reward, in 1642, of telling parliament an unwelcome truth.[1]

"I trust," said one who called himself a charitable judge,

> ". . . you shall never twice be paralleled that a third[2] should be found amongst them so hypocrizing . . . as to betray as much as in you both lay, the cause of both God, the Church, and the country, wheeling and veering about, . . . not content with what the kingdom had appropriated lately unto your deserts, . . . poisoned with the dregs of that cup [of the Straffordian faction]."

Yet in fact Dering was no royalist and certainly no Straffordian. His tragedy, like that of many other English people, was that he could not side whole-heartedly with either party in the passionate dispute. Though, like others in the county, he sympathized with the pietistic and mystical element in puritanism, he could not abide its rancours. As for the aspersions of his puritan enemies, they merely confirmed him in severing himself from them. He could not support men who cried away with "episcopacy, away with the burden of liturgy, . . . away with . . . a national church, . . . away with all the distinction of clergy and laity, it is popish. . . ." They would not learn moderation, as he wished, and they made him afraid in demanding that "popular parity" which "may hereafter labour to bring the king down to be but as the first among the Lords, and . . . the Lords down into our House . . .," and so break the "well-ordered chain of government, which from the chair of Jupiter reacheth down by several golden links, even to the protection of the poorest. . . ." When released from the Tower on 11 February 1642, Dering therefore returned to Kent, and to the society of men like Sir Roger Twysden, whose simplicity could hardly believe that the "merciful House . . . full of

[1] *Ibid.*, pp. xliii–xliv; CJ, II, p. 411; *Verney Papers. Notes of Proceedings in the Long Parliament . . .*, ed. John Bruce, Camden Society, XXXI, 1845, p. 152; CSPD, 1641–3, p. 273. Dering had not in fact named any members of the House, but he had given the initials of several which it was not hard to identify: e.g., "S.A.H." no doubt referred to Sir Arthur Heselrige.

[2] In this phrase the writer is linking Dering's defection with that of Lord Digby.

wisdom" should so misjudge him. The king had tentatively offered Dering the lieutenancy of the Tower, but he was quite consistent with his own principles in refusing it. "So much for courtship," he wrote to his wife at Surrenden Dering, "but I will be thy country-fellow again."[1]

Meanwhile, uncertainty and unrest were also spreading far and wide in the county of Kent itself. The prevailing sentiment of the shire was now anti-parliamentarian, if not positively royalist. The ever-present fears of invasion were much heightened by the arrival of troops from the continent, and the requisition of Kentish forces for Ireland. Opposition to parliamentary taxation and disputes among the lathal commissioners appointed to collect it were rife, and the collection of poll-money was much in arrear. In January 1642 a sermon was preached in Canterbury Cathedral that "the people of England had deserted the king;" and when Charles I accompanied the queen on her way through Kent to Holland, in February 1642, a wave of royalist sentiment flooded the county. Many gentry, like Dering's brother-in-law Anthony Percivall of Archcliffe, were graciously received by the king and knighted. Others came to see his Majesty riding upon Barham Downs, and all were impressed by his gracious bearing. "The Lady Percivall knelt to kiss his Majesty's hand; he helped her up and saluted her, and so did the queen. . . ."[2]

But a nucleus of parliamentarians was also emerging in the county. Sir Anthony Weldon of Swanscombe, destined shortly to become chairman of the County Committee, was informing against his local rector, publicly traducing Sir John Culpeper when Charles I appointed him Chancellor of the Exchequer, and gleefully exposing the scandal of the gunpowder monopoly. Sir Michael Livesey of Eastchurch, another man of violent temperament, and a later regicide, was informing against his recusant neighbours, and endeavouring to organize a petition

[1] E. 135. 43; E. 197. 1, pp. 164–6; BM, Stowe MS 744, f. 15; KCA, Dering MSS, Dering to Lady Dering, 24 Jan. 1641/2; Proc. in K., p. xliii.

[2] *The Petitions of the Mayors, Bailiffs, Jurats, Freemen, and others, Inhabitants of the Cinque Ports*, March 1642; cf. CJ, II, pp. 145, 402, 420; BM, Add. MS 44846, f. 11v.; Add. MS 28000, ff. 381, 382v.; Rushworth, IV, p. 484.

amongst the Kentish puritans to counterblast Sir Edward Dering's petition in favour of moderate episcopacy.[1]

(ii) *The Kentish Petitions of 1642*

It was to these conditions of unrest and dissension that Sir Edward Dering returned after his expulsion from the House of Commons in the opening months of 1642. The time was ripe for the launching of a new county petition, in answer to that of Sir Michael Livesey, which purported to express the views of the whole county, but in fact was the work of a small puritan clique and was based upon a stereotyped model sent down from London. In order to obtain the free support of the shire, the new petition was to be promoted by the Grand Jury at the forthcoming county assizes. It was the launching and ultimate suppression of this document that S. R. Gardiner regarded as the final signal of Civil War. On Monday, 21 March 1642, an excited concourse of gentry and countrymen began to flock into Maidstone, led by Sir Edward Dering, Sir Roger Twysden, Sir John Sedley of St Clere, Sir George Strode of Squerryes, Richard Spencer of Orpington, and Thomas Blount of Wricklesmarsh. On the following day, as they sat at supper in the Star Inn, the usual meeting-place of the gentry, they commenced their discussion of the proposed petition. On Wednesday, in response to Judge Malet's suggestion (for which there was apparently no precedent) that, instead of yeomen chosen by the sheriff, the gentry should offer themselves for the Grand Jury, Dering, Sedley, Strode, Spencer, Blount, and fourteen others stepped forward, and Dering was appointed their chairman.[2] During the evening, on Twysden's

[1] Proc. in K., pp. 48–9, 206–26 (Weldon was behind these petitions); *DNB*, s.v. Sir Anthony Weldon; CJ, II, p. 34; Notestein *op.*, *cit.*, pp. 55–6, 541. As many as 70 recusants had recently been convicted in Canterbury (*ibid.*, p. 288); but in general in Kent there was neither the same fear nor the same oppression of recusants as in puritan counties like Essex and Suffolk: cf. Everitt, *Suffolk and the Great Rebellion*, p. 11.

[2] BM, Add. MS 28000, f. 149; Twysden's Journal, I, pp. 200–2; CJ, II, p. 502. The Maidstone assizes covered West Kent only; the East Kent gentry were not generally involved in the petition, apart from a few who were visiting friends or kinsmen in West Kent. For East Kent, the assizes

advice, a committee of the Grand Jury and Bench met privately to discuss each clause of the proposed document, and the petition was then drawn up, with great care, by Dering and Strode. On 25th March, under the committee's direction, Dering propounded it publicly in the presence of 2,000 people, and Augustine Skynner, the new knight of the shire, who had been elected in Dering's place, promised to forward it in the House of Commons, Strode's and Dering's suggestion of sending a copy to the king being rejected. When the new petition was "delivered at the Bar by the Grand Inquest," however, nine of the jurymen, much to the surprise of the promoters, disowned it. They were led by Thomas Blount and they had already signed Livesey's petition: they seem, in fact, to have joined the new movement with the intention of undermining it. Unable, therefore, to present their document in open court in the name of the Grand Jury, the remaining ten jurors, with Judge Malet's connivance, "published it upon the Bench when the judge was withdrawn from the Court of Pleas to the Court of Nisi Prius. And in this manner the several articles . . . were voted by all that were present except some few."[1]

The terms of this celebrated county petition provide a clear statement of the general religious and political convictions of the community of Kent. They were both temperate and conservative; mildly royalist, or at least non-parliamentarian, but essentially local in outlook. In secular matters they demanded,

---

were held at Canterbury. Owing to the congregation of gentry in Maidstone and Canterbury at such times, the assizes had come to resemble a kind of informal county 'parliament' in this period: the verdict of the Grand Jury on political matters was regarded as the decisive 'voice' of the county. A similar development had taken place in other shires by this date, but it was more clearly marked in Kent than in some other parts. The Kentish Rebellion of 1648 was organized at the Canterbury assizes in the same way as the Kentish Petition of 1642 was organized at Maidstone. The activities of the Grand Jury gave each event the semi-formal sanction of the county community. It was the fear of this, in the exacerbated state of county feeling, that led to Sir Anthony Weldon's quite valid objection to holding the assizes at Canterbury in 1648. For the same reason, the West Kent assizes following the Rebellion were not held at Maidstone but were transferred to Sevenoaks.

[1] CJ, II, pp. 502–3, 507; Twysden's Journal, I, pp. 203–5; LJ, IV, p. 676; HMC, XII, ii, p. 311.

in the first place, that militia offenders be tried within the county, and that "our sea-forts may be repaired and our magazines renewed." They also desired "an especial law for the regulating of the militia of this kingdom, so that the subject may know how at once to obey both his Majesty and both Houses of Parliament, a law whereby may be left to the discretion of governors as little as may be:" so that nothing might be "left to any arbitrary power," and "the precious liberty of the subject . . . may be . . . preserved. . . ." They also asked that "his Majesty's gracious message" for maintaining these liberties, and his own "just and regal authority," might be taken into speedy consideration; and they laid bare "the sad condition that we and the whole land are in, if a good understanding be not speedily renewed between his Majesty and both Houses of Parliament."[1] The ecclesiastical demands of the petition comprised no fewer than eight of the seventeen clauses. Episcopacy, an institution "as ancient in this island as Christianity itself" and "the most pious, most prudent, and most safe government," though not claimed to be *jure divino*, should be "preserved . . . for the peace of the church." They asked that the liturgy,

"celebrated by the piety of the bishops and martyrs who composed it, established by the supreme laws of this land . . ., confirmed by the subscription of all the ministry . . ., and with a holy love embraced by the most and best of all the laity . . . may . . . be enjoyed quiet and free from interruptions, scorns, profaneness, threats, and force of such men who daily do deprave it and neglect the use of it. . . ."

Such profaneness and neglect by clergy should be punished in ecclesiastical courts; there must also be a "severe law made against laymen for daring to arrogate to themselves and to execute the holy function of the ministry. . . ." They also desired that differences concerning religion and ceremonies be referred to a synod of "pious and judicious divines" chosen by all the clergy, "because all the clergy are to be bound by

[1] E. 142. 10; Twysden's Journal, I, p. 208. The phrase "just and regal authority" is significantly vague: S. R. Gardiner seems to me to overstress the petitioners' support of the royal prerogative: *History of England . . ., 1603–1642*, 1899, x, pp. 180–2.

their resolutions, and the determination of this synod [is] to bind us all, when you have first formed them into a law."[1]

When the promoters of this petition left Maidstone, only a month elapsed before the date on which they had agreed to meet again, at Blackheath, with their followers, in order to present it to parliament. The clerk of assize, a Maidstone attorney named Pope, was instructed to "make and deliver out copies . . . to be dispersed through Kent" for subscription; one Thomas Fawcett printed it; and the gentry who had been present at Maidstone undertook the organization of the subscription. In the north-west of the county Richard Spencer of Orpington was in charge of the proceedings, and Sir George Strode of Squerryes made "several scandalous speeches" in behalf of the petition, sending a copy of it to Judge Malet for the earl of Bristol, and perhaps for the king. From Roydon Hall in the Weald Sir Roger Twysden rode on Sunday, 27th March, through Mereworth Woods to obtain the support of his friends and neighbours in Holmesdale. His neighbour Thomas Stanley of Hamptons in the Weald secured the signatures of many of the townsmen of Maidstone. At Pluckley, Sir Edward Dering gathered his parishioners together after evensong, and propounded the petition to them in the body of the church. Many parish clergy, like Dr Richard Shelden of Appledore-cum-Ebony and Theophilus Higgons of Hunton, also played an active part in the organization.[2]

It was impossible, however, to organize such a movement without the cognizance of the House of Commons, against whose present leaders' most cherished political intentions it was principally directed. Either by accident or by design, a

[1] E. 142. 10. Gardiner's comment (*op. cit.*, pp. 181–2) is misleading: "Questions at issue were to be determined not, as the petitioners proposed, by an assembly of divines chosen by the clergy, many of whom had been instituted under Laudian influence, but by an assembly of divines chosen by parliament." The last thing the Kentish petitioners wanted was determination of ecclesiastical questions by *Laudian* clergy, and the petition makes it quite clear that they wished them settled by parliament as well as clergy.

[2] Twysden, *Certain Considerations*, p. liv; Twysden's Journal, I, p. 210; CJ, II, pp. 501, 503, 516, 518, 510; LJ, IV, pp. 678, 701; CSPV, 1642–3, p. 35. J. M. Kemble is misleading in describing these promoters of the petition (Twysden, *loc. cit.*) as "the *Cavaliers* of Kent."

certain Francis Jones had been present at the assizes, and it was he who communicated these subversive activities of the Kentish gentry to the House of Commons. At once, a hasty conference was arranged with the House of Lords, and the earl of Bristol and Judge Malet were sent for and summarily committed to the Tower.[1] On the following day, without warning, and much to their surprise, Sir Roger Twysden and Sir Edward Dering were summoned to appear before the House of Commons. The two cousins who had opposed one another in 1640 were now once again united. Next morning they met each other at Roydon Hall and made their way to London together, where they were joined by Pope the attorney, Shelden, Higgons, Strode, and Spencer, and were committed to custody.[2]

Meanwhile, Thomas Blount had informed parliament, in detail, of the proceedings at the Maidstone assizes, and a bewildering series of examinations, confessions, and accusations ensued. Richard Spencer pleaded that the petition was "but an embryo . . . never preferred to the House, . . . and that, since he found it to be distasteful to the parliament, he endeavoured to stop it." Sir Roger Twysden regretted anything "displeasing to this honourable House," and withdrew the copies he had sent out. But Sir George Strode of Squerryes was less complaisant. He refused to surrender the county's right to present the petition, and though it was burnt by the hangman, "the subscribing of it . . . went on cheerfully." New informers therefore came forward or were summoned to give evidence, among them Sir Michael Livesey of Eastchurch and Sir Thomas Walsingham of Scadbury, Twysden's cousin Richard Browne of Singleton Manor, and Sir John Sedley of St Clere. When these measures also failed, the leaders were again examined, first upon thirty interrogatories, then upon nine more on oath, in order to force them to incriminate one another. Finally they

[1] CSPD, 1641–3, p. 368; CJ, II, p. 501. Bristol had received his copy of the petition less than 24 hours before his arrest: LJ, IV, pp. 677–8.

[2] BM, Stowe MS 184, f. 49; Twysden's Journal, I, pp. 211–12; CJ, II, pp. 501, 503; LJ, IV, p. 676. No cause was assigned for their arrest, which elicited a typical comment from Twysden: "I am sure I have heard [this practice] enough condemned in others. See Coke's Instit. 2, 52, §4 the Cause."

were impeached, and in an absurd speech the Lord Keeper declared the petition

"a desperate design to put not only Kent, but, for aught is known, all Christendom too into combustion; carrying the sails full swoln with spite, arrogancy, and sedition. . . . He said many arguments he might use in aggravation of them, from the eminency and power of the person [Sir Edward Dering], the arrogancy of his mind, the acrimony of his spirit, and from the Topic Place of *Kent*, which former ages have found obnoxious to these infelicities. . . ."

"Some may perhaps admire," Twysden ironically remarked,

"why the two Houses were so transcendently incensed? . . . Why they took so unheard of ways in their proceedings? . . . Why they . . . encourage petitioning in some, yet make this a crime so heinous as it is certain a lawyer of the House went so far as to say there were in it things not far from treason . . . ?"

The simple reason was that the Kentish appeal provided moderate opponents of parliament everywhere with a clear manifesto. Hitherto the puritan leaders had worsted them at every turn: but now other shires endeavoured to obtain copies of the county petition and began to follow the example of Kent.[1]

In fact, by arresting the originators of the movement, the parliamentarian leaders simply handed over the organization of opposition in Kent to hotheads. With a little more tact and caution, the moderates who had set the county petition on foot might have been won over. If they had been pacified, the subsequent rule of the County Committee would have been far easier, and the control of parliament itself more secure. Instead, the House of Commons, in repulsing them, only estranged the county as a whole and incited a party of youthful Kentish Cavaliers, angry at what they regarded as an insult to both Kent and the king, to attempt to seize control of the shire. There was little in common between these new Kentish

[1] CJ, II, pp. 502–3, 507, 526, 533, 543, 557; Twysden's Journal, I, pp. 212–13; LJ, IV, p. 710, V, p. 19; CSPV, 1642–3, pp. 35, 38–9. The three leaders who were impeached were Dering, Strode, and Spencer.

leaders and the original promoters of the petition. All were young men, with none of that experience in local government which had made men like Sir Edward Dering aware of the need of moderation in maintaining order in the county. They had no sympathy whatever with either the scholarly interests or the pietism of men like Sir Roger Twysden and Sir George Sondes of Lees Court. Many of them were either heads or younger sons of impoverished Kentish families, with little stake in the land themselves, and no interest in the careful estate management so dear to the heart, and necessary to the stability, of families like the Sondeses and Twysdens. They therefore seized the petition and continued to promote it, not because they agreed with its relatively mild demands, but in order to defy parliament in the most flagrant manner possible and secure the adhesion of the county to the cause of a persecuted king. Essentially, they were Cavaliers and royalists, whereas men like Dering, Twysden, and Sondes were dyed-in-the-wool moderates and provincials.

In the Weald, these new promoters of the Kentish opposition to parliament were headed by Dering's neighbour George Chute of Surrenden Chute and his friend Richard Lovelace of Lovelace Place. Lovelace, the Cavalier poet, had recently returned to the county from service with the northern army against the Scots. Along the Medway they were led by Sir William Boteler of Teston, gentleman-pensioner of the king, and in Holmesdale by his friend Sir William Clerke of Ford Place: two neighbours who were destined to die in arms together at Cropredy Bridge. Over the Downs from Ford Place, the Cavaliers were headed by Sir Thomas Bosvile of Eynsford, who like Lovelace had recently returned from the north, where he had been knighted by the king, and by Sir Leonard Ferby of St Paul's Cray Hill. Across the Medway from Teston lived Sir John Mayney at Linton Place, newly made a baronet and, like his friend Lovelace, ready to sacrifice his family patrimony on behalf of the king. Two miles away, at Wiarton Place, lived another impoverished family, the St Legers, and three miles east again, at East Sutton Place, the young son, also recently knighted, of Sir Robert Filmer. Round Maidstone the new group was led by Sir John Tufton of Le Mote, the eighteen-year-old cousin of the earl of Thanet and son-in-law of the recusant Wottons of Boughton Malherbe; and at Aylesford by Mayney's brother-in-law Paul Richaut, whose family were wealthy newcomers, as eager as any to devote their wealth to the king. In East Kent, around St Albans Court, the Cavaliers were headed by Anthony Hamond; near by, at Bishopsbourne on the Lesser Stour, by Hamond's brother-in-law Sir Anthony Aucher; and two miles downstream by the impoverished Palmers of Bekesbourne, who like the St Legers had long held minor office under the crown. It is remarkable how closely related were the members of this small group of Cavaliers, and how similar were their precarious economic fortunes.[1]

It was not likely that such a group of angry, and it must be confessed frustrated, young men would be restrained by any of that respect for the formalities of the law which had characterized the moderates. On 19 April 1642, the new quarter sessions opened at Maidstone. As Thomas Blount and his colleagues were drawing up a new petition as a parliamentarian answer to the petition of the moderates, Richard Lovelace and his friends suddenly strode into the court-room, and "in a furious manner cried No, No, No; and then, with great contempt of the court, clapped on their hats and said . . . that . . . [there were] many falsities therein [in Blount's petition], and . . . they were ashamed of it." Flourishing the new parliamentarian document over his head, on his sword's point, the Cavalier poet dramatically rent it in pieces. The meeting broke up in confusion, and the promulgation of Blount's counter-petition was necessarily postponed.[2]

Ten days later the meeting of the promoters of the original petition of Kent was due to take place at Blackheath. Little

[1] AC, x, p. 211, xviii, p. 67; *DNB*, s.v. Richard Lovelace, Sir Paul Rycaut; BM, Harl. MS 163, f. 99; E. 240. 20; Hasted, ii, pp. 130–1, 534; CJ, ii, pp. 511, 745, 747, iii, p. 216; John Aubrey, *Brief Lives*, ed. A. Clark, 1898, ii, pp. 37–8; G.E.C., *The Complete Peerage*, entries under Thanet, Wotton of Marley; G.E.C., *Complete Baronetage*, ii, p. 151; Dorothy Gardiner, ed., *The Oxinden Letters, 1607–1642*, 1933, pp. 289–90.

[2] BM, Harl. MS 163, f. 99. Twysden records that a number of justices attended these quarter sessions who did not normally do so: Twysden's Journal, ii, p. 180.

caring that parliament had forbidden the promulgation of this petition and flatly refused to receive it, Lovelace and Boteler sent their agents to the Heath early in the morning to prepare for the expected multitude of petitioners. Of the thousands who eventually came to the rendezvous, 280 were chosen to carry the Kentish petition to the House in defiance of the Commons' wishes. Richard Lovelace and Sir William Boteler led them, carrying the now notorious document in their hands,

"marching two in a rank; and when they came in the Borough, the chain was drawn athwart the bridge, and Captain Bunch with his company at the bridge sought and demanded of them their intent, and the two foremost told them that they came to deliver their petition to the parliament, and their petition was read; and Captain Bunch asked them why they came armed, and they told him they had no arms but the arms of gentlemen and delivered their swords there."[1]

Next day a small party of the Kentish Cavaliers was admitted to the House, and Lovelace presented the petition; they withdrew, and it was read. He and Boteler were recalled, interrogated, and committed to the Gatehouse and Fleet forthwith. The rest of the Cavaliers were treated with somewhat patronizing moderation. ". . . You cannot be ignorant," they were told,

"what opinion both Houses have formerly expressed of the same petition: yet considering you are young gentlemen, misled by the solicitation of some not affected to the peace of the kingdom, . . . they are willing that you should be dismissed; hoping that you may hereafter prove good members of the commonwealth."[2]

But instead of benefiting by this unwonted lenience, the Kentish Cavaliers "departed full of wrath," dispersing "rumours to

[1] E. 145. 6. According to Secretary Nicholas, about 500 gentlemen of Kent brought the petition (CSPD, 1641–3, p. 316); but he probably exaggerates. The peculiar phonetic spelling of the above quotation in the original suggests that it was written by a Cockney, no doubt an eye-witness of the incident.

[2] BM, Harl. MS 163, f. 99; CJ, II, pp. 549–50. It was during his imprisonment on this occasion that Lovelace wrote his celebrated lines, "Stone walls do not a prison make . . ."

the scandal of parliament," plotting "for this purpose to meet at the assizes," and declaring

"that they will come back very soon in greater strength and numbers for the purpose of compelling parliament to return again to the straight path of the laws, to preserve for the Protestant church its ancient pastors, and to assure the king, their lawful sovereign, the tranquil possession of the prerogatives enjoyed by his predecessors."[1]

In the face of these threats of the Kentish Cavaliers, Thomas Blount found it necessary to expedite the organization of his own counter-petition. He and his friends spent only five more days in securing signatures to it, and the document was presented to the House of Commons on 5 May 1642. Many Kentishmen said that Blount's petition was a mere intrigue of the House of Commons with a handful of local puritans. In this they exaggerated, but it is suspicious that, contrary to the usual custom, permission was given to subscribe it subsequently to its presentation to the House. Its parrot-like phrases in fact afford little insight into county opinion; while the burning issues of the day, connected with the liturgy and episcopacy, together with the question which troubled so many consciences of "how at once to obey both his Majesty and both Houses of Parliament," were simply ignored.[2]

The battle of petitions was not yet over, however. No valid case could be made out against either the moderates or the Cavaliers for presenting the original Kentish petition; and before long they were perforce released from confinement and allowed to return to their homes in the county. When the next summer assizes opened at Maidstone, moderates like Twysden and Spencer arrived in the town, along with the Cavaliers Mayney, Chute, Clerke, Bosvile, Richaut, Tufton, and Filmer. Dering alone had not yet been set free, but he had

[1] CSPV, 1642–3, p. 55.

[2] *To the Right Honourable the Lords and Commons . . . The Humble petition of many of the Gentry, Ministry, Freeholders, and other Inhabitants of the County of Kent . . .*, 1642; LJ, v, p. 44; CJ, II, p. 558; HMC, v, p. 21. Six thousand are said to have signed this petition; but this must be compared with the 40,000 said to have supported the royalist petition: both figures, no doubt, an exaggeration.

managed to escape from custody and he was hiding in a friend's house near by. When these Kentish gentry once again arrived in the county-town, accompanied by Judge Malet and a great concourse of countrymen, Robert Barrell, the minister of All Saints, preached a fiery assize sermon "incensing the county against the . . . parliament." On hearing of these tumults in Kent, the House of Commons hastily appointed a committee of Kentish members of parliament to go down into Kent and sit on the Bench of Justices, in order to preserve the county in peace and a "right understanding" of its proceedings. This unprecedented step, however, was a serious tactical blunder. In addition to its chairman Vane, the committee appointed by the Commons included moderates like Sir Edward Partheriche and Sir Thomas Peyton, who seem to have acted from the first in collusion with Judge Malet. Possibly instigated by them, the judge refused either to admit the committee to the Bench or to publish parliament's order against the Commission of Array, since it came not "unto him by the Great Seal." Resenting the infringement of their authority as "a great aspersion laid on this county," the Kentish justices, led by Twysden, supported Judge Malet. "We do not know what place may be suitable to the authority and trust they [the committee] represent," they coolly told parliament; "nor that we have power to place any on the Bench not sent thither by the like authority we sit there." On the afternoon of the 23rd July, led by Vane, the committee therefore sat on the Bench without the formal leave of the local justices. Vane propounded "somewhat [that] tended to the good of the king, peace of the county, maintenance of the laws, and religion;" and while the judge was replying to him, "so loud acclamations were heard, and such fear of stirs began to be apprehended, the judge told him if it went on so he should be forced to adjourn the court." Vane was apparently forced by his fellow-committee-men to desist, and the meeting broke up in confusion.[1]

Full of resentment against parliament, the Kentish Cavaliers then drew up yet another petition, now boldly addressed not to the House of Commons but to the king, and a list of

[1] Twysden's Journal, II, pp. 181–6; CJ, II, pp. 686, 698; E. 202. 40; E. 109. 35; E. 112. 36.

"Instructions to the Knight of the Shire." At this juncture, however, faced with the prospect of open and active opposition to parliament, an institution which, whatever its errors, was still the legally constituted body to which they looked for redress, the Kentish moderates hesitated.[1] Led by Sir Roger Twysden himself, and encouraged by his wily cousin Sir Henry Vane, they refused to associate themselves with the Cavaliers' list of "Instructions," which was forwarded to the House of Commons on 2nd August.[2] "We, the Commons of Kent," this hotheaded document ran,

"require you, Master Augustine Skynner, as our servant, to certify to that honourable House, that you found the country in full peace, . . . and that you desire in our names to know the particular of that Information [of tumults in Kent] . . . and the informer, that this county may have full reparations in honour against so scandalous an aspersion cast upon them; and that the informer, of what quality soever, may receive condign punishment."

The Houses were peremptorily asked to "give his Majesty full satisfaction in his just desires;" to deliver Hull to him; to lay "aside the Militia until a good law may be framed" protecting the subject's liberty; to adjourn parliament to an "indifferent place where His Sacred Person" and the Houses may meet in safety; and to restore the navy to the king forthwith. Meanwhile, the Cavaliers openly informed his "Sacred Majesty" of their "loyalty of heart . . . with all love and faithfulness to our country," while he absolved them from allegiance to the Houses, and ordered his reply to be read in all the parish churches of Kent.[3]

[1] Twysden's Journal, II, pp. 186–7; Rushworth, IV, p. 642. Some of the members of the parliamentary committee had not left the county and were present at these proceedings, no longer as observers from the Commons, but as fellow-countrymen of the petitioners.

[2] CJ, II, p. 700; Twysden's Journal, II, p. 186. The *DNB* (s.v. Sir Roger Twysden) is incorrect in stating that these "Instructions" were "prepared under Twysden's guidance:" he refused to read them to the Bench when asked to do so. As his whole life showed, he was as much opposed to Cavalier as to puritan ideas.

[3] Twysden's Journal, II, pp. 187–8 and footnote; Rushworth, IV, pp. 642–3; J. M. Russell, *The History of Maidstone*, 1881, p. 251; CSPD, 1641–3, p. 314 (where the above document is incorrectly assigned to April 1642).

The refusal of the Kentish moderates to support the Cavaliers at this critical juncture was deeply significant. Their dilemma was cruel. Faced with an open conflict between king and parliament, they could find no historical precedent to guide them, and could do nothing but remain neutral. In the eyes of the parliamentarian leaders, however, neutrality was as iniquitous as royalism. Sir Edward Dering could not be found; but as soon as Sir Henry Vane returned to London, Twysden, Spencer, Strode, and Malet were once more arrested, along with the Cavaliers Mayney, Clerke, Tufton, Ferby, Filmer, Richaut, St Leger, and Chute. In the battle of petitions, parliament was determined to have the last word. Sir John Sedley of St Clere patched up his family quarrel with Sir Henry Vane, and set about organizing yet another county petition. Its conventional parliamentarian phrases were no real indication of Kentish feelings. The petition was presented to the House of Commons on 30 August 1642.[1]

(iii) *The Fight for the County*

The time to petition, however, was now past. The king had raised his standard at Nottingham, and the Civil War had virtually begun. In Kent, as in other counties, either the Commission of Array or the Militia Ordinance must be executed forthwith. Kent was in fact one of the last counties to declare for parliament, and its decision was ultimately forced upon it from outside the shire.[2]

The immediate occasion for the procrastination of the county was the refusal of the Lord Lieutenant, the earl of Leicester, to grant commissions to his deputies under the Militia Ordinance. Leicester was by nature indecisive. As Lieutenant of Ireland he had declared himself

[1] Twysden's Journal, II, p. 189; CJ, II, pp. 744–6; E. 202. 42; E. 115. 1; LJ, V, pp. 332–3.

[2] Of the counties which, ostensibly, supported parliament, Hants., Essex, Sussex, Northants., Leics., Suffolk, Cambs., Herts., Dorset, Norfolk, and Derbyshire had executed the Militia Ordinance apparently by mid-July 1642.—CJ, II, pp. 596, 597, 612, 614, 632, 647. It was another month before it was executed in Kent.

"environed by such contradictions as I can neither get from them nor reconcile them. The parliament bids me go [to Ireland] presently; the king commands me to stay till he dispatch me. The supplies of the one, and the authority of the other, are equally necessary. . . . The parliament . . . is not confident of me; . . . the king . . . is as little confident."

In Kent, the earl repeatedly refused to grant his commissions "because some [of the gentry] have refused them and others, principal gentlemen of that county, think it not a fit time now to execute the Militia [Ordinance] there, by reason the country is now distempered. . . ." Finally, when "commanded to put in execution the militia presently," Leicester preferred to "deliver up his commission of lieutenancy and be excused." His resignation was accepted.[1]

The Lord Lieutenant's hesitancy was symptomatic of that of the county as a whole. Many of his own deputy lieutenants, such as the Honywoods of Evington and Scotts of Scots' Hall, who later supported the County Committee, were no more eager to execute the Ordinance without royal sanction than the earl himself. In a county like Suffolk, where the gentry were predominantly puritan, such hesitation would have seemed an impious distrust in Providence. But in a county where genuine puritans and Cavaliers were relatively few, it was inevitable that there should be much heart-searching before a decision was arrived at. "I would be most glad to hear the best human advice I know, which is yours, in this point," wrote the distraught Henry Oxinden of Deane to his cousin Henry Oxinden of Great Maydeacon: "and to be informed of the examples of wiser men, and amongst them what Sir James Hales and Ned Monins intend to do."[2] Where society was so

[1] R. W. Blencowe, ed., *Sydney Papers*, 1825, p. xxi; CJ, II, p. 675; LJ, V, p. 227. Leicester's successor, the earl of Pembroke, was not appointed till 10 August 1642; LJ, V, p. 280; CJ, II, p. 713. Pembroke's appointment was merely nominal. He had no connexion with the county and never interested himself in its affairs: a fact which further weakened parliamentarian influence.

[2] BM, Add. MS 28000, f. 213. Of these four men Monins and Oxinden of Deane became committeemen, and Oxinden of Maydeacon a temporary captain in one of the county regiments; but all four, typically enough, sup-

inbred, it seemed a crime to draw the sword between neighbouring families and cousins.

For a time, after the failure of the battle of petitions and the resignation of the Lord Lieutenant, it seemed that the king's own efforts to secure the adherence of Kent would be successful. The Commission of Array was in fact set on foot in Kent before the parliamentarian Militia Ordinance, and on 16 July 1642 a "great meeting" of the leading families of East Kent was held at Dean Bargrave's house, near Canterbury, in order to promote its execution. Many men who subsequently became members of the County Committee, at this stage sincerely supported the Commission, partly because they wished to maintain local order, and partly because Charles I's recent visit to the county had stirred their loyalty.[1] In the west of the county, support for the king seems to have been even more widespread than in the east. Writing from Leeds Abbey, Henry Oxinden of Deane informed his cousin at Maydeacon that the Commission would "find obedience of five gentlemen for one and of the major part of the yeomen in these parts. . . ." In Maidstone, the people "wished all their heads off that would not obey" it; and at Knole the earl of Dorset and Sir John Sackville began laying up arms for the king in "caves and cellars." At Aylesford Friary, Cobham Hall, Birling Manor, and elsewhere, Richauts, St Legers, Ropers, Nevilles, and other Cavalier and recusant families were also collecting arms and setting the Commission on foot. Sir John Sackville was appointed official receiver of the royalists' contributions, and sent Secretary Nicholas a lengthy list of Kentish gentlemen who offered £1,000 or more for the king's armies.[2] Extravagant reports circulated that the Cavaliers had offered to raise

ported the Rebellion of 1648. For the contrast of Kent with Suffolk at this decisive period, see Everitt, *Suffolk and the Great Rebellion*, p. 15.

[1] BM, Add. MS 28000, f. 213; LJ, v, p. 213. The king had sent a declaration to the sheriff of Kent, apparently against the Militia Ordinance, at the time of the Kentish Petition: CJ, II, p. 506.

[2] BM, Add. MS 28000, f. 220; E. 112. 32, p. 4; E. 116. 33; AC, XXXIII, pp. 125–7; E. 202. 39; E. 202. 44; CSPD, 1641–3, p. 368; CJ, II, p. 714; E. 113. 18; LJ, v, pp. 293, 295; *A Catalogue of the Moneys, Men, and Horse already subscribed unto by several Counties of this Kingdom . . ., 1642*. In this last document, Kent is the only southern or eastern county listed; it is

20,000 men in the county, and in mid-August it was rumoured that the king himself would march into Kent and join them.[1]

Over against these groups of royalists, a small but active nucleus of parliamentarians was also emerging in the county. Apart from Sir Anthony Weldon, Sir John Sedley, and Sir Michael Livesey, this consisted of scattered groups of minor gentry, later destined to become Independents or Republicans. Amongst these men were Thomas Belke of Canterbury and Thomas Plumer of Milkhouse, who raised volunteer troops amongst their puritan neighbours in Canterbury and the Weald. In north-west Kent, the parliamentarians were headed by Captain Willoughby, whose party of one hundred "well-affected and stout youngsters" secured Woolwich dockyard, captured seventy-five pieces of ordnance, plundered the house of a local recusant, and found a trunk "filled with plate, which they conceived could not be less worth than 1,000 pounds," and "another trunk in which was many popish books, . . . beads, and priests' garments. . . ." Willoughby's soldiers dressed themselves up in the priests' attire, and carried their booty by torchlight to London. At Dover, where shiploads of horses and men were arriving for the king from the continent, young Richard Dawkes offered to adventure his life in capturing the castle.[2] He was offered a captain's commission, and at two o'clock at night on 21st August he scaled the walls with ten men, disarmed the sleeping guards, secured the porter's lodge, beat on his door till the keys were surrendered, locked the gates against the king's soldiers, and searched for ammunition. When dawn broke, although "the chiefest sort of the people in that town . . . threaten[ed] to raise the trained band upon him, and to starve them out"—firing ordnance and con-

said to subscribe £1,000, but other sources suggest that several men in the county subscribed this sum. According to Nicholas, Sir Edward Hales, who still sat in the Commons, had offered the king £1,000; but when taxed with this by the House, Hales denied it, sardonically remarking, "he is not a man so easily to part with money, especially on such an occasion."—E. 113. 18.

[1] HMC, *Franciscan*, p. 145.

[2] CJ, II, pp. 714, 717; E. 115. 13; E. 110. 14; E. 115. 8. Dawkes may have been a member of the foreign congregation in the town: his name was often spelt Daux.

fiscating the ammunition sent by those well-affected to parliament—Dawkes was relieved by a small party from Canterbury. During the following days, with the earl of Warwick's support in the Downs, Captain Dawkes advanced "his own money to provide fat oxen and fat sheep with bacon, butter, yea bread, beer, and all things else that's fit for men, likewise for timber he doth not spare, to mount his guns. . . ."[1]

The situation that faced parliament, in Kent, in the autumn of 1642 was thus a tricky one. Its own supporters had secured certain keypoints in the county, but were powerless to win the allegiance of the community as a whole. Weldon and Livesey were influential but unpopular, and Livesey, as a comparative newcomer, was only distantly connected with the family clans who controlled Kentish society. Belke, Willoughby, Dawkes and their kind came of native, but minor, families, and lacked the territorial influence necessary to govern the shire. The vast majority of the gentry were still neutral or mildly royalist, but anxious above all things to preserve the precarious framework of local society. Obviously, parliament could not tolerate this situation indefinitely in a county of such strategic importance. Early in August 1642 a packet of royalist correspondence fell into its hands, revealing the imminence of a local Cavalier *coup*. Immediately Colonel Edwyn Sandys was despatched into Kent to suppress it. Sandys was a member of one of the puritan families of the county, but he seems to have acted entirely on the initiative of parliament, and his troops were raised in London, not in Kent. In the first of his two successive expeditions into the county, he marched down to Sevenoaks on Sunday, 14th August, in order to scotch the Cavalier group headed by Sir John Sackville at Knole. It was during the time of service when he arrived in the town, and Sackville was

"laid wait for as he was at church. . . . The town of Sevenoaks stood a while in his defence, endeavouring to rescue him from them . . .; but when they perceived that the other who came to apprehend him were too strong for them, they fearing

[1] E. 115. 8, pp. 7–8; LJ, v, pp. 313–14. CJ, II, p. 731, says 30 men were appointed to assist Dawkes in securing the castle, but 20 deserted.

to endanger themselves in such a combustion . . . suffered them to carry him away. . . ."

Sandys then crossed the narrow valley on the eastern edge of the town and entered Knole itself, where he took five wagon-loads of arms and, grossly exceeding his commission, ransacked the house for money and supplies. "There are above forty stock locks and plate locks broken open," wrote the steward to his absent master, the earl of Dorset,

"which to make good again will cost £10. There is of gold branched belonging to the coach . . . as much cut away as will not be made good for £40. . . . And in my Lord's chamber 2 long cushion cases embroidered with satin and gold and the plumes upon the bed [tester?] to the value of £30. They have broken open six trunks, in one of them was money, what is lost of it we know not. . . ."

After thus sacking Knole, Colonel Sandys returned to London, and Sir John Sackville was committed to the Fleet.[1]

Five days later, accompanied on this occasion by Sir Michael Livesey and a body of 200 troopers and 300 dragoons raised in London, Colonel Sandys once again came down into Kent. This time he was provided with a full commission to disarm all malignants and secure all forts, castles, and stores or arms. His first port of call was Cobham Hall, near Rochester. At his approach, the duchess of Richmond "through fear sent out word to us that we should have the magazine delivered unto us, which, when we had it, we loaded five wagons and sent them to London. . . ."[2] At Rochester, Sandys's troops overcame the county guard on the bridge, and imprisoned Lord Teynham and other gentry coming into the town to execute the Commission of Array. On Wednesday, 24th August Sandys's men

[1] E. 112. 32, pp. 3–4; AC, XXXIII, p. 126; LJ, V, p. 293; HMC, XII, ii, p. 321.

[2] E. 116. 33; E. 239. 9; E. 115. 10; HMC, XII, ii, p. 322. The duke of Richmond, who was absent, had instructed his steward "to take no steps to preserve his goods at Cobham." Though loyal to the king, his cousin, Richmond consistently sought to avoid falling foul of the ruling powers in Kent in 1642–60.

"went to the cathedral . . . in the midst of their superstitious worship . . ., marched up to the place where the altar stood, and staying awhile, thinking they would then have [c]eased their worship . . ., but seeing they did not, the soldiers could not forbear any longer to wait upon their pleasure, but went about their work they came for. First they removed the Table to its place appointed, and then took the seat which it stood upon . . . having two or three steps, . . . and brake that all to pieces . . ., plucked down the rails, and left them for the poor to kindle their fires. . . ."

The ships in the Medway were taken and the castle at Upnor, a few miles downstream, where the captain was playing bowls and the garrison were "most or all of them forth at harvest." At Chatham Captain Pett delivered up the dockyard and 300 pieces of ordnance about to be conveyed to the king.[1]

In Holmesdale, between Maidstone and Sevenoaks, Sandys scotched a cluster of recusant families headed by the Nevilles of Birling Manor. He and his men searched the house

"where Mrs Littleboy and her daughter worshipped the picture of the Queen of Heaven, and the Crucifix, which was pictured upon the rafters of the house, for it was not ceiled, which pictures they took away, with some other popish books, and broke down the altar: but we found no ammunition nor money. We searched up and down for vaults and caves but found none. After a little time of discourse with her daughter, we . . . departed."

Across the Medway, at Aylesford Friary, Sandys arrested Sir Peter Richaut, and

"brought away with him in and about his coach good store of money and a trunk full of plate, which was discovered by one of his maids, which when the old Lady heard who discovered it, she threatened to be the death of her; whereupon our Colonel commanded her to be brought away . . . and so she was preserved. . . ."

Upstream, at Barham Court, unable to effect an entrance to the mansion, Sandys held one of Sir William Boteler's servants

[1] E. 116. 33; E. 115. 10; CSPD, 1641–3, pp. 374–5; HMC, v, p. 46.

against the door of the house and ordered his dragoons to fire on him till it was beaten down. When the steward refused to deliver his master's plate and money, Sandys "cruelly . . . beat him with his pole-axe" and

"to enforce the discovery from him, with drawn swords they prick him . . . from one room to another. At last, being come to the dining chamber, Colonel Sandys causes a dozen of candles to be lighted, and so to be held to and under the steward's hands, and lighted match to be applied between his fingers, for the space of a quarter of an hour, Sandys himself all the while looking on, . . . until both his hands were shamefully burnt. . . . The rest of the servants . . . they prick with their swords, beat with their pole-axes to the endangering their lives . . . to extort a confession. . . . They broke up every door, plundered every trunk and chest, and examined every dark place from the closet and cabinet to the powdering-tub and oven: nay, the cellars escaped not their fury; what they could not drink . . . they let out and poured upon the ground."[1]

Next, Colonel Sandys's troops secured the "malignant town" of Maidstone, and on the way to Canterbury searched the earl of Thanet's house at Hothfield and found "good store of ammunition, both pikes, armour, and head-pieces, swords, gunpowder, bullets, and match. . . ." Some plundered Calehill, Sir Robert Darell's home near by, and at Surrenden Dering they marched off with the family plate. At Canterbury, Sandys set a watch on the cathedral close, "to the great affright of all the inhabitants." At two o'clock in the morning, he sent to Dr Paske, the subdean, for the keys of the cathedral, and took the "arms of the church and the store-powder of the county."[2] Next morning, declaring that "the foundations of the cathedral churches were naught," his troops entered Christ Church and

"giant-like began a fight with God Himself, overthrew the communion table, tore the velvet cloth from before it, defaced the goodly screen . . ., violated the monuments of the

[1] E. 116. 33; HMC, v, p. 46; E. 103. 3, pp. 6–8; cf. E. 115. 10.

[2] E. 115. 10; E. 116. 33; E. 116. 22; HMC, v, p. 48. Sandys had once owed his life, when indicted for rape, to the intercession of Dean Bargrave of Canterbury.

dead, brake down the ancient rails and seats with the brazen eagle that did support the bible, . . . mangled all our service books and books of common prayer, bestrowing the whole pavement with leaves thereof; a miserable spectacle to all good eyes . . .; for many did abhor what was done already . . . Upon the arras hangings in the choir, representing the whole story of our Saviour, . . . observing divers figures of Christ, (I tremble to express their blasphemies), one said, Here is Christ, and swore that he would stab Him. . . ."

When they "had done their pleasure," they departed singing "cathedral prick-song as they rode over Barham Downs towards Dover, with prick-song leaves in their hands, and lighted their tobacco-pipes with them."[1]

At Dover, Colonel Sandys's troops furnished themselves "with about seven thousand pounds, all which we have made bold with out of the houses of recusants." One party marched into Thanet and the Downs about Lynsted to secure such recusant families as the Ropers and Finches; while others returned through Romney Marsh and the Weald, where a group of Commissioners of Array were active. Some of them met again at Maidstone, collected the prisoners from Upnor Castle, and loaded their arms on to wagons; the rest rejoined them at Deptford. They then returned to London, which "we found the welcomest place," at the end of August.[2]

To all appearance, Colonel Sandys's mission was completely successful.[3] Parliament was at last supreme in the county. Such Cavaliers as had not been arrested, like Richard Lovelace and Sir Anthony St Leger, left Kent as quickly as they could, joining the king with regiments or troops raised from among their labourers and tenantry.[4] Under the pressure of events, semi-neutrals and moderate parliamentarians, like the Scotts

[1] E. 116. 22; E. 532. 12, p. 19 [mispaginated, between pp. 23 and 24]; HMC, v, pp. 48–9.

[2] E. 115. 10, p. 4; E. 116. 33; HMC, v, p. 47; E. 202. 41; Hasted, XII, p. 19.

[3] But cf. E. 240. 45 and CJ, II, pp. 731, 840, 851, for the continued anxiety of parliament in relation to the county.

[4] Cf. E. 116. 30; E. 239. 18; E. 239. 19; Thomas Sprott, *Thomae Sprotti Chronica*, ed. T. Hearn, 1719, pp. xliv–xlv.

of Scots' Hall and Honywoods of Evington, perforce agreed to accept commissions from the new Lord Lieutenant, the earl of Pembroke. They were ordered to search suspicious persons and places, seize horses and arms, counteract the Commission of Array, fortify strategic places, execute the Propositions for bringing in money and plate, clear parliament from "false aspersions," and execute the Militia Ordinance forthwith. On 16th September some of them met at Rochester, with Sir Edward Hales of Tunstall as their chairman. Two days later they informed Speaker Lenthall that this initial work of subjugation was complete: officers' commissions had been given, days of muster appointed, repairing of beacons commenced, and summonses for subscriptions sent out. By these means many of the old county families, with whom the real power of the community lay, were induced to lend their tacit support to parliament in the interests of law and order, and an embryonic County Committee was formed.[1]

(iv) *The Pattern of Parties, 1642*

With the success of Colonel Sandys's expedition, Kent came permanently under the yoke of parliament until the year 1648. This more or less enforced loyalty concealed a good deal of inward disunity and heart-burning; but after the increasing confusion of the two previous years, a kind of unstable equilibrium had been established. What then were the lines upon which the Kentish gentry, in the last resort, had divided? The story is more subtle and complex than in a largely puritan county, like Suffolk, or a county divided initially on class lines, like Northamptonshire, or by ancient family feuds, like Leicestershire. The Kentish gentry had not divided on precise lines of class, wealth, antiquity, family rivalry, religion, or abstract political principle. The families through whom Charles I had ruled the county—Walsinghams, Boyses, Sedleys, Twysdens, Derings, and Filmers, for example—were found in

[1] CJ, II, pp. 724, 726 (for D.L.'s' names); LJ, V, pp. 329–31; HMC, XIII, i, p. 62. Hales was appointed chairman because of his seniority only, it seems: within a few weeks he had fallen foul of parliament. See also p. 109, n. 2, *supra*.

equal abundance on either side during the Civil War. The essential clue to the understanding of party division in Kent, and of the subsequent tangle of relationships between these parties, consists in the fact that there were not *two* parties in the county, but *three*. The word 'party' is itself misleading, if it suggests a body of men united by well-defined principles and a stable organization; the word 'group' would be more suitable. Much the largest of the three groups in the county was the moderates, who shaded off into mild 'parliamentarians,' supporting the County Committee, on one hand, and mild 'royalists,' temporarily joining the king in 1642 or waiting hopefully at home, on the other. On either wing of this group were two small groups, hardly more than cliques, of genuine Cavaliers and parliamentarians. At the outset of the war only the two latter groups, and perhaps only a minority amongst them, envisaged the political issues involved in simple terms of king *versus* parliament. Let us analyse each of these three groups in turn.

The genuine parliamentarians in Kent were mainly men of strong and indeed violent personality. Several of them came of families with a long tradition of opposition to the crown, like the Sandyses of Northbourne Abbey. Some had suffered at the hands of James I or Charles I, like Sir Anthony Weldon, who had lost his office, or like the Heymans of Somerfield, who were imprisoned and mulcted, or the attainted Brookes, who in 1640 were still endeavouring to regain the Cobham title and inheritance which they had forfeited in 1603. Some, at least, like the Walsinghams of Scadbury, seem to have been in economic difficulties; others came of the type of family always found at the centre of local feuds, like the Riverses of Chafford, Sir Michael Livesey of Eastchurch, and Sir John Sedley of St Clere.[1] Few of these parliamentarians seem to have had strong religious convictions. The puritanical enthusiasm of Richard Culmer was a liability rather than an asset to the cause, and that of the three leading Independents in the county—Sir Henry Vane of Fairlawne, Sir William Springate, whose daughter became the wife of William Penn, and John Dixwell of

[1] Cf. E. 37. 1; CSPD, 1636–7, pp. 47, 52; 1638–9, pp. 494–5; Twysden's Journal, III, pp. 161, 175–6, *et passim*. See also p. 80, n. 1, *supra*.

Broome Park—was as antipathetic to their colleagues on the County Committee as it was to their political enemies. The most striking characteristic of these parliamentarians, however, was the fact that only four of them—Sir Henry Heyman, Sir John Sedley, Sir Thomas Walsingham, and Sir Henry Vane—came of old county families; while almost all still retained, or had recently held, some mercantile, legal, or official position unconnected with the county. Dixwells, Riverses, Liveseys, Garlands, Springates, Sandyses, and Blounts were all comparative newcomers to Kent: lawyers, merchants, grantees, an unscrupulous archbishop, and two lord mayors were among their antecedents.[1] Such a group was not likely to control the county for long without some degree of support from the older landed families of the shire, who outnumbered them by at least six to one.

The Cavaliers of the county came from a rather different *milieu*. Many of them belonged to families with a long tradition of service to the crown. There were great peers among them, like the duke of Richmond, knights like the St Legers of Boughton Monchelsea, and small gentry like the Bowleses of Chislehurst and Brasted. Most of them still held some official position, like John Philipot, who was Somerset Herald, Sir John Marsham, who was one of the Six Clerks in Chancery, Arnold Braemes and Sir Peter Richaut, who were members of the royal Fishing Association, and the Palmers of Bekesbourne and Moyles of Buckwell, who held minor naval appointments. Several of them were recusants, like the Ropers, Guldefords, Nevilles, and minor branches of the Finch family; though in general the recusants of the county kept their heads low and endeavoured to remain neutral. On the whole, the Cavaliers were younger men than the parliamentarians. As soon as the war began they left Kent to join the king with regiments or troops raised among their labourers and tenants: John Boys of Bonnington, for example, Sir John Mayney of Linton Place,

[1] E. 128. 37; E. S. Sandys, *History of the Family of Sandys . . .*, 1930, I, p. 9, II, pedigrees A, C, D; Hasted, *passim*; *The Records of the Honorable Society of Lincoln's Inn, Black Books*, 1898, II, pp. 327–30; *DNB*, s.v. Edwin Sandys, Sir Edwin Sandys, Sir Michael Livesey, John Dixwell, Sir Anthony Weldon, Thomas Blount. Sandys usually spelt his name Edwyn.

the plundered Sir William Boteler of Barham Court, his friend Sir William Clerke of Ford Place, and the poet Richard Lovelace of Lovelace Place.[1] A few of them, it must be confessed, were drunken debauchees, like Richard Thornhill of Olantighe, whom Dorothy Osborne called "the veriest beast that ever was," and Dorothy Denne a "lewde, . . . dishonest, wicked" man. Others, like Francis Finch dreamed away their lives in romantic poems addressed to "our bright queen, and England's sun, . . . our sovereign and his bride." The older Cavaliers, like Sir John Culpeper, hung their hopes upon his Majesty's "exemplary piety and great justice," which rendered his ears open to the just complaints of his subjects.[2] The one characteristic which the Cavaliers held in common with the parliamentarians, and which distinguished them from the moderates, was that they were often relative newcomers to the shire and derived part of their income from some other source than the land. In other words, neither parliamentarians nor Cavaliers represented the deepest interests of the county.

The moderates formed a more heterogeneous group. Their distinguishing characteristics were, on one hand, their more or less complete identity with the ancient Kentish gentry, and, on the other, their incapacity to adhere firmly to either king or parliament. At the beginning of the war they themselves were subdivided into three distinct groups or sections. A number of them at first joined the king's garrison at Oxford, though it is clear that they did so with reluctance. Their ambivalent attitude is depicted in the words of Sir Edward Dering. "In my own house," he said afterwards, "[I enjoyed] so

[1] CSPV, 1642–3, p. 174; W. H. Bowles, *Records of the Bowles Family*, 1918, pp. 23, 167; E. 156. 6, pp. 4–5; CSPD, 1639–40, *passim*; CCC, *passim*; KCA, U. 120. C 4–6; E. 116. 30; AC, x, p. 210; *DNB*, s.v. Sir Warham St Leger, Sir John Marsham, John Philipot, Sir Paul Rycaut (Richaut was the more usual family spelling), Dudley Digges, Sir John Boys, Richard Lovelace.

[2] BM, Add. MS 28003, f. 173; G. C. Moore Smith, ed., *The Letters of Dorothy Osborne to William Temple*, 1928, p. 177; E. 196. 8; *Musarum Oxoniensium*, 1643, contains two poems, each of 16 lines, by the brother-Cavaliers Francis and John Finch, in honour of the queen: both were of Balliol College.

happy a privacy as that nothing could add to the sweet satisfaction thereof but the sight and company of my children. . . . My wife at chosen times came into my study, and made my stolen commons a feast with her society. . . ."[1] Summoned to attend the king at York, however, Dering went "willingly, but out of my own house and from my own country the most unwilling man that ever went." For "truth to confess, I did not then like one side or the other so well as to join myself with either. A composing third way was my wish and my prayer." Before many months passed, Dering found, in consequence, though he "dare not say [so], that the king's promises [were] forgotten and unperformed." He could not sympathize with the extravagant royalism of some of the clergy, and with his puritan ancestry he feared deeply the advancement of papists. "All my care," he said, on returning to Kent in 1644, "was not to trespass against any inward thoughts, and I hope I have in no one action been guilty thereof. . . ."[2] Closely similar to the undecided attitude of Sir Edward Dering was that of the earl of Dorset, of Knole. With his estates sequestered, his mansion plundered, and his son and heir imprisoned, Dorset was doubly unfortunate in also falling into disfavour with the king for advocating a policy of reconciliation. He bitterly deplored the

"shamble of men's flesh made, . . . yet I am in despair that hereafter will bring amendment, since . . . men, money, horse, and arms are furnished and found out daily, to foment and nourish this most odious division, which if it do not by God's mercy and good men's piety presently meet with some . . . accommodation, infallibly mankind must be much diminished in this land. . . . Whosoever shall be so unhappy as to survive the approaching summer [of 1643] shall see . . . more barbarities to be committed than ever yet any of our chronicles mentioned . . . I beseech God turn all hearts to peace and repentance. . . ."[3]

[1] E. 40. 5. He refers to the time when he had escaped from prison in 1642 and was in retirement at Surrenden Dering.

[2] E. 40. 5; E. 51. 13, preface.

[3] E. 83. 19; E. 83. 45; E. 249. 2; C. J. Phillips, *History of the Sackville Family*, n.d., I, p. 345.

The second group of moderates at first took an opposite course to men like Dorset and Dering, and accepted uncomfortable seats on the County Committee. According to Sir Roger Twysden, there were many "men of wisdom, honesty and judgement" in the county who were "at first led away by the protestations, promises, and pretences" of parliament, and who only gradually came to realize the real aims of the puritan leaders in the House of Commons. It was sometimes not until such men visited London and, like Henry Oxinden of Deane, found it "divided into so many sects and schisms, . . . some whereof deny St Paul, . . . others say that there is no national church, . . . another will preach against the keeping of holidays . . . and in their pulpits vilify and blaspheme our Saviour's name," that they experienced the gradual change of heart which eventually turned them away from the Committee.[1] In fact, in studying the Great Rebellion, it is easy to exaggerate the extent to which provincial people were generally conscious of the political problems of the period. If the issues often seemed obscure in the House of Commons, they sometimes seemed impenetrable in the countryside. Much of the private family correspondence of the time shows that both gentry and commonalty were less concerned with political principles than may be supposed. In Kent many appeared at first to conform to parliament; but in reality, locked in their own thoughts and the narrow family circle of the shire, they were largely unaware of the ultimate issues in which their support involved them. They accepted places on the Committee mainly in the interests of maintaining local peace, and because it came naturally to them to sit in the seat of county government. The story of their gradual disillusionment and ejection from the governing circle of the shire is told in the following chapter.

The great majority of the Kentish moderates joined neither king nor parliament, however, but endeavoured from the outset to maintain an attitude of rigorous neutrality. They remained at home on their estates, but they refused to support the County Committee, and many of them ended up as

[1] Twysden's Journal, II, pp. 195–7, and cf. IV, p. 138; BM, Add. MS 28000, f. 163.

prisoners within the moated walls of Leeds Castle or Westenhanger House. They had neither leader nor spokesman; but their attitude of mind is accurately portrayed in a tract written by Sir George Sondes of Lees Court. ". . . I was bound by many several oaths to my king," says Sondes,

"which I did not so readily know how to dispense with. Yet I never was so great a royalist as to forget I was a freeborn subject. Our king I was willing to have him; but not our tyrant, or we his slaves. . . . I was never against reducing of bishops to their pristine function of taking care of the churches, nor of the rest of the clergy, to take them off from secular employments. . . . Nor was I ever against taking away monopolies and arbitrary impositions, and imprisonment of the free subject; nor against lessening the exorbitancy of favourites, who like drones sucked and devoured all the honey which the commonwealth's bees with much toil gathered."

But Sondes was "ever for order and government, both in church and state. Parity speaks nothing but confusion and ruin. God is the God of order, and therefore of His own courtiers He hath degrees. . . ." Quite consistently, Sondes went with parliament

"so long as it was for king and parliament, and I think did them as faithful service as any. But when it came to parliament and no king, and parliament against king, then I boggled, I knew not what to do. I was contented to sit still and not do. . . . And though I have suffered enough [through sequestration of his estates], yet I never acted anything against the state, never was in any plot or petition against them."

". . . For my part," he concluded, "as long as I live I will endeavour honestly, not only in my words, but in all my actions, and as much as in me lies, labour to have peace with all men."[1]

Despite their initial division into three sections, the moderates of the county were essentially in unison with each other in their basic convictions. During the previous fifty years, the

[1] Harleian Miscellany, x, pp. 55–6, 65.

development of the English economy had given rise to a kind of self-assertive individualism which was alien to a society where the sense of kinship and community was so intense as in Kent. In the eyes of moderates the railing spirit of many puritans "did not only not further, but extremely disgrace and prejudice their cause;" while the new lights of the sectaries ran counter to all their prejudices in favour of orderly institutional government. Consequently, though they never came to accept royalist theories, the moderates became increasingly antagonistic to parliament, because to them its policies seemed, rightly or wrongly, to undermine the world of obstinate, inarticulate custom in which they lived and moved and had their being.[1]

Such was the structure of parties in Kent at the outset of the Civil War. Quite clearly, if Sir Edward Dering had found it hard to retain control of the community in 1640–2, parliament was not likely to find it any easier during the following six years. In fact the expedition of Colonel Edwyn Sandys had left behind it a legacy of bitterness and hatred which parliament was never wholly able to overcome. Though to all appearance successful, and in a few places, such as Ashford, welcomed, it concealed a seething mass of discontent which broke out in many sporadic insurrections during the Civil War. Sandys's senseless cruelty to the servants of Sir William Boteler at Barham Court was a particularly bad error of judgement, and turned many neutral people against him. At Rochester the citizens had refused him supplies; at Maidstone the malignants had shut up their shops and "burned so inwardly with malice and hatred that they could no longer forbear . . . to speak malignant words against parliament. . . ." At Dover Sandys's troops "found ourselves least welcome of any place we yet came to, for scarce anyone would vouchsafe to us a good look. . . ." At Canterbury, despite a large puritan element in the town, even the city's members of parliament complained of the "many outrages in the cathedral church, worthy condign punishment. . . ." No wonder an outsider observed, on Sandys's return to London, "That county of Kent have angry hearts." Like every other major political occurrence in Kent during the

[1] *Ibid.*, pp. 40, 33, 56; E. 197. 1, *passim*. Cf. pp. 219–30, *infra*.

Great Rebellion, the events of 1642 showed that they were "a people that are sooner drawn by gentle means than any way enforced; their affection must flow uncompelled."[1]

[1] HMC, v, p. 47; XII, ii, p. 322; E. 116. 33; E. 115. 10; E. 202. 44; E. 128. 27; cf. E. 116. 22; E. 532. 12, pp. 9 sqq.

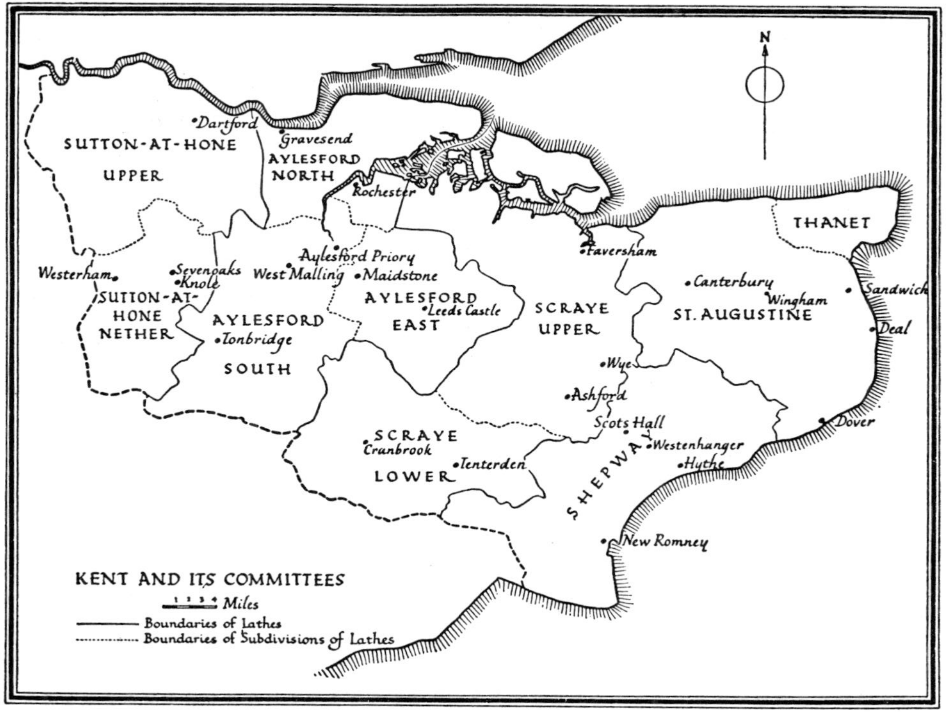

KENT AND ITS COMMITTEES

V

THE COUNTY COMMITTEE, 1642–8

IN EVERY COUNTY under the control of parliament, a committee of the leading parliamentarian gentry of the shire was set up at the end of 1642 or early in 1643 to govern the local community. In some counties, committees composed of the deputy lieutenants of the shire had already been in existence, informally at least, for a couple of generations. They were now simply given whatever official status the two Houses of Parliament were able to accord them by their own ordinances. In Suffolk, such a committee of the gentry had met at regular intervals at least since Queen Elizabeth's reign; by 1642 it had worked out its own detailed code of forms and precedents for the government of the county. There is no evidence at present that the deputy lieutenants of Kent had formed themselves into such a committee at this date. Certainly *ad hoc* meetings of the gentry had been held long before 1642; but it is evident that not until some months after the Civil War began was there a regular committee *institution* in Kent, with a distinct life of its own. The gentry of Suffolk, in county affairs at least, were more politically minded and more businesslike than their cousins in Kent. Efficient administration came naturally to their orderly puritan temperament. It was no accident that the Eastern Association and the New Model Army were such efficient organizations: they owed much to the admirable organizing abilities of the Committee of Suffolk.[1] In Kent, by contrast, the wayward propensities of the gentry continually chafed at the procrustean system of government forced upon them by parliament.

It must be admitted that parliament was faced with a particularly difficult task in Kent. With no clear county leader, with little sympathy towards puritanism except in some towns and cloth villages, with a highly complex social structure, and with an intensely insular outlook, Kent was no easy county to control. Essentially parliament's problem was twofold. First,

[1] Cf. Everitt, *Suffolk and the Great Rebellion*, pp. 22, 28, 30–1.

how was it to secure the allegiance, or at least tacit acquiescence, of that body of major gentry who held the wealth and power of the county? Who, in other words, was to be the leader of the shire? In Suffolk and some other counties the problem was resolved by the fact that the county leader was a prominent member of the House of Commons or the House of Lords: there was a natural, personal link between the puritan leaders in parliament and the community of the local gentry. In Kent there was no such link, since all the county's members of parliament were either royalists or political ciphers. One of the main reasons for the intractability of the county during the Civil War, and especially the unco-operative spirit of its genuine parliamentarians, was the fact that the man who eventually emerged as chairman of the County Committee, Sir Anthony Weldon, neither sat nor wished to sit in the House of Commons.

The second problem that faced parliament in controlling Kent was the endemic lawlessness and the anglican—or at least anti-puritan—sympathies of most Kentish parishes. For the parish was the ultimate basis of the Committee's activities, and if government broke down in any one village, confusion rapidly spread over the surrounding district. In all parts of Kent anglican ministers continued to function during the Civil War: and in consequence the ecclesiastical policy of parliament was thwarted, the presbyterian classis it wished to set up remained a dead letter, and the leaven of opposition continued to work unseen in almost every village and most manor-houses. The whole lathe of St Augustine, for example, was frequently tossed by furious squalls of anti-puritanism, culminating in the maiming of parliamentarian ministers like Richard Culmer and the notorious series of murders perpetrated by Squire Adam Sprakeling in 1648–52. The lawlessness of the Isle of Thanet was such a thorn in the side of the Committee that at one time it was proposed to form it into a separate county, with its own sheriff and officers: it already had its own local Committee.[1]

[1] Cf. BM, Add. MS 28000, ff. 278–86; E. 532. 12, p. 11; E. 625. 8, *passim*; Richard Culmer, jr, *A Parish Looking-Glass for persecuted Ministers*, 1657, *passim*; *Culmer's Crown cracked with his own Looking-Glass* [1657], pp. 1, 4–6; E. 888. 1, Part II, Dedication.

If the proposition had taken effect, Thanet would have taken from Rutland the title of the smallest county in England.

It was principally the failure of parliament to solve either of these problems satisfactorily that led to the Kentish Rebellion of 1648. It was the union of the discontent of the gentry with the lawlessness of the parishes that made the rebellion so formidable. The feudal power of the gentry in their parishes was sufficient to swing the county round and overthrow the power of both parliament and Committee.

(i) *Structure and Expansion of the Committee*

Such were the local peculiarities and problems in response to which the County Committee of Kent developed its three most striking characteristics: namely, its evolution from existing institutions, its complexity of structure, and the immensity of its labour. In many respects it developed differently from similar institutions in other counties. Certainly, as a result of the extent, the populousness, the lawlessness, and the strategic importance of the county, it became one of the largest and most powerful county committees in the realm: it was the Committee, moreover, and not parliament, that became the supremely important institution to most Kentish people between 1642 and 1648. The first fact to notice about its structure is that in Kent there were three kinds of committee: the General Committee, or County Committee proper, the Sequestration Committee, and the Accounts Committee. In all counties these three bodies were set up, at least in theory; but in other parts they rarely seem to have developed so vigorous and independent a life as in Kent. The two former institutions only will be dealt with in this section, and first the General Committee.

In each of the western counties of England the general committee was simply created by a distinct ordinance of parliament; in Kent a multiplicity of ordinances throughout the 'forties, conferred further powers upon it—powers of sequestration, assessment, indemnity, martial law, and so on—but there was never an act of creation. What then was its origin? Quite simply the commission of deputy lieutenancy—the committeemen themselves assert this.[1] The development into 'the county committee' was quite gradual. In the Commons Journals and State Papers can be traced the unconscious change of style from "deputy lieutenants" through "deputy lieutenants and committees" to "committees" and finally "Committee of Kent;" in both parliament and county they were often called the committee of deputy lieutenants.[2] But for brevity and convenience the style "Committee of Kent" became most usual, and as it became a distinct institution, with a permanent headquarters and secretariat, the most accurate. The evolution was more than nominal. Though much of the administrative machinery of the County Committee was original, it was not an entirely new creation: it was also a development from the petty sessional divisions and the embryo civil service (with a treasurer and other officials) which the J.P.'s had been forming well before 1640; from the elaborate administration of Charles I's Ship Money and other subsidies; from the administrative experience of the gentry and officials of the naval fringe; and above all from the existing parochial machinery and the immemorial division of the county into five lathes.[3]

It was the lathes which gave shape to the complexity of the Committee; for besides the central body, just as each lathe had always had its own group of deputy lieutenants, so each now

[1] BL, Tanner MS 62, f. 561; Add. 44846, f. 20v. The South-Eastern Association Ordinance (F and R, I, p. 333, 4 Nov. 1643) purports to set up a 'Standing Committee,' but the Committee had already been in existence for a year. Both inside and outside the Committee there was some disquietude regarding the legitimacy of their authority at this date. In theory it derived from the authority of Pembroke, the Lord Lieutenant, but he neither entered the county nor attempted to influence its politics. There was never a confirmatory act, but the ordinances in F and R (especially that of 4 Nov. 1643) confirmed their powers in fact.

[2] Cf. CJ, II, III, V, CCAM, CSPD, 1625–49, *passim*; Richard Culmer, jr, *op. cit.*, pp. 12, 14.

[3] KCA, West Kent Sessions Order Book, 1625–51; BM, Add. MS 19398, f. 159; Add. MS 33512, f. 89; Weller Papers, p. 16; W. Lambarde, *A Perambulation of Kent*, 1826, p. 22; TRHS, 3. IV, 1910, M. D. Gordon, 'The Collection of Ship Money in the Reign of Charles I', pp. 146–7; CJ, II, pp. 231, 232. Orders and ordinances were issued to the hundredal constables to publish "in every parish throughout your hundred, in the church, either by the churchwardens or clerk of each parish:" Add. MS 19398, f. 159.

had its own committee: the size of the county demanded it. Moreover each of the old subdivisions of the lathes of Scraye (Upper and Lower), Aylesford (North, South, and East), and Sutton-at-Hone (Upper and Nether) had separate committees; by 1645 there was one for Thanet; and Canterbury, a county in itself, had its own committee, separately nominated.[1] The ten lathal bodies were subcommittees of, not personally separate from, the central body; but for many lathal members the size of the county precluded constant attendance at the latter (especially when Knole, in the extreme west, was the headquarters) and hence some degree of separate existence, fruitful of discord, was inevitable. And though all subcommitteemen were members of the central Committee, there was a definite hierarchical tendency. In each division a leading committeeman of the county gentry came to be regarded as a sort of lathal head or intendant: in Aylesford South, for example, Sir John Sedley of St Clere in Holmesdale; in Sutton-at-Hone Nether Sir John Rivers of Chafford in Penshurst; in Shepway Sir Edward Scott of Scots' Hall, where he provided his committee with liberal headquarters.[2] Scott and his kinsman Thomas Rooke, who lived with him and became the lathal treasurer, ruled their lathe together till 1648, just as Sir Anthony Weldon ruled the county.[3]

Most, if not all, of the subcommittees eventually secured a fixed headquarters for their meetings and secretariat, but initially even the central Committee was peripatetic and its meetings arranged *ad hoc*: "we have agreed to meet at the Crown at Rochester on Tuesday next, by noon," they wrote in March 1643; in May they met at Bexley, in June at Bromley and Gravesend.[4] But well before the end of the year they had fixed their headquarters at Knole, the sequestrated house of the earl of Dorset; about October 1644 they removed to Aylesford Friary, the rambling mansion by the Medway of the delinquent

[1] SP. 28: 157, Richard Beale's and Colonel Bothby's Account Books, *passim*; BM, Add. MS 33512, ff. 88–9.

[2] *Ibid.*; HMC, *Pepys*, p. 203, calls Shepway "Sir Edward [Scott's] Lathe;" Weller Papers, *passim*.

[3] SP. 28: 159, 160, Thomas Rooke's Account Books.

[4] E. 55. 4; CJ, III, p. 144; CCAM, p. 150; AC, III, p. 145.

Richauts; and about January 1646 to hired quarters in Maidstone. Their fixture at Knole marked the development from an *ad hoc* committee to an institution; the peripatetic stage of meeting anywhere and "visiting the wavering places" was over; the Committee was established.[1] The same change is discernible in the lathal committees. They did not always meet in sequestrated mansions; in some lathes they hired premises, as in Aylesford North at Rochester; in several they met at inns, as at the Star in Maidstone; in Aylesford South at the Swan in West Malling; in St Augustine at the Lion in Wingham, and the Bell in Sandwich; and in Canterbury at the Chequer.[2] For their prisons the committee used Knole, moated Westenhanger, and Leeds Castle, across whose broad lake no prisoner could hope to escape.[3]

Unlike the General Committee, the Sequestration Committee, which administered sequestered estates, came into being through a definite act of creation—through the ordinance of 1 April 1643 which appointed all such committees.[4] Although its membership was practically co-terminous with that of the General Committee, its meetings, its functions, and its secretariat were separate and rendered it a separate institution. Structurally it was very similar: though not stipulated in the ordinance, the division into eleven lathal bodies (each with its sequestrator, treasurer, agents, and collectors) under a central body (with its solicitor-general, treasurer, agents, and collectors) was again inevitable. Meeting in their own lathe, the committeemen were better informed of their neighbours' estates and more accessible to tenants than a single central body, which met in the same premises as the General Committee, could be. In some lathes, to facilitate the tenants' payment of rents, they met peripatetically: in St Augustine's they

[1] SP. 28: 130, Bowles's Account Books; SP. 28: 157, Beale's and Bothby's Account Books; AC, IV, p. 139; CSPD, 1645–7, p. 350; Weller Papers, p. 6.

[2] BM, Add. MS 34167, f. 32; Add. MS 33512, f. 94; Sandwich Muniments, S/N. 2, f. 55; Richard Culmer, jr, *op. cit.*, pp. 12, 14.

[3] KCA, U. 120. C4–6; BM, Add. MS 28001, f. 19; A. G. Matthews, *Walker Revised*, 1948, p. 215. Westenhanger was Viscount Strangford's mansion, Leeds one of the Culpepers'.

[4] Harleian Miscellany, IX, pp. 519 sqq.; F and R give the date as 27 March.

sat usually at the Chequer in Canterbury, at the Red Lion in Wingham, or at Deane, Sir James Oxinden's house; but they also met at Chillenden, at Barham, at Deal, at the Flower de Luce in Eythorne, at the Dolphin in Sandwich, and at Dover Castle. Meetings were held twice a week by the central Committee, and for a lathe, the Order Book of St Augustine's records thirty-nine meetings in 1644–5, twenty-five in 1645–46.[1] Like the General Committee, however, and despite its creation rather than evolution, the Sequestration Committee inherited much from existing county institutions, and operated through them. All the committeemen were J.P.'s, the sheriff published their orders, the borseholders summoned the delinquents' tenants, and the trained bands dealt with any serious opposition.[2]

That is not the end of committee complexity, for in 1644 the Accounts Committees were set up.[3] At the height of committee rule there were thus three kinds of committees of the county, a separate organization for Canterbury, and more than twenty subcommittees.

Functions. It was the problems and the duties of the County Committee that necessitated this complexity. The duties of the General Committee imposed in the original commission of deputy lieutenancy were confirmed in greater detail—and much wider powers were granted—by the ordinance of 30 May 1643 and its accompanying instructions to the Lord Lieutenant and deputy lieutenants: the basis of all subsequent authority. The Committee's *raisons d'être* were the provision of the sinews of war and the provision of armed forces (treated below),[4] but the other powers and duties mentioned in the instructions include: securing papists and the ill-affected; committing opponents to prison, without bail if necessary; apprehending all contemners of the ordinance; disarming those who

[1] SP. 28: 210, Order Book of St Augustine's Lathe Committee; KCA, U. 455. 04, account by Lambarde Godfrey of the countess of Thanet's fifth part; BM, Add. MS 5494, ff. 264, 273, 279; CSPD, 1645–7, p. 350; Twysden's Journal, *passim*; Harleian Miscellany, IX, p. 542.

[2] SP. 23: G: 158, f. 109 (J.P.'s not on the Committee assisted the committeemen); SP. 28: 210B, Order of County Sequestration Committee to Shepway Lathe Committee; KCA, U. 455. 04; CCC, p. 324.

[3] See pp. 172 sqq. [4] See pp. 155 sqq.

refused to contribute; creating magazines; administering "such covenant or protestation . . . as shall be agreed upon;" and informing the county of "the care . . . of the parliament to provide for his Majesty's safety, and that they do not, nor never did intend any evil against his Majesty's person, his crown or dignity." The deputy lieutenants were "enjoined constantly to convene once every month at least, in some one convenient place of the said county during the time of these public distractions, so that all orders and ordinances of parliament may be better divulged and intelligence given and received to and from parliament. . . ."[1]

The immensity of the labours of the twenty-odd committees of Kent need cause no surprise. If the experience of the central Committee and Sutton-at-Hone Upper can be taken as typical, they may well have been sending out 20,000 letters and packages annually in the peak years 1643–5.[2] The functions allotted to the Sequestration Committee still further extended their power. In effect the property of all delinquents was nationalized, without compensation, and all rents and profits were paid to the Committee. By ordinance 'delinquents' included only papists and those attending or assisting the king, but the Committee interpreted the latter category very broadly. There was little, indeed, in Kent which now lay outside their province, specifically or by implication, if they chose to exercise their powers to the full.

Jurisdiction. And they did so choose. Nor were they content with so much. Their gradual engrossing of power till the culmination—and catastrophe—of the 1648 Rebellion is striking. Naturally it brought them into conflict with other jurisdictions in the county; but with Sir Anthony Weldon as their chairman there was little question of compromise, and one by one these jurisdictions were reduced to submission. Sometimes it brought the Committee into conflict with parliament, too; but for that also Sir Anthony was prepared; for though faithful to parliament, he was more faithful to Kent, and most of all to himself.

[1] BM, Add. MS 44846, f. 20v.; E. 104. 22; LJ, VI, p. 73.

[2] Each committee spent over £100 p.a. on posts (SP. 28: 235). The average cost per package was about 2s.

Weldon was now an elderly man, perhaps nearly seventy. As the head of the Weldons of Swanscombe and the friend of leading parliamentarians, he might well have sought a seat in the House. But he lacked the friendships, and perhaps the desire, to secure election, and the sphere he marked out for himself was the county. A life of disappointment at court had embittered him against governments. Until James I's reign his ancestors had for several generations held the offices of Clerk of the Kitchen and Clerk of the Green Cloth.[1] But in 1617, accompanying that monarch to Scotland, he wrote a scandalous paper against James's native country. "The air might be wholesome but for the stinking people that inhabit it. The ground might be fruitful had they wit to manure it. Their beasts be generally small, women only excepted, of which sort there are none greater in the whole world."[2] Though not published, the manuscript was discovered, and the king of the Scots was too small-minded to ignore it. Sir Anthony was dismissed and the seeds of an implacable enmity were sown. He proceeded to write the yet more scandalous *Court and Character of King James* and *Court of King Charles*. Their theme was simple: each succeeding stage of government since Elizabeth's golden age was worse than the last. James was a fool, Charles a villain. Salisbury was bad, Buckingham was worse, Strafford was unspeakable. Every conceivable scandal was adduced to illustrate the story. There was no philosophy in it. His virulence against the episcopate might imply presbyterianism. Possibly, if he had a religion, he was an old-fashioned Elizabethan puritan; he admired Archbishop Abbot. But probably, since he was the friend also of Catholic Windebank, his ecclesiastical antipathy, like his politics, was due merely to feuds with his neighbours. For Bishop Neile of Rochester his venom was indescribable; and Sir Roger Twysden, who had once worsted him at law, he persecuted with implacable malice when he became chairman of the County Committee.[3] "Yet I cannot deny him," said Sir Roger,

[1] *DNB*, s.v. Sir Anthony Weldon.

[2] *Secret History of the Court of James the First*, 1811, II, p. 75.

[3] *Ibid.*, I, pp. 302, 386–8 *et passim*; CSPD, 1634–9, *passim*; Twysden's Journal, II–IV.

"to have been a person had noble principles, yet shadowed with many vanities, if not vices; a good friend where he took, no less an enemy; in which notion he had long looked on our name; one, I dare say, did not in his heart approve the actions of the two Houses, yet the desire of rule brought him to run with the forwardest."[1]

It was that "desire of rule" which lay behind the Committee's engrossing of power. With the judicial jurisdiction Weldon had little difficulty, for the committeemen were J.P.'s, and the sheriffs and mayors usually committeemen. Hence the normal work of the justices, including economic matters, repair of highways, poor relief, and plague regulation, continued to be done under the aegis of the County Committee.[2] It seems probable that the Committee controlled the appointment of new J.P.'s, and it is certain that justices, sheriffs, and parish officers were ordered to assist the Committee in its duties, and that the publication of parliament's ordinances was usually entrusted to the sheriffs.[3] On their own behalf, alleging "the great discouragements they lie under, through many vexatious suits that people well-affected to the parliament are liable unto for services done to the parliament," the committeemen obtained in December 1647 an act appointing a Committee of Indemnity in Kent, composed of their own members. Such suits were thus brought within their own control and they secured a large exemption from normal process of law.[4]

With the jurisdiction of the Cinque Ports, highly conscious of their autonomy and cohesion, the Committee had considerable difficulty, but proved eventually successful. The friction was not political, for the senior port and ringleader, boastful

[1] *Ibid.*, III, p. 146.

[2] KCA, West Kent Sessions Order Books, 1625–51, 1652–70, "Book Containing Lists of Prisoners and their Offences, 1627–74," *passim*; BM, Add. MS 33512, f. 91; Sandwich Muniments, Letter Book 1295–1753, f. 84; Richard Culmer, jr, *op. cit.*, pp. 12–16. Often their respective jurisdictions were hard to distinguish: where local disputes were involved, two committeemen might be sitting as D.L.'s or J.P.'s or both. The suppression of supernumerary alehouses, for example, was undertaken by both: Add. MS 33512, f. 96.

[3] Sandwich Muniments, Letter Book 1295–1753, f. 146; CCC, p. 324; LJ, v, pp. 329–31; F and R, *passim*.

[4] E. 520. 19; CJ, v, p. 341.

Sandwich, was noisily, though emptily, parliamentarian. The pulse of opinion can be taken in the thousand-odd letters of the corporation during the period. From the beginning it was declared that the deputy lieutenants' attempts to act in any way within their region were "contrary to the liberties, customs, and freedoms of the ports and their members." The trouble came to a head over the propositions for the South-Eastern Association in January 1643. Refusing to co-operate, the ports bluntly told the Committee that they already bore vast charges in watching the coast, which the county did not share; that if they sent their men on the county's service they would be defenceless during invasion; that if they came under the county's charges and commands their liberties would be infringed, and it "were undoubtedly a query whether our charters were not thereby forfeited."[1]

But despite the wishes of Sandwich national developments began to break their solidarity, and the Committee exploited their disunity. The royal forces were advancing through Sussex, and the southern ports of Lydd, Hythe, and Folkestone were pitifully weak. Declaring they had so often acted with the county that their privileges were in any case long since infringed, and trusting that it was not the intention of parliament to annul their charter, these towns decided to support the Association. The Committee eventually overcame the opposition of the rest by mere importunity of demand, and in this they were assisted by the fact that Sir Edward Boys of Fredville, one of their leading members, was baron of Dover, lieutenant of Dover Castle, and popular in the ports as their parliamentary champion. With Sandwich even he had some difficulty. In August 1643 he had a great quarrel with the corporation, but by January 1644 he had brought them to heel. In February 1645, in the impressment of troops, they were reckoned as a hundred of St Augustine's Lathe, though the deputy lieutenants excused their action by saying:

"we shall be forced to press from the plough's handle the most of them [to be levied in the lathe], which in this time of

[1] Sandwich Muniments, S/N. 5, ff. 189 sqq., 194–6; BM, Add. MS 33512; cf. AC, XXVIII, p. 64.

the countryman's being cast much behindhand in their seasons (which must be both yours and our livelihoods) by reason of the long and tedious frost, we are enforced to desire your aid." In April 1646 the recorder of Sandwich informed the town flatly that their militia was under the authority of the county.[1] Generally, by operating through the existing machinery of government in each port separately instead of dealing with them as a whole, the Committee of "Kent and the Cinque Ports," as it was sometimes called, achieved a *de facto* union of the towns with the lathes by the summer of 1643.[2] By August 1645 they were able, tactfully, to sway the by-election at Hythe, and a committeeman, Thomas Westrowe of Mersham, was returned.[3]

Similar opposition might have come from the Committee of Canterbury, but it was largely avoided by appointing some of its leading members to the County Committee—Sir William Mann, Sir John Roberts, Avery Sabine—and in December 1644 the deputy lieutenants of Kent sought power to act also as lieutenants of Canterbury.[4] Similar methods brought under the control of the Committee the naval fringe of Kentish society, which centred on Rochester. This city's originally separate committee was united with that of the county in 1643; the vice-admiral of Kent, Sir Thomas Walsingham (whose family had represented the city in every parliament since Elizabeth, and Sir Thomas himself seven times) was a leading committeeman; the castle was owned by Sir Anthony Weldon himself; and the administrative experience of the naval officials was much used by the Committee: Charles Bowles, keeper of the outstores, was commissary of the county, Peter Pett became a committeeman, and Thomas Whitton (Bowles's deputy) and John Swynoke (clerk of the Ropeyard at Woolwich) were committee officials.[5]

1 Sandwich Muniments, S/N. 5, ff. 227–8; S/N. 2, f. 55; Letter Book 1295–1753, f. 138.

2 BM, Add. MS 33512, ff. 88–90, 94; Sandwich Muniments, S/N. 5, f. 212; E. 104. 22; HMC, VIII. i, p. 8.; CSPD, 1645–7, p. 287.

3 G. Wilks, *The Barons of the Cinque Ports and the Parliamentary Representation of Hythe* [1892], pp. 82–3.

4 CJ, III, p. 733.

5 SP. 28: 130, Bowles's Commissary Account Books; CSPD, 1644–50, *passim*.

One of the greatest offences to the Committee was the new jurisdiction of the excise officers. All taxation but this was under the dictatorship of Sir Anthony Weldon, who found no pleasure in the authority of others. It was not entirely beyond his control, for the local assessors were the borseholders, who were also servants of the Committee.[1] But the excise officers themselves were outside his purview. An excuse to gain control of them was made when, universally abhorred, and universally suspected of embezzlement, they did all they could to avoid accounting for their receipts to the County Committee like other fisal officers. And for a while they secured the ear of the central Committee of Accounts, ever fearful of offending the House.[2] "If you shall encourage them in it," the Accounts Committee for West Kent wrote to the latter in March 1646, it

"will much redound to our disparagement and the country's [i.e. county's] dissatisfaction. . . . If their accounting shall be deferred . . . they may be gone and shifted as they have been three or four times in two years, and then their miscarriages unpunishable and unquestionable."

The Canterbury Committee wrote in the same month seeking immediate power to call them to account, since

"we find the present examination of them of so great concernment . . . for the advancement . . . of the state's revenue . . . and the earnest expectation of the commonalty of the county, who ardently await that business. . . . There are witnesses now ready to testify their knowledge in that business, who [should it be longer retarded] might not be in a capacity of doing the state that service."

The clamour was successful, the power was granted, and in June they wrote again:

"there can be no greater satisfaction to the whole body of the county, who have with much devotion long expected it, and (we are confident) will yield us all assistance in the business itself. [We send our committeeman] Anthony Hamond [who]

[1] BM, Add. MS 34167, ff. 32, 34.
[2] SP. 28: 252A, Central Committee Letter Book, f. 66.

can fully inform you of how great consequence it is, and how much the people's eyes are engaged upon the issue of it."[1]

Finally, and most important of all, there was the jurisdiction of the Church, with which the Committee was never so successful. But that is too long a story to deal with here.

It was not only in the case of the excise men that the Committee's determination to engross power within the county brought them into conflict with the supreme jurisdiction of parliament. In the government's letters flattering their faithfulness there is doubtless some sincerity; where their own interests were concerned the Committee were ready enough to accede. But the general tone is one of continual friction and independence; for decentralization was their aim.[2] The Tudors had had trouble, the Stuarts had more trouble, and parliament had most of all, because it was the weakest of all, in governing by the one means available before the nineteenth century: the county gentry.

They would have had less, however, if Sir Anthony Weldon had not been chairman of the Committee. It was he who was behind the Committee's successful demands in 1644 that the forts should be placed in the hands of the county gentry. He was behind the incessant complaints of "the extraordinary and unsupportable charges of this county."[3] In May 1644, for example, he and the rest of the Committee wrote:

"The case of our county differs from all others, for, [whereas they have been assisted from the common fund], what we do and have done at most excessive charge hath been and is all out of our own purses, without any additional help, when [there is] nothing [that] hath been required of us, as well to defend others as ourselves, that hath not been cheerfully undergone. . . . We repent not of any service for the public,

[1] SP. 28: 256, loose letters of John Parker to William Prynne (31 March 1646, June 1646), and of CAC to LAC, 14 March 1645/6.

[2] Dering's scheme for the reorganization of the Church (E. 197. 1, pp. 155–61) foreshadowed some of their ideas on decentralization: virtually autonomous county churches were to be set up—episcopal, but largely responsible to the 'county elders,' i.e. the gentry.

[3] E. 19. 11; HMC, XIII. i, p. 163; CJ, III, p. 733.

yet we must be accountable to our county, who wholly entrust us with their persons and purses . . . for—besides the soldiers' pay—arming, ammunition, etc., have cost the county £20,000, with little or no help from any but ourselves."[1]

In November 1644 they sought the immediate payment of £2,358 per month for their troops' expedition into Sussex.[2] In October 1645, in response to further demands of the House, Weldon and the rest of the Committee wrote again:

"representing that upwards of £9,700 *per mensem* besides the militia and other necessary charges is charged on the county, which not only disables them from undertaking new charges, but which they will not be able to continue, and complaining that while these charges take away one third of the revenue of the county, Sussex escapes with a tenth, sixteenth, or twentieth part."[3]

In March 1646, after a year of unprecedented exactions and repeated demands for arrears, the Committee was "still £1,479 4s. 5½d. in arrear of the first four months' pay [for the New Model], the whole last four months' assessment, and £500 of the Scottish loan: at which we wonder," wrote the Goldsmiths' Hall Committee. They had sent down William Hale, their agent, to bring before them all committeemen or officers who "obstruct the service," but Lambarde Godfrey, the county treasurer, "took distaste at the warrants of the [central] Committee . . . and said their Committee was no ways inferior to it . . . Mr Hale said he had as good bring up all Kent as any of the Committee, although they obstruct the business."[4]

Eventually the arrears were duly paid in, but even in July 1648, with Committee government crashing about his ears in the Rebellion, Weldon wrote to Lenthall blaming "the extraordinary and unproportionable burthen . . . upon this county, made use of by the malignants to exasperate the people against the parliament."[5]

[1] CSPD, 1644, p. 147.
[2] E. 19. 11.
[3] HMC, XIII. i, p. 296.
[4] CCC, pp. 34, 780; cf. CSPD, 1645–7, p. 193. Lambarde Godfrey was grandson of William Lambarde and brother of Sir Edmund Berry Godfrey.
[5] HMC, XIII. i, p. 472.

Taxation was not the Committee's only issue with the central government. Weldon was also behind its policy of severity and sequestration in dealing with delinquents, and resolutely opposed the policy of composition and relative lenience advocated by the central Committee for Compounding in London. Parliament, uninfluenced by county rancours, unaware of county problems, and seeking quick returns, supported the central Committee. Composition, by which, on payment of a fine varying from one-third downwards, delinquents could regain their estates, was more efficient and kept control in central hands. The County Committee was opposed to it because of the centralization which it entailed; because many of the 300 malignants whom they scotched by sequestration between 1643 and 1649 were thereby set at large, and formed a nucleus of opposition; and (since sequestration moneys were retained in the county and compositions passed to the central coffers) because it involved a loss of county income, and an increase in assessments, which they, as well as royalists, had to pay.[1] Hence they often complained that "the discharge of chief malignants" by composition was "injurious to the cause."[2] They complained after the 1643 rebellion when 230 people were allowed to compound for trivial sums.[3] They desired that the rebels of 1645 "be made speedy examples of your justice, who have already so surfeited upon your mercy that they grow wanton and insolent." They desired that the rebels who rose at Canterbury on Christmas Day, 1647, should be tried by the County Committee under martial law; and when parliament insisted on trial by commission of Oyer and Terminer, and the bill was twice thrown out by the Canterbury jury, so that the rebels escaped unscathed, the recriminations of the committee-men against parliament, led by Sir Anthony Weldon, were drowned only by the clangour of the great Rebellion of 1648.[4]

If the Committee did not always secure its demands, it could often ignore the orders of the central Committee for

[1] Numbers of royalists sequestered in 1643–9 are based on the account books of the lathal Sequestration Committees in SP. 28: 210, SP. 28: 158, and on CCC.

[2] CCC, p. 840.

[3] SP. 28: 157.

[4] BL, Tanner MS 57, f. 60; MS 60, f. 99.

Compounding. On one occasion, having refused to free Sir Alexander Culpeper from sequestration, they were ordered to "show cause in 10 days why they do not [do so] . . . or they will be reported to the House."[1] On another, when ordered to stay sequestration of the earl of Thanet, Weldon replied from Knole:

"The causes wherefore his Lordship's estate is sequestered are so many as either he deserves it, or else no other. . . . What hath been made of his estate [in rents and sale of timber] for the present we know not, and will ask a long time to give the Honourable Committee satisfaction . . . but we are confident not so much as his crimes merit. . . ."[2]

On many occasions, despite a stream of orders and protests of the central Committee for Compounding, delinquents remained sequestered for years. Sir Roger Twysden of Roydon Hall obtained order after order in his own behalf—all to no purpose: he remained sequestered till Sir Anthony Weldon was dead. John Heath of Brasted Place, the heirs of Sir Alexander Culpeper of Hollingbourne, and Laurence Bing of Offham suffered in the same way.[3]

Not till 1648 did there come a change. The Rebellion had taught the County Committee to co-operate and the central government to admit their problems. Compounding was extended, but entrusted to a special county committee to operate, and the proceeds devoted to the Committee's expenditure in suppressing the Rebellion. The numbers of the sequestered fell sharply: in St Augustine, for example, from 29 in 1643–5 to 12 in 1649.[4] Behind this change of policy lies a long story, which a study of the membership of the committee will reveal.

[1] CCC, p. 1058.

[2] SP. 23: G: 223, f. 877.

[3] SP. 23: G: 114, f. 1184; BM, Egerton MS 2978, ff. 242–3; Twysden's Journal, III, pp. 167 sqq.; CCC, pp. 1058, 1472, 1942.

[4] SP. 28: 210, Edward Boys's Sequestration Account Books for St Augustine.

(ii) *The Committeemen*

Who were the men behind Sir Anthony Weldon, and how did he gain his ascendancy?

The growth of the Committee's power, complexity, and labours, was reflected in the growth of its membership. In February 1643 there were a mere 24 members, by June 38, and by November 59; and from then until the 1648 Rebellion between 58 and 68. Thereafter—in April–May 1649—the committee suddenly rose to 94, and remained between 88 and 99 till the Restoration.[1] It was the largest County Committee in England, but when its lathal divisions are remembered, not so excessive: each subcommittee, controlling on an average 40 parishes and 100,000 acres apiece, had about five members before 1648, and eight thereafter.[2] Altogether, by 1660, 274 men had at some time sat on the Committee. There had then been great fluidity in its composition: in fact only eight members had survived from 1643 to 1660 without a break—a low figure even allowing for deaths.

The initial division into parties in Kent was not a social cleavage, and with negligible exceptions all on the Committee were of gentle extraction. Nevertheless there was a notable change in its social composition. In February–March 1643 22 per cent of the committeemen were baronets, 33 per cent knights, and 45 per cent esquires; by December 1652 the proportion of baronets had fallen to 5 and knights to 6 per cent, whereas esquires had risen to 77 per cent, and 10 per cent were mere gentlemen. The tendencies should not be exaggerated, since some esquires were eldest sons of titled gentry, and some were later created knights or baronets. But not all: the figures undeniably indicate a gradual secession of county families and influx of parochial gentry. Equally important is the fact that, though committeemen were always inhabitants of Kent and the majority were of families long established in the county, the preponderance of indigenous families

[1] See Appendix, Table IV. This and the following analyses are based on the Committee lists in F and R, LJ, V, CJ, II. The figures for the Canterbury Committee are included, though in fact separately appointed.

[2] Till the end of the war those appointed to the Committee were also usually appointed D.L.'s: LJ, V–VI, CJ, II–IV.

tended to diminish. In February 1643 75 per cent of the members were of indigenous families (i.e., in Kent before 1485); in November nearly 70 per cent; in April–May 1649 62 per cent. Newcomers (i.e., after 1603) were always few, but increased slightly: at these dates 12, 14, 17 per cent. These two gradual changes in the social composition of the Committee seem slight, and the dominance of well-to-do and solidly Kentish families throughout is undeniable; but they are significant, and for more interesting reasons than at first sight appears. It was not simply a class cleavage.

Parliament's problem was how to control the county. The essence of the difficulty—the lack of a single dominant family like the Barringtons in Essex or the Barnardistons in Suffolk—necessitated, as has been mentioned, rule through the county gentry, that is the group of twenty or thirty leading families of Kent. Charles I himself had found this. For justices, for captains of trained bands, and on multifarious commissions, he had used men like Sir Edward Scott of Scots' Hall, Sir Edward Boys of Fredville in Nonington, Sir John Honywood of Evington in Elmsted, Sir Thomas Godfrey of Heppington in Nackington, and Thomas Seyliard of Delaware.[1] And on the Committee there were eight of the Boyses, including their leader Sir Edward of Fredville—Boyses of Willesborough, of Elmington, of Betteshanger, of Trapham in Wingham; six of the Scotts, including their leader Sir Edward of Scots' Hall; five of the Honywoods, including theirs, Sir John of Evington; five of the Seyliards, including theirs, John of Delaware; and four of the Godfreys, including theirs, Sir Thomas of Heppington; and so on. The power of such family groups and their lateral connections, ramifying throughout the county, necessitated their inclusion in its government. But from parliament's viewpoint they had many disadvantages. For they were all deeply rooted in Kent; they tended to think in terms of the county rather than the nation; they demanded devolution as the price of their allegiance; and in politics they were marked, if not obsessed, by moderatism. The clue to parliament's problems, and to

[1] PRO, 35 Assizes 79, 80, 81, 82, 83; Ind. 4212 (Entry Book of Commissions, Patents, etc. (Chancery), 1629–43), *passim*; CSPD, 1627–40, *passim*.

party formations, lies in the gradual divergence of those who held the power in Kent—these county gentry—from those who held the reins of government.

How could parliament, then, control the county gentry? Since the parliamentary leaders had no social connection with Kent, as the Pym-Hampden-Cromwell group had with the eastern counties, the one means open seemed to be through the parliament men on the Committee. Unfortunately, not only were they a small minority, but, since the secession of Sir Edward Dering and Sir John Culpeper, the Kentish members of parliament had themselves become notorious for their hankerings after a moderate solution to the Civil War. Out of sixteen one had already been expelled from the House, three were never appointed to the Committee, and six more, rarely active, were soon omitted from it.[1] By the spring of 1643 Sir Thomas Peyton and Sir Edward Hales, the ringleader of the moderates, had seceded from Westminster.[2] In September complaint was made of Sir Francis Barnham for non-attendance at the House, and in December for disaffection in the county. In the summer Sir Norton Knatchbull had been sequestered and fined 1,000 marks for neglecting "the service of the House" and refusing to "meet and join with the Committees [of Kent] in the putting in execution the ordinances for raising of monies;" in the autumn he hesitated long in taking the Covenant; in November some scruple stuck with him still that he could not yet take it; four days later, still undecided, he was "suspended the House;" he did not take it till February 1644. Sir Edward Partheriche and Sir Humphrey Tufton shared his hesitancy. Again and again in 1643 the Committee complained to the House of the slackness of parliament men in attending its meetings; and so late as 1647 fines were set on seven Kentish members of parliament for repeated absences.[3]

[1] Thomas Webb, William Harrison, John Harvey, Benjamin Weston, Sir Humphrey Tufton, Sir Francis Barnham, Sir Edward Hales, Sir Edward Partheriche, Sir Thomas Peyton.

[2] BM, Add. MS 44846, f. 12v.; CJ, III, pp. 80, 256. Hales retained an uncomfortable seat, though sequestered and fined, till 1648.

[3] CJ, III, pp. 43–390, *passim*; HMC, XIII. i, pp. 702, 713. All these men retained their seats, but like Hales were inactive in the House. This prevented the election of more wholehearted 'recruiters' in their place.

Even reliable men, like Sir Edward Boys, governor of Dover Castle, were frequently absent, or like Sir Edward Master of Canterbury, lived too far off for constant attendance at both House and Committee. So the parliament men were practically useless as a means of controlling the greater county gentry.

This gave these twenty or so insular families their opportunity. Parliament never appointed a quorum to act as a 'standing committee' as in some other counties; but, as was inevitable among 60–70 men, a distinct, though unofficial 'core' of people who guided Committee policy soon emerged from the 'general body.' Let us first examine the core and then the general body of committeemen.

The composition of the core was highly unstable. At first, as Committee letters and attendances show, it was composed entirely of members of the county gentry. Of sixty members only about twelve regularly attended the central Committee; in a typical lathe—St Augustine—only four out of fifteen: Sir James Oxinden of Deane, John Boys of Trapham, senior, Sir Richard Hardres of Upper Hardres, and Sir Edward Monins of Waldershare.[1] The rest were lesser men; they attended rarely; and they merely followed the policy of the core. Led by their chief and eldest member, Sir Edward Hales, the core naturally reflected, in its early stages, the moderatism of the county gentry from whom it was drawn. But from the beginning there were a few discontented extremists within it: men of years and experience mostly, with a family tradition of opposition to the crown, like Sir Henry Heyman and Colonel Edwyn Sandys; or men always at the centre of local feuds, like Sir John Sedley of St Clere; or disappointed courtiers in economic difficulties, like Sir Thomas Walsingham; and combining nearly all these traits their leader, Sir Anthony Weldon, whose "desire of rule brought him to run with the forwardest."[2] Inevitably there was rivalry between this group and the moderates.

[1] BM, Egerton MS 2978, f. 239; SP. 28: 210, Order Book of St Augustine's Lathe Committee. Names are always entered in correct social order and Sir Richard Hardres accorded his baronetcy, though granted in 1643 and in theory disallowed by parliament.

[2] BM, Add. MS 34163, f. 138; cf. E. 37. 1; E. 78. 21; E. 122. 9; CSPD, 1635–40, *passim*; Twysden's Journal, III, *passim*; E. A. Webb, G. W. Miller, J. Beckwith, *The History of Chislehurst*, 1899, p. 149.

The theoretical and national basis of that rivalry, as far as there was one, turned on the absolute or qualified support that either group was prepared to accord the two Houses apart from the king. But for most men the basis was less theoretical and national than practical and local. The 'extremists,' eager to sever the sheep from the goats, desired sequestration and imprisonment not only of all royalists but of all neuters, as they termed the king's inactive sympathizers. The 'moderates,' on the other hand, wished to leave as many as possible, and in particular those numerous neuters, alone; for among neighbours they had no wish to sharpen discords and define divisions. By the beginning of 1643 the rivalry had resulted in the expulsion of the original chairman, Sir Edward Hales, and the establishment of Weldon as supreme. In July 1643 came Sir Francis Barnham's defection. Within two months Sir Robert Honywood, the elder, of Petts in Charing, followed him. By September 1643, when the Committee had been established at Knole and had become a distinct institution, renewed differences between some of the deputy lieutenants resulted in their supersession by further ardent supporters of Weldon, including his own son Captain Ralph and Sir William Springate.[1]

Who now composed the core? With Weldon there were about ten men. They still included such moderates and heads of ancient Kentish clans as Sir John Honywood of Evington, Sir Edward Scott of Scots' Hall, and Sir James Oxinden of Deane. But also among them were Sir Michael Livesey, Thomas Blount, and Sir William Springate—men of an altogether different stamp and the only members of the core who were newcomers to Kent.[2] The two former, colonels of Kentish

[1] BL, Tanner MS 62, ff. 222, 468, 487–8, 534; Twysden's Journal, *passim*; CJ, III, *passim*; Weller Papers, *passim*; HMC, V, p. 108; CSPD, 1641–7, *passim*. Honywood was not sequestered, for Sir Henry Vane, a close family friend whose sister had married his son, "charmed Sir Anthony Weldon in [his] regard."

[2] Evidence for this and subsequent lists of the 'core' is based mainly on: (1) correspondence of the Committee in State Papers Domestic; BL, Tanner MSS 56–64; KCA, U. 350 (Dering MSS); BM, Add. MSS 28000–28004 (Oxinden correspondence); Add. MS 44846 (Peyton letters); Weller Papers; (2) Commonwealth Exchequer Papers, SP. 28: 130, 157–60, 197, 210, 234, 235; (3) Thomason Tracts in BM; (4) Twysden's Journal.

regiments, were the two men excepted from the king's offers of pardon to Kent in November–December 1642.[1] The uncompromising enthusiasm of Blount, who lived at Wricklesmarsh, near Greenwich, was especially valuable to the Houses in controlling the tumultuous and highly royalist parishes of the London fringe.[2] As for Livesey, he was at feud with parliament, at feud with Sir William Waller his superior officer, and at feud with Captain Ralph Weldon his inferior; according to his enemies he was the "plunder-master general of Kent;" according to his colleague Springate he shamelessly feathered his own nest; and he became a regicide.[3] Springate himself was high-principled, and, as a dedicated puritan, fully conscious of the fact. Other committeemen looked on him as mad, said his wife, "because he reproved their carnal wisdom in managing of things, and told them it was the cause of God and they should trust God in it." One of the milder members, possibly his wife's uncle Sir Edward Parteriche, had been appointed with him and others to search recusants' houses and "destroy their pictures and trumpery," and Springate,

"coming one day . . . to visit [him], as he passed through the hall . . . spied several superstitious pictures, as of the crucifixion of Christ, and of His resurrection and such like, very large, that were of great ornament to the hall . . . He drew out his sword and cut them all out of the frames, and spitting them upon his sword's point went into the parlour with them,"

and presented the mangled remains to his host's wife.[4] It was hard for mild parliamentarians like Sir Edward Partheriche and Sir Edward Scott to remain in the core with such men as that. And as the Springates and Liveseys, like Cromwell and Vane

[1] E. 128. 37.
[2] E. 278. 21; E. 278. 30.
[3] BL, Tanner MS 51, f. 50; *Somers's Tracts*, 2nd edn, 1812, VII, pp. 59, 432–6; CJ, IV, p. 27.
[4] *Gentleman's Magazine*, 1851, part II, pp. 368–72. In opposition to their uncle Sir Edward Partheriche, with whom they lived, Springate and his wife became disciples of Thomas Wilson of Otham, an extreme puritan. She remarried Isaac Penington and became a Quaker; her daughter married William Penn: cf. *DNB*, s.v. William Penn.

in the House, became increasingly prominent on the Committee, the others drifted to its fringe, and gradually out of it altogether.

The inevitable crisis between them came in the winter of 1644–5, during the formation of the New Model Army. In the previous winter the Committee had been united against the formation of the South-Eastern Association, but political realities and the king's advance through Hampshire towards Kent had forced them to forgo some measure of county autonomy and join with the three other south-eastern counties for mutual defence. The same issues—centralism versus county autonomy and an extreme policy versus a moderate one—faced the Committee once more in the winter of 1644–5 over the New Model. And the same political reality—the necessity to defeat the king outright—was leading several of the core, under Weldon, to come to terms with parliament. As the county unit had given way to the unit of association in 1643–4, so now Weldon began to see that the unit of association, at least for the moment, must give way to that of the nation. But not all of the core and the Committee agreed with him. Some—leaders of the lathal Committees like the powerful Sir Edward Scott—had been antagonized by his attrition of their powers in their lathes. And the insularity of the gentry remained potent. Hence, in the Committee appointed after the formation of the New Model, thirteen of the original committeemen were dropped and twelve new members appointed. Moreover, while many of the former leaders like Scott and Oxinden were anglicans, in the New Model crisis Independency raised its head, and one of the new men, who rapidly became prominent, was the lay leader of the Kentish Independents, Robert Hales of Howlets in Bekesbourne.

It was not only political but personal divisions, however, that led to the gradual exclusion of the 'county gentry' from the core of the Committee. Two men of such animosities and ambitions as Sir Anthony Weldon and Sir John Sedley of St Clere could not long remain together. Sir John's feuds with tenants and neighbours continued unabated through the 'forties.[1] His feuds with other committeemen began as early

[1] BL, Tanner MS 69, f. 133; CJ, III, p. 160.

as December 1643 and were redoubled in the county election of 1645, when no less than five rival committeemen sought election.[1] In June 1646 he was at loggerheads with a "seditious and turbulent spirit" (his own words), John Baldwin of West Malling, a former committee official.[2] In December came the inevitable clash with Sir Anthony Weldon, when Sedley was arrested, for "divers miscarriages," by the Committee itself. For the time he was released by parliament, who in January 1647 appointed a committee to consider his petition and the differences between him and the County Committee, and to "use the best ways and means they shall think fitting . . . to reconcile the parties, and compose the differences between them; and make a conclusion of the business without reporting to the House, if they can." There followed an interminable series of attendances upon parliament, involving the Committee in expenditure of £267 in order "to assert their own authority . . . and the justnesss of their proceeding in displacing the said Sir John Sedley from military commands."[3] But he had friends in the House, and by April it was clear that parliament intended to do nothing. Sir Anthony Weldon, however, was not so easily fobbed off: baulked of accomplishing his will as a deputy lieutenant, he would yet secure it as a J.P.

Now as a justice Sedley had procured a bill of indictment against another committeeman, William Kenwricke, "for his troopers' taking of three horses . . . at the first rebellion in Kent . . . for the service of the state. . . ."[4] It was a trivial matter, but more lay behind it: Kenwricke was the protégé, adjutant, and neighbour of Weldon's friend Colonel Sir Michael Livesey. The course Weldon and his confrères adopted was extraordinary. As "his Majesty's Justices of Peace for the county of Kent" they met on 27 April 1647 and drew up a remonstrance to parliament:

"finding our endeavours for the settlement of peace in the said county . . . much disturbed by the counteractings and

[1] Weller Papers, p. 42; CSPD, 1645–7, pp. 138, 155; cf. CJ, III, pp. 273, 275.

[2] HMC, VI, p. 120 b.

[3] SP. 28: 130, Charles Bowles's Account Book, 1646–7, ff. 8–12; CJ, V, pp. 6, 55.

[4] Rushworth, VI, p. 479; Whitelock, II, p. 139.

illegal proceedings of certain Justices . . . and much apprehending the great inconvenience arising and dangers which may ensue thereby, [we] thought it our duty to present the same to your wisdoms for redress, that so we might deliver ourselves from the blame which otherwise by our silence might justly be charged upon us."[1]

This time, having heard such Weldonian phrases before, parliament listened. There had been a rebellion when they had ignored them in 1643. Sedley was instantly "called to the Bar in the House . . . and upon full debate, though Mr Holles and Sir William Waller pleaded hard on his behalf, he was voted to be put out of Commission of Justice of Peace, out of the militia, and made uncapable of bearing office in State and Commonwealth."[2] Increasingly those like Sedley—one of the most influential of the county gentry—who thought in terms of county politics were being forced from the core by those who, for various reasons, now looked to the state and thought nationally.[3]

The core had now changed. Weldon, Livesey, Blount remained. But the milder men, the great men of the county gentry like Sir James Oxinden and Sir Edward Scott, do not appear as signatories of the remonstrance against Sedley. What sort of men supplanted them? Though all were armigerous, they were all 'parochial gentry.' Though among them Robert Hales of Howlets, Thomas Seyliard of Seyliards, and Thomas Broadnax of Godmersham were as deeply rooted in Kent as any, most of the rest were newcomers to the county: Thomas Plumer and Sir Michael Livesey came of a Tudor lawyer and a London merchant; Augustine Skynner, John Dixwell, William Kenwricke, Thomas Westrowe, Thomas Blount, Augustine Garland, and John Parker (two mere gentry, two of mercantile, three of legal origin) were all post-Tudor. Several, like Lambarde Godfrey, had served an apprenticeship as Committee

[1] KCA, West Kent Sessions Order Book, 1625–51, ff. 168, 169.

[2] *Clarke Papers*, I, p. 27.

[3] BM, Add. MS 28001, f. 247. Sedley did his utmost to regain favour, but having sowed the wind he reaped the whirlwind: he was twice sequestered and at least once fined on the false allegation of assisting the 1648 Rebellion: E. 518. 14; CCC, pp. 1926–7.

officials. Six of them, since Committee work involved more and more litigation, were gentlemen-lawyers. The majority of them—for since the New Model the core had come increasingly into line with national developments—were Independents. And among them were the three Kentish regicides—Livesey, Dixwell, and Garland.[1] The county gentry, moderatism, and insularity had vanished from the core of the Committee together.

But the county gentry and moderatism had not yet been forced from the general body of the Committee, and the next developments came there. The reins of government were still held by Weldon and his confrères, but the wealth and influence of the county, represented by the county gentry, were now held by the general body. Hence the politics of the core now diverged from those of the county gentry. The latter, of indigenous families, moderate and still anglican, thought in terms of the county, and sought salvation there; the former, of newer families, extremist and puritan or Independent, looked more and more to parliament and army to secure their ideals. Only Sir Anthony Weldon, the chairman, had been able to keep the two divergent sections of the Committee together; but with the exclusion of the county gentry from the core he could do so no longer. The greatest asset of the Committee—the ramification of these families throughout Kentish society, bringing it into the sphere of the Committee's rule—became its liability when they were excluded from the core and subjected to the influence of royalism.

For though technically parliamentarian, such families had many royalist relatives. One of the Honywoods, for example, was imprisoned as a royalist officer in Windsor Castle. One of the Boyses, Sir John of Bonnington in Goodnestone, was the

[1] KCA, West Kent Sessions Order Book, 1625–51, ff. 168, 169; BL, Gough Kent MS 19; Tanner MS 51, f. 50; SP. 28: 210; BM, Add. MSS 28001, 44847, 44848, *passim* (letters of Hales and Dixwell); E. 888. 1 (cf. Dedication to Robert Hales); CSPD, 1654, pp. 386–7; CJ, III, p. 377; *Papers of the New Haven Colony Historical Society*, VI, 'Dixwell Papers', pp. 337–74, *passim*; *DNB*, s.v. Sir Michael Livesey, John Dixwell, Augustine Garland. "Gentlemen-Lawyers:" the lawyers of English towns were often drawn from the minor gentry on their fringes; Lambarde Godfrey, son and heir of Thomas of Hodiford in Sellindge, practised in Maidstone.

king's governor of Donnington Castle. The Scotts were related to the Derings, the St Legers of Boughton Monchelsea, the Nevilles Lords Abergavenny of Birling Manor, the Diggeses of Chilham Castle, and the Bakers of Sissinghurst—all Oxford royalists. The Oxindens were related to Sir Thomas Peyton, one of the royalist conspirators of the Interregnum; Sir Edward Partheriche to his neighbours Sir John Culpeper, Charles's Chancellor of the Exchequer, and the recusant Wottons of Boughton Malherbe; Sir Richard Hardres—created a baronet by the king while a committeeman—to the Diggeses and Sir George Sondes; and so on.[1] Even during the war such relationships were rarely disrupted. Henry Oxinden of Great Maydeacon, a parliamentary captain, freely corresponded with Sir Thomas Peyton and Sir Anthony Percivall, saw to their estates while they were in prison, and entertained Sir Thomas when released. Sir John Honywood, William James, and other committeemen remained close friends of Sir Roger Twysden when he was imprisoned and sequestered. War was far from total, and it was certainly inconvenient—and there was a strong feeling even during the war that it was unchristian—to remain at constant enmity with half your neighbours. So in their manor-houses, the centres of county life, family gatherings took place, as in the homes of the Oxindens of Deane and Great Maydeacon, where royalist and parliamentarian were meeting one another; especially when the first war was over and Oxford Cavaliers like Sir Anthony St Leger and Sir John Boys returned to Kent.[2] In 1647 the Committee spent £55 for "keeping watch . . . for the . . . dispersing of the great concourse of . . . soldiers then flocking daily . . . in and about Maidstone from . . . the king's army subdued and surrendered, and such persons as had been formerly in several insurrections in the county."[3] Such intercourse profoundly affected party feeling and allegiance.

[1] W. Berry, *Pedigrees of the Families in the County of Kent*, 1830, *passim*; J. R. Scott, *Memorials of the Family of Scott of Scot's Hall*, 1876, *passim*; LJ, v, p. 590.

[2] BM, Add. MSS 28000–28003, 44846, *passim*; Sandwich Muniments, Letter Book 1295–1753, f. 146; Twysden's Journal.

[3] SP. 28: 130, Bowles's Account Book, 1647–8.

Hence in 1648, corrupted by royalism, the county gentry proved too strong for Weldon. Rebellion broke out; within a few weeks the Committee disintegrated; and before the end of the year, a brokenhearted man, he was dead.[1] When the Committee re-emerged after the Rebellion had been crushed, there were still a few sons or minor branches of the county families upon it. But of almost every one the head, the chief branch, withdrew its support: e.g. Sir Edward Scott of Scots' Hall, his kinsman Humphrey Scott, Sir John Honywood of Evington, Sir Thomas Godfrey of Heppington, Sir Richard Hardres of Upper Hardres, Sir James and Henry Oxinden of Deane, the three chief Boyses—John of Fredville (heir of Sir Edward), and John and Edward of Betteshanger; and so on: all withdrew.

Committee and parliament were thus compelled to find a new answer to the old problem of controlling the county. The core of men willing to take their cue from national politics remained: Sir Michael Livesey, Thomas Blount, Robert Hales, and the rest. But the general body altered profoundly. Instead of the baronet or knight and his connexion of friends extending over several parishes, there stepped in several minor squires and gentry, separated as far as possible from that connexion. Nearly every parish in Kent had from one to half-a-dozen such minor men: essentially parochial, not county, gentry.[2] Few were Independents; it was enough that they were willing to do the work required of them.[3] So the numbers of the Committee shot up from 60 to 100, and included men like Richard Amherst of Horsmonden, Thomas Foach of Wotton, Henry Paramore of Paramore in Ash, Michael Belke of Coperham Sole. They were as deeply rooted in Kent as the Honywoods

[1] AC, LI, p. 127.

[2] Hasted records several hundreds such, and monuments and floor slabs in Kentish churches many more.

[3] Apart from a few notorious cases (Vane, Algernon Sidney, and the regicides Dixwell, Livesey, and Garland) the evidence of republicanism is scanty. The important evidence in Charles Nichols's correspondence (BM, Add MSS 44847–44848) suggests that, outside a few favoured towns and Wealden villages, Independent communities in Kent were mainly small and isolated. Nichols and his patron, Robert Hales of Howlets in Bekesbourne, were its leaders, and Howlets was its centre.

or Boyses of the county gentry and the old Committee, but, lacking their influence, they were unable to bargain with parliament, and found their powers more rigorously centralized from the start.

Hence the explanation of the social changes in Committee composition is more complex than the mere influx of lesser families suggests. It denotes the supersession of the county gentry, the eclipse of moderatism, a blow to local independence, and a strong tendency to centralization. But would the new Committee, with its minor gentry and its newcomers, be able to hold the county? It would not. The way was prepared for the major-generals.

(iii) *Revenue and Expenditure: the Committee Ascendant*

A study of the Committee's chief function—the provision of the sinews of war—not only reveals the Committee at work, but also demonstrates its fiscal efficiency, the burden of its administration, and some of the factors in party bitterness. Revenue and expenditure, both of taxation under the general Committee and of penal levies on royalists under the Sequestration Committee, are here examined separately.[1]

Revenue. The chief source of revenue was the weekly assessment, but two levies that foreshadowed it should first be examined.[2] In September 1642 began the collection of money, plate, and horses subscribed under the declaration of 9 June,

[1] This section is based on the eighty order books, day books, and account books of the central and lathal County Committees, and some hundreds of parochial account books, in SP. 28: 158–60, 234, 235, 252, 253, 255–60. Of these the most important are Bowles's, as county commissary and receiver-general (SP. 28: 130, 234), Beale's and Bothby's as county treasurers (SP. 28: 157), Rooke's series for Shepway (SP. 28: 158–60), Shetterden's and Joseph's for Sutton-at-Hone Upper (SP. 28: 159, 259), and Boys's for St Augustine (SP. 28: 158, 210).

[2] Revenue not under the Committee's control—from crown lands, customs, and excise—is excluded. The last was less heavy than might be supposed: Nicholas Toke of Godinton (with an income of £370) and Sir Roger Twysden (with at least £800) paid only 6s. a quarter: BM, Add. MS 34167, ff. 32, 34; E. C. Lodge, ed., *The Account Book of a Kentish Estate, 1616–1704*, 1927 (British Academy Records of the Social and Economic History of England and Wales, VI), *passim*.

known as the Propositions. Treasurers were appointed for each lathe and collectors for each parish, and the proceeds were brought to Rochester. In Shepway Lathe Sir Edward Scott was the organizer, and his kinsman Thomas Rooke the efficient treasurer; the 736 subscribers contributed £2,485 (£805 of it in plate) and 35 horses. Most of the twenty-three hundreds were unenthusiastic and subscribed under £100 (Newchurch only £2), but three, including Sir Edward Scott's Bircholt Franchise, subscribed over £400. Thomas Rooke carefully begins each account with its leading squire: the Scotts set the example with the gift of six horses and £270, including £150 worth of the family plate; in Philborough the Broadnaxes gave £50 in plate, and in Stowting Sir John Honywood another £50. In Sutton-at-Hone Upper Lathe, with no dominant gentry like the Scotts, Daniel Shetterden received but one-third as much as Thomas Rooke, and, though it included the London fringe, most parishes were apathetic—West Wickham contributed but five shillings. Over half—£445—was contributed by ten local gentry, and it included Shetterden's own £100; not a single merchant's name appears.[1]

It was this apathy which parliament attacked in 1643–4 with the assessment of the fifth and twentieth parts on personal and real estate of all who had not contributed money and plate.[2] It was administered by the County Committee, but the area within twenty miles of London (broadly corresponding to Sutton-at-Hone Upper), and all people with property in the capital, were assessed there by a special committee of seven members. Based on hearsay evidence in a period of uncertain allegiances, assessments were often ridiculously high: upon his London property, which consisted of a single house in Red Cross Street, Twysden was rated at £400—more, he thought, than its capital value. Consequently they were rarely paid in full, but their yield was considerable: in the 33 ascertainable cases dealt with by the London committee £14,834; in those dealt with by the County Committee probably much greater—between March and September 1644 alone £11,405. The overlapping of jurisdictions involved many in a double mulct;

[1] SP. 28: 159, 160; Weller Papers, *passim.*

[2] F and R, I, pp. 145–55.

those who refused to pay both, like Sir Roger Twysden, were deemed 'neuters' and sequestered.[1] It also led to friction between the County Committee and the central Committee, especially when the latter attempted in 1644 to assess Kentish deputy lieutenants. "You well know that the service of deputy lieutenant," the County Committee replied haughtily, "draws on a charge sufficient to free from further payment. . . . We beg that no tickets may be granted against any deputy lieutenant, and that [this one to Sir Edward Monins] may be recalled. . . ."[2]

In February 1643 began the weekly (later monthly) assessment, and this continued throughout the period to 1660. Though the tax was new, its administration was based on long experience in collecting subsidies, on parliament's earlier levies, and especially on Ship Money and local assessments (e.g. for church property).[3] The total sum required, to be levied on both real and personal estate, was first apportioned by parliament between the counties. Then the County Committee appointed two, three, or four assessors in each hundred to ascertain the total county income (i.e. the income of all persons in the county), and fixed the poundage rate necessary to bring in the sum required from Kent: e.g. 1s. 5d. in the pound on real estate and 4d. on personal. Then they apportioned the county total between the lathal committees, and they the lathal total between the hundreds and parishes. Then collectors were appointed, and collecting began: the parishioners paid their assessments to the parish or hundredal collectors, they to the treasurers of the lathes, and they to the county treasurer at Knole. At every stage there was frequent consultation to arrive at just assessments, and abatement was granted where unfairness appeared. And at every stage careful records were kept: assessment books were issued by the Committee to the assessors, account books and collecting bags and boxes,

[1] SP. 28: 157, Bothby's account book; KCA, U. 120. C4–6; Twysden's Journal, III, pp. 153–5; CCAM, *passim.*

[2] *Ibid.*, p. 491.

[3] Cf. BM, Add. MS 44846, f. 11v.; Rushworth, II, pp. 260–1; Maurice Ashley, *Financial and Commercial Policy under the Cromwellian Protectorate*, 1934, pp. 72–3.

even pens and ink, to the collectors; nothing was levied without the issue of a warrant or voucher by two deputy lieutenants, and nothing received without the issue of an acquittance.

Central and lathal officials like Thomas Rooke, Charles Bowles, and Richard Beale, and most parochial collectors and assessors, were drawn from the minor gentry so numerous in Kentish parishes: Alchorns, Fissendens, Bathursts, and Woodgates among them. Charles Bowles, their head, eventually secured the three chief offices of the county *in commendam*. The junior scion of an ancient family of Kent and Lincolnshire, he had been trained under his relatives the Rochester Petts in the dockyard, and his exquisitely written account books attest his pride in his work. As receiver-general of the county he gathered all receipts from taxation; as treasurer to the Committee he controlled the third part of revenue retained by the county; as commissary to the deputy lieutenants he had charge of all expenditure. His influence was felt throughout the Committee, and gradually lathal books, such as Thomas Rooke's, dropped their interesting irrelevancies and assimilated themselves to his rigid form, with its medieval 'charge' and 'discharge,' its roman numerals, and its elaborately analysed accounts and 'abstracts.'[1] In such work parochial gentry earned that administrative experience which stood them in good stead in the 'fifties, when their own hour came, and the 'county' gentry were eclipsed.

Was the tax so efficient as this elaborate mechanism suggests? What was its total yield? Kent, Norfolk, and Suffolk were the three most heavily burdened counties, and the total assessed on Kent between 1643 and 1648 was at least £391,000.[2] But

[1] SP. 28: 130, 158–60, 234; W. H. Bowles, *Records of the Bowles Family*, 1918, pp. 1–8, 16.

[2] F and R. The total is calculated from the ordinances relating to Kent: (1) Feb. 1643–Feb. 1645, £1,250 a week ($\frac{1}{18}$ of the country's total—but many counties assessed were under royal control); Feb. 1645 (New Model Ordinance) to March 1647, £7,070 a month (over $\frac{1}{8}$ of total—17 counties); then till March 1648, £4,763 1s. 1d. ($\frac{1}{13}$ of total—all counties); (2) additional assessments: 4 Nov. 1643 for S.E. Association, unspecified sum; 18 Oct. 1644, for 12 months for Ireland, £208 6s. 8d. a week; 21 Feb. 1645, for 4 months for Scottish Army, £1,825 3s. 4d. a month; 16 Feb.

was so much in fact received? The answer is not simple because of the lacunae in the account books. The 600-odd payments to Charles Bowles as receiver-general between 1647 and 1649 total £146,229. Nearly half came from the two eastern lathes of Shepway and St Augustine; one quarter from Scraye Lower, Aylesford South, and Sutton-at-Hone Upper (which included the rich London fringe but paid only 9 per cent of the total); and the rest from the remaining six divisions, including Canterbury's mere 2 per cent.[1] (These proportions illustrate the strength of landed wealth in Kent:[2] the wealthiest lathe, Sir Edward Scott's Shepway, was purely agricultural.) It is fortunate that for Shepway Thomas Rooke's complete series of twenty-nine assessment account books from 1644 to 1651 has survived. His total receipts for the lathe were £124,491, of which half was paid during the first two and a half years when, at the end of the war, assessments were very high—2s. 6d. in the pound on real property (by 1649 they had fallen to 1s. and below). Calculated from his proportion of the total in Bowles's books (nearly one-quarter), the county total during the seven years was probably about £570,000.[3] Assessments, then, were probably yielding well over £100,000 p.a. (Sir Anthony Weldon asserted over £116,000),[4] during the last two years of the war, declining to under £50,000 p.a. by 1649, when they began to rise again. It seems quite certain that the total assessment of approximately £391,000 between 1643 and 1648 was reached: the efficiency of the tax was remarkable.

1648, for 6 months for Ireland, £1,587 13s. 8¼d. a month. In Sept. 1645, when the burden was greatest, it was estimated by the Committee at "£9,700 and upwards a month."—AC, v, p. 122.

[1] See Appendix, Table v.

[2] A typical assessment shows Greenwich (£385) and Lewisham (£346)—though the two wealthiest Thames-side parishes—paying less than many Shepway parishes such as Lydd (£582), and in their own lathe less than Dartford (£397): SP. 28: 158, 159, 160, Rooke's and Joseph's account books.

[3] Joseph's eight similar books for Sutton-at-Hone Upper imply a county total of £325,000 for 1645–9.

[4] HMC, XIII. i, p. 296.

What proportion did assessment bear to the total income of the county, upon which it was based? In October 1645 Weldon claimed that it was one-third; but he had an interest in exaggeration and the above-quoted poundage rate of 2s. 6d. suggests about one-eighth. In the one ascertainable instance over a long period, that of Nicholas Toke, esq., of Godinton in Great Chart (a 'neuter' and not likely to be favoured), it was only 5 per cent of income: he paid £281 in the fifteen years from March 1645 to the Restoration. The increased taxation in fact made no change in the way he managed his prosperous estates during or after the war: an illustration of that remoteness from war and its miseries which made many small and peaceable Kentish squires foolhardy in the 1648 Rebellion.[1]

No such efficiency marked sequestrations: that was why the central government wished to supersede them by composition. The mountains laboured and brought forth a fiscal mouse. Receipts by Samuel Avery for the central government from sequestered estates in Kent in 1643–9 totalled but £22,618 (a total, however, exceeded only by Suffolk's £40,917, London's £33,268, and Essex's £28,651).[2] In theory this represented two-thirds of total net receipts (i.e. total receipts less expenditure on estate management, including debts and mortgages), one-third being retained by the county. But the twelve surviving lathal account books show that a far higher proportion was retained in fact.[3] In St Augustine Edward Boys's net receipts were £5,339, of which Avery received only two-fifths; from Sutton-at-Hone Upper he received but an eighth. Prob-

[1] Lodge, *op. cit., passim.* His average annual taxation remained almost the same during the first six years of the Restoration: cesses to parliament, £18 14s. 4½d. p.a., cesses to king £17 10s. 6d. p.a. Cf. BM, Add. MSS 28000–28004, letters of Henry Oxinden to Thomas Denne of Wenderton Manor.

[2] BM, Add. MS 5478, account book of Samuel Avery and others of receipts from sequestrations. Total receipts were £209,548. The figure for Colchester is here included in the Essex total, and for Canterbury in that for Kent, the two places being separately listed in the account book. The Suffolk total given in the account book is wrongly added and is here corrected.

[3] SP. 28: 158, 210, account books of Aylesford North, 1643–7, of St Augustine and Sutton-at-Hone Upper, 1643–49, and of Barber, Fance, and Woolfe.

ably £70,000 is a conservative estimate of total net receipts by county and government. (The average net yield from each sequestered person was only £172 in St Augustine, the highest George Browne's £1,337.) As much again, moreover, was swallowed in costs of estate management, which in the duke of Richmond's case actually exceeded total receipts: such was the wastefulness of the administration.

Composition, by which sequestered royalists paid a fine and regained their estates, was more fruitful, and, as the yield of sequestration fell (in St Augustine from £3,075 p.a. in the first three years to £224 in the last), the yield of compositions increased and probably exceeded that of any other county.[1] The harvest following the 1648 Rebellion increased the number of compounders to 595 and total receipts to at least £105,597: the highest included the duke of Richmond of Cobham Hall, £9,856; the earl of Thanet of Hothfield Place, £9,000; and Sir George Sondes of Lees Court, £3,450.[2] Favourable composition instead of sale, in fact, was a concession to the 1648 rebels to induce surrender. Hence outright sales in Kent, for laymen, were few, comprising only fourteen small properties.[3] They were augmented by the sale of sequestrated woods, which was separately administered by the Committee of Woods: an offshoot of the county Sequestration Committee of which little is known. Purchasers were local people, and their lots minute. When Pyne Wood in St Augustine was sold, 87 purchasers (including Sir James Oxinden and Sir Thomas Palmer) came from such parishes as Wickhambreaux and Thanet Minster and bought from one yard to two acres each at £6 to £8 per acre. The Committee's total revenue was only £786 in St Augustine in 1643–5, and thereafter less or nothing; the county yield perhaps £5,000.[4] Sales of ecclesiastical land were far more profitable, and the episcopal property of Canterbury and Rochester realized £82,990—one-eighth of the total for

[1] CCC. The total yield for England for 1651, when compositions were at their height, was £98,486 (*ibid.*, v, p. xxxi).

[2] Based on SP. 28: 157 (list of 230 compounders following the 1643 rebellion of Kent), CCC. The fines in a few cases are not known.

[3] I. J. Thirsk, *The Sale of Delinquents' Estates during the Interregnum* (London Ph.D. thesis), 1950, pp. 123–4. All were smaller than a manor.

[4] SP. 28: 210, Edward Boys's Wood Account Book, 1643–5.

England and probably more than in any other region.[1] Capitular lands may have realized a similar sum.[2]

Probably, then, the total net receipts from sequestration, composition, and sale were somewhere about £350,000,[3] compared with a yield from assessments of perhaps £700,000 in the same period 1643–52.

Expenditure. In theory the central government's share of assessment revenue was two-thirds; in practice, since Weldon preferred to keep as much as possible under his own vigilant eyes, and out of parliament's more easy-going control, it was but one-third or less, especially after the formation of the South-Eastern Association in 1644, which involved the county in heavy expenditure.[4] How was the county's two-thirds spent? For January 1644 to June 1645, when the Committee reached the zenith of its power, Commissary Charles Bowles's highly elaborate account book—of 200 large folios—has survived. Upon it the following account is largely based. His total expenditure of £88,125 falls into three categories, here examined separately: military disbursements on Kentish troops under Sir William Waller (the South-Eastern Association's general) outside the county; military disbursements within the county; and disbursements on administration.[5]

The first accounted for seven-eighths of the total—£77,414

[1] EHR, XXIII, 1908, G. B. Tatham, 'The Sale of Episcopal Lands during the Civil Wars and Commonwealth', pp. 104 sqq. Only Winchester (£89,343) exceeded this, but its lands were probably more scattered through various counties than those of Canterbury and Rochester. Nearly all were sold before 1652.

[2] The Kentish figure is not known but may be estimated from the fact that sales of capitular lands in all England realized £455,621, and the income from those of Kent when sequestered was one-sixth of the total.—W. A. Shaw, *A History of the English Church during the Civil Wars and under the Commonwealth*, 1900, II, pp. 515, 516.

[3] Estimated: sequestration £70,000, woods £5,000, composition £106,000 plus, sale of sequestered lands £160,000 plus.

[4] In 1644–5 the county retained approximately £102,000 out of £150,000: SP. 28: 130. Its expenditure exceeded this by £15,000.

[5] SP. 28: 130. In addition the County Committee spent £9,145 through its treasurers (before Bowles secured that office), and the lathal committees about £15,000. Where possible these are also included in the following account.

—for this was the year of Waller's campaigns before the New Model was formed. Of this sum, £45,530 went to the four Kentish regiments: £22,950 to Sir Michael Livesey's horse, £15,269 to Colonel Ralph Weldon's foot, £6,016 to Colonel Samuel Birch's foot—all in the south-west—and £1,295 to Sir William Springate's in the Arundel siege. Seventeen other special troops and companies on services such as the Arundel siege accounted for £14,652. All forces were captained by such parochial gentry as Bevill Cruttenden, James Greenestreete, Edward Peake, and Robert Gibbon, ancestor of the great historian: all of indigenous, minor families. Few were pronounced puritans, but Springate had chosen one such, John Swynoke, a family friend, as his clerk. The Swynokes, like Springate and his wife, were at the heart of puritanism in Kent; each Sunday in the 'thirties they used to walk from Maidstone to hear the ejected Thomas Wilson secretly preaching in Otham Rectory, to which they had themselves presented him.[1] They too came of an old though minor family; their name was a corruption of the town-name Sevenoaks. As Springate's clerk, John received 5s. p.d. and "£4 13s. 2d. for making up the accounts of the regiment"—exceptionally high pay for a clerk, 1s. p.d. being usual. Captains usually received 10s. p.d., chaplains 8s., marshals 6s., quartermasters 5s., lieutenants 4s., wagon masters, trumpeters, ensigns 3s., farriers, saddlers, troopers 2s. 6d., drum majors and sergeants 1s. 6d., drums and corporals 1s.

On arms and ammunition the Committee spent £13,880, and Bowles devotes thirty folios to details of every conceivable kind of arms, ammunition, clothing, horse-furniture, and wagon, and to stocking, cleaning, repairing, and marking weapons. Their purchase was one of the many tasks of Jonathan Tilecoate, the Committee's invaluable messenger, who was allowed £43 for his journeys from Knole to London, and also bought extensively in Maidstone and Sevenoaks. The chief magazine was at Knole (later at Aylesford Friary) with sub-

[1] G. S[wynoke], *The Life and Death of Mr Tho. Wilson*, 1672, *passim*. On one occasion, while he was preaching, officers from the Council came to arrest him. As they entered the room, the concourse rose, and in the confusion he slipped through a door in the hall-screen and escaped.

sidiaries at Canterbury, Rochester, Dartford, Scots' Hall, and Leeds Castle. The raising of horses, as well as the punishment of offenders, was in the hands of the provost-marshal, who received 10s. p.d., his deputy 5s., and his nine troopers 2s. each. Many horses were commandeered in the county; the rest, bought locally or at Smithfield, cost £3,735.[1] Shoeing cost £21 and "bleeding, drenching, and curing sick horses returned from the army" £7. Medical attention to sick and wounded men accounted for £185, besides what each regiment spent (Ralph Weldon, for example, had given his surgeon a horse and £18 "to furnish his chest with physical drugs and medicaments").

Military expenditure within the county totalled £6,984. More than half (£4,156) went to garrisoning Tonbridge Castle: £2,220 in pay and £1,936 in refurbishing the dilapidated building, to which Bowles devotes 85 extraordinarily detailed folios. Watching the passes and "frontshires of the county," patrolling by the trained bands, and a guard at the assizes accounted for £1,321. The expenditure on guarding the Committee is eloquent of its dangers: upon the special patrol for its region, the court of guard at Sevenoaks Market House, the Committee's bodyguard at Knole (75–150 men), and its guard in St Nicholas's church on a fast day, £1,869 was expended.[2]

Committee administration, which accounts for the remaining 4 per cent (£3,727) of Bowles's expenditure, comes under five heads: Debts and Interest, Rents, "Travelling and Incident Charges," Household, and Salaries. The first consisted of interest on £4,785 lent mainly by Kentish gentry, including royalists like Sir John Baker of Sissinghurst. Rents amounted to only £60; none was paid for Knole, which was under sequestration, but some adjoining fields were rented of Lady Sackville, with whom the Committee evidently remained on good terms at Knole.

Travelling and Incident Charges (£691) are miscellaneous. Those by the central Committee, for example, include: allow-

[1] KCA, U. 120. C4–6.

[2] Most lathal expenditure was also of this type. In Shepway Thomas Rooke spent £6,589 in 1644–5 on local guards, "scouting the country," and billeting troops.

ances of 10s. p.d. to committeemen attending parliament concerning the South-Eastern Association;[1] payments to the Committee postmasters (£109), for carriage of money from Knole, mainly to Kentish regiments (£97), for carriage of prisoners and horses between Knole, Canterbury, Maidstone, etc. (£161); and many gifts of a few pounds, e.g. to goodman Skinner for "looking to Knole Parkgate," to messengers for bringing "letters of concernment," to John Grimsell for discovering the Dover Castle Plot, and to the ringers at Sevenoaks "for ringing news of Arundel victory." Lathal Incident Charges include items for dispersing tax books to collectors, writing and dispersing orders to be read in churches for keeping Christmas a fast day, dispersing the Committee's official account of the Dover Castle Plot to be read in churches, writing twenty-nine orders "to prohibit [crowds] collecting in churches," carriage of missives to the constables to keep strong watches, and to the deputy lieutenants to hasten their assessments and exercise their companies, and for carriage of money from Scots' Hall to Knole.

Expenditure on the Household (£3,091) relates to the "seraglio," as their enemies called it, maintained at Knole by the Committee. The extravagance of the Committee's housekeeping, alleged and otherwise, was a cause of much envy and hatred in the county. According to one popular legend the devil himself on one occasion appeared amongst them in the midst of their carousals. Certainly their domestic expenses were more lavish than those of some counties; but it must be remembered that the extent of the county necessitated an elaborate organization. The meetings of the Committee at Knole were held in the room now known as the Poets' Parlour, through a later earl of Dorset's patronage of Dryden, Rochester, Shadwell, and other authors. Many other rooms in the house were converted into a kind of hotel for the committeemen's permanent residence. The existing furnishings were employed, but £153 was spent on sheets, table linen, and carpets, and £22 on silverware, candlesticks, glasses, jugs, and drinking-horns, etc. Additional beds were brought from Kippington, Thomas Farnaby's sequestrated house on the other

[1] The office of committeeman was unpaid.

side of Sevenoaks. Timothy Stone of Sevenoaks was employed as locksmith, a "mason for mending the forge," and a carpenter for "mending the great gate;" general repairs were undertaken by the Sequestration Committee. The provisioning of the Committee was in William Trevis the steward's hands and cost £1,921. Of this, £1,295 was spent in 54 such weekly payments as: 2 loads of hay £3, 5½ quarters of oats £3, 20 quarters of malt £22, 10 quarters of wheat £16, 1 bag of hops (216 lbs.) £4 2s. 6d., Cheshire cheese £5 3s. 8d. Hay, straw, and oats for the committeemen's horses figure largely, bought from such local people as William James of Ightham Court Lodge and Lady Sackville. The Committee brewed their own beer from local malt and hops; they spent £7 in repairing the brewhouse and £10 in repairing the vessels; Thomas Alemente, a Sennockian, brewed there at £1 for four brewings. Cider also appears, a gift on occasion from Chafford, Sir John Rivers's house in the Weald. Gifts of "a doe sent to the Committee" and turkeys and pigeons were not infrequent—from the countess of Leicester at Penshurst, the sequestered duke of Richmond's keeper at Cobham, and Lady Sackville; the carter was always rewarded with a shilling or two. Fruit was bought from Richard Randall, the gardener at Knole, to whom on occasion Sir Anthony Weldon made a gift of £2 or £3. Fuelling is sometimes included in Trevis's expenditure, but at least £119 was spent in addition on charcoal, faggots, and wood, cut in the park and bought from Lady Sackville; coal is never mentioned. Candles were purchased locally from Thomas Tydman, but paper, wax, quills, pens, parchment, penknives, and sealing wafers apparently not. Less usual items were entrusted to Jonathan Tilecoate to purchase in Maidstone or London, particularly the "several sorts of wine for the Committee," on which he spent in eighteen months no less than £86.

Salaries totalled £502. Charles Bowles, the commissary, received £200 p.a., his clerk £30, Andrew Lydall the Committee clerk and Thomas Barrome the agent £60 each, Jonathan Tilecoate the messenger 4s. 6d. p.d., the scouts 2s. 6d., and the doorkeeper 1s. The Sackvilles' own servants attended the Committee, but were given £39 gratuity "for cleaning the chambers, lighting fires," etc., and William Sparks £1 "for his pains in helping the cook at general Committees." The chaplain received £69 and a nag, and £1 17s. 4d. was paid for the "carpenter and others employed in taking away the rails and levelling the ground in the chapel at Knole." Thus purified for the Committee, the medieval chapel was devoted to the ministrations of Samuel Annelley and Joseph Bowden. "Here is the model and line of your work," preached Bowden on one occasion: "banishment for banishment, sequestration for sequestration, . . . blood for blood, . . . double unto her according to her works. . . . If they have cut off God's people's ears, . . . we may warrantably cut off their heads."[1]

Another account book of Charles Bowles (for 1647–8) shows that with the end of the war Committee expenditure fell sharply—to a mere £2,938: military expenditure from £77,414 to £820 (all disbursed within the county on guarding passes and suppressing tumults); administrative from £3,727 to £2,118 (Travelling and Incident Charges fell to £358, but legal expenses, e.g. in Sir John Sedley's case, added £359).[2] Lavish housekeeping was over: the Committee had removed to premises rented at £74 p.a. from the Swynokes and others in Maidstone, and spent upon it only £327 (£305 in diet allowances to committeemen at 6s. 8d. p.d.). Salaries stood at £483; there were now no domestic servants, but personal servants of committeemen sometimes received diet of 6d. p.d.

If all levels are taken into consideration—parochial, hundredal, lathal—the salaries paid in administration and taxation between 1644 and 1647 witness a fair efficiency in the rule of the general Committee. There were probably fewer than fifty lathal and county officials altogether, receiving under

[1] E. 10. 3, p. 20. Bowden was minister of Ashford. His sermon was against anglicans, not papists. The chapel was apparently used for daily prayers, St Nicholas's church only on fast days.

[2] SP. 28: 130. Comparison cannot be exact since this book covers a slightly shorter period. This account book has now been published by the Kent Archæological Society (edited by the present author) in *Kent Records: a Seventeenth Century Miscellany*, 1960, pp. 115–52.

2 per cent of the Committee's income in salaries; parochial and hundredal collectors and assessors added perhaps another 1 or 2 per cent.[1] The total expenditure at all levels on committee administration—on debts and interest, rents, travelling and incident charges, housekeeping, and salaries—was perhaps 7 per cent of income, and certainly well under 10 per cent.

By comparison sequestrations once again appear inefficient.[2] Disbursements were of two kinds: towards charges of state and county, and—more than half the total—upon estate management. Full figures of the former have not survived, but in the lathes of St Augustine and Sutton-at-Hone Upper they totalled £9,416 from 1643 to 1649. Of this £5,969 went to the general County Committee and the treasurers at Guildhall: some of it raided by the former when hard-pressed, much earmarked for payment of garrisons, regiments, and repair of harbours and castles. (At Dover the castle garrison was paid from Sir William Boteler's estate and the harbour repairs met from Sir William Campion's.)[3] The remaining £3,447 was disbursed by the two lathal committees themselves: on raising horse £1,691 (each sequestered estate being charged with so many); on carriage of money and letters, on paper books, parchment, purses, and wallets £192. Salaries were in theory fixed by the ordinance appointing the Committee, but after April 1644, when officials threatened to leave their employment if they were not raised, the Committee itself fixed them for each lathe at: solicitor general, 6d. in the pound on gross receipts, collector 3d., agent 2½d., treasurer 2d., clerk 1½d., £16 p.a. to all officials "for their trouble and charge in riding up and down the country," and 12d. in the pound reward "for rents discovered" on sequestered estates now freed from sequestration. In St Augustine and Sutton-at-Hone Upper this

[1] Lathal high collectors, sub-collectors, and clerks were paid by the lathes (from ½d. to 3d. in the pound). From 1644 to 1651 this amounted to 1 per cent of total receipts in Shepway (£1,224).

[2] The following paragraphs are based on the order books and account books of the Sequestration Committee in SP. 28: 210.

[3] SP. 23: G: 10, f. 738; SP. 23: G: 16, ff. 65, 265; SP. 23: G: 27, f. 46; SP. 23: G: 100, ff. 525–30; SP. 23: G: 158, ff. 243–4; CJ, III–VI, *passim*.

totalled £1,522: 16 per cent of net receipts compared with only 7 per cent for collecting assessments.

The same inefficiency marked the disbursements on estate management, and it was this perhaps more than the fact of sequestration that made royalists intransigent in 1648: the damage took years, perhaps generations, to repair. Inefficiency was not surprising, for no one, especially in a county of small estates, had experience of managing such agglomerations of property; sequestration, after all, was virtual nationalization. Admittedly exploitation was not always ruthless. At Canterbury Cathedral the pumps and cisterns were kept in order, the cathedral vaults cleaned, a stone causeway laid from the south gate to the porch, the cloisters paved, the library, upper windows, tower arch, and roofs repaired, new clappers and ropes bought for the bells, and so on.[1] On the estates of Sir Thomas Peyton, Lord Teynham, and the earl of Northampton, the roads, sea walls, dikes, sluices, and fences were kept in order, and considerable sums were spent on carpenters' and glaziers' bills, and on lime, sand, bricks, and tiles.

Nevertheless sequestered properties fell into decay. Despite Thomas Monins's repairs, the Canterbury Chapter spent £12,000 on repairing the cathedral at the Restoration, and found some of their farm buildings "ready to fall down." On Sir Roger Twysden's estates, only unremitting care of every field and acre, every coppice, frith, and spring restored his property to prosperity in the 'fifties.[2] After his return from prison to Knowlton Sir Thomas Peyton found his "whole time . . . swallowed up in the business of farming, which notwithstanding will never repair the breaches made in my fortunes by the evil of persons and times." Mary Hawkins of Nash Court, recusant, complained that Langdon Farm "has been allowed to decay ever since the sequestration in 1643; some of the buildings are fallen down, and others ready to drop." In 1648 Bishop Warner's property at Monkton in Thanet was so "misused . . . that now it will not let at all. . . ." When Allington Castle and her palace in Canterbury were granted to

[1] BL, Gough Kent MS 19, ff. 148–84.

[2] SP. 23: G: 212, ff. 395–9; BM, Add. MS 34162 (Twysden's estate account book); Hasted, XI, pp. 349–50.

Lady Wotton as her 'third,' they were so "ruinated" that she pleaded to be relieved of them.[1]

In a heavily wooded county it was perhaps "the wasteful spoil of . . . timber and woods which had been for many years carefully preserved by your petitioner and his ancestors" that aroused greatest resentment. Ignorant and short-sighted silviculture of "gifts easily destroyed, but with difficulty repaired" permanently injured the royalist's income.[2] No coal came from Newcastle during the war and great quantities of timber were felled for fuel in Kent and London; much went to repairing the castles; and much of the timber used in the dockyards came from Kent, shipped down the Medway from the Weald, or from the line of small northward ports—Milton Regis, Otterham Quay, and Faversham—which, on the edge of recusant country, drew from many sequestered estates.[3] The earl of Thanet alone reckoned his timber losses at £2,226, including "143½ acres of coppice wood felled [at] £10 the acre." Other complainants included Sir George Sondes of Lees Court, Sir Peter Richaut, concerning woods at New Hythe, Sir Robert Darell, woods in Little Chart and Charing, Sir Thomas Peyton, woods round Knowlton Court, and Sir Roger Twysden, woods and copses in the Weald.[4] Again and again, when they had wrung an order from the Committee in London to "forbear the cutting down or spoiling any timber," the Kentish Committee ignored it.[5]

A further cause of resentment was the encouragement the Committee gave to informers. Sometimes they used professional spies, like Thomas Beauchampe, to whom they gave £10 for informing against the recusant Ropers of Lynsted.[6]

[1] SP. 23: G: 10, 133, 158, ff. 179, 188; BM, Add. MS 44846, f. 36v.; CCC, p. 2930; CCAM, p. 264. Recusants were allowed to retain one-third of their property; this usually included the manor-house.

[2] SP. 23: G: 223, f. 876; Twysden's Journal, III, p. 159.

[3] BM, Add. MS 5491; Add. MS 5494; CSPD, 1644, p. 554; EcHR, 2nd Ser., VI, 1953–4, D. C. Coleman, 'Naval Dockyards under the Later Stuarts', pp. 148–50.

[4] KCA, U. 435. 04; SP. 23: G: 9, f. 39; SP. 23: G: 125, f. 579; BM, Add. MS 44846, f. 27v.; KCA, Darell MSS; CCC, p. 1253; Twysden's Journal, II.

[5] E.g. BM, Add. MS 34174, f. 47; CCC, *passim*.

[6] SP. 28: 210B.

More often they played on the susceptibilities of tenants. Some royalists were sequestered two or three times, others for ten or fifteen years, and with conflicting demands on their allegiance tenants often could not tell to whom their rents, and their loyalty, were due. Most remained surprisingly, pathetically, faithful to their landlords; but there was often one who, for money, could be induced to inform. The Derings of Surrenden Dering, who would have starved but for the charity of their tenants, and the Filmers of East Sutton Place, both discovered this to their cost. "One J. B[usher]," Lady Filmer recorded, "the only neighbour or tenant that ever my husband hath had any suit with in all his lifetime . . . did most untruly inform some of the Committee that my husband had hid some arms in the parish church." So the Filmers were sequestered and Sir Robert was imprisoned in Leeds Castle.[1] A tenant of Sir Thomas Peyton's, to whom he had once "given out of my purse above £100," did "with impunity . . . revile and scandalize me to . . . all the world: besides the glory and triumph he hath conceived already to himself of having cast a present tenant of mine and right honest man into prison, for that, he knows, and all men too, he had no right unto. . . ." It was not only the gentry who suffered. James Branford of Strood, an "ignorant, harmless man," was blackmailed with threat of sequestration by his neighbour Peter Birch for refusing to pay £6 for a £4 debt.[2]

Everywhere, as a result of sequestration, the bonds of society were weakened, the "well-ordered chain of government" broken, and parochial lawlessness let loose. When the war was over and the earl of Dorset returned to Knole, his steward told him that

"all the outwoods upon Seal Chart are not worth above £20: my reasons are [that] in the time the soldiers lay thereabouts, continuing no small time, they pulled up and sold above 300 rod new hedge. The poor and of a better sort are yeomen so thievish and unconscionable that all the care [that] can be taken will not, without arresting some of them, and send[ing] them to prison, reform them. I have made many journeys to

[1] SP. 23: G: 223, f. 751; BM, Stowe MS 184; KCA, U. 120. C4–6.
[2] SP. 23: G: 158, ff. 231–3; BM, Add. MS 44846, f. 17.

one poor old Justice (and he dwells six miles from me) but to little purpose, the poor of Senoke [Sevenoaks] are grown so insolent."

Nor was it only the poor who grew insolent. Many Kentish gentry were themselves tenants of one another or of the Church, and some, like Richard Porter of Lamberhurst, esq., a relative of Sir Roger Twysden, and tenant to the Filmers, proved equally obstreperous.[1] Ultimately the disruption of society recoiled upon the Committee's head, and was a major factor in the inefficiency of their management of sequestration. When they laid their hands on Stockwood, for example, they found it so "spoiled by the poor of Canterbury . . . that we were forced to sell it, or else it would have been all spoiled." Their tenants on the estates of Bishop Warner, Sir Edward Dering, Sir Thomas Peyton, and Sir Nathaniel Finch destroyed timber, refused to repair the buildings, and "ploughed up the ancient meadows and pastures."[2]

Behind this disruption, behind the severity, behind the exploitation of estates, and the use of informers, are found, not the Committee as a whole, but the small group of members led by the implacable Sir Anthony Weldon. The bulk of the committeemen, on the other hand, always sought to temper the wind to their relatives the shorn lambs. But "had you any one enemy in the Committee," said Sir Roger Twysden (whom Weldon persecuted to pay off old scores), you were undone, "if you could not approve and run mad in complying with their horrid ways. . . ."[3]

(iv) *The Accounts Committee and Committee Disintegration*

Meanwhile bitterness had begun to poison relationships even within the Committee, as a study of the Accounts Committee will show. But first that body itself must be described.

Structure and Functions.[4] The General and Sequestration Committees were virtually one institution; the Accounts Com-

[1] KCA, U. 120. C4–6; U. 269. C61. 2.

[2] SP. 28: 210, Boys's Wood Account Book; cf. CCAM, p. 264.

[3] Twysden's Journal, II, p. 209. Cf. also pp. 141–2, *supra*.

[4] This section is based on the day books, order books, letter books, and papers of the Accounts Committee in SP. 28: 158, 160, 234, 252–8, 260.

mittee was quite separate, and its function was to audit the accounts of those bodies. Originally the County Committee itself had audited its officers' accounts, periodically calling in the books they had issued, checking them with the vouchers and acquittances, "signing of every page and then cancell[ing] all their several warrants" for payments.[1] By April 1644 the central Committee of Accounts in London took over the task, but the County Committee were too busy to attend to their demands and pleaded "the large extent and circuit of this county, and the many several divisions therein which [we] must successively visit." Hence in January 1645 the central Committee suggested the creation of a county committee of accounts, and, having been promised the concession of appointing it themselves, the general County Committee readily acceded. It would extend yet further their own power, and enable them to show (in Sir Anthony Weldon's words) that "all the water runs the right way, or if it hath broken out where that brack is."[2]

Subdivision, as in general and sequestration business, was unavoidable, and jealousies as well as convenience led to separate Committees for the East and West Divisions of Kent. The East, i.e. the three lathes of St Augustine, Shepway, and Scraye, containing 44 hundreds, further divided itself into eight subcommittees, sitting at Dover, Margate, Wye, Sandwich, Hythe, New Romney, Faversham, and Tenterden, under the central one at Canterbury, where they hired premises for £8 p.a. in Burgate. By this subdivision, they said, "not only the persons accomptable will be much eased but the accompts themselves will be also more punctually examined, the tenants to the sequestration, witnesses, and members of this Committee being at no great trouble or charge" in travelling and the like.[3] In the West, less easily settled, there was a feud between

[1] SP. 28: 260, Bowles to Domville, 18 Sept. 1656; Weller Papers, pp. 6, 17–18.

[2] SP. 28: 255, Weldon to LAC, n.d., Sequestration Committee to LAC, 8 April, 18 Sept., 9 Oct. 1644; SP. 28: 252A, Letter Book of LAC, f. 27.

[3] SP. 28: 257, Dover Accounts Committee to CAC, 12 Jan. 1648; BM, Add. MS 5494, f. 270. The subdivision of the East Division took place, after much complaint at long travelling, in Dec. 1646: some parts of it were 40 miles from Canterbury.

the majority meeting at Rochester and a minority who started meeting separately at East Greenwich. For some months the central Committee in London tried to reconcile their differences, and suggested Gravesend as a compromise. Though complaining it was "far more remote" from them than from Rochester, Sutton-at-Hone Upper, under London influence, agreed; but, under Weldon's influence, Rochester refused even to negotiate and, since the county was stronger than the London fringe, it remained (with its five subdivisional Committees) the West headquarters.[1] The Committees met at least once a week, except in August, when they adjourned so that sub-collectors employed in harvest work might not be prejudiced by a call to account.

The first task of each Division was to compile a book listing all collectors since "the last Ship Money of 1639." Their names ran into hundreds: in five years there had been thirty-three collectors in Westgate alone and thirteen in Molash.[2] Armed with this information, the officials traversed their regions to draw up "Enquirers' Returns," based on information which any one chose to supply about committee officials. Royalists like Archdeacon Kingsley and the Boyses of Bonnington in Goodnestone were consulted, and the feuds of committeemen and officials like John Pollen and Alderman Lade of Canterbury exploited. Matters to be enquired into included: what sequestered goods have been taken and from whom, which sold, by which sequestrators and "their indifferent value;" what sequestration moneys have been paid, by whom, on what terms, for what period; and so on.[3] When completed, the returns were brought to Canterbury or Rochester and compared with one another and with the officials' account books.

[1] SP. 28: 158, loose paper listing divisions and commissioners' names; SP. 28: 252A, LAC Day Book, ff. 9, 10, 19; SP. 28: 252B, f. 2; SP. 28: 253B, LAC Letter Book 1646–9, *sub* 19 June 1646 and 15 March 1646/7; SP. 28: 256, *sub* 22 June 1646; SP. 28: 257, *sub* 23 Jan. 1647/8. The Rochester Accounts Committee (hereafter RAC) rented a house from their treasurer, John Philpott, for £10 p.a.

[2] SP. 28: 160, Book of Collectors' Names of East Division. That no distinction was made between taxes before and taxes after the breach with the king illustrates the continuity of the fiscal system.

[3] SP. 28: 260, Particulars Enquirable by the Committee for Accounts.

Each lathe, hundred, and parish was examined in turn, and warrants were issued to each collector—e.g. to Richard Gore of Rushbourne Barton, a remote farm on the edge of Blean Forest, "to appear . . . to perfect his accompts," first of all at the subcommittee, then at Canterbury or Rochester. There Gore's books were left for a fortnight, every payment being checked with its 'acquittance' and every 'abatement' with its order under the hands of two deputy lieutenants. In his case they agreed; he was recalled to Canterbury, his account "cleared and posted" by Nicholas Bix the treasurer, and his books and acquittances returned to him.[1]

Each division was allowed a register (at £50 p.a.), an accomptant (£50), a clerk (£40), a messenger (13s. 4d. per week and horse allowance), a door-keeper (5s.), and a treasurer (unpaid); and each subcommittee its own clerk and messenger.[2] The register was the Committee's key officer, preparing warrants, composing letters, negotiating with other bodies, present at all meetings, and "privy to all their transactions."[3] Men with the varied gifts necessary were rare, as the Canterbury Committee found. Their first, Thomas Kitchell (paid £30 p.a. above establishment), survived only one month; for the general County Committee accused him of former delinquency, and the Accounts Committee, though bitterly complaining, could not yet flout the authority that created them. Their next, John Fry, gent., was temporary.[4] Their third was one Tracy Pauncefote. Once "registrar under the Judges for Probate of Wills," Pauncefote's unctuous language and his gesture in demanding a salary of £150, instead of £50, impressed them: "we think it most necessary," they wrote. They were themselves

"gentlemen skilful in the examination of accompts but not in the digestion of them into methodical forms. . . . We find

[1] SP. 28: 252B, CDB 'C', ff. 19, 32, 48.

[2] Expense of administration was not great compared with that of the General and Sequestration Committees: for RAC only £307 in its first two years.

[3] SP. 28: 235, John Fry's 'Note expressing what service I have performed.'

[4] SP. 28: 252A, LAC Letter Book, ff. 71, 77, 80; SP. 28: 252B, CDB 'B,' f. 5; SP. 28: 255, CAC to LAC, 6 Oct., 22 Nov., 13 Dec. 1645.

the county hath expended very great sums of money and the accompts are so various and disorderly [that without Mr Pauncefote] we shall not know how to return you [the central Committee] perfect information."[1]

When, in 1647, they found Thomas Golde, their treasurer, paying him certain unauthorized sums, Pauncefote's suave effrontery once more deceived them. In May, "he acquainting them with the urgency of his business" in London, they even gave him a fortnight's leave and an advance of salary. But city streets had greater attractions than Kentish dens and orchards. Seven months passed and Tracy Pauncefote neither returned nor wrote, till, hearing in November of their anger, and gracious to the last, he "acquainted them that some urgent occasions both public and private have detained him" and "resigned his employment into their hands."[2] He had in fact been negotiating his advancement and became register to the London Committee, where his talents were doubtless better appreciated. At Canterbury John Fry again became register.[3]

Committee Disintegration. A study of the Accounts Committee helps to answer two fundamental questions. Why did the Committee disintegrate in 1648? Did committeemen and officials use their opportunities to feather their own nests? Ultimately these are the same question, but to begin with we may take the first alone.

One clue has been found in the membership of the general Committee, in the friction between the 'general body' and the 'core.' Another lies in the mere multiplication of committees: as they reached maturity, the organization lost flexibility; as they extended themselves into every corner of the county, they began to invade each other's territory. A third lies in the discontents implicit in committee rule. Some committeemen grew weary of unpaid labours. Others, like Thomas Weller, who was greatly the loser by his forced lease of Tonbridge Castle to the county, became disgruntled. Many,

[1] SP. 28: 258, Tracy Pauncefote to LAC; SP. 28: 252B, CDB 'B,' ff. 45–6, 77; SP. 28: 256, CAC to LAC, 9 Dec. 1646.

[2] SP. 28: 252B, CDB 'C,' ff. 12, 31; SP. 28: 257, CAC to LAC, 5 Feb. 1648. Golde retained his post but was reprimanded.

[3] SP. 28: 253B; SP. 28: 258.

like John Wright, to whom the recusant George Loane owed £1,000, could not obtain satisfaction of debts because estates were under sequestration.[1] But the most embittered cleavage was between the General and Accounts Committees. Why was this?

The first clue again lies in membership—in the complete distinction of the members of the Accounts Committee from those of the general Committee which originally appointed them. The latter was not permitted to appoint its own members to the Accounts Committee, it could not in practice remove any once appointed, and additional members were not appointed by it at all but co-opted. Since all the great county gentry who were trustworthy were already on the general Committee, the Accounts committeemen were drawn from the parochial gentry—from families who came to form the backbone of the reorganized County Committee of the commonwealth. The thirty-one members of the Canterbury Committee comprised no baronets, only one knight, and three esquires; the rest were mere gentry. Some were 'mercantile gentry' of the towns, such as Robert Master of Canterbury and Thomas Waad of Dover, though most were drawn from old Kentish families like those of Sir Christopher Harfleete of Hackington (of Anglo-Norman origin) and Thomas Denne of Dennehill (armigerous at least since Henry III).[2] The same pattern is found among the twenty-six members of the Rochester Committee.

As in the general Committee, with the constant increase of work, the membership expanded and a group of extremists emerged. At Canterbury only five of the thirty-one attended regularly and these five directed policy. Their chairman was the violent Thomas Denne, who ruined his co-parliamentarian

[1] Weller Papers, pp. 42–3, 48; CCC, p. 1684. Thomas Philpott of Sutton Valence, though a parliamentarian, petitioned the Committee for seven years and did not even receive an answer: BL, Tanner MS 55, ff. 143, 147.

[2] SP. 28: 234, 'Names of additional committeemen;' SP. 28: 252B, CDB 'B' and 'C'; SP. 28: 235, CDB 'D'; SP. 28: 255, Samuel Shorte of Tenterden to LAC, 20 Oct. 1645; Hasted, IX, pp. 344–5. Social conventions are carefully observed in the Day Books: e.g. Harfleete, as a knight, always comes first in attendance lists.

Henry Oxinden of Great Maydeacon in lawsuits, and whom even his children found "subtle, fraudulent, faithless, and setting all on fire of contention."[1] In fact, though formed of different families, the leading group of the general Committee and that of the Accounts Committee—each with its minor gentry and lawyers, its extremists and Independents—came more and more to resemble one another. But why did they not then tend to harmony? Because the purpose of the Accounts Committee was to discover fraud.

Had the general committeemen and their satellites, then, been fraudulent? This is not a simple question to answer. The *prima facie* evidence (mainly common report), the evidence of the Accounts Committee itself, and that of the subsequent history of committee families must each be examined. The first, when lumped together, looks black. Some committeemen, it was said, escaped taxes.[2] A number hunted for comfortable places: Edward Boys of Betteshanger, Henry Oxinden of Great Maydeacon, John Dixwell of Broome, and Thomas Hales of Howlets in Bekesbourne all sought that of woodward to the archbishop's lands; and no means of influence remained unexploited by any of them.[3] Parliamentary informers of the lowest type certainly took bribes from delinquents to desist from prosecution. It was said that parliament had given Sir Thomas Walsingham "a great part of the Lord Dorset's estate." It was certain that Augustine Skynner bought extensive tracts of episcopal and royalist lands; that parliament granted Weldon £500 for his services to the County Committee, and Sir Henry Heyman £5,000 for his family's sufferings in the 'thirties; and that even Sir William Springate testified to Sir Michael Livesey's base gains.[4]

[1] SP. 28: 252B, CDB 'B'; SP. 28: 235, CDB 'D'; BM, Add. MS 28002, f. 300; Dorothy Gardiner, ed., *The Oxinden and Peyton Letters, 1642–1670*, 1937, pp. xxii–vii. The five members of the core were Thomas Denne, esq. (104 meetings), Nicholas Knight, gent. (110), Allen Epes, gent. (93), Robert Master, gent. (72), William Reeve, gent. (63). The average attendance was four, the highest twenty-one, the lowest nil (once) and one (once).

[2] Twysden's Journal, II, p. 202; CCAM, pp. 53, 491.

[3] BM, Add. MSS 28001–28003, *passim*.

[4] CCAM, pp. 1332–3; HMC, VI, p. 120b; *Somers's Tracts*, 2nd edn, 1812, VII, p. 59; CCC, p. 2859; *DNB*, s.v. Sir Anthony Weldon, Sir Peter Heyman.

So it is not surprising that the illiterate but official spy of the London Accounts Committee, Hugh Justice, should regale his employers with a lurid story after visiting John Mosley, "innkeeper at the sign of the Golden Cock" in Dartford. From Mosley, who had "been under the lash" of the County Committee, Justice learned that

"Mr Jesope [treasurer for sequestrations in Sutton-at-Hone Upper] has got a great estate, it is thought, and has good store of moneys in his hands; they carry their business so close it cannot be easily discovered what money they have by them, one Mr Shoterton [Shetterden] of Eltham [treasurer] before Mr Jesope, a man of a great estate got in these times . . . Mr [Lambarde] Godfrey [sequestrator-general of the county] dwells at Maidstone, a man that has played the knave much and got a great estate from nothing, and Mr Charles Bowles [commissary and receiver-general] likewise, both committeemen and rules the Committee as they please; you will find them to be a great obstructor . . . of the business, they will be loth to come to accompt. . . . There comes in great sums daily to the Committee; I cannot learn what use they put it to but their own private uses. . . . About Canterbury Mr Boyses [? Edward Boys, sequestrator of St Augustine] is thought has got a great estate since these times and deceived the state much; . . . he has bestowed £2,000 upon building. Mr Cogan [treasurer of Canterbury] fled from Canterbury . . . he has got a great estate. Captain Richard Sandall [Sandwell] sequestrator for the Isle of Tennent [Thanet], he and the other before named have played the knave much. . . ."

And so on.[1]

But all this tavern gossip of "great estates" comes from hostile sources, and is remarkably vague. From his subscription on 'the Propositions' Daniel Shetterden was clearly wealthy before his treasurership. Even Boys's £2,000 upon building, by no means exorbitant for a squire, was honestly come by as likely as not. Did the discoveries of the Accounts

---

The alleged grant to Walsingham is a distortion of the fact of his keepership of Eltham Park.

[1] BM, Add. MS 5494, ff. 287–8; cf. f. 285.

Committee substantiate common report? With few exceptions they did not. Petty peculation, of a few shillings or pounds, occurs. Sir John Roberts was accused of keeping £33 of his troops' pay, of taking a "Barbary mare, . . . a bow, and . . . a quiver of arrows" from sequestered Sir George Sondes; and Robert Lade, a Canterbury alderman, of embezzling £183.[1] But all the Committee's bundles of 'discoveries' amount to little compared with the many thousand pounds involved. As far as it goes the evidence shows comparative honesty. Parliamentarians received no more tax abatement than royalists. They did not monopolize purchases at the Committee's auctions of sequestered goods: at the Sackville sale, Lord Buckhurst, the heir, bought back far more than any parliamentarian.[2] They were not favoured in the Committee's leases of sequestered property: John Maplisden obtained his lease of Allington Castle, when the property was 'posted,' only by offering £40 more than anyone else.[3] Only three committeemen appear in a six-page list of Committee tenants in 1650, whereas recusants and royalists included, among many others, Sir Thomas Culpeper, Francis Lovelace, Sir Roger Twysden, and even the bishop of Rochester.[4]

But how much slipped through the mesh of the Accounts Committee? This question cannot be fully answered, but much may be guessed from the subsequent history of the families above mentioned. It is certain that they and their alleged wealth in no way came to dominate the county. Of the two who rose meteorically, the Bankses made their money as scriveners, not as committeemen, and Charles Bowles, though he could have speculated with what passed through his hands as receiver-general, could hardly have embezzled undetected.[5] Of the

[1] SP. 28: 252B, CDB 'B' and 'C'; SP. 28: 257, CAC to LAC, 6 Jan. 1647; BM, Add. MS 5494, ff. 275–7, 283.

[2] KCA, U. 269.

[3] SP. 23: G: 158, ff. 175–81. A paper was posted up announcing that "if any one have a mind to deal for the same let them . . . give in, in writing under hand and sealed up, the most they will give [within] 14 days."

[4] SP. 23: G: 158, ff. 259, 264; BL, Gough Kent MS 19.

[5] SP. 28: 258, loose paper, Bowles to Ufflett; W. H. Bowles, *Records of the Bowles Family*, 1918, pp. 16, 27 sqq. The Bowleses soon left Kent. Their wealth eventually came to the Spencer-Churchills.

three lawyers, Robert Hales gained a baronetcy, but his wealth was largely inherited; if Lambarde Godfrey and Edward Boys added to their inheritance, it may equally have been by their legal practice, and their lines soon became extinct. Of the rest, the Moninses and Heymans merely retained their place as leading county gentry, and the Shetterdens, Jesopes, and Sandwells theirs as parochial gentry; the Weldons sank from knights to armigers; the Walsinghams, after three centuries at Scadbury, sold all their estates in the 'fifties; Lady Springate was forced to sell her own and her husband's Kentish estates; John Dixwell and Sir Michael Livesey, as regicides, were attainted, lost all their property and died overseas in obscurity; and Augustine Skynner, though the friend of royalists and the purchaser of bishop's lands, died in a debtor's prison—because he had mortgaged his estates to buy them.[1]

But if committeemen had been relatively honest stewards, why were they opposed to the Accounts Committee? Again the clues lie in Committee membership. Partly it was because it was responsible, not to themselves, but to the London Committee: so that the 'county gentry,' the natural leaders of Kentish society, were not only losing power in the general Committee, but were excluded altogether from controlling the Accounts Committee.

It was also because, just as the general Committee had sought to engross power, so now did the Accounts Committee. In the consequent clashes the London Committee became the unhappy mediator; for though willing to support its satellite, it was anxious to avoid offending parliament, Sir Anthony Weldon, and the general County Committee. The chief point at issue was the claim of the Accounts Committee to enforce payment from collectors in arrear; without such power its orders were clearly of little value. But the County Committee, asserting that the ordinance of appointment conferred no such authority, refused to admit the claim.[2] The crisis came in July 1646, when, having paid his £69 arrears to the Canterbury

[1] SP. 28: 260, Sir Thomas Walsingham to LAC, 8 March 1653/4; *DNB*, s.v. Sir Michael Livesey and John Dixwell; Hasted, *passim*.

[2] SP. 28: 255, loose paper of Tracy Pauncefote; SP. 28: 256, CAC to LAC, 15 Aug. 1646.

Accounts Committee, Jeffery Sandwell, high collector in Thanet, produced a letter of the general Committee ordering repayment. Canterbury refused to obey the order, and sent Tracy Pauncefote to the London Committee for support. But no answer came, and the County Committee proceeded to levy the sum by distraining Thomas Golde, treasurer to Canterbury, who therefore again wrote to London:

"Be pleased seriously to consider . . . how much we are publicly disturbed in the execution of our service, and by it rendered so contemptible in the eyes of the rest of the county (who greedily take any examples that cross us in the execution of the ordinance) that, if we be not upheld by you, we may . . . never probably bring about that service to which we are appointed."[1]

To this the London Committee replied:

"Truly we conceive that both they and you have transgressed the bounds of your authority. . . . We know not how to remedy you herein, only for Mr Goule [Golde], we conceive he hath a very good action at law against them [the County Committee] for it, which accordingly we would have him prosecute."[2]

This reply was useless; but the Canterbury chairman, Thomas Denne, was persistent. "Since we received a commission from you," he wrote to the London Committee,

"we have endeavoured to follow the ordinance by which we act, and we cannot but wonder that . . . we should be tied from receipt of any money. . . . By the additional ordinance, page six, it is very clear that we may receive any money found in arrear . . . and we have expressed our reasons . . . in the paper annexed. . . . We desire your speedy answer to us in this particular, and your prescription of certain rules for us to go by. And truly until we shall receive your full determinate

[1] SP. 28: 252B, CDB, f. 12; SP. 28: 256, CAC to LAC, 11 and 18 July 1646.

[2] SP. 28: 253B, CAC Letter Book 1646–9.

resolution therein, we shall suspend the execution of the service."

The Rochester Committee made the same stand, the London Committee eventually gave way, and the County Committee, with ill grace, was forced to submit.[1]

Finally, it was galling for men like Weldon and Springate, who had made great sacrifices of money, time, and energy for the parliamentary cause, to be called to account for trivial sums before Sir Christopher Harfleete and Thomas Denne, who had not borne the heat and burden of the day; still more to be informed against by royalists and disreputable spies. Their cases dragged on for years, and the brusque methods of the Accounts Committee aggravated their hardships. Innocent and guilty were alike alienated. Sir John Roberts, often peremptorily ordered to attend about Sondes's horses, as often angrily refused, and when the Accounts' officials visited "his house upon Thursday [8 April 1647] . . . he opened his stable door and shewed them the black horse and said they were a company of fools and meddled with that they had nothing to do withal."[2] When Daniel Shetterden, falsely informed against by Michael Heath, was ordered to appear, he replied: "I know not that I have in my hands one penny belonging to the state. But there is about £30 disbursed by me more than received . . . which were but reason I should have repaid me. It was enough I bestowed my labour in that service." When Thomas Francklyn's case came up, he was already dead, so his son and heir was summoned, but found to be "a captain in the state's service, has not been in England for three years;" so his widow was then summoned, who replied, "I never saw any accounts of my first husband's. I administered and fully paid his debts as far as the estate would allow;" so her second husband, Ralph Weldon, was summoned, and the Committee did "much marvel he took no notice" of their orders. He took no notice, either, of their demands to satisfy his father Sir Anthony's alleged debts to the state, till stung to answer that he "had not anything to the value of one penny from him, but have in honour to him paid out of my own estate of his debts

1 SP. 28: 256, CAC to LAC, 1 Aug. 1646; SP. 28: 257, RAC to LAC.
2 SP. 28: 252B, CDB 'B,' ff. 22–3, 50, CDB 'C,' ff. 2–3.

£500." Out of his own estate he had also expended £6,000 upon his Kentish regiment at Plymouth, which apparently was never repaid him. Not a noble reward for a family which, whatever its failings, had served parliament with fidelity and sacrifice.[1]

Minor gentry and yeomen, who became the parochial organizers of the 1648 Rebellion, were also among the damnified. Often appointed five or six years since to collect a single assessment, they had perhaps lost their acquittances or cess books, ill-written or wrongly added them, abated a friend without valid order—and were now called to account for long-forgotten sums. If they could not remember, they must pay, like Michael Hills of St Cosmas-and-St Damian-in-the-Blean, given a fortnight to do so; or Joseph Seyward, committed to Canterbury Westgate for non-payment of his arrears; or John Osborne, "whose cess [book] is lost," granted a month to pay, "whereof not to fail at his peril;" and scores of others like them. Occasionally they ignored all threats, like Thomas Stowes, who in April 1648 "notwithstanding the former order of the 27th of April [1647] . . . did still persist in his neglects of gathering his assess. It is therefore now . . . thought fit that the fine of £3 more be added to the former fine of 40s."[2] Or they might be like the distracted treasurer of Canterbury, John Cogan, who, after a dozen or so audits, prayed the Committee to consider "how much he hath been troubled with giving many accompts, and that you would be pleased to afford him such directions as may give satisfaction . . . for his future quiet, so that he may with his grey hairs go in peace to his grave."[3]

Such was Kent and its County Committee on the eve of the Rebellion of 1648—that impossible rebellion, to contemporaries, which began the Second Civil War. "In a straggling disarmed county," said Roger L'Estrange,

"within two days' march of an experienced, successful army, under the very nose of the county militia, . . . they made in

[1] SP. 28: 257, letter of Shetterden; SP. 28: 253B, Order Book of LAC, *passim*; SP. 28: 259, Mary Weldon to LAC, n.d., Ralph Weldon to LAC, 10 Feb. 1652/3; CJ, VII, p. 419.

[2] SP. 28: 252B, CDB 'C'; SP. 28: 235, CDB 'D.'

[3] SP. 28: 260, loose paper of John Cogan.

12 days 12,000 men effective, . . . gave an amuse and diversion to their adversaries, . . . gave themselves the glory of beginning an action wherein the whole nation stood at gaze and durst not second them. They made war *alone* upon the masters . . . of three kingdoms. . . . Our age produces not any where persons . . . of a more primitive worthiness than in Kent."[1]

Some of the complex causes of rebellion have now appeared. Genuine royalism was present, for the king was in captivity; but its influence was comparatively feeble. It was against the Committee rather than parliament that practically the whole county rose. "It hath pleased God," they said, "to confound and destroy us by . . . a numerous offspring of Committees . . . in a ruin so acute and violent as nothing but the wickedness of the last age could have invented. . . ."[2]

But "scarce ten" even of the committeemen remained faithful.[3] The ancient, indigenous gentry like the Twysdens and Honywoods—rooted in their lands, moderate, anglican, insular—had been embittered by sequestration if they were royalists, and elbowed out of their leadership of Kentish society if parliamentarians. Control of the County Committee had passed from these county gentry to other men. It had passed to the small group of extremists, mainly of new and unpopular families like Sir Michael Livesey the regicide, national and Independent in outlook. But the ultimate control of Kentish society had not passed to these extreme men, and when in 1648 the county gentry united as they had never done since 1640, nearly all Kentish society was drawn together in their wake. Were they not all one family? Rebellion was not impossible, as contemporaries thought; it was inevitable.

[1] *L'Estrange his Vindication*. L'Estrange was one of the outsiders who came to join the Rebellion from other counties.

[2] E. 7. 26, p. 15. The tract is probably by a Thanet royalist.

[3] E. 448. 5.

VI
THE COMMUNITY AT WAR, 1642–7

One of the principal problems, as we have seen, that faced both parliament and king during the first Civil War was that of uniting the independent political life of the counties under their control in a single organic whole. Until this problem was resolved, there was no real prospect of peace. It was principally because parliament solved it before the king, by forming the New Model Army, that it was the eventual victor. The nature of the problem varied greatly from place to place, according to the character and geographical position of each shire. In the Midlands, where counties were relatively small and less insular than elsewhere, the problem was in some ways more easily resolved than in the peripheral areas of England. In East Anglia, a common social and economic heritage provided the basis for the political union of the several counties in the Eastern Association. In the South of England, there was no sense of common loyalty between the shires; the Association in which they were united by parliament was of little importance, and the community of Kent, in particular, was out of sympathy both with its sister-counties and with London.[1]

In fact, the geographical position and the genius of Kent gave rise to a highly peculiar situation. The county experienced little or nothing of the devastation of armies during the Civil War; neither king nor Cromwell ever came within its borders; but it never knew real peace. Compelled to contribute to the parliamentarian cause, and eventually to submit to association, its restless temperament continually chafed at the parliamentarian yoke, and this encouraged Charles I both to foment rebellion within the county and to endeavour to force a way into it through Sussex or Surrey. The group of Cavaliers who had left the county in 1642 repeatedly urged the gentry at home to rebel, at the same time demanding commissions from

[1] Cf. Everitt, *Suffolk and the Great Rebellion*, pp. 16, 18, 20–2. For Kent's relations with its sister-counties, cf. G. N. Godwin, *Civil War in Hampshire*, 1904, *passim*.

the king to march into the county, blockade the Thames, and link with royalist forces from the north. These grandiose ambitions of the Cavaliers were never fully realized; but they resulted in a recurring pattern of rebellion and defeat. Whenever the local royalists revolted, the Kentish Oxonians promised them assistance, and the king's forces made a thrust towards the county from Berkshire or Hampshire. Each time, the rebels were defeated, the royalist forces repulsed, the reins of parliament and Committee drawn tighter, and the union between the four south-eastern counties made more complete. The complicating factor in this situation was the reluctance of the County Committee itself to submerge its loyalty to the shire in loyalty to the Association and the state. Eventually, the pressure of parliament, and the constantly recurring threat of insurrection, led the core of the Committee under Sir Anthony Weldon to relinquish their localism and agree to union with Sussex, Surrey, and Hampshire. The price of their surrender to parliament, however, was the alienation of the old county families, without whose tacit support the rule of parliament and Committee was ultimately impracticable. In this way, the success of the union eventually led to the overthrow of the Committee and the *volte face* of the county in 1648.

(i) *The Rebellion of 1643*

There is no need here to trace the whole tangled tale of plots and counterplots which the local royalists and the Kentish Oxonians set on foot between 1642 and 1646. Only the principal risings need be mentioned. One of the earliest took place at the end of 1642, when Sir William Brockman of Beachborough, near Hythe, endeavoured to raise a rebellion in the county. He was sent a Commission of Array by the king, while the earl of Thanet was despatched with a regiment through Sussex in an effort to support him. The revolt collapsed when a vital letter of the royalists fell into parliamentarian hands, and Sir William Brockman was arrested. Within ten days Thanet ignominiously surrendered at Bramber Bridge in Sussex, and requested "an accommodation."[1]

[1] E. 129. 6; Rushworth, v, p. 70; E. 244. 9.

It was this revolt that led parliament to make its first effort to link the four south-eastern shires in an Association like that already established in the eastern counties. In order to do so, hasty meetings were called, in January 1643, with a couple of committeemen from each county, and puritan ministers like William Jemmet of Faversham preached sermons in favour of the Association from their pulpits.[1] At this stage, however, the proposals for Association met with little success. They had originated with parliament, and not in the several shires themselves, and there was as yet little sense of urgency among the members of the four County Committees. In the South, as elsewhere, most people were still hoping for a peaceful solution of the war and extreme measures were deprecated. In Kent there was little response when the drum was beaten, and "two or three of the chiefest in every parish" went "from house to house to encourage men in the service." Some who responded to the new call to arms "altered their minds" when they came to the appointed rendezvous, and refused to go beyond their county boundary. The Cinque Ports declared that they had "ways enough of expense at home," and that "if a foreign enemy (much to be suspected and feared) attempts to invade us we shall be without strength." After lengthy wrangling, Sir Anthony Weldon and the committeemen themselves refused to admit the claim of the Houses to march Kentish troops beyond the borders of the county. Finally, when the king heard of this opposition, and ordered his proclamation forbidding the association to be read—according to parliament illegally—in all churches and chapels, the four south-eastern counties backed out of the proposal altogether, because they were reluctant to displease the king. The spring of 1643 passed quietly away, and for the time being no more was heard of the South-Eastern Association.[2]

Pym had now decided to employ other means of galvanizing

[1] Sandwich Muniments, Letter Book S/N. 5, ff. 189–96; W. Boys, *Collections for an History of Sandwich in Kent*, 1892 [i.e., 1792], II, p. 754; CJ, II, p. 974; E. 249. 20, preface.

[2] Sandwich Muniments, Letter Book S/N. 5, ff. 189, 212; BM, Add. MS 33512, f. 84; Weller Papers, pp. 25–6; *His Majesty's Proclamation forbidding his Subjects of Kent, Surrey, Sussex, and Hampshire to raise any Forces . . .*, 16 Feb. 1643; CJ, II, p. 986; LJ, V, pp. 630–1; E. 246. 39.

the efforts of the parliamentarians in the South-East of England. He had recently learned that Edmund Waller, whose royalist plot came to light at the end of May 1643, had many friends and kinsmen in Kent; for his family had originated in the county, at Groombridge Place. One of his friends, Sir George Strode of Squerryes, had been sent a Commission of Array by the king, and Pym learned that the Kentish Oxonians, putting themselves under Hopton, hoped once more to march through Sussex, join this party in Kent, link with the queen's forces marching from Newark into Essex, and sever the Thames below London. This grand design collapsed, of course, upon the discovery of Waller's plot; but in the hysteria which followed the discovery, each member of parliament was required, on 6th June, to take a "Sacred Vow and Covenant" by which he was to declare:

"whereas I do, in my conscience, believe that the forces raised by the two houses of parliament are raised and continued for their just defence . . . against the forces raised by the king, . . . I will . . . assist the forces raised and continued by both houses of parliament against the forces raised by the king without their consent. . . ."

A few weeks later, at the end of June 1643, the Committee of Kent was ordered to administer this covenant to every person of age in the county. It was to be taken in the parish churches under the supervision of the minister, with the churchwardens' assistance. The ministers were instructed to keep written registers of those who subscribed and those who refused it.[1]

Doubtless Pym had judged aright of the temper of opinion in the capital; but he had made a grave blunder in his estimate of that of Kent. The signal for rebellion, a serious rebellion, was now raised. Faced with the Covenant, it was difficult to pretend any longer, as the moderates had tried to pretend, that one was not fighting against the king. Some of them, led by Sir Edward Hales, left the Committee altogether; whilst many Kentish ministers, still smarting under the iconoclasm of Colonel Sandys and the intrusion of lecturers into their pulpits

[1] E. 55. 8; E. 105. 8; CJ, III, p. 118; Sandwich Muniments, Letter Book S/N. 5, ff. 222–3; E. 56. 10.

by parliament, declared that their meat was taken out of their mouths and, "if it were possible, our souls, by rigid and unlawful oaths, forced out of the arms of our blessed Saviour and Redeemer. . . ." They refused to co-operate and began to preach seditious sermons. There were many other people in Kent, moreover, neither committeemen nor royalists, who, like William Stede of Stede Hill, abhorred the Covenant "and resolved rather to die than to be so false to God, my king, the church, the nation, and my own conscience" as to take it.[1]

The well-known Kentish Rebellion of 1643, which followed this attempt of parliament to administer the Covenant in the county, was organized with the same speed, and by the same kind of semi-feudal organization, as the elections of 1640 and the petitions of 1642. Barely a month elapsed between the administration of the Covenant and the defeat of the rebels. The refusal of the rector of Ightham to subscribe the Covenant at the end of June was followed by the "murder" of one of the parishioners who had turned out to prevent his arrest. Within a few days the whole countryside began to gather "in a tumultuous and seditious manner" at Sevenoaks.[2] The surrounding hills, still thick with the unenclosed chartland forest, gave the rebels cover, and the open commonland of the Vine formed a natural rendezvous. The little market town controlled both the entrance to the county from Oxford and the vital Darent Valley, with its road to the Thames and its command of the three roads into the county from London. Thomas Farnaby of Kippington, the celebrated Carolean schoolmaster, and William Loane, the recusant lord of the manor of Sevenoaks, led the rebels in the town. They were supported by nearly all the gentry of Holmesdale and the Darent valley: Peckhams of Wrotham, Mannings of Westerham, Gilbournes of Otford, Polhills of Shoreham, Harts of Lullingstone, Bathursts of Horton Kirby, and a son of Sir Thomas Walsingham of Scadbury, one of the members of the County Committee. In the

[1] E. 7. 26, p. 14; E. 249. 29; E. 61. 15; R. H. Goodsall, *Stede Hill: the Annals of a Kentish Home*, 1949, p. 58. The words quoted in the last sentence of the paragraph are those of William Stede of Stede Hill, but are typical of those of many other Kentish people.

[2] E. 61. 11; CSPV, 1643–7, p. 2.

valleys of the Eden and Medway to the south, another group of gentry gathered their tenantry and servants: Childrens and Horsmondens, Rogerses and Bettenhams, Stanleys of Hamptons, Skeffingtons of Dachurst, Streatfeilds of Chiddingstone, and Campions of Combwell. At Aylesford, the only Medway crossing between Maidstone and Rochester, a subsidiary rendezvous was formed, under the aegis of the Dukes, the Maplisdens, the Crispes, the Biggeses of Maidstone, Thomas Felles of Chart Sutton, and William Stede of Stede Hill. On the downs south of Faversham, a third gathering was covertly supported by Sir Edward Hales, and openly by his grandson and heir, Edward Hales of Tunstall Place. They were joined by their cousin Sir James Hales of The Dongeon, and by the Alchorns of Bredhurst, the Hugessens of Lynsted, and the Owres, Faunces, Strughills, and Odiarnes.[1]

Significantly enough, these rebel leaders were almost all representatives of old-established Kentish families; the newer gentry of the county, nearer to London, lent the insurrection no support. In other words, the rebels were essentially moderates rather than Cavaliers, and their grievances were primarily local. Everywhere, they were seconded by their local parish ministers: Nicholas Gibbon and Henry Hammond, the learned rectors of Sevenoaks and Penshurst; the two Grimeses at Ightham and Hadlow; Daniel Horsmonden at Ulcombe; David Nash at Temple Waltham; Sir Edward Dering's two cousins, Henry Dering at Lower Halstow and Edward Ashburnham at Tonbridge; Dean Bargrave's nephew, William Jarvis, at Sturry; and John Jeffreys, the ejected vicar of Faversham.[2] In many parishes the rebellion became entangled with local squabbles and long-standing family feuds. At Swanscombe and Stone, the Chase family probably joined the rebellion out of personal revenge against Sir Anthony Weldon, who had preferred a petition against them to the Committee for Religion in 1641.

[1] CJ, III, pp. 181, 185, 208; *DNB*, s.v. Thomas Farnaby; SP. 28: 157, Accompt of fines on 1643 Rebels; E. 61. 22; E. 61. 25; SP. 23: G: 158, ff. 140, 227; E. 249. 30; CCAM, p. 1277; *Certain Informations, sub* 25 July 1643; HMC, v, p. 108; Goodsall, *loc. cit.*

[2] E. 61. 25; E. 249. 29; E. 61. 11; Henry Hammond, *Works*, 2nd edn, 1684, I, p. iv.

At Maidstone, all the "vain company in the town" supported the rebels. At Tonbridge one Chalklin, who bore "an old and inveterate malice" against his neighbour Thomas Weller, spread false rumours against him, "whereupon the rude multitude presently were enraged and swore to destroy all that ever [Weller] had and to pull [his] wife out of her bed by the hair. . . ."[1]

By such methods, a motley crowd of perhaps 4,000 rebels gathered round Sevenoaks, including "all but a very few" of the trained bands. The roads into the county from Oxford and London were secured. Emissaries were dispatched to the king, who was persuaded by the Kentish Oxonians to order the rebels to secure the crossings of the Thames, and seize the ships and dockyard at Rochester. Meanwhile, an advance party of the king's forces reached Guildford in an attempt to raise Surrey and Sussex, and the king's cousin, the duke of Richmond, was expected to appear in his native county and lead the rising. A proclamation declaring all who took the Covenant traitors was received in Kent with wild enthusiasm, read by the ministers in their pulpits, and nailed to the church doors.[2]

The cause of parliament looked black. The Kentish rebels, it was true, were an ill-armed and undisciplined band; but they were descendants of those men who in past centuries—under Wat Tyler, Jack Cade, and Sir Thomas Wyatt—had marched on London and made its citizens tremble. Moreover, the military fortunes of the two Houses were at this moment everywhere in eclipse. Their armies had been defeated at Adwalton Moor, at Lansdown, at Roundway Down, and at Bristol. Somerset and Devon had succumbed to the king, and the queen had reached Oxford with her supplies from overseas. Hopeful Cavaliers began to cross into Kent from East Anglia, and timid parliamentarians took flight for London. Some of the committeemen declared themselves neutral; others were imprisoned; and many were unable to pass the rebels' guard in order to reach the temporary meeting place of the Committee

[1] SP. 28: 157, Accompt of fines on 1643 Rebels; Weller Papers, pp. 31–2, cf. p. 33; AC, XVII, p. 365; *Gentleman's Magazine*, 1851, II, p. 368.

[2] E. 61. 15; E. 61. 22; E. 61. 13; *Certain Informations, sub* 26 July 1643; E. 249. 29.

at Wrotham. Those who arrived allowed many "prejudicial delays in forbearing to use the forces drawn together." Sir Edward Hales supplied the rebels with match and powder; Sir Francis Barnham neither "appeared nor assisted;" the activities of Sir John Rivers were decidedly suspicious; and the son of Sir Thomas Walsingham, one of the committeemen, joined the rebels. Captain Thomas Blount declared that, by "his commission, he alone, without another deputy lieutenant, could not act anything." Captain Richard Lee and his guard at Rochester, "through waiting and fear, were almost at their wits' end." Even Sir Anthony Weldon, who bravely resolved to live and die with the thirty men of his "ragged regiment" who remained faithful to him at Dartford, where the magazine had been seized, told the House of Commons that "if we should have drawn any blood, we no question must have undergone the censure of all the misery the county must suffer by this insurrection."[1]

In these circumstances, the Kentish parliamentarians at first resolved to defeat the insurrection by exploiting the rebels' weaknesses. They still held Rochester Bridge, the dockyard, and the ships in the Medway; whilst they were aware that the rebels were not only ill-armed, but ill-led and disunited.[2] The three rendezvous's at Sevenoaks, Aylesford, and Faversham had not co-ordinated their plans, and were hamstrung by the characteristic Kentish difficulty—a cleavage between the moderates and the Cavaliers. The latter, led by Francis Skeffington, a younger, landless son of tne Skeffingtons of Dachurst, welcomed the prospect of a battle in Kent for the king. They despised both Committee and parliament, and refused all compromise. The former, led by Thomas Stanley of Hamptons, had no real desire to see the king's predatory armies enter the county, and would have welcomed a local and peaceable solution of their grievances. If the Covenant were abandoned, the moderates were ready to negotiate with the Committee. The Committee therefore induced parliament, "out of their tender

[1] BM, Egerton MS 2647, f. 70; E. 249. 29; E. 249. 30; CJ, III, pp. 176, 185; Weller Papers, pp. 29–30; BL, Tanner MS 62, ff. 175, 179; BM, Egerton MS 2647, f. 55; HMC, V, p. 97; E. 61. 25.

[2] Cf. E. 61. 22; E. 61. 25; *True and Exact Relation.*

compassion," to offer them indemnity if they would lay down their arms and return home. On the 17th or 18th July, the parliamentarian emissary, Sir Henry Vane the elder, came down into Kent and called a hasty meeting of the committee-men at his house at Fairlawne. Sir John Sedley of St Clere, his son Sir Isaak Sedley, and their friends William James of Ightham Court Lodge and Thomas Weller of Tonbridge Castle attended. Fairlawne, St Clere, Ightham, Wrotham, and Tonbridge were all within a few miles of one another and of the rebels' principal rendezvous at Sevenoaks. Next day, armed only with parliament's offer and their own courage, the five committee-men rode through the deserted woods to Sevenoaks.[1]

There they propounded their terms to a great concourse of rebels, and at first "many . . . seemed willing to lay down their arms." But others, led by Thomas Farnaby and a local demagogue, one Gransden, gradually whipped up a "great controversy" until, through "the violence of the rude multitude," Thomas Weller was suddenly seized upon and "shut up in a chamber. . . . And certain base fellows bound themselves with an oath presently to kill me [Weller], and accordingly came with their drawn swords into my chamber, swearing great oaths they would run me through. . . ." With "much persuasions" Weller tried to convince them of the sincerity of parliament's offer; but Gransden suddenly rushed "into the chamber tearing his hair, and tumbling himself upon the bed, swearing and raving like a madman, and telling me that Sir Henry Vane, Sir Isaak Sedley, and Mr James were in great danger to be murdered upon the Vine, and that if no course was taken they would be slain . . . 'Mr Gransden,'" Weller solemnly replied," '. . . you see you can bear no more rule than another man. If those noble gentlemen's blood should be spilt . . . [who have come] to give you all reasonable satisfaction . . . the odiousness of the fact will . . . bring utter desolation on yourselves, your houses, families, wives, and children, which will be burnt and destroyed in revenge of such a horrid act.' Upon this all those which were present swore they would all die before such gentlemen should miscarry, and

[1] Weller Papers, pp. 26 sqq.; AC, XVII, pp. 365–6; E. 64. 11; LJ, VI, p. 143; Rushworth, V, p. 277; E. 249. 29.

accordingly presently run down the stairs . . . and within some short time" released them, and left the committeemen to a safe but ignominious escape.[1]

The County Committee did not yet give up their efforts at appeasement, however. Hasty meetings were again called at Wrotham, though this time without the sanction of parliament, and the negotiations were resumed by means of the good offices of Thomas Stanley of Hamptons. Possibly Stanley saw Vane privately at Fairlawne, for their estates lay adjacent to one another, and certainly late on 22nd July he and a few other rebels came to Wrotham to present their requests in a petition and to ask the Committee to mediate with parliament.[2] Their main demands were as follows: first, that they may have the Common Prayer continued amongst them (as now established by Act of Parliament) till it be abrogated or corrected by another Act of the king, Lords, and Commons; second, that they may have no new ministers imposed on them, till those who are now over them be found guilty of some crimes which may render them incapable of their places;[3] third, that they may not have their goods distrained, or any taxes imposed upon them, contrary to the liberty of the subject; and fourth, that they may not be compelled to take the Covenant. Next morning, Stanley records, the Committee met again at six o'clock. After consultation between themselves and a long debate with the rebels' delegation, they agreed, he says,

"to send our petition to the parliament this day by a messenger of their own with their letters of recommendation . . .; and as touching our letter for a cessation of arms until an answer from the two Houses to our petition, they have thereunto agreed, so we will do the like, as also keep our soldiers from plundering and violence."

[1] Weller Papers, pp. 27, 28.

[2] AC, XVII, pp. 365–6. No complete copy of the petition has been found. The following text is based on three summaries, in E. 61. 15, E. 249. 29, and E. 64. 11.

[3] E. 64. 11 says: "That all their ministers whom the two Houses have displaced might be returned unto their cures . . ."

"Let me entreat you," Stanley wrote to his fellow-rebels, "to send me a letter by this bearer which may testify your consent to avoid all acts of hostility and plundering . . . that I may give an account unto the deputy lieutenants. The God of peace direct you all for His glory and our comfort." Unfortunately, in Stanley's absence the leadership of the rebellion had fallen into the hands of the hotheads. His earnest messages received no answer, and Vane and the County Committee, who sat till sundown awaiting one, naturally concluded that their offer had been rejected. Having now received a peremptory order from parliament to proceed immediately by force, they terminated the negotiations and at last ordered Sir Michael Livesey to advance against Aylesford.[1]

That evening the Houses heard how the Committee had endeavoured to act the role of mediator without their consent, and indignantly refused to receive any petition whatsoever from the rebels until they laid down their arms. But it was no time to punish trimmers on the Committee. Troops were immediately dispatched to Reigate to forestall the king's advance through Surrey. A second regiment under Colonel Browne was sent towards Sevenoaks, and a third to the assistance of Richard Lee at Rochester. Sir John Roberts was ordered to advance from Canterbury against Faversham, and Sir Thomas Barrington and Captain Temple, who had already heard of "the huge alarm . . . out of Kent," sent troops across the water from the more faithful county of Essex. Thomas Stanley was in despair. Before leaving his house at Hamptons and finally returning to the rebels' camp, he wrote to his colleagues once more. "I protest I have . . . bestowed all the faculties of my wit and understanding," he said, "for a good accommodation between them and us, for the peace . . . of this county in danger to be destroyed by these unhappy distractions. . . . A reasonable satisfaction is far better than a miserable devastation." "I advise you . . .," he added later, "by all means to lay down your arms, to release Sir Thomas Walsingham and Lieutenant Lee, and to lay hold on the pardon sent unto you in the declaration of parliament, which if ye do

[1] AC, XVII, pp. 365–6; E. 61. 22; E. 63. 13; LJ, VI, p. 146; CJ, III, pp. 178, 179.

not ye are undone. This is [the] counsel of your loving friend. . . ."[1] Stanley was right. Despite the king's promises to the county and the urgent protests of his Council, the royalists had resolved to march towards Gloucester and leave Kent to its fate. Of this decision, however, the Cavaliers at Sevenoaks knew nothing. They scoffed at Stanley's provincial caution, and prepared for battle.

Twenty-four hours later they rued their folly. It was a Sunday following forty-eight hours of rain, and the crowd of disheartened rebels—scarcely an army—had already begun to lose heart. At Bromley Browne waited in vain for the promised county forces to join him; but he need not have troubled. When he reached Sevenoaks, all but five or six hundred of the insurgents had "slipped away . . . to their own dwellings. . . ." The rest he soon drove down the steep wooded hills towards Tonbridge, where they broke down the bridge over the swollen Hilden Brook and turned to face him. Some, probably led by the faithful Stanley, who had now rejoined them, endeavoured to treat.[2] The more resolute, urged on by the "very malignant" townsmen, and expecting help from Aylesford, began to fire. Colonel Browne then drew his men

"into battalia, resolving to fight it out without hearkening to their conditions, when, after a most gallant charge by such gentlemen as voluntarily came to accompany us,[3] we gained the broken bridge, . . . making it passable by long planks laid over it. We then drew our men into several divisions towards the town and charged them again. . . . After three hours and a half very hot fight, with the loss of five or six men . . . and thirty or forty wounded, . . . we entered the town by force. We found about twelve of their men dead in the town, and

[1] BM, Egerton MS 2647, f. 55; *Certain Informations, sub* 27 July 1643; AC, XVII, pp. 365–7.

[2] E. 61. 25; *Certain Informations, sub* 25 July 1643; HMC, V, p. 97; *True and Exact Relation*; Rushworth, V, p. 277.

[3] These included Sir John and Sir Isaak Sedley of St Clere, Sir Henry Vane (apparently the elder), and William James of Ightham Court Lodge.—Weller Papers, p. 32.

believe there are many more in hop-gardens and hedges, . . . beside many wounded."[1]

Thence the parliamentarian troops pursued the rebels to the Medway, where

"many of them left the bridge and leapt into the river and were drowned; others that got over the river left the highways and betook themselves to by-paths and hedges; but if night had not overtaken us we had taken, in all probability, all their horse (as we did a great part), and few of their foot had escaped."

Within the town the parliamentarian troops found the streets deserted and the doors of the houses locked against them. Two hundred unfortunate countrymen were discovered and taken prisoner, and others were "pursued . . . upwards of six miles" into the country.[2]

The expected advance of the rebels from Aylesford had at last begun; but it was now too late. The men at Tonbridge had rung the bells backwards to summon them, but they were still ten miles away when the town fell: ten miles of miry Wealden lanes, with Sir Michael Livesey and Sir William Springate in pursuit. They shut themselves in the little town of Yalding while Livesey,

"planting his ordnance, . . . summoned them, promising they should enjoy the benefit of the parliament's declaration if they would submit and lay down arms. They at the first were adverse, . . . but the pieces playing upon them so affrighted them, that some of them fled, . . . yet the major number stood upon their guard. He gave a false alarm, which distracted them, which Sir Miles perceiving, sent for two of the chief of them, who presently submitted. . . ."

In the town Livesey found sufficient muskets, pistols, pikes, and gilt swords to arm six hundred men. Three hundred prisoners—gentlemen, commanders, and others—were sent to the church.

[1] E. 61. 25; HMC, v, p. 97. The quotation is Browne's own account; others confirm it, but put parliament's losses higher.

[2] *True and Exact Relation*; E. 61. 26; E. 61. 25; HMC, v, p. 97; Rushworth, v, p. 277.

The remaining gatherings of rebels were soon disposed of. At Sittingbourne "the mutineers all ran away" at the approach of Sir John Roberts, and Sir Edward Hales was imprisoned in Dover Castle. The scattered groups along the Darent were suppressed by Captain Twistleton, and those in the Weald by Livesey and Springate. As quickly as it had appeared, the rebellion of 1643 melted away again into the woods and fields from which it had sprung.[1]

It now only remained to punish the rebel leaders and reinstate the County Committee. Ever eager to extend his power, particularly against neutrals, Sir Anthony Weldon was not the man to let such an opportunity for self-aggrandizement slip by. On 25th July he wrote to the House of Commons:

"God of His infinite mercy, and by the care and endeavours of the honourable parliament, hath quenched this great flame even ready to consume the whole county. This hath been the only time to distinguish betwixt the well- or ill-affected: in which many noble gentlemen, with part of their trained bands, have so really expressed their forward zeal in their country's service, that . . . for their encouragement [we desire] some largesse may be given out of some great men's estate . . . who have been so forward to foment and promote this wicked design."[2]

Three days later, the following resolutions were passed by parliament:

"1. That all those . . . in that insurrection should be disarmed . . . and their arms to be sent up to London. 2. That all such as stood as neuters, and did not use their utmost endeavour to suppress that insurrection, shall be also disarmed . . . 3. That there shall be full reparation to all such as have been any way sufferers . . . by opposing that insurrection out of the others' estates.[3] 4. That divers of the chief actors . . .

[1] E. 63. 13; *True and Exact Relation*; E. 249. 30. The latter says Hales was imprisoned in the Tower. Some of the rebels fled into Sussex, and occupied Rotherfield and Winchelsea.—Weller Papers, p. 32.

[2] BL, Tanner MS 62, f. 186.

[3] London also was to be reimbursed out of sequestrated Kentish estates for its assistance in suppressing the rising.—CJ, III, p. 187.

shall be sent for . . . and 'tis believed will be turned over to be tried by a Council of War. 5. That . . . 30 others of the most active in that business shall be drawn forth, and cast lots, every third man of them to be hanged . . ."[1]

One week later the new Committee of Sequestration in Kent was set up, and the general County Committee was purged of waverers like Sir Francis Barnham. Colonel Browne quartered his regiment on the site of the rebels' old rendezvous at Sevenoaks, and under his protection the Committee now took up its residence at Knole, on the edge of the town. The punishment of the ringleaders was swift: Haleses of Tunstall, Hugessens of Lynsted, Polhills of Otford, Bathursts of Horton Kirby, and Farnabys of Kippington were among them. Most were imprisoned and sequestered, some were heavily fined, and Thomas Farnaby narrowly escaped deportation.[2] The remaining 230 leading rebels, despite Weldon's protests, were let off lightly: though most of them were gentry, their fines totalled only £2,893 and four-fifths of them paid under £10 apiece. Of the clergy only a few implacable royalists were ejected. So far as Kent was concerned, the Covenant was relegated to discreet oblivion, and the use of the prayer-book was for the most part winked at. In London the Venetian ambassador reported that "the men of Kent . . . preserve the most favourable disposition towards his Majesty, ready to come to the fore when they are encouraged and assisted."[3]

(ii) *The Struggle of 1643–5*

The following winter of 1643–4 was the time of Waller's repulses in Hampshire, and the quarrel with Essex; of Pym's death, and of the Solemn League and Covenant. Neither the malcontents in Kent nor the Kentish royalists at Oxford had learned the real lesson of 1643: the impossibility of any real conjunction between them. Before long the old pattern of local risings and Oxonian encouragement began to re-emerge.

[1] E. 249. 30.

[2] F and R, I, pp. 247–8; *True and Exact Relation*; BM, Add. MS 33918, f. 40; E. 249. 30; *DNB*, s.v. Thomas Farnaby.

[3] SP. 28: 157, Accompt of fines on 1643 Rebels; CSPV, 1643–7, p. 6.

Winchester fell to the royalists in November; Hopton renewed his advance into Sussex; and on 9th December Arundel Castle, thirty-odd miles from Kent, was taken. The next objective of the royalists was Winchelsea, on the border of Kent, where a group of Kentish rebels had fled and "nested themselves" after their defeat at Tonbridge, and now urged the corporation to repudiate parliament and claim the protection of the royalist Lord Warden, the duke of Richmond. An advance party of royalists, led by Sir Edward Dering was expected from Oxford, and the parliamentarians dreaded "what a party may join with them" in the area. From Basing House, in Hampshire, that "receptable of the malignants of Kent, Sussex, and Surrey," the young son of Lambarde Cooke of Mount Mascall in Kent was sent into the county. Cooke was "a great favourite of Prince Rupert's," observed a parliamentarian, who ". . . rides upon an excellent grey mare, wears a white hat and a red coat, long hair and brownish;" he came into Kent "to discover the affections of the people how they stand affected to the king; for, believe me, there is a design to send 1,000 horse amongst us suddenly . . . I pray God preserve us in these bad times."[1]

Faced with renewed danger, Weldon and his henchmen this time drew closer together and at last conceded the necessity of associating with Sussex, Surrey, and Hampshire. "Though an evil spirit hath long deluded" the four counties, said a parliamentarian, "now their eyes begin to be opened. . . ." To "give the plough peaceable passage at home," they called musters of the trained bands, and guards were placed along the "frontshires" of the county of Kent. The earthen ramparts erected on the Oxford road at Westerham may still be seen, crumbling beneath the beeches of Squerryes Park on the Surrey border: an abiding witness to the insularity of county life in the seventeenth century. In November 1643 the dormant South-Eastern Association Ordinance was resuscitated, revised, and promulgated. Within one month 800 horse and

[1] BL, Tanner MS 62, f. 468; E. 77. 32; E. 76. 19; E. 77. 9; E. 73. 2; Weller Papers, pp. 36–7. Royalist news-sheets show a detailed knowledge of events in Kent which cannot have been derived from the parliamentarian press: the presence of the royalist garrison at Basing House facilitated communication between the county and Oxford.—E. 73. 2.

1,200 dragoons were drawn up at Sevenoaks, ready to march with the trained bands of the county to the siege of Arundel. Meanwhile, in December, an advance party was sent to guard the little market-town of Westerham; situated as it was on the Oxford road, it was "the only key of that county this winter-time, because the Wild of Kent is now become unpassable by reason of the deepness and foulness of the ways that lead through those parts."[1]

Emboldened by the danger of the times, the new puritan ministers of the county ardently supported the Association in their sermons. The new lecturer at Sandwich, by repute a local "maker of washing balls," burnt the prayer-books in St Peter's church and prayed that the sword might "not be sheathed again till it be fully glutted in the blood of the malignants."[2] As for the activities of the new Six Preacher at Canterbury, Richard Culmer, who was appointed a commissioner for "the utter demolishing . . . of all monuments of superstition" in the cathderal, they can only be given in his own words. "Many window-images . . . were demolished . . .," he says,

"many idols of stone, thirteen representing Christ and His twelve apostles . . . were all cast down headlong, and some fell on their heads and their mitres brake their neck. . . . And then . . . the commissioners fell presently to work on the great idolatrous window . . . [with] the picture of God the Father, and of Christ, . . . and the picture of the Holy Ghost in the form of a Dove, and of the 12 apostles; and . . . seven large pictures of the Virgin Mary, in seven several glorious appearances, as of the angels lifting her into heaven, and the sun, moon, and stars under her feet. . . . Their prime cathedral saint, archbishop Thomas Becket, was most rarely pictured . . . with cope, rochet, mitre, crozier. . . . Now it is more defaced than any window in that cathedral. Whilst judgement was

[1] Weller Papers, pp. 36–7; E. 77. 27; F and R, I, p. 333; Sandwich Muniments, Letter Book S/N.5, ff. 256, 257; BM, Add. MS 5491, f. 165. S. R. Gardiner (*History of the Great Civil War, 1642–1649*, 1904, I, p. 250) appears to assume the immediate implementation of the South-Eastern Association Ordinance, but in fact it remained dormant till February 1644.

[2] E. 80. 8.

executing on the idols in that window, the cathedralists cried out . . ., Hold your hands, holt, holt, heer's Sir, etc. A minister [Culmer himself] being then on the top of the city ladder, near 60 steps high, with a whole pike in his hand rattling down proud Becket's glassy bones . . ., to him it was said 'tis a shame for a minister to be seen there. . . . Some wished he might break his neck, others said it should cost blood. . . ."

And so Culmer's account goes on, page after page; for the devastation lasted three days. The only remarkable fact is that so much escaped—more indeed than in any other cathedral, except York Minster.[1]

In spite of the zeal of men like Culmer, however, Sir Anthony Weldon and his adherents encountered many obstructions in setting the South-Eastern Association on foot. The dangers that led him and his followers to support the Association only made the moderates of the county hesitate. The security of the county was imperative: but could one honestly enter an Association to defeat one's sovereign and destroy one's church? Compelled, under parliamentary pressure, to take the Covenant, men like Sir Norton Knatchbull scrupled, hesitated, and withdrew. Faced with the prospect of Association, a number of the committeemen began to resort to measures calculated to undermine the ascendancy of the County Committee itself. According to their enemies, some of the deputy lieutenants endeavoured to "work their own ends by appearing most zealous," while they "diligently meet and talk much that nothing may be concluded. . . ." At Dover the parliamentarian marshal who had captured the castle in 1642, Captain Dawkes, was "wrought to . . . treachery" by his Cavalier brother, and himself "wrought the most part of the soldiers to become neuters, and divers disaffected in the town to be of his party. . . ."[2] As a result of Richard Culmer's

[1] E. 532. 12, pp. 20–2. E. 79. 8 and *Culmer's Crown Cracked with his own Looking-Glass* [1657], p. 4, add further details. William Somner, the Canterbury antiquary, had written a guide to the cathedral, and Culmer utilized this "card and compass to sail by in that cathedral ocean of images."—E. 532. 12, p. 21.

[2] E. 73. 2; E. 67. 22. His plot was betrayed to the governor by one of his adherents.

activities, a riot broke out at Canterbury, where some of the townsmen threatened Culmer's life, and one tried to stone him. The clergy of the town proclaimed the iconoclasts "worse than Jews and Turks," and peppered their sermons with such seditious phrases as: "O Lord, give the king more hands to fight for him;" "an impious and rash vow is called a Holy Covenant;" "fomenting of an unnatural civil war is called advancing the true religion"; "bad zeal is a work of the flesh; such zeal have they who would pull down bishops," who may need to be "snuffed" but not extinguished.[1]

The discontent of the county came to a head early in 1644 among the 4,000 troops gathered at Sevenoaks ready to march to the assistance of Sir William Waller. The anger of these men at being ordered to leave the county reflected the feeling of the shire as a whole, and they were encouraged to mutiny by the townsmen themselves. "When our country did appear in full glory," Sir Anthony Weldon told the Commons' Speaker,

"to attend the commands of the deputy lieutenants, not only to defend their own but to go into any other associated counties where any service might be done for the publique, . . . Captain Chyld['s] company did not only in a mutinous manner refuse to follow their colours, but secretly whisper into the ears of all the other to mutiny with them. . . . Some of them offered to draw upon their officers, and the deputy lieutenants understanding thereof, riding up to them, were not without danger of their lives."

In a second letter, Weldon reported that

"Russell, a sergeant, . . . after we commanded the captain to beat the drum, twice faced about from his captain with 50 men, not above 10 following the captain, as it were in scorn of the deputy lieutenants, captains, and officers, and no question intended a second rebellion, for he brake open the magazine doors, to have seized that, which was prevented. . . . After that, a second time, this fellow in scorn led away and the next morning carried at least 60 in a rebellious manner,

[1] *Culmer's Crown Cracked with his own Looking-Glass* [1657], p. 4; Richard Culmer, jr, *op. cit.*, p. 6; E. 532. 12, p. 11.

divulging as he went, not one man would stir. . . . The black-bearded fellow told us, we did fight against the king, who loved Kent, and intended no hurt, nor ever offered to invade us: this with a loud and public voice . . ."

In these dangerous circumstances, it was imperative for the County Committee to act against the mutineers without delay. Their two ringleaders were seized and executed, and "the rest, partly out of fear, partly out of shame," returned to their colours. A few days later the Kentish regiments of the newly-formed South-Eastern Association left the county with the local trained bands, led by the county gentry, and marched to the siege of Arundel Castle in Sussex.[1]

Whilst the issue between county loyalty and loyalty to the state was thus being fought out on the parliamentarian side, precisely the same issue was facing the royalists themselves, both in Lord Hopton's army and among the Kentish gentry who supported him at Arundel. Hopton himself was now in Hampshire. The frozen fields which had enabled him to advance in the autumn had begun to thaw. The roads in the Weald were flooded, the intended advance to Winchelsea was abandoned, and the disunities within the royalist army were acute. Hopton's Cornishmen had left him; his Irish recruits were mutinous; his command was in dispute; and in mid-December he was defeated at Alton.[2]

For some time there had been a good deal of heartburning among the more moderate gentry who had hitherto supported the king. It was precisely at this juncture that their misgivings came to a head, in the defection of Sir Edward Dering and a number of other Kentish gentry who had joined the royalist garrison in Arundel Castle. Men like Sir Edward Dering had never been happy with the king. They ad joined his forces in 1642 from a sense of loyalty to his person rather than from any fundamental agreement with his principles. At Oxford, Dering's scrupulous conscience had constantly been distressed both by the reckless politics of the Cavaliers and the immoral

[1] SP. 28: 130, Bowles's Commissary Account Book; BL, Tanner MS 62, ff. 532, 488, 468.

[2] CSPV, 1643–7, p. 51; Gardiner, *op. cit.*, I, pp. 252–4.

atmosphere of the royalist capital. Moderate episcopacy was there as much in disfavour as in London, while the counsels of papists were followed, and Irish troops were employed in the slaughter of English protestants. Dering himself was slowly dying of a painful disease, and had vainly petitioned the king to release him from his commission. His estates at home were sequestrated; his family manor-house was deserted; his wife and children, on the verge of starvation, were living in a farm-house on the charity of old family tenants.[1] Not surprisingly, the arrival of the Kentish regiments outside the walls of Arundel Castle, led by his own cousins and nephews, finally unnerved him. These nephews and cousins were themselves equally distressed at the prospect of fighting their kinsmen. "I was . . . grieved," wrote Henry Oxinden of Great Maydeacon, ". . . to see men of the same religion, of the same nation, so eagerly engaged one against the other, as if they had beleft they had done Almighty God good service in . . . destroying the workmanship of His own hands." While the siege was in progress, Sir Edward Dering therefore slipped out of the castle, rowed down the river, returned to Oxford, and resigned his commission. Articles were preferred against him, and in an absurd charge he was "voted . . . the chief cause of the two great losses the Lord Hopton hath sustained at Alton and Arundel," by "persuading the king's Majesty to put the Lord Hopton upon that design, he promising to be certain of raising the greatest part in Kent for the king. . . ."[2] Meanwhile, on 1 February 1644, parliament published an offer of pardon to all delinquents who took the Covenant and compounded. On the following day, the first of a swelling stream of refugees to return to the county, Sir Edward Dering set out for Kent. After a lengthy exchange of letters with the County Committee, in which Augustine Skynner, the knight of the shire who succeeded to his seat in parliament, pleaded earnestly in his behalf, Dering submitted to the two Houses. The conditions exacted from him were harsh—harsher than he had been promised—but it was imperative to provide for his wife and

[1] E. 31. 21; E. 33. 4; *DNB*, s.v. Sir Edward Dering.

[2] BM, Add. MS 28000, f. 303; E. 79. 26; E. 81. 20; E. 29. 17; E. 81. 17.

children without delay, for he had only a few more weeks to live.[1]

In the passion of civil war, the defection of Sir Edward Dering was everywhere greeted with execration, except amongst his own circle of kinsmen in Kent. Neither in 1642 nor in 1644 had many people the patience or insight to see the essential consistency of purpose behind the apparent change of heart. Personal ambition had no doubt played a part in his electoral campaign in 1640; but his dominant motive had been the desire to serve his countrymen, by representing their grievances to the House of Commons, especially their desire—none the less real for its vague idealism—for a return to "primitive episcopacy." Personal loyalty to the king had played a part in his promotion of the Kentish Petition of 1642; but once again service to the county and its desire for moderation was his principal motive. Personal affection for his own family, at the approach of death, was one of his guiding feelings in 1644; yet evidently uppermost in his mind was his distress at the reckless, rootless, godless life of the Cavaliers and the Court. The truth was that Dering, like so many others, in Kent and elsewhere, was too conservative and too provincial to wrestle successfully with the terrible conflict of loyalties in which the country was caught during the Great Rebellion. Whether in parliament or at Oxford, his heart remained embedded in that circle of cousins and neighbours around Surrenden Dering who found their life, not in national politics or warfare, but in the careful management of their estates, the adornment of their manor-houses, the local government of the shire, and that peculiar blend of studious pietism and antiquarian learning so characteristic of the county. His real sphere of action was the shire and not the state. As S. R. Gardiner observed, he was one of the many Englishmen who could neither find a party to support nor embody their ideals in any practicable policy.[2] As a consequence, though he was guiltless

[1] E. 31. 10; E. 32. 1; E. 32. 11. Several news-sheets refer to a submission by Dering of c. 2 January (E. 81. 14): this must refer to his correspondence with Waller of that date, which was certainly followed by a temporary return to Oxford till 2 February.

[2] *DNB*, s.v. Sir Edward Dering.

of the absurd charges brought against him by the king, his defection was not without effect upon the royalist cause. It gave vent to that *malaise* and failure of nerve which, from the early months of 1644, led an increasing number of moderates to leave the king's headquarters and return to their native shires.[1]

In Kent, the defeat of Hopton and the defection of men like Sir Edward Dering undoubtedly strengthened the hands of the County Committee. A year of unprecedented fiscal and military burdens ensued, in comparison with which the king's much-complained-of exactions in the 'thirties seemed trivial. Nevertheless, though the South-Eastern Association, with Sir William Waller as its general, was now firmly established, and a handful of men like Sir Anthony Weldon in each county sincerely supported Waller, the strife between county loyalty and loyalty to the nation was by no means over. The Association of the south-eastern shires in no way resembled the powerful union of counties behind Manchester and Cromwell: partly because Waller lacked the necessary qualities of leadership and social prestige—he came originally of the same minor Wealden family as Sir Hardres Waller and Edmund Waller the poet; partly because there was no joint Committee like that which governed the Eastern Association from Cambridge; and partly because the area lacked the economic cohesion and sense of community which characterized East Anglia.[2] In fact, as the danger from royalist attack began to recede, following the royalist defeat at Alton and surrender at Arundel, the old jealousies of the four counties began to re-emerge.

Once again, it seems, the chief culprit was Kent. Early in 1644, Sir Anthony Weldon himself complained yet again of the fiscal burdens laid on the county, and raised once more the vexed question of the county's authority to grant commissions. By parliamentary ordinance, the right to grant commissions was vested in Sir William Waller; but under Weldon's instigation the Committee of Kent now reasserted the anachronistic claim of the county to lead the van in battle and to

[1] E. 33. 27 reports that the earl of Westmorland and others followed his example; cf. also CCC, p. 832.

[2] Cf. Everitt, *Suffolk and the Great Rebellion*, pp. 22, 30–2.

control its own forces. "First we conceive ourselves," they told parliament,

"enabled with this power by two several ordinances . . . Secondly my Lord General [Essex] never questioned the exercise of this power, but permitted us to constitute our several officers; . . . yea, Colonel [Ralph] Weldon [Sir Anthony's son] . . . refused in modesty and upon the same grounds a commission from his Excellency. . . . Thirdly our several officers and commanders (we shall forbear their expressions) refuse the employment under any other commissions, being gentlemen of great quality and worth of this county. . . . And lastly we . . . have . . . already granted the several commissions. . . . Without which [power] we must be necessitated to desist from further action in this kind, leaving it to the agitation of others, whose endeavours we wish more successful. . . . If [it is] referred to our own disposal, we . . . dare confidently engage ourselves [that our regiments] shall be the glory and pattern of his [Waller's] army to imitate."[1]

On this occasion, however, parliament was adamant. For the time being Kent, like the other three counties, was forced, with ill grace, to submit. "Sir," they indignantly wrote to the Commons' Speaker in February 1644,

". . . we must be silent. . . . But surely, Sir, there is not the same reason for the other associated counties as for ours; nor was any ordinance granted to them upon those occasions ours were; . . . nor have the other associated counties moulded theirs [*sc.*, their regiments] to the same form ours now is, we having generally given the Covenant to all, those others to some or none. . . . We shall endeavour the obeying your commands, . . . but dare not promise that assurance in any other than in what we hitherto have settled them. . . ."[2]

In fact the problem was not yet solved; and with the Committee raising and paying the forces, parliament supervising, and Waller commanding them, new troubles were bound to arise. When Waller ordered the Kentish regiments into the

[1] BL, Tanner MS 62, f. 561.

[2] *Ibid.*, f. 573. This letter, in Weldon's own hand, is typical of his quick-tempered style.

West in the spring of 1644, the County Committee accordingly wrote once more to the Committee of Both Kingdoms.[1] Waller's removal, they said, "leaving an enemy behind without any other guard, must be a danger, if not a destruction, to some part of our county;" and, even if to the enemy's utter destruction,

"we confess we desire not to purchase their ruin at so dear a rate. . . . My Lords, the case of our county differs from all others. . . . We must be accountable to our county, who wholly entrust us with their persons and purses, . . . and to send out such forces from our own defence and all upon our own charge . . . will argue so much improvidence as we shall lose all credit with our county. . . ."

For the moment the Committee of Both Kingdoms quietened the Committee of Kent by promising that "their forces now abroad shall not be employed except for their own security, and requesting the continuance of their horse for some time longer, which after the first month will be taken into pay by the state." "The people, perhaps, may groan under the burden," they added blandly, some weeks later, but "we doubt not but your wisdoms will easily instruct them . . ."[2]

These persuasions of parliament were followed by a few weeks of comparative peace. But in the summer of 1644 the old problem was raised once more, this time by mutiny within the ranks of the county regiments themselves. Some of the Kentishmen with Sir William Waller at Abingdon, with others from Essex, professed themselves disgusted with the general's maladministration of the money contributed by their counties, and on 23rd June Waller wrote to the Committee of Both Kingdoms in London. "I am necessitated to inform you," he said,

[1] The background to their demands was yet another plan of the Oxonians to invade Kent (and this time Essex too), which the Venetian ambassador described as "the sole and safe means of destroying this poisonous plant [of parliamentarianism] at the root" (CSPV, 1643–7, p. 113). On this occasion the County Committee effectively revived the legend of the 'unconquered county,' like the rebels in 1648, resolving that "as they were born freemen so they will die, and with their lives and fortunes maintain their religion and liberties against the Oxonian invaders."—E. 42. 16.

[2] CSPD, 1644, pp. 147–8, 152, 222.

"of the mutinous carriage of Sir Michael Livesey and Sir Thomas Piers, who, without acquainting me with their discontents, have falsely suggested to the Committee of Kent that I abused and slighted their regiment . . . and that I should put them upon the hardest duty and worst quarter. Yesterday, without any notice given to me, four troops of that regiment marched away by their command. The rest, I am informed, for they have private counsels of their own, will follow speedily."[1]

Upon the remaining Kentish colonel Waller set a guard, and the captain of a supernumerary troop he imprisoned. But when the Committee of Kent heard of this action, they at once wrote from Knole, in great anger, to the Committee of Both Kingdoms. "We received early this morning a letter from Captain [Edward] Scott, that he was imprisoned," they said;

"we receive even now one from our Colonel that he is under restraint. . . . We cannot but entertain these proceedings with amazement. . . . Captain Scott we ever intended to recall, though upon your command we had designed the stay of his troop under another captain commissioned by us . . ., and wherefore he should be committed for obeying our commands, having no dependence on Sir William Waller's associated forces, as we understand not, so can we make no fair construction of that action. The truth is we have observed for a long time a plot of the malignants to blow up this county into a high discontent, which we have done our best to prevent, but fear it will not be. Let the sin and shame light upon the authors, we are free from it; nor have we ever declined any of your commands, though to our excessive charge."[2]

A few days later, the mutinous regiments returned to Kent and were there fêted by the County Committee. Before long the regiments of Essex, Hertfordshire, and London followed the example of those of Kent and likewise returned home. Despite Waller's military successes of the summer, he was now forced to shut himself up in Abingdon with a mere 1,400 men.

[1] CSPV, 1643–7, p. 126; CSPD, 1644, p. 370.
[2] *Ibid.*, p. 377. The style betrays Weldon's authorship.

The times were grave. Essex was marching to his destruction at Lostwithiel. The great issues between Manchester and Cromwell, soon to be resolved by the formation of the New Model, were now being fought out in the two Houses of parliament. In Kent, these issues were reflected in a seemingly interminable squabble between Sir Anthony Weldon and Sir Michael Livesey on one hand, and Sir William Waller and the parliamentarian government in London on the other. Letter after letter was dispatched from London into Kent to persuade the County Committee to return Livesey's regiments to their general, and to raise new ones to augment them. It was only through the parliamentary influence of Sir Michael Livesey and the personal generosity of Sir William Waller that the quarrel was patched up at all.[1] By then Waller had come to realize, like Cromwell, that a mere association of shires was not the answer to the invincible obstinacy of local loyalty. The only solution to the Civil War was the formation of a *national* army, on an entirely new model, in place of the loose association of county regiments with which Waller and Cromwell had fought hitherto.[2]

It was these continuing dissensions among the parliamentarian leaders that gave the royalists their last opportunity to effectuate their old ambition of forcing a way into Kent, fomenting a local rising, blockading the Thames, and surrounding London. While the reorganization of the Roundhead army was being discussed in parliament, and the New Model was being formed under Sir Thomas Fairfax and Oliver Cromwell, the king had endeavoured to reorganize his own army under Prince Rupert. The consequent "designs in Kent" formed a part, though but a minor one, of the revised royalist strategy of the following winter of 1644–5.[3] In fact, the king's chances of success were now remote; but the plans of the Cavaliers were as elaborate as ever. Dover Castle, Rochester, and the ships in the Medway were to be seized by stratagem; a force

[1] *Ibid.*, pp. 384, 386 sqq., 394 sq.; cf. pp. 427, 506, 522, 534; *DNB*, s.v. Sir Michael Livesey.

[2] Cf. Everitt, *Suffolk and the Great Rebellion*, pp. 32–5.

[3] Cf. C. V. Wedgwood, *The King's War, 1641–1647*, 1958, pp. 381–2, 404 sqq.

was to land in the county from Calais; a rising was once again to be organized at Sevenoaks; the new regiments being raised for Fairfax were to mutiny and join the rebels; and Hopton was to advance into Kent through Surrey.[1]

The plot to seize Dover Castle originated in the county itself, and was promoted by the survivors of Captain Dawkes's conspiracy of 1643. The promoters included Dering's brother-in-law Sir Anthony Percivall of Archcliffe, and his old friends Edward Kempe, Richard Master, Humphrey Mantell, and John Reading. Most of these men were already well known to the County Sequestration Committee, and as early as mid-summer 1644 they had secretly dispatched one Bray to the Kentish Cavaliers at Boarstall House, near Oxford. Clad "in the habiliments of his profession, and with his carpenter's rule and leathern apron" about him, Bray "easily passeth the Courts of Guard, without being suspected anywhere of any further journey than to or from the next neighbouring town or village to his work or home." His first visit to Oxfordshire was unsuccessful, owing to the king's absence; but when he eventually reached Boarstall House he was welcomed by Sir William Campion of Combwell, Edward Master of Willesborough, George Chute of Surrenden Chute, Richard Thornhill of Olantighe, and George Kingsley, son of the archdeacon of Canterbury: a group of Kentish Cavaliers who were close friends and kinsmen of the little group which Bray had left behind him in the county. These men introduced Bray to Secretary Nicholas, and they agreed on the following plan of action on the 29th November 1644. Two or three conspirators, including one Startup and one Hayes, were to

"have used means to be entertained as soldiers in the castle, who, at a time appointed, should have a merry day with the other sentinels and soldiers, at the drinking of some bottles of wine, to be sent in as a present to them by Mr Graunt, the operation of which wine, to be compounded by Mr Graunt himself, should have been to cast such as drunk of it into a

[1] E. 25. 6, *passim*; CSPV, 1643–7, p. 140. As before, the initiative came from the county; but the Venetian ambassador remarked—in cipher—that "those most devoted to his Majesty" at Oxford favoured an advance into Kent as "the only stroke that can win him back his crown. . . ."

sleep for six hours' space. But if this failed, whilst the rest were at their cups, the new-come soldiers should have led in a party, some with scaling ladders . . . and others at the barbicans; . . . at which instant the prisoners in the castle, by the help of a false key, which was made by one Onion, formerly the castle smith, and was in the hands of one Colonel Haggaster, a papist, then a prisoner, should have broken out upon the soldiers, and altogether with the rest have seized upon the guns and guard. At which time likewise a sufficient strength from the town and neighbouring parts should be ready for an entrance."[1]

A Commission of Array was to be sent by the king to the royalists at Dover, whom Captain Increased Collins, a former lieutenant of the castle, was to command. Another Commission was to be sent to Rochester to secure the parliamentarian ships, and a third to raise rebellion in the region about Sevenoaks. Arms and supplies, together with 500 troops, were to be dispatched from Calais, and the rising was to be "forthwith seconded by an invasive power . . . under the command of Mr Richard Thornhill, now made High Sheriff by the king, and commander of the earl of Cleveland's Brigade of Horse. . . ."[2]

Unfortunately for the royalists, neither Rochester nor Sevenoaks was ready to rise in time. Increased Collins, recently released from prison, dared not jeopardize his bail by accepting the command. Neither Thornhill nor the promised troops from France arrived, and before the seizure of Dover Castle could be effected one of the conspirators had taken fright and betrayed the whole design to the County Committee. The Commission of Array to the rebels at Dover was thereupon seized, and about eighty royalists were apprehended and sequestered. From the examinations of these delinquents, Sir Anthony Weldon skilfully wove a narrative of the conspiracy.[3] The Committee ordered that, on Sunday 26 January 1645, "in

[1] E. 25. 6, pp. 8–11. This is the official account of the conspiracy by the County Committee, based upon its examinations of the participants.

[2] E. 25. 6, p. 10; E. 22. 7; E. 22. 9; E. 22. 12; E. 258. 7; E. 22. 8.

[3] E. 26. 12; E. 25. 6, p. 12; SP. 28: 210 B, St Augustine's Sequestration Order Book, f. 43; E. 25. 2. Increased Collins was tried for his life for not revealing the plot.—CSPD, 1660–1, p. 89.

the morning before the sermon, the ministers of the several parishes throughout this county shall openly read [it] . . ., and shall lay open unto the people the vileness of the same and . . . openly declare their own abhorring of the said plot. . . ." The Committee also desired that "all who are of a willing mind then present do, in token of joining with the minister, stand up from their seats." It was

"further ordered that the several ministers do often . . . take occasion both in their prayers and sermons to praise God . . . for all . . . defeatings of plots, . . . and to inform the people thoroughly that, in comparison of these things, their estates and lives . . . ought not to be valued or esteemed by them. . . ."[1]

Upon the defeat of the conspiracy at Dover, the royalists changed their tactics and in April 1645 attempted a surprise attack on the Committee itself. The Committee had by now removed its headquarters from Knole to Aylesford Friary. Led by the Harts of Lullingstone Castle, their nephews the Giffords of Eynsford, and their cousins the Millers of Wrotham, the Cavaliers of the county adopted the same methods of organization as those employed by the rebels of 1643. They were in fact supported by many of the delinquent families who had promoted the earlier rebellion. Their demands also were similar: freedom from "illegal taxes," the right to use the prayer-book, and to refuse the Covenant. Their troops consisted of about 500 mutinous soldiers, who had been impressed for Fairfax's armies and were angry at being forced "from the plough's handle." They were also joined by a motley company of countrymen, coney-stealers, highwaymen, "and the veriest rogues in all Kent, such as their custom was always to drink and roar as long as their money lasted, and then, out, and rob, and steal, and so to drinking and whoring again. . . ." Lullingstone Castle, in the Darent Valley, was garrisoned and fortified; a number of neighbouring hamlets were plundered for horses, arms, and packs of linen; the local villagers were commanded "in the king's name to come into them for the king;" and Sir John Culpeper was alleged to

[1] E. 25. 6, pp. 3–4.

have promised "that they should be seconded by a party from [Oxford]."[1]

Faced with this second threat, Sir Anthony Weldon and the two Houses of Parliament acted with immediate vigour. The trained bands were called out by the Committee, a party of Fairfax's horse was dispatched into the county, and Colonel Thomas Blount of Wricklesmarsh "caused to be beaten an alarm on the top of his own house, and summoned in the country all about. . . ." At the approach of the parliamentarian troops, the undisciplined countrymen were unable to 'body' their motley companies in time, and abandoned Lullingstone. Some fled on horseback towards Maidstone; "some were taken in their beds; and others straggling up and down; and divers of them returning home." The rest fled into the woods and hills, and "stole out . . . by night, and so escaped."[2]

Meanwhile, the Kentish regiments in Surrey, having apparently heard of the troubles at home, mutinied and hastened back into the county. There they encouraged the new regiments, which were drawn up ready for Fairfax at Sevenoaks, to mutiny. They were also joined by some of the rebels who had fled from Lullingstone Castle. The houses of a number of the surrounding committeemen, including Weldon's, were plundered; certain "narrow passes" of the county were made good; and the mutinous troops set out to march to Rochester, apparently intending to secure the parliamentarian ships in the Medway, and to surprise the County Committee on the way. As they marched thither, however, they were themselves surprised by the trained bands of East Kent, under Colonels Newman and Kenwricke, and promptly defeated.[3]

With the defeat of the Kentish Rebellion of 1645, the king's last hope of entering the county vanished.[4] Sir Anthony

[1] E. 278. 8; E. 278. 13; E. 278. 15; E. 278. 30; E. 260. 15 ("Rollington" is Lullingstone); E. 260. 20; E. 260. 17; E. 278. 19; E. 278. 18; E. 279. 8.

[2] E. 260. 17; E. 278. 15; E. 278. 8; E. 278. 18; E. 278. 30; E. 278. 12; E. 278. 13; E. 278. 19.

[3] CSPD, 1644–5, pp. 411–61, *passim*; E. 260. 23 ("Newnham" is Newman); E. 260. 26; E. 279. 12 (possibly "houses" here should read "horses").

[4] So late as February 1646 the king wrote to Henrietta Maria: "I shall . . . draw into a body by the end of this February 2,000 horse and dragoons; with these I resolve to march into Kent, where I am confident to possess some

Weldon and his henchmen on the County Committee were now fully convinced of the necessity of subjecting county loyalty to the state. They bent all their energies to the support of the newly-formed national army under Fairfax and Cromwell; and before long the fiscal burdens upon the county rose to the unprecedented height of £9,700 a month. The moderates upon the Committee were either forced to agree with the Weldonians or ejected; while Sir Anthony himself utilized the rebellion as an excuse for further spoliation of 'neuters' and 'malignants.' It was high time, said the parliamentarian *Mercurius Britanicus*, to provide a "sickle to cut down the tares in that fruitful county of Kent." The Weldonians had in November 1644 petitioned for power to sequester all those who defamed parliament, who dissuaded others from contributing to the cause, who resigned military commands which they had held before the war, who did "nothing voluntary to evidence their affection to the common cause," who refused either of the Covenants or took them with reservations, or who attended anglican services ("lazy, superstitious usages") outside their own parishes.[1] Hitherto, parliament had considered these demands too extreme to accede to; for they would in fact have empowered their promoters to sequester many of the committeemen themselves. After the rebellion, however, Sir Anthony Weldon pressed his cause in the Commons once more, and this time parliament was induced to listen. "By God's infinite mercy," he said,

"we are now past our third rebellion. The two first have yet passed without the punishment of any, except imprisonment only. If this pass so, we must expect monthly rebellions,

---

important place . . . (not being out of hope of Rochester) . . ." (*Charles I in 1646*, Camden Society, LXIII, 1856, ed. T. Bruce, pp. 14–15). These remarks, of course, were merely an example of Charles I's invincible optimism.

[1] HMC, XIII, i, p. 296; E. 278. 21; E. 19. 11. According to CSPV, 1643–7, p. 157, however, this extreme petition "was actually promoted by the most seditious parliamentarians," that is members of parliament. Since the extreme group in Kent at this date were not M.P.'s, it is possible they were not the real promoters; but the petition throughout smacks of Sir Anthony Weldon's style.

if not hourly, when undoing well-affected men is held but a recreation. We shall therefore humbly desire that you will be pleased to let some of these be made speedy examples of your justice, who have already so surfeited upon your mercy that they grow wanton and insolent."

Accordingly, one week later, an ordinance was passed constituting the Committee of Kent "Commissioners and [a] Council of War . . . for punishing . . . those in the late rising. . . ." A wave of fresh sequestrations in the county followed.[1] For the two succeeding years the power of Sir Anthony Weldon in the county was all but absolute.

The moral of the tangled tale of events in Kent between 1643 and 1645 is a simple one. The history of Kent in these years shows with remarkable clarity the problems that faced both king and parliament in converting the stubborn provincialism of an English county into loyalty to the state. The same battle was being fought out, with varying success, in most other shires at the same time. In the parliamentarian areas of the country, this success was most complete in East Anglia, because of the natural cohesion of the area and its predisposition in favour of puritanism. Even there, however, there was much opposition both to parliament and to Cromwell personally.[2] In Kent, the apparent success of parliament and Sir Anthony Weldon in winning the support of the county was temporary and superficial, because it was not spontaneous but enforced. With his immense energy, his eagle eye, and his iron discipline, Weldon was able to raise regiments, levy taxation, and rule the county with, on the whole, remarkable efficiency; but he could not change its heart. He lacked any strong connexion with those galaxies of old county gentry in whose hands the power of the community ultimately resided. His violence, arrogance, and spleen were the worst means possible to convert the anglicanism of these families into puritanism, or their provincialism into loyalty to the state. The community was pacified, but it was not at peace.

[1] E. 19. 11; BL, Tanner MS 60, f. 99; E. 260. 17; F and R, I, pp. 674–5.

[2] Cf. Everitt, *Suffolk and the Great Rebellion*, pp. 28–34.

(iii) *The Revival of Royalism, 1645–7*

Quite clearly, the apparent *volte-face* of the county in 1648 arose from no sudden change of heart, but from a revival of loyalties temporarily obscured, but not fundamentally altered, by the repressive measures adopted by the County Commitee. Sir Anthony Weldon might profess amazement, when the rebellion broke out, that "the fair face of such a faithful county" should be "turned of a sudden to so much deformity and ugliness;" but in fact he knew well that its parliamentarian appearance had never been more than skin deep.[1] The history of this re-emergence of the power of local sentiment between 1645 and 1647 is marked by no outstanding political events. Its secret lies in the gradually changing relationships between the four main political groups in the county: the Weldonians and moderate committeemen on one hand, and the Cavaliers and neutrals on the other.

The clue to this changing relationship lies in the fact that in Kent, as in other counties remote from fighting, the Civil War was not a 'total' war. In most parishes a good deal of social communication still took place between members of opposing parties. Politics touched men's lives only casually and occasionally. Even within the Committee, abstract principle rarely disturbed the details of administrative routine. Only Sir Anthony Weldon's clique were consistently conscious of the political barriers separating them from neutrals and delinquents. On most Kentish estates, the labour of seedtime and harvest and the squabbles and friendships of the parish remained the principal concern of the gentry. Henry Oxinden of Great Maydeacon, though a captain of the trained bands, was far more concerned with property disputes than politics, and more ready to come to the aid of distressed royalist kinsmen than to support the County Committee, from which he derived his commission. His brother-in-law, the delinquent Sir Thomas Peyton of Knowlton, was at this date engaged less with the misfortunes of the king than with the mangling of his own property by another delinquent, Sir Edward Hales of Tunstall: he married his daughter to one of the regicide Dixwells, who

[1] *Clarke Papers*, II, p. 15.

were his neighbours at Broome Park, and his stepson to a daughter of the parliamentarian colonel, Edwyn Sandys.[1] Even on sequestrated estates, the ancient customs of the locality often continued unaltered. On the earl of Northampton's manor at Sutton-at-Hone, the manorial courts were still held and the stewards and jurors still came to their annual rent-day dinner, which was now paid for by the County Committee. At Wingham and in Canterbury, the charities of royalists like Sir Thomas Palmer and Lady Wotton were still paid by the committeemen to the poor. Though the estates of the archbishop and the dean and chapter were sequestrated, regular payments were made to the housekeeper and pensioners of the archbishop, to the prior of St John's Hospital, to the prebendaries of Christ Church, to William Pyseing "one of the singing men," to John Bailey for keeping the library, to the master of the King's School, the clerk of works, the porters, doorkeeper and vergers, and to the bellringers "for keeping the boys in order in the time of public meeting."[2]

In all parts of Kent, the allegiance of the gentry was thus determined less by abstract principle than by local circumstances, and above all by the activities of the County Committee. Friends and enemies agreed that it was largely "upon their own score," and not the king's, that the county rose in 1648, and rather against "the violent part of the Committee," the Weldonians, than against parliament as such. The promoters of the Kentish Manifesto of May 1648 attributed their troubles, not to parliament, but to "the provocation of a conscious and enraged Committee," which they charged

"with increasing the taxes of the county above the due proportions, and only for maintaining their own private luxury and pride; with usurping a power over the estates and fortunes of the freemen of this county not granted to them by any power of parliament; with a tyrannical and embittered spirit . . . to

[1] BM, Add. MS 44846, f. 71 *et passim.*

[2] SP. 28: 210, Joseph's and Shetterden's Account Book, ff. 1–16; SP. 28: 210 B, Order Book of St Augustine's Lathe Committee, f. 39, and Edward Boys's Account Book, ff. 34–49; BM, Add. MS 5494, ff. 266, 268; BL, Gough Kent MS 19, ff. 141 sqq.

the exasperating of the people's hearts into all animosity, and overthrowing of all love and peace in this county. . . ."[1]

In a letter "from a gentleman in Kent giving satisfaction to a friend in London," the County Committee was described in 1648 as eventually having

"no scantling of any rule but such as proceeded from their own unlimited proud thoughts and passions. Hence they exercised their cruelty more than once over the lives and fortunes of their poor countrymen for offering to shake off their intolerable yoke of slavery, and would have obtained a fixed standing rule . . . from the parliament (had it not been denied), whereby they sought to endow themselves with a power would have shamed the most notorious tyrants this kingdom ever knew. Hence also they erected to themselves a seraglio at Knole, and after at Aylesford, maintaining their state and princely economy at the sad charges of the county; living at the height of pride and luxury, till in the terror of their own consciences they broke up, when the devil himself came to appear amongst them (which is most true) as a committee-man."

Indeed, if the two Houses had not themselves given a stop to the Committee's "exorbitant proceedings," the county would have "suffered much more under the torment of these men's projected designs: wherein we acknowledge ourselves also to have been secured in the temper and moderation of the Houses."[2]

A few further instances of the activities of the extremists on the Committee will reinforce those given in Chapter V, and show that these accusations, however exaggerated, were not entirely without foundation. For no other reason than to secure the rich benefice of Edward Powell of Chiddingstone for one of his kinsmen, Squire Seyliard of Delaware had Powell imprisoned in Leeds Castle,

[1] *L'Estrange his Vindication; The Manifest of the County of Kent*, [26 May] 1648; cf. E. 459. 12 (*A brief Narration of some arbitrary Proceedings of the Committee . . . of Kent*).

[2] E. 449. 34, pp. 1–2. The story of the devil appearing to the Committee of Kent became notorious at the time.

"where he lay three years and eleven months without seeing the face of any accuser . . . And he [Seyliard] came with a guard of soldiers [to the rectory] and . . . most barbarously carried out a sister of Mr Powell's (who had that day taken physic) and set her in a chair in the frost and snow, to the great hazard of her life."[1]

Another delinquent

"was so plundered, chased, and vexed . . . that, being above 80 years old, with often removal and want of accommodation, it shortened his life. . . . Before his death [he] was sent to by the Kentish Committee . . . for a tax of £2,000. . . . His nephew (who was his heir) went to this Committee, desiring the sequestration might be taken off his estate, shewing them they had been so deeply pillaged that 'twas impossible to raise one, much less £2,000. The noble knight Sir Anthony Weldon replied . . . that he should not think to get his estate unsequestered; and whereas (quoth he) you say you are unable to pay one thousand pound, you shall pay two, and ought to pay us three, for we have killed your uncle for you, and caused you to be heir. . . ."

This story, of course, is related by a royalist; but it is highly characteristic of Weldon's grim sense of humour.[2]

Perhaps the worst example of Sir Anthony Weldon's attitude to neutrals was his treatment of the gentle but obstinate Sir Roger Twysden of Roydon Hall. Long since defeated at law in an old family feud, Weldon now took the opportunity, says Twysden, of "revenging that by power, he failed of doing by justice. . . ." There was no real case against Sir Roger, and many times the Committee for Compounding in London ordered stay of his sequestration. But Weldon and his splenetic friend Sir John Sedley of St Clere always managed to find a way round the orders of the London Committee. They trumped up a case by cumulative evidence, perjured themselves in support of it, and asserted that Sir Roger Twysden

"hath been refractory to all proceedings of parliament; not only in himself, but in animating his neighbourhood [in the

[1] BM, Egerton MS 2985, f. 323.

[2] E. 37. 1.

petition of 1642] . . . His holding correspondence by letters intercepted, both to priests in his own county and strangers abroad, of ill consequence; . . . his absenting himself is, by the ordinance, one of those characters for sequestration; if all this together be not sufficient to sequester him, . . . we confess we understand not how to proceed upon that ordinance; but shall be very tender hereafter, when such an account is required for so notorious a delinquent. . . ."

None of these allegations against Twysden was legally valid; several were false, and most were gross misrepresentations of fact; but Twysden remained sequestered. When Lady Twysden, though "great with child, and a very weak body, thought fit to attend the Committee of Kent for her fifth part," they "used her very harshly and . . . the chairman [Weldon] told her 'as soon as ever this half year was past, they would have all the rents, and she nothing of them.' " It was not until 1649, says Twysden, that "Sir Anthony Weldon now dead, and Sir John Sedley's power, by his own carriage, taken off; my woods, the great eyesore, destroyed; I found the Committee of Kent not so eager against me, and my addresses more facile to the parliament. . . ."[1]

Equally implacable, in the east of the county, were Weldon's two henchmen John Boys of Wingham and Edward Boys of Goodnestone. The object of their persecution, as innocent as Twysden until they drove him to desperation, was their neighbour Sir Thomas Peyton of Knowlton Court. "I must needs tell you," Peyton writes in 1644 to John Boys's aged father, Edward of Betteshanger, that

"I find myself more aggrieved by some of near relation to you than I think any man ever was since Christianity was professed . . . I may truly conceive myself and mine pursued not only to disherison and want, but also to death itself. . . . Among others things [your son] was pleased to say, when hearing of my address to the Committee at Knole, . . . that if I offered to justify myself, he would produce letters under my own hand should tame me . . . I desire not in anything herein to asperse

[1] BM, Add. MS 34163, f. 138; Twysden's Journal, III, pp. 146, 160, 171–3, IV, pp. 137–8, 184.

the legitimate power derived to your son as deputy lieutenant by any ordinance of parliament; but find fault with that studied and contemplated opposition from him to whatsoever favour I may be admitted. . . ."

On receiving this letter, Edward Boys the elder apparently tried to mollify his son's animosity. But John Boys remained unappeased, and his letter to Peyton elicited the following reply. "You cover your . . . implacable affections," said Peyton,

"with a pursuance of ordinances and obedience to superior commands, wherein also you . . . have . . . to answer for neglect, . . . which I may interpret thus: I have yet a name and being in the world, and hopes of better times, and you think you have neglected some piece of your office and calling to let this be. . . . All along to the present time . . . I have been assaulted by you in words, counsels, and actions, not without evident suspicion of private disaffections, which yourself . . . confess."[1]

The correspondence with Edward Boys of Goodnestone, who succeeded John Boys as sequestrator of the Lathe of St Augustine, runs in the same vein. "You have carried yourself towards my affairs," wrote Peyton, "quite contrary to . . . those gentlemen [of the Committee] . . . who appointed you to be chancellor . . ., making some of my tenants with menaces and ill language fly their houses."[2]

Such miserable examples of injustice and rancour are indeed too numerous to mention. That delinquents like the earl of Thanet or Sir Edward Dering should suffer at the hands of the Committee was not altogether surprising, since both had been in the king's quarters at Oxford. But the Twysdens and Peytons of the county had as yet done nothing whatever to assist the king, and yet were treated with even greater severity. According to Peyton their crime consisted merely in doing "nothing voluntary," through "natural commiseration of public calami-

[1] BM, Add. MS 44846, ff. 29 v., 31.

[2] *Ibid.*, f. 32 v. 'Chancellor' was not Boys's official position, but in using the term Peyton was appealing to his sense of equity and his power to adapt the letter of the law to the needs of the particular case in hand.

ties," for either side in the dispute. They "suffered . . . to satisfy the exorbitant passions of some"—namely, the Weldonians—"the effects of whose power tended to have corrupted the temper of every peaceable man." It was not surprising, then, that in January 1647 there was "a great combustion" in the House of Commons "about an appeal to the parliament against the injustices and oppressions of the Kentish Committee, who have attended at Westminster by special order about it; but it is a business of so high and tender concernment to the very parliament itself, that it's not fit to come to a public hearing."[1] The public hearing of the case was yet to come—in the Rebellion of 1648.

While these predatory activities of the more extreme committeemen were driving the neutrals towards active opposition, the influence of the moderates upon the Committee was being exerted in favour of the neutrals. Broadly speaking, both neutrals and moderates were identifiable with the indigenous gentry of the shire, and the force of kinship greatly modified the lines of party division in the county. In Kent, moreover, the influence of moderate anglicanism, which by 1640 had so penetrated the mind of the community, continued throughout the war and reinforced the modifying influence of kinship. Most of the committeemen resolutely opposed both the attempt of the Weldonians to sequestrate the anglican clergy and the efforts of parliament to set on foot a presbyterian *classis*. "We do find the ministers in general," they wrote on the latter occasion, "and the major part of the gentry to be desirous yet awhile to wait." Accordingly, under the aegis of the Committee itself, anglican ministers remained unmolested in hundreds of Kentish parishes where they would have "been cast forth as unsavoury salt, had a commission come down to proceed against such ministers, as in Wales."[2] In West Kent, the sequestrated earl of Westmorland still presented anglicans to the benefices in his gift. In the Weald, the puritans of Brenchley had to walk seven miles to East Peckham to have their children baptized by a puritan minister. In Thanet, Richard Culmer

[1] BM, Add. MS 44846, ff. 67, 67 v.; BL, Clarendon MS 29, f. 72.

[2] BL, Tanner MS 59, f. 77; for the Weldonians' viewpoint, cf. HMC, XIII, i, pp. 704–5.

found all the parish clergy 'neuter,' and the orders of parliament protecting him against persecution useless. At Penshurst, the new minister set up by parliament was attacked by the parishioners for supplanting the anglican Henry Hammond, prosecuted for libel by the earl of Leicester, and found guilty by a Kentish jury when the parliamentarian judge declared him innocent.[1] At Canterbury, even the court of the archbishop continued to function without molestation.[2] In fact, wherever "a pious and painful ministry" was settled by the two Houses, many men, "from a principle of contentious upholding of the present liturgy," forsook their own churches for those of anglicans near by.[3]

Among the milder men of both sides, the prevalent tradition of moderate anglicanism often became exalted rather than extinguished by the strife and tension of war. When sequestered from Penshurst, for example, Henry Hammond employed his leisure hours in writing *The Christian's Obligation to Peace and Charity*. When sequestered and exiled, Sir George Strode of Squerryes wrote his *Discourse of Holy Love*, as he informed his family, that "your hearts [may be] replenished with the Spirit of Love, and your feet conducted in the right paths of charity. . . ." More than once the parliamentarian Sir Edward Partheriche wrote from the House of Commons to allay "the many divisions and uncharitable riots" in his borough of Sandwich. The imprisoned Sir George Sondes recalled that

"God was not in the fire or the boisterous wind, but in the soft and gentle voice. And Christ says, Learn of Me, for I am lowly and meek. These boisterous and fiery-spirited men, I much doubt whether the Spirit of God be in them or no. I am and ever was far from deriding or scoffing at any of them, . . .

[1] A. G. Matthews, *Walker Revised*, 1948, p. 222; A. R. Cook, *A Manor through four Centuries*, 1938, p. 28; Richard Culmer jr, *op. cit.*, p. 14; J. Maudit, *The Practices of the earl of Leicester against the Minister of Penshurst . . .*, 1660; J. Maudit, *A Defence of the Minister of Penshurst . . .*, 1660.

[2] BM, Add. MS 28003, f. 229. It was still functioning, as "the late archbishop's court," in 1654, when Thomas Denne, a committeeman, cited Henry Oxinden of Maydeacon before it "in a plea of covenant breakage:" a curious illustration of the tangled skein of contemporary politics that a Republican should cite a former colleague before an episcopal court in theory extinct.

[3] E. 69. 11.

but leave them to stand or fall to their own Master. The way that I . . . propose to myself to walk in is . . . short but full, Christ His own way and this is it: to love the Lord thy God with all thy heart, and with all thy soul, and thy neighbour as thyself. . . ."[1]

When Henry Oxinden and Clement Barling of Denton fell out, neither side could rest till amity was restored. "Love is easily entreated," wrote Barling to Thomas Oxinden, Henry's son, "and . . . my love . . . presseth me to hearken to your prudent advice in making another overture for . . . reconciliation, notwithstanding late refusals . . ., which as I bless God I regard them not, so I hope they shall never stick in my heart or be mentioned. . . ." "Sir," Barling wrote to Henry Oxinden himself, "[we] have hitherto lived in peace, and I hope shall so continue . . . by the beam of your favour breaking forth upon your honest-hearted neighbour, . . . that like Christians we may be serviceable to each other in love. . . ."[2]

As a consequence of this spirit of moderation, relatively few royalists and neutrals in the county were unable to find some member of the Sequestration Committee to befriend them. The Derings of Surrenden were saved from disaster by the intercession of the parliamentarian Augustine Skynner of East Farleigh Hall, who had succeeded Sir Edward as knight of the shire. Sir Roger Twysden eventually regained his estates through the mediation of such "worthy friends" as William James of Ightham Court Lodge: a committeeman, said Twysden, who desired not "to have done mischief in general to any man" and "for justice sake and old acquaintance" pleaded his cause before the Sequestration Commissioners. Sir Thomas Peyton of Knowlton considered the presence of his brother-in-law, Henry Oxinden of Great Maydeacon, amongst the parliamentarians "as a virtue between two extremes to moderate the severer inclination of others." "The world are everywhere busy," he added,

"to advance out of every little power they are invested with. . . . You have chosen a more angelical office of guarding

[1] E. 1382, Dedication; Sandwich Muniments, Letter Book, 1295–1753, f. 146; Harleian Miscellany, x, *Sir George Sondes his Plain Narrative*, p. 56.
[2] BM, Add. MS 28002, ff. 291, 225.

and defending [MS torn] from these evils. . . . 'Tis not the nearness of doors nor the confining of inheritances makes us neighbours; but the acts of love and charity which exercise their offices in all places. . . ."

The wives of the committeemen too were not unamenable to the pleas of delinquent gentlemen, as Thomas Stanley of Hamptons found when he received a demand for £30, for which he was "altogether unprovided." "Good sweet Madam," he wrote to his neighbour Lady Sedley, "help me now in this pinch of need. . . ." In all parts of Kent, as Sir Thomas Peyton observed of his own district, " 'tis known and seen that . . . there is retained among men of different opinions, in these dividing times, the seeds of ancient amity and good-will. . . ."[1]

It was the subtle influence of this ancient amity and good-will that eventually reunited the moderate committeemen with the neutrals and delinquents of the county. Their reunion was expressed in a multitude of ballads and poems reviving the story that Kent had never been conquered by William the Norman, and in a passionate desire to restore "the liberties of the county" by freeing their estates from "the violent part of the Committee." Their pleas for a restoration of the liberties of the county harked back to the Eyre of Kent in 6 Edward II, when the "community of the whole county" had "prayed the Justices that they might be allowed their customs which they had ever been used to have, . . . founded upon gavelkind and upon other manners or customs which were not in accordance with the common law. . . ."[2] Their ballads and poems reverted to the days when the county was an independent kingdom, and when it had refused to yield to the foreigner's yoke. In all parts of England popular legend at this time attributed every form of oppression to the yoke of the Conqueror; it was natural that in Kent this sentiment should now become assimilated with the much older tradition of the 'unconquered county.' The following doggerel lines are typical of many from the tracts

[1] SP. 23: G: 228, f. 52; Twysden's Journal, III, pp. 148–9, 158, IV, p. 138; BM, Add. MS 28000, f. 327; Add. MS 44846, f. 26 v.; AC, XVII, p. 368, and cf. pp. 364–5.

[2] Selden Society, XXIV, Year Books of Edward II, V, *The Eyre of Kent, 6 & 7 Edward II, A.D. 1313–1314*, I, 1910, p. 11.

and broadsheets which circulated in Kentish farms and manor-houses in 1647–8:

> "Your hearts, no doubt, are same, brave Kentishmen,
> Fighting for that which you pretended then [in 1066],
> Your liberties, laws, privileges, rights . . .
> Shall those victorious state-triumphant bays
> Which decked your fanes and temples in those days
> From you receive their winter, and decline
> Through your remissness in this feverish time? . . .
> Retain your pristine prowess and make good
> That ancient-line all-uncorrupted blood
> Which ye derive from them from whence ye came,
> And who have chalked the way to crown your fame . . ."[1]

It was the return of the Cavaliers from Oxford in 1647, and the release of the local royalists from Leeds Castle that sparked off the grievances of the reunited moderates of the county in the Rebellion of 1648. The power of the Cavaliers derived from their determination to transmute these essentially local grievances into thoroughgoing royalism. "Kent will be loyal to their king," so their motto ran, "should all the kingdom else prove wicked." With the Cavaliers' return, many family gatherings took place in the manor-houses of East and West Kent. Ominous "meetings of the county" occurred in Canterbury, and a "great concourse" of disbanded royalist troops was held at Maidstone.[2] Royalist families like the St Legers, Lovelaces, Mayneys, Diggeses, Skeffingtons, and Richauts mortgaged their estates to raise funds for the king. By Christmas 1647 there were few people outside Sir Anthony Weldon's own circle who remained at heart loyal to the County Committee. Fundamentally there was little in common between the Cavaliers and the moderates; but from the viewpoint of parliament adversity had made them dangerous bedfellows.

The ensuing Rebellion of 1648 possesses a historical significance beyond Kentish history, however. According to some

[1] *Halesiados: A Message from the Normans to the General of the Kentish Forces*, 1648.

[2] E. 446. 21; SP. 28: 130, Bowles's Account Book, 1647–8; BM, Add. MS 28001, f. 132.

contemporaries, it formed part of a concerted plan to reinstate the king, and was organized either in London or from St Germain.[1] In this opinion contemporaries were certainly mistaken. Leading participants in the rebellion, like Sir Thomas Peyton and Matthew Carter, were unaware of such a connexion. The rising at Canterbury which touched off the rebellion preceded the plans laid at St Germain by several months. Throughout the insurrection, moreover, the county was uncompromisingly hostile to every outside effort to co-ordinate its activities with risings elsewhere. The view of an anonymous Kentish gentleman was undoubtedly correct in stating that the rebellion "was a plain committee-war, without the least premeditate design or plot against the parliament or the present peace and security. . . ."[2] Nevertheless, though of local origin, the Kentish rising was of more than local significance. It was symptomatic of a major crisis in the royalist party as a whole. Its ultimate failure was due to that cleavage between Cavaliers and moderates, between court royalism and country royalism, which was apparent at this date in many parts of the country. This cleavage was one of the chief obstacles to the settlement of the kingdom in 1648, and it made the rule of the protectorate possible in the 'fifties. It was not until the lessons of division had been learned, through years of exile and bitterness, that the restoration of the House of Stuart could be accomplished.

[1] This also seems to have been the view of S. R. Gardiner. But Gardiner's remark (*Civil War*, IV, 1901, pp. 132–3) that the "royalist leaders in Kent," in May 1648, "having made up their minds that an isolated rising would be an act of madness, resolved to await the Scottish invasion and the consequent withdrawal of Fairfax to the North" misrepresents the statements of Clarendon upon which it is based (*History of the Rebellion*, ed. Macray, 1888, IV, pp. 332–3). Clarendon asserts that the Kentish rising was not designed "by those who did take care of the king's affairs, and who did design those insurrections which happened in other parts of the kingdom." He adds that "what fell out there was by mere chance and accident, that could neither be foreseen or prevented." The royalist leaders to whom Gardiner refers as resolving to await the Scottish invasion before rising are stated by Clarendon not to have been in Kent at the time, but to have lain "privately in London" specifically "to avoid all cabals in their country. . . ."

[2] *L'Estrange his Vindication*, *passim*; Carter, *passim*; E. 449. 34, p. 8; E. 459. 12, *passim*.

VII

THE COMMUNITY IN REVOLT, 1647–8

(i) *Christmas at Canterbury, 1647*

THE CHAIN OF EVENTS which culminated in the rebellion of the county in 1648 had its genesis in a riot at Canterbury, on Christmas Day 1647. At that date, Canterbury was much the largest town in Kent, more than twice as large as its rival Maidstone, and one of the most populous towns in England. Probably only the streets of Norwich, Bristol, York, Exeter, Ipswich, Newcastle, the two university towns, and possibly Yarmouth were more crowded.[1] To the south of the city, in the fertile valleys of the Great and Lesser Stour, manorial gentry probably clustered more thickly than in any comparable area of England, and their life was closely bound up with that of the town. Many of these gentry possessed property in Canterbury, or were connected with the clerical families of the Close, and not a few with the corporation. Their religious sentiments chimed in with those of most of the townsmen, who, despite important Walloon and puritan elements, were predominantly anglican. In the churches of the city and its dependent villages, services were still often held according to the rites of the Church of England, and the proscription of religious festivals had been largely winked at. In 1647, however, in consequence of "sundry seditious sermons" and "dangerous speeches . . . darkly implying threats against the parliament and a course to be taken with the Roundheads about Christmas," the County Committee refused to countenance any further contempt of the parliamentarian ordinance. An order was published throughout the county requiring strict observance of the injunction proscribing the festival.[2]

[1] Cf. C. A. F. Meekings, ed., *Dorset Hearth Tax Assessments, 1662–1664*, Dorset Nat. Hist. and Arch. Soc., 1951, pp. 108–10.

[2] BL, Tanner MS 58, f. 672; cf. E. 520. 21. In their letters to Sir John Culpeper at St Germain, the leaders of the riot denied that it was due to

It was this order that sparked off the riot. The temper of the shire was now far less complaisant, after two years of nominal peace, than it had been in the dark days before Naseby. The Committee might storm; but the county, as one contemporary observed, was convinced that that body had reached its "climacterical and fatal year," and refused to listen. The local people were "so eager . . . of a sermon that day by such as they approved of, that the church doors were kept with swords and other weapons, defensive and offensive, whilst the minister was in the pulpit."[1] When the mayor of Canterbury, a man of a "rough and unkind nature," proclaimed that a market should be kept, only twelve shopkeepers obeyed him, and they were at once

"commanded by the multitude to shut up again; but refusing to obey, their ware was thrown up and down and they at last forced to shut in. . . . The sheriff laying hold of a fellow, was stoutly resisted; which the mayor perceiving, took a cudgel and strook the man, who . . . knocked down the mayor, whereby his cloak was much torn and dirty. . . . The mayor hereupon made strict proclamation . . . that every man depart to his own house. The multitude hollowing thereat, . . . the alderman and constables caught two or three of the rout, and sent them to jail, but they soon broke loose, and jeered Master Alderman. Soon after issued forth the commanders of this rabble, with an addition of soldiers into the High Street, and brought with them two foot-balls,"

thus "drawing together on a sudden great numbers of rude persons not only of the city but of country-fellows, strangers from the parts adjacent, whereby they speedily grew into a tumult." The crowd that gathered surged through the streets crying "Conquest!"[2] Some "set up holly-bushes at their doors like your country alehouses, and gave entertainment with, Nothing to pay, and, Welcome, gentlemen." The gates of the city jail were set open and the aldermen were chased and beaten

"any designed rising for the king," and asserted that it was merely a matter of local grievance at the mayor's action.—BL, Clarendon MS 31, f. 96.

[1] E. 449. 34, p. 2; E. 421. 22; E. 421. 30.

[2] E. 421. 22; E. 449. 34, p. 2.

into their houses. The puritan minister, Richard Culmer, fleeing from the Saracen's Head, was pelted with mud, and his life was threatened in the place near the cathedral where he had beaten down the "great figure of Christ" in 1643.[1]

During the week-end, countrymen flocked into the town from neighbouring parishes. On Monday morning a heated argument with "a busy prating" puritan led to pistol shots and a sudden clamour of "murder." Crowds again surged through the streets of the city, and the battle-cry was first heard, "For God, King Charles, and Kent." "Master sheriff, . . . striving to keep the peace, was knocked down and his head fearfully broke; it was God's mercy his brains were not beat out. . . ." The rebels "beat down all the windows of Mr Mayor's house, burnt the stoups at the coming in of his door. Master Reeve's windows were broke; Master Page and Master Pollen . . . and others were sorely wounded." The godly ministers of the city and the members of the Accounts Committee were maltreated, imprisoned, or "laid in irons." Within a few hours, the Cavaliers claimed, this "random rout" was reduced to martial order. The city magazine was seized, 1,000 men were armed, courts of guard appointed, passengers examined, and the city gates shut against the approaching committeemen and trained bands. Similar bodies of rioters were gathering in Thanet and in the downland to the south, and, incited by "malignant ministers," in the parishes along the Thames in the north-west of the county. From the Isle of Wight news was received of the king's attempted escape from Carisbrooke Castle on the 29th December. Believing that Charles was about to make his way towards Kent, the Cavaliers openly declared their readiness to join their assistance with the Scots, "release the king's Majesty out of thraldom and misery, . . . restore him to his just rights, . . . and . . . endeavour the preservation of the honourable constitution of parliament . . . and all the just privileges thereof. . . ."[2]

The last clause of this declaration of the Cavaliers was

[1] E. 421. 29; E. 421. 22; Richard Culmer, jr, *op. cit.*, pp. 29–30. The mayor was a brewer, and the populace made free with his beer.

[2] E. 421. 22; E. 421. 29; E. 449. 34, p. 2; E. 520. 20; BL, Tanner MS 58, f. 672; E. 422. 23; E. 421. 23.

intended as a sop to parliament, and as a bait to the more moderate members of the Committee of Canterbury. Well aware that the allegiance of the milder committeemen, such as Sir William Mann, was beginning to waver, the Cavaliers perhaps hoped that such a saving clause of the rights of parliament would now secure their overt support. At this stage, however, the more responsible citizens were unwilling to face a siege, and the moderates on the Committee hesitated. Sir William Mann, Francis Lovelace, Avery Sabine, and other moderate committeemen met the Cavaliers at the Town Hall, and, in virtue of their office, offered the rebels indemnity and mediation with parliament if they would lay down their arms. The Committee of Canterbury was thus able to save the life of the mayor, and it hoped by this means to keep the Committee of the County at arm's length until the issue became more settled. Sir Anthony Weldon, however, was too astute to be deceived by the bland assurances of Sir William Mann. He and his adherents "gathered together with their confederate friends, chaplains, and other instruments of war," and took their stand with the trained bands of the county before the city walls. A lengthy correspondence took place between the County Committee, the Committee of Canterbury, the corporation, the Cavaliers, and the leading citizens of the town. Early in January 1648, isolated and frightened, the rebels of Canterbury were forced to capitulate.[1]

The capitulation of Canterbury was followed by the swift vengeance of Sir Anthony Weldon and his henchmen. During the following weeks many special meetings of the County Committee were held in Canterbury, Faversham, and Sittingbourne to examine the rebel leaders. It is significant of the change in the balance of power in the county that, by this date, none of Weldon's supporters came of the old landed families of the shire: all were relative *nouveaux-riches* of legal or mercantile origin, such as Thomas Plumer, Thomas Blount, William Kenwricke, Augustine Skynner, Richard Beale, Sir John Rivers, and Sir Michael Livesey. Their account books record the many sums they spent in setting their guards, sum-

[1] BL, Tanner MS 58, ff. 645, 653, 672–4; Clarendon MS 31, f. 96; E. 421. 22; E. 449. 34, p. 3.

moning witnesses, and heating and lighting their chambers. The city gates of Canterbury were broken up and burnt; stretches of the town wall were pulled down; ordnance was mounted upon the ramparts; and the command of the militia was transferred (so Weldon hoped) to "trusty hands." When the work was complete, a deputation was sent to parliament desiring a commission of martial law to try the rebels. Meanwhile, Sir Michael Livesey conveyed Sir William Mann, Francis Lovelace, Avery Sabine, and about forty others to Leeds Castle, where, if the commission were refused, they might be left to languish for the time being in oblivion.[1]

The following winter and spring of 1647–8 was a time of great turmoil in all parts of the county. Near London, John Lilburne staged a meeting of Levellers from the capital, East Anglia, and the Midlands. In some of the coastal castles the parliamentarian governors declared themselves "to be neutral and to look after themselves." At Dover, a town "exceedingly malignant, and by reason of the decay of trade and poverty of the seamen, rude and barbarous beyond belief," yet another plot was laid, by Walter Braemes of Blackmansbury, to seduce the governor and betray the castle to Prince Charles. The plot came to nothing, but John Boys of Fredville, a local gentleman, was unwisely superseded by the unpopular William Brafield as governor. At the county assizes, a recent sentence of the House of Lords was nailed upon the gallows in contempt. At local musters defaulters became so numerous that the Committee asked parliament for power to levy a "pecuniary mulct . . . with a power of levy thereof by distress and sale." Reinforced by troops sent from parliament under Colonel Hewson, the committeemen made an official progress through the county in order to set matters at peace. Everywhere they came, however, they now began to find "themselves laughed at and by mean people affronted. . . ."[2]

[1] SP. 28: 130, Bowles's Commissary Account Book, 1647–8, ff. 24–9; BL, Tanner MS 58, f. 673; Clarendon MS 31, f. 96; E. 449. 34, p. 3; E. 423. 17; Richard Culmer, jr, *op. cit.*, pp. 29–30.

[2] E. 423. 23; CJ, v, pp. 438, 559; CSPV, 1647–52, p. 16; E. 448. 5; E. 435. 39; CSPD, 1648–49, p. 37; E. 449. 34, pp. 5, 9; E. 522. 14; BL, Tanner MS 58, ff. 653, 673, 731.

Meanwhile, in January 1648 those Cavaliers who had managed to slip through Weldon's net in Canterbury published a declaration justifying their riot.[1] At Leeds, the rebels imprisoned in the castle were regarded as martyrs, and their petition to parliament desiring a legal trial was rapidly circulated throughout the county. Weakened by their interminable quarrel with the army and well aware of the "injustice and oppressions of the Kentish Committee," the Commons were at last disposed to listen to their grievances. At the end of January, the Committee of Kent was summoned to attend at Westminster by special order. This meeting was followed by a lengthy correspondence between the Committee and the Commons, in which Sir Anthony Weldon insisted that the rebels should be tried by the County Committee, by commission of martial law. Trial by normal commission of oyer and terminer, he rightly claimed, would necessitate a packed jury and consequently bring the cause of parliament into disrepute. The "strong malignity of the distemper in these places . . .," he declared, "is able to convert this kind of physic to the nourishment . . . of the disease, . . . and by consequence will prove the destruction of the body."[2] Parliament, however, was now tired of Sir Anthony Weldon's arrogance. Believing that procrastination would allay the Kentish distemper, it ordered the prisoners to be tried in the normal way at the county assizes in May. The ensuing weeks showed that parliament had misjudged the situation. The continued imprisonment of most of the rebels untried, and the release of Sir William Mann and his two colleagues on bail, confirmed Sir Anthony Weldon's forebodings. When the assizes began on 10th May, and Serjeants Wilde and Cresheld, with the Kentish members of parliament, were sent down to Canterbury to act as commissioners, "the malignity of the humour [of Kent], increasing by insensible

[1] E. 421. 23. This declaration purports to be by many thousands in Kent and Canterbury; internal evidence suggests that it was drawn up by the Cavalier leaders.

[2] E. 421. 23; E. 449. 34, p. 4; *L'Estrange his Vindication*; BL, Clarendon MS 29, f. 72; Tanner MS 57, f. 60; Tanner MS 58, f. 673. For the fundamental reasons for Weldon's objections, which subsequent events justified, see p. 95, n. 2, regarding the place of the assizes in the political life of the county.

degrees, at last had putrified and corrupted almost the whole county, gentry and all."[1]

Cavaliers, moderates, and neuters were at last united, and they were not taken by surprise or without a carefully thought-out plan of action. Like the petition of 1642, the county petition which led to the Rebellion of 1648 was organized at the assizes. Two separate trials were held, one at the Town Hall for the city, and the other in the Castle Yard for the county. The juries were carefully chosen from supposedly well-affected inhabitants, and Sir Michael Livesey and Colonel Gibbon were placed on guard at either place with their respective regiments. For some days past, there had been "great resort . . . to Canterbury by gentlemen and others to see the issue." Feeling in the city ran so high that the House of Commons forbade the minister of the French church to preach, though he was a former pillar of the parliamentarian cause.[2]

In these inflammable circumstances the parliamentarian judge would have been well-advised to use a little diplomacy. In giving his charge against the accused at the Town Hall, however, Serjeant Wilde was so "full of blood-thirstiness that the people were ready to destroy him." Serjeant Cresheld, or Creswell as he was popularly called, seemed

"somewhat more honest, and at the close of his charge bade, 'God save the King,' at which the people gave such a shout as put Wilde and Livesey half out of their wits, saying that it was not safe for them to sit there without a stronger guard. . . . So they sent presently for ten companies and troops . . ., but none came save only a part of Foach's troop, the rest would not stir. The next morning they put in their bill of indictment against six which they took to be chief ringleaders, but the jury found it *ignoramus*; whereupon Wilde caused the witnesses to be re-examined at the bar, and very much importuned and pressed hard the business to the jury, who went out again, and returned a second *ignoramus*, at which Wilde was very much offended, and the counsel refused to proceed any further but adjourned the Court until July next, saying, That if they had

[1] BL, Clarendon MS 31, ff. 80, 96.

[2] E. 449. 34, p. 4; BL, Clarendon MS 31, ff. 80, 96; E. 522. 27.

had a jury from hell, they could not but have found the bill . . . This bloody villain Wilde . . . was not ashamed to urge the statute of 25 Edward III to Serjeant Cresheld as sufficient to hang these Kentish gentlemen; but Cresheld honestly told him, he durst not consent to condemn them upon this statute, because it is . . . levying war against our Lord the King, . . . which they were no ways guilty of. . . ."

Similar scenes took place at the same time in the Castle Yard, where the people openly cried out, "A King! A King!" A troop of parliamentarian horse was called in to awe the jurors; but a report of the city jury's return was passed round the court, and the county jurors also returned *ignoramus*. And thus was "converted that intended tragedy," says Roger L'Estrange, "into a scene of mirth."[1]

At once the people of Canterbury "began to talk another language; to contemplate the mortality even of a perpetual parliament; and fleshed . . . upon a Committee, . . . determined next to fly at all, and step in boldly to the rescue of their invaded liberties." Rumours flew that the jurors were to be tried —imprisoned—perhaps hanged—"for their contempt in not giving a verdict according to the sense of the House." The Cavaliers were ready to exploit the excitement, and framed and subscribed a petition to parliament in conjunction with the Grand Jury. As "the knights, gentlemen, and franklins of the County of Kent, the most free people of this late flourishing nation, by the wisdom and valour of our ancestors, delivered from the laws

[1] E. 443. 7; BL, Clarendon MS 31, ff. 80, 96; *L'Estrange his Vindication*. L'Estrange, the well-known journalist and pamphleteer, came of a Norfolk family but was a close friend of young Edward Hales of Tunstall. His account of the Rebellion, in which he played an active part throughout, is one of the most detailed and colourful. He consistently exaggerates his own influence, however, and he was far from being the architect or originator of the movement in Kent, as a casual reader might suppose. He was a dominating figure amongst the 'foreigners' who joined the rising, but their importance was marginal, not central, to the action as a whole. In all probability it was he who induced the plutocratic Haleses to support the rising so liberally with money, and who promoted the leadership of Edward Hales in its early stages. There is reason to think, however, that the Haleses' financial assistance may also have been linked with the fact that many Kentish gentry had become indebted to them during the past few years under the stress of Civil War, sequestration, and perhaps other factors. See also pp. 275–6, below.

of a conqueror, and to these late days of unhappy confusion . . . enjoying the same through all the reigns of the most glorious and victorious kings," they desired, first, a personal treaty to settle both the king's and parliament's just rights; secondly, the disbandment of the army; thirdly, government by known and established laws; and fourthly, "that, according to the Petition of Right our property may not be invaded by any taxes or impositions whatsoever." Of these demands, the last not unnaturally rendered the petition immensely popular. The parliamentarian commissioners were forced to adjourn the court before the petition could be presented to the Grand Jury, who had however already signed it. The committeemen who still supported Weldon beat a hasty retreat to Maidstone, where they drew up "a most precipitate order" declaring the petition to be seditious, sent out more troops to suppress it, and dispatched a recriminatory letter to parliament for insisting on trial by the common law.[1] "In discharge of . . . our trust we did then," in January 1648, they said,

"in all faithfulness . . . declare our thoughts how fruitless and dangerous it would be to attempt to cure of so strong a malady in this place by such a medicine. . . . Delays so destructive, in cases of this nature, to public peace and safety . . . are unavoidably incident to the formalities of the common law, [so] that usually before the plaister can be sp[r]ead, venom and infection hath so overspread that it often comes too late. We . . . shall leave it to the wisdom and consideration of the honourable House to provide what future remedy you think fit."[2]

But the recriminations and orders of the Committee, "instead of suppressing, gave life to the petition." In a single day

[1] *L'Estrange his Vindication*; BL, Clarendon MS 31, f. 80; *The Manifest of the County of Kent*, [26 May] 1648; *The Petition of the County of Kent*, 18 May 1648 (MS copy in BM, Thomason Tract Collection, 669. f. 12. 28); E. 441. 25; BL, Clarendon MS 31, f. 96; E. 449. 34, p. 5. The eleven committeemen who issued the above order included Sir Anthony Weldon, Sir John Rivers, Richard Beale, Thomas Seyliard, Lambarde Godfrey, William Kenwricke.

[2] BL, Tanner MS 57, f. 60.

200 gentry subscribed the document in Canterbury, and sent copies "all the county over for hands." On the 29th May these copies were to be brought to Rochester, and all that intended to accompany it to parliament were to meet at Blackheath the day following. Of the committeemen, out of about seventy "scarce 10" forbore to sign the petition. Some, upon parliament's orders, tried to muster the county forces, but found that all but a few score of each regiment defaulted. In one regiment the mutineers dismounted their commanding officer and compelled him to drink the king's health. Not knowing "what to do nor where to sit in safety," most of the committeemen who remained loyal to parliament "rode in all haste out of the country [*sc.*, county] to tell their several tales to the parliament and army."[1] Only a handful of stalwarts, like Sir Henry Heyman and Sir Anthony Weldon, with their homes surrounded by rebels, remained to stem the rising tide of revolt. "Never was the fair face of such a faithful county," Weldon wrote in despair to the Committee at Derby House,

"turned of a sudden to so much deformity and ugliness. If your Lordships do think that by flinging water on our flame you shall extinguish all, believe me it will not do, but make all parts in flame the more. . . . You may cast away many gentlemen [of the Committee] that have served you formerly . . ., but where to find such [i.e., substitutes] is not easily to be advised. . . . If you suffer us to perish for want of aid you shall wish aid had come in time."[2]

(ii) *The Organization of Revolt, 1648*

The historical sources for the Kentish Rebellion of 1648 are more copious than for the whole of the rest of the period put together: a fact which affords an indication of the impact of the rising upon contemporaries.[3] It was not the rising of a

[1] E. 449. 34, pp. 5–6; Carter, p. 14; BL, Clarendon MS 31, f. 80; E. 443. 41; E. 448. 5; CSPD, 1648–49, pp. 67–9.

[2] *Clarke Papers*, II, p. 15.

[3] The principal *corpus* consists of some dozens of pamphlets, together with scattered references in several scores of news-sheets and newspapers of the time, in the Thomason Tract collection in BM. There are also many other relevant tracts in the BM, of which the full-scale accounts by Roger L'Es-

single clique or class of the community. It was the revolt of a whole countryside, like that of Cornwall in 1497, and like the Northern Rebellion of 1536. It was a rising of thousands of countrymen spurred on by lingering legends of Cade and Wyatt, and largely unaware of the miseries of warfare or the problems of the nation at large. It was the last, in fact, of the great local insurrections of English history.

From the launching of the county petition, barely three weeks elapsed before the proposed meeting of the county at Blackheath, and no plans had been formulated beyond it. Twenty thousand people were said to have signed the petition, but nine out of ten of them had as yet no thought of outright revolt. Only the clear intention of parliament and Committee to employ force against them induced them to subscribe the "Engagement" of self-defence which, within a few days, was subjoined to the original petition by the Cavaliers.[1] "We do solemnly and religiously oblige ourselves," this Engagement ran,

> "with our lives and fortunes to oppose effectually what person or persons soever shall presume to interrupt us in the just and legal presentment of our humble desires to the two Houses. . . . And further, in case any single person shall be for this Engagement prosecuted, all of us [are] to rise as one man to the rescue."

This Engagement, the first definite act of defiance to parliament, was followed by a "Remonstrance showing the Occasion of the present Arming of the County of Kent." "We are menaced and persecuted into this extremity," the Remonstrance declared, "by spirits so implacably distempered, that Sir Anthony Weldon vowed that he would not cross the street of Rochester to save one soul that subscribed the petition. And it was a

---

trange and Matthew Carter are of special importance. Of the participants themselves there is much information in the records of the parliamentarian Committee for Advance of Money and Committee for Compounding in PRO. The Rebellion also figures largely in CSPD, and in the Tanner and Clarendon manuscripts in BL.

[1] BL, Clarendon MS 31, f. 96; E. 449. 34, p. 6; E. 453. 37; E. 459. 12.

proposition of [Richard] Beale's to hang two of the petitioners in every parish. If this be not enough to admonish others," they said, "it awakens us. . . ."[1] Although many people feared that the defiant style of the Remonstrance "was bolder than became the growth of our affairs," and apparently refused to support it, virtually the whole adult male population of the county—27,373 people—are said to have signed a declaration in which the county threatened to arm itself in defence of the petition, "if thereunto reduced by any troublesome interposition. . . ."[2] In consequence of this declaration and the Engagement, the subscription of the petition and the arming of the county henceforth proceeded together.

Of those who signed the petition and declaration, we know the names of nearly 600. Among them were nearly all the indigenous Kentish families who had formed the backbone of the moderate party since 1640. Precisely the same kind of feudal organization, moreover, came into play as in the elections and the earlier rebellions of the shire. Each of the leading county families secured the support of his cousins and friends among the minor gentry, and they in turn brought their sons, servants, bailiffs, labourers, and tenants to the particular rendezvous of their region, whether Canterbury, Maidstone, Faversham, or Rochester. In some parishes the gentry supported the petition simply because their neighbours invited them to do so; for "good fellowship," as Clarendon observed, "was a vice generally spread over that country" of Kent. In other towns and villages, as at Cranbrook, the local squire "summoned the people in the street with a loud voice, as well as by trumpet, saying he was for the king." Elsewhere, as at Northfleet, the whole male population of the village turned out to support the rising, and the lanes were left

[1] *A Remonstrance showing the Occasion of the present Arming of the County of Kent*, 1648 (to which the "Engagement" is subjoined); *L'Estrange his Vindication*; cf. E. 459. 12.

[2] *L'Estrange his Vindication*; E. 443. 9. As always with the numbers alleged to have signed petitions and declarations, the figure of 27,373 must be treated with reserve; but there is no reason to doubt that some thousands did sign the declaration. Such documents were quickly printed and distributed in large numbers through every parish in the county, where they were often signed in the church and in inns and houses.

deserted save "only [for] the women, making sad moan. . . ."[1] In the Lathe of St Augustine the former committeeman Colonel Sir Richard Hardres of Upper Hardres brought the complete regiment of the lathe to the rendezvous. In Canterbury the French church, hitherto a buttress of parliament, raised and paid two companies from amongst its congregation. In many parts, "under the several pretences of horse-races, wrestlings, and maypoles," the "frothy humour of the giddy multitude" was exploited. In the parish churches the petitioners listened to popular sermons hallowing the "blood of the martyrs of Kent," and in countless villages ballads and pamphlets were spread broadcast:

> "Retain your pristine prowess and make good
> That ancient-line all-uncorrupted blood . . .
> That Kentishmen were never conquered yet."[2]

Support for the petition was organized in four distinct areas of the county, separated from one another by tracts of sparsely populated down or marshland. Five-sixths of the rebels came from the east and centre of the county, and relatively few from the desolate sheep-pastures of Romney Marsh, the puritan cloth villages of the Weald, or the parishes bordering the metropolis.[3] Three-quarters lived in the wealthy and thickly populated eastern half of the county, and more than one quarter in the easternmost lathe of the shire, that of St Augustine. The valleys of the Great and Lesser Stour which run through the centre of St Augustine's, south of Canterbury,

[1] SP. 23: G: 158; Carter, p. 75; *L'Estrange his Vindication*; CCAM, pp. 1221, 1315–16, 1417; CCC, p. 2602; E. 445. 26.

[2] Carter, p. 65 [68]; BL, Clarendon MS 31, f. 94; CSPD, 1648–9, p. 73; cf. E. 445. 15; *Halesiados*, 1648. The "martys of Kent" were those killed by parliament in former rebellions.

[3] Sutton-at-Hone Upper furnished 10 per cent of the petitioners, Nether 3 per cent, the Weald 3 per cent, and Romney Marsh 1 per cent: except the Marsh and part of the Weald these areas are in West Kent. The list of petitioners' names upon which this and the following paragraphs are based has been compiled from: BL, Tanner MS 57, f. 135; E. 445. 26; E. 446. 9–11; E. 448. 5; E. 448. 18; E. 448. 20; E. 449. 12; E. 450. 8–9; E. 461. 3; CCC; CCAM. The Wealden villagers might have lent more support to the rising if many of them had not been cut off by floods: it was an exceptionally wet season.

were probably more thickly strewn with manorial gentry than any comparable area of England; they were almost unanimous in their support of the petition. Under the leadership of Sir Thomas Peyton of Knowlton Court and Sir Richard Hardres of Upper Hardres, they were headed by a group of twenty closely-related families: amongst them Hardres's brother-in-law Sir Thomas Godfrey of Heppington, and his cousins Sir James Hales of The Dongeon, the Oxindens of Deane, the Bargraves of Bifrons, and the Palmers of Bekesbourne; Sir Thomas Godfrey's uncle Sir John Honywood of Evington in Elmsted; the Bargraves' cousins the Boyses of Bonnington and Uffington; the Oxindens' cousin Sir Thomas Palmer of Wingham; Sir Thomas Palmer's son-in-law Arnold Braemes of Blackmansbury; Braemes's brothers-in-law Thomas Harfleete of Bekesbourne and Anthony Hamond of St Albans Court; Harfleete's cousin Sir Christopher Harfleete of Milton Septvans; Hamond's cousin Sir Anthony Aucher of Bishopsbourne; and Sir Anthony's brother-in-law Robert Hatton of Oswalds in Bishopsbourne. Supporting these county families in St Augustine's were their many kinsmen among the minor gentry and clergy of the shire, such as the Austens of Eastry, the Engehams of Bridge, the Paramores of Paramore in Ash, the Hobdays of Barham, the Houghams of Chislet and Ash-by-Wingham, Prebendary Blechynden of Canterbury, and Archdeacon Kingsley.

Many of these gentry, like the Oxindens and Hardreses, had been prominent members of the County Committee, for in St Augustine's nearly all the committeemen were "either fled, or imprisoned, or revolted."[1] Four of the rebel families were headed by former Cavaliers from Oxford, including Sir John Boys of Bonnington, the king's former governor of Donnington Castle. Also amongst the rebel leaders in St Augustine's was a handful of debauchees, like Richard Thornhill of Olantighe, "the veriest beast that ever was," and Adam Sprakeling of St Lawrence-in-Thanet, whose notorious series of murders culminated in that of his wife and became a Kentish *cause célèbre* in the 'fifties.[2] The great majority of these petitioners in East

[1] *L'Estrange his Vindication.*

[2] E. 697. 10; Richard Culmer, jr, *op. cit.*, p. 31. Sprakeling murdered his neighbour Richard Langley of St Lawrence-in-Thanet shortly before the

Kent, however, represented families of moderate inclinations who had suffered much from the persecutions of the extreme group in the County Committee. They had little or nothing in common with men like Sprakeling, Thornhill, or even Sir John Boys. Amongst the most active of them was Anthony Hamond of St Albans Court, who raised 300 foot in half a day, more, says Carter, "than ever were listed by one man in so short a time;" while "every gentleman . . . subscribed . . . some a hundred pounds, some eighty, some fifty, some forty, some more, some less. . . ."[1]

Another group of petitioners, comprising one-eighth of the total number, were seated in the countryside bordering the headwaters of the Stour, around Surrenden Dering. It was this region which had most firmly championed Sir Edward Dering in 1640, and the group was now led by his brother-in-law, the earl of Thanet. Having written "to all gentlemen he knew had any power," Thanet "secured above a thousand men in that part. . . ." He was supported by various branches of the Dering family seated at Egerton, Eastwell, Boughton Malherbe, and Wickins in Charing; by four of Dering's cousins among the Darell family of Calehill; by Zouche and Sir William Brockman of Beachborough, Dering's brothers-in-law; by his neighbours the Knatchbulls of Mersham-le-Hatch, the Mantells of Monks' Horton, and the Lovelaces of Lovelace Place; by many minor gentry like the Osbornes, Belkes, and Broadnaxes; and by the principal chronicler of the rebellion, Matthew Carter of Great Winchcombe.[2]

North-west of the Stour lands, in the fertile country about "busy Maidstone," a further sixth of the petitioners were seated. Once again they were headed by a knot of closely related knights and baronets, cautiously supported by the king's

storming of Maidstone; he was hanged for murdering his wife in 1653. The Sprakelings, like a number of other Thanet families—for example, their kinsmen the Proudes and Hobarts—were infamous for their violence and their feuds. The same wild strain came out in the gentle Henry Oxinden of Maydeacon's son and heir, who inherited the blood of the Sprakelings and likewise ended up as a murderer.

[1] Carter, pp. 36–8; cf. CSPD, 1648–9, p. 226.

[2] Carter, p. 68 [69]. For Carter cf. Hasted, *op. cit.*, VII, p. 373; *DNB*, s.v. Matthew Carter.

cousin, the duke of Richmond at Cobham Hall. Unlike those of St Augustine and the Stour area, however, the ringleaders in this region were Cavaliers rather than moderates. Led by Sir Anthony St Leger of Wiarton Place and Sir John Mayney of Linton Place, the Sedleys of Aylesford, the Culpepers of Preston Hall, the Fludds of Gore Court, and the Barnhams of Boughton Monchelsea Place met together at Maidstone and appealed by letter to the influential gentry of the district. "All the gentlemen of the country," they wrote to the delinquent Sir Robert Filmer at East Sutton Place, "both East and West are engaged, . . . and we hope that you, who have been ever a well-wisher to such an act, will not now draw back."[1] The rendezvous of the region, under pretence of a horse-race, was at Coxheath, on the brow of the unenclosed heights above Linton and Boughton Monchelsea. Thither the squire and rector of Addington in Holmesdale sent their tenants and relatives, furnished with arms and money, persuading the villagers both in public and private to support the petition. They were followed by seven of the Tomlyn family, both gentlemen and yeomen, "plundering the well-affected" as they went. They were also joined by many of the minor gentry of the district, such as the Maplisdens and Bestbeeches, who had sat on the County Committee but had suffered from the recent prosecutions of the Accounts Committee.[2]

Yet another group of petitioners gathered in the valleys of the downland north and east of Maidstone under the wing of "wilful and purse-proud" old Sir Edward Hales of Tunstall Place. This wily and ambitious plutocrat still posed as a parliamentarian, but he allowed his grandson to finance the petitioners (it was claimed) to the extent of £80,000. Having acquired by marriage much of the inheritance of the Cromer family and the recusant Wottons of Boughton Malherbe, the Haleses were among the wealthiest gentry in the county, and much the richest in these rather infertile valleys of the Downs.[3]

[1] KCA, U. 120. C. 4–6; U. 120. C. 5/2.

[2] *Clarke Papers*, II, p. 16; SP. 23: G: 9, ff. 30, 31; SP. 23: G: 158, ff. 138, 139; CCAM, *passim*.

[3] Dean and Chapter Library, Canterbury, Hales MSS; *L'Estrange his Vindication*.

They were supported by their friends and kinsmen the Haleses of Faversham and Hugessens of Lynsted, and by many obscure parochial gentry like the Adyes of Doddington, the Harfields of Huckinge, the Bunces of Throwley, Otterden, and Stalisfield, and many another minor Kentish family in the remote parishes of Selling, Sharsted, Wormshill, Stockbury, and Boughton-under-Blean.[1] Other petitioners in this area came from the marshland parishes to the north of Tunstall, such as Teynham, Luddenham, and Oare, and from the islands of Elmley, Sheppey, and Harty. Many of these gentry, like the Pordages of Rodmersham and Ospringe and the Bryans of Luddenham Manor, were recusants; for under the influence of the Ropers of Lynsted this was the principal catholic region of Kent. From Watling Street a number of Cavaliers travelling from London to Dover turned aside through the orchards to Tunstall, and a handful of "outlandish men," some of them family friends like Roger L'Estrange of Norfolk, crossed the water from Essex and East Anglia.[2] From the time of the king's defeat, as the eyes of the royalists began to turn towards France and Holland, there was "great resort of ill-affected persons in Kent, it being the place to which all resort that either go beyond the sea or return. . . ."[3]

The three principal problems that faced the Kentish petitioners initially were the capture of the county magazines, the seizure of the castles round the coast, and the securing of the navy lying in the Medway and the Downs. In each of these tasks their success was facilitated by the defection of the parliamentarians who had been left in command. At Westerham the committeeman William Bothby delivered up to them the "whole magazine of arms left in his charge. . . ." At Aylesford Friary some of the garrison "crept away" and others were

[1] SP. 23: G: 158, ff. 109, 110; CCAM, pp. 1211 sqq., 1315–16, 1326. Typically, John Adye sent his servant, John Milburne, to the rendezvous with ten days' pay, and after the rebels' defeat gave him £2 "for his loss and suffering in the said service."

[2] SP. 23: G: 158, ff. 95, 98, 108; *L'Estrange his Vindication*; Clarendon, *History of the Rebellion*, ed. Macray, 1888, IV, p. 334.

[3] CSPD, 1649–50, p. 140. The quotation is from a letter of May 1649, but the conditions described had obtained since the king's defeat and the prince's departure overseas.

"chased . . . out of the county." At Canterbury, Scots' Hall, and Faversham the magazines were secured with equal ease, and at Sittingbourne the country people "rose upon [Sir Michael Livesey] and chased him divers miles," imprisoning Nicholas Bix and seizing the magazine left in his care.[1] At Rochester the rebels set a guard on the bridge, armed "the streets in the manner of a court of guard at every door," secured the *Fellowship*, *Sovereign*, and *Prince*, removed the arms, ordnance, ammunition, and victuals from the ships, engaged with the self-appointed commissioners of the dockyard and seamen, who unanimously joined them, and besieged Captain Peter Pett in the dockyard. In the Thames-side parishes, stores, arms, and shipping were also taken and roads and river were blockaded. As Sir Anthony Weldon helplessly watched these latter proceedings from his house at Swanscombe, he told the Committee at Derby House that he expected "hourly to be seized, which must cost the seizers, or some of them, their lives, for I shall not be their prisoner to be led in triumph as poor Mr Box [Bix]" was: he would certainly be lynched. Around the coast the castles garrisoned for parliament were "by the concurrence of those within invited to the common interest of the country." Upnor and Tonbridge castles were also delivered up, whilst at Leeds, where some of the gentry were still imprisoned for their part in the riot at Canterbury the previous Christmas, the garrison was on the verge of mutiny.[2]

Of all the strongholds in the county, the only place left to protect parliament's friends was Dover Castle; and this was virtually surrounded by the rebel leaders of the lathe of St Augustine. In the town of Dover itself the petitioners were led by Arnold Braemes. When Captain Brafield, the parliamentarian governor, sent down for supplies, he found "nothing but delays of purpose that [the castle] might be destitute of

[1] CCAM, pp. 1216, 1230; BL, Clarendon MS 31, ff. 88, 96; E. 445. 13; E. 448. 5; *Clarke Papers*, II, pp. 14, 16 ("Box" is probably a mistranscription for Bix).

[2] E. 443. 41; CJ, v, p. 606; *Clarke Papers*, II, p. 15; E. 445. 9; E. 445. 21; CSPD, 1648–9, pp. 79, 80, 88; BL, Clarendon MS 31, f. 96; E. 448. 5; E. 449. 34, p. 9; Carter, pp. 54–8, 66–7.

victual when the intended siege should come." Brafield was forced upon his own credit to get in "meal, wheat, . . . salt, beer, cheese, butter, peas, and sheep," while the petitioners' forces, led by Anthony Hamond and Sir Richard Hardres, approached Dover from the north, and took the outlying forts of Archcliffe and Dane's Mount. Within the castle was one of the few members of the County Committee still loyal to parliament, Sir Henry Heyman of Somerfield, who, under pretence of entering the castle for refuge, quietly took control from Brafield, organized its defence, and skilfully played for time by entering into negotiations with Sir Richard Hardres. Hardres and Heyman were near kinsmen of one another and had formerly sat together on the County Committee. The blunt honesty of the former, however, was no match for the dissimulation of his crafty cousin. Their correspondence is amusing. In a series of the politest possible letters, Heyman affected to disown any parliamentarian sympathies, declaring that the

"burden of intolerable guilt of innocent blood and unparalleled misery of this gasping nation had overwhelmed his conscience with a cloud of despair of any other safety than the old Roman rule, *Per scelera semper, sceleribus tutum est iter*; knowing indeed himself to have been as zealous a promoter and accessory to the calamity as any confederate in the Grand Junto. . . ."

And yet he was unable to perceive, he said, the wisdom of the petitioners in "drawing together in a warlike posture. But you are abroad," he added ironically, "I cooped up, and so you may know more than I can apprehend, till a new light, which is said in this age to be frequent, appears to me; however, I pray the Lord heartily it may be for the kingdom's good. . . . My respects," he concluded, "to all our good friends."[1]

While these abortive negotiations were in progress at Dover, news suddenly came that the fleet in the Downs had dismissed Rainsborowe in a pinnace to parliament and declared themselves for Kent and the king. The long-simmering discontents

[1] BL, Tanner MS 57, ff. 102, 104; E. 448. 5; E. 449. 34, p. 9; Carter, pp. 48 sqq.

of the navy need not engage our attention here. They were connected with the displacement of the earl of Warwick as admiral, the withdrawal of Sir William Batten's commission, and the appointment of Rainsborowe, a landsman, to succeed him. The mutineers were not fundamentally royalist, however, and they did not cast off all subjection to parliament. "That which is the greatest motive to the disturbance of the seamen is that these parts are wholly for the king," Rainsborowe told the Admiralty Commissioners. They had been encouraged to mutiny by Sir Henry Palmer and Thomas Harfleete of Bekesbourne, and Richard and Robert Bargrave of Bridge. The ships concerned were largely manned by Kentishmen and were in close touch with the Kentish inhabitants ashore. To many of the sailors Palmer, as a former naval official, was already well known. Taking advantage of Rainsborowe's absence on shore, Palmer and his colleagues smuggled letters and copies of the County petition into the ships, inviting them to join with them. As soon as the ships "saw but one troop of horse on the shore, they rose instantly, secured their commanders, and declared themselves for our petition." The four Kentish gentry boarded the ships, and agreed with the men to "communicate counsels and designs, and not to resolve without the joint consent of both parties, and further to defend and save harmless one another . . . with the utmost hazard of our lives and fortunes." When this news of the naval revolt reached Dover, it made all the town "drunk with joy." Sir Richard Hardres left a small blockading force before the castle, contemning it as a "place of little concernment," and "with colours flying, of white answerable to the candid innocence of a peace-making engagement," marched to the "business of far greater concernment" off Deal. "I am right glad," replied Sir Henry Heyman, with a parting shot, "to hear . . . that you now give the true value to this place."[1]

As the Kentish petitioners grew more confident of success, however, the fundamental disunity in their ranks began to come to light. The question which hitherto neither Charles I nor parliament had been able to answer began to trouble them

[1] E. 448. 5; BL, Clarendon MS 31, ff. 96–7, 108; E. 445. 30; E. 445. 32; BM, Add. MS 5494, f. 288; HMC, XIII, i, p. 457; Carter, pp. 40, 51.

also. In a county with no single dominant family, who was to be the leader of the shire? The presence of half-a-dozen rival leaders, scattered through several different regions of the county, led to constant friction and jealousy. When Sir Edward Hales and his grandson at Tunstall dispatched invitations to ask the city of Canterbury to join them in massing and forming the county's divided forces, the city replied that "they would look to themselves. It should seem," added Roger L'Estrange, a friend of the family, in recording the incident, that "there were others of that opinion too."[1] In order to counteract these divisive tendencies, the petitioners eventually agreed to form a committee of the gentry, or rather a couple of committees, sitting at Rochester and Canterbury. These two bodies, comprising 40 or 50 members apiece, met daily and reached decisions "by resolution upon the question." Each member was required to bind himself "not to discover or betray any debates or resolutions" of the Committee. Of one of their meetings an agenda paper has survived, and the following is a summary of it: to appoint officers of trained bands and auxiliaries; to appoint one officer to deliver out arms, only to deliver them when well-informed who demands them, and to note their names; whether it is necessary to fortify Rochester with a line of forts and to garrison Tonbridge Castle; to secure the chief opponents of the petition; to decide which bridges to fortify; and to take special order regarding intelligence.[2]

In practice, the formation of these two Committees rather canalized than healed the differences between the petitioners. Probably they helped to overcome the divisions between the different regions of the county; but their incessant wrangles

[1] *L'Estrange his Vindication*. The independence of these regions is shown by their ignorance of each other's plans. L'Estrange's account shows little acquaintance with events further east in Kent or in the Stour Valley, which occurred simultaneously with those in north-east Kent with which he was connected.

[2] E. 445. 40 (2); Carter, *passim*; *L'Estrange his Vindication*; HMC, XIII, i, p. 460. The text I describe as an 'agenda paper' is part of a tract printed from papers found in the pockets of prisoners taken at Maidstone. It is not described as an agenda paper in the tract, but internal evidence suggests that this was its origin. Since no other papers of the Committee have survived we know very little of its functioning.

brought into the open the cleavages between the moderates, the Cavaliers, and the outsiders who had arrived from other counties. The chief troublemakers were these outsiders. They came into Kent from many different parts of the kingdom and even from overseas. Sir Robert Tracy was a Gloucestershire man; William Filiol was of Dorset; Sir George Lisle came from Essex; Sir Barnaby Scudamore had been the king's governor at Hereford; and Sir Bernard Gascoigne was an Italian. When the royalists were banished from London by parliamentary ordinance, this group was joined by bands of Londoners who despoiled the inhabitants of Deptford, blockaded the river, seized ships, stores, and arms, and secured Woolwich Dockyard. Finally, several hundred watermen and apprentices came into the county from the capital.[1]

Although the Cavaliers from other counties never numbered more than a tithe of the Kentishmen, they increased daily as the news of the "flames in Kent" spread abroad. What they lacked in numbers, moreover, they made up in violence and abandon. Some of them came into the county without money, and expected the generous young Edward Hales to provide for them; others came without horse or arms, and could not be furnished; whilst all required shelter and a share in the county's sorely taxed food-supplies. Though there were "persons of skill in the art of war" among them, "yet many of them expecting to be courted into the business, not being taken notice of" either returned home again or remained to plague the Committee with their demands. Some, in fact, like Sir George Lisle, were men of high character and integrity; but many were "lofty, desperate, and discontented-minded spirits," and the popular verdict described one and all as a "company of strange officers and soldiers." Sir Gamaliel Dudley was denominated a "most vile profane wretch," and the rebels from the London suburbs as "those mad souls." The only support which the outsiders found in the petitioners' Committee came from Roger L'Estrange, who was a bosom-friend of Edward Hales, and from the relatively small group of Kentish Cavaliers. The link between the local Cavaliers and the

[1] E. 445. 22; E. 446. 18; CCC, p. 2847; BL, Clarendon MS 31, f. 92; E. 446. 20; E. 445. 21.

outsiders was partly a personal one, since many of them had been together at Oxford; it was also one of principle, since both groups saw the necessity of co-ordinating the events in Kent with similar risings elsewhere, in particular with the plans of the royalists in London and the activities of Langdale and Hamilton in the North of England.[1]

As we have seen, there was little real sympathy between these Cavalier groups and the moderates of the county. Adversity had driven them together, but it could not unite them. The moderates were not without a certain sentimental attachment to the king, and if he had appeared in the county they would have welcomed him. When one Cornelius Evans landed at Sandwich, and called himself Prince Charles, he was lodged in state at the house of one of the jurats, clothed by local gentlewomen, feasted with delicacies "like a prince," and liberally provided with money. The local people flocked to kiss his hand, and the mayor "delivered him up his staff with great joy."[2] Yet the moderates had no real wish to be drawn into an organized royalist army. Rather than "disgust their enemies," they refused to force the negative engagement of the Cavaliers—that is, the promise not to bear arms—upon the few remaining Kentish parliamentarians of the county: for no man should be disarmed or penalized, they thought, merely for refusing to subscribe the petition. They went so far as to make it a capital offence throughout their quarters "to disturb the interest of any [man] for his affection to the parliament." For the most part they refused to have anything to do with the unrest in East Anglia, the Welsh Marches, or the South-West, though many counties borrowed copies of the Kentish petition. Although "pressed hourly almost" by L'Estrange's friends "to dispatch commissioners to negotiate an association" with their neighbours in Essex and Surrey, they neglected the construction of the proposed bridge of boats with Essex, and delayed joining the Surrey petitioners until they were forced to submit to parliament.[3]

[1] E. 445. 22; E. 449. 34, p. 11; Carter, p. 96; E. 446. 18; E. 445. 30; cf. E. 446. 29.

[2] BL, Clarendon MS 31, f. 97; E. 445. 13; Carter, pp. 42–6; E. 443. 26.

[3] *L'Estrange his Vindication.*

Aware of these differences between the Cavalier clique and the bulk of the petitioners, and advised by the scattered remnants of the parliamentarian County Committee that moderation might regain the allegiance of the latter, parliament made tentative efforts to play upon these divisions and detach the moderates from the Cavaliers. In its first attempt, three members of the Commons who were also members of the Committee were sent down to Maidstone with a force of 800 foot, and an offer to redress "the peevish differences betwixt the county and the Committee, . . . and consideration of all their regular requests for the future." After some desultory skirmishing with the petitioners, the committeemen arranged an armistice upon the basis of the *status quo*, with a view to discussing terms of surrender. Unhappily, the committeemen were neither trusted by the petitioners nor wholly loyal to parliament. The armistice was observed only at Maidstone, not at Canterbury or Rochester, and a group of irresponsible Cavaliers ordered their men to pillage the committeemen's lodgings and encouraged the parliamentarian troops to mutiny. Their efforts were so successful that within two days, so it was said, "there were not six persons left together" of the 800 parliamentarian soldiers. The committeemen were forced to return to London and the negotiations collapsed.[1]

A few days later, however, a sudden turn of fortune gave parliament a second opportunity to appease the petitioners. The particular circumstance that induced the earl of Thanet, at this moment, to desert the royalist cause is obscure. But although Thanet's descendants, with unconscious irony, assumed the words *Semper fidelis* as the family motto, in memory of him, this "ambidextrous" brother-in-law of Sir Edward Dering had in fact deserted the king on a former occasion, in 1643. He had already paid an immense composition fine, amounting to no less than £9,000, and was doubtless reluctant to pay more. While he was hesitating whether to continue to support the petitioners, "divers gentlemen living in those parts where he dwells came to him and [said] . . . that if they may

[1] *Ibid.*; E. 446. 1; KCA, U. 120. C 4–6; E. 445. 18; Rushworth, VII, p. 1129. Apparently these deserters joined the petitioners. The son of one of the M.P.'s and the father of another were already among the rebels.

have liberty to petition the parliament, which they claim as their privilege, and may have indemnity for what is passed, it will satisfy them. . . ." With this message Thanet called upon his cousin the earl of Pembroke in London, and he, as the absentee lord lieutenant, pleaded the cause of Kent and of Thanet in the House of Lords. Meanwhile, seeing they had been deceived into offensive action against parliament by the 'foreigners,' a group of petitioners in north-west Kent underwent a similar change of heart, and deputed one of their ministers, Mr Sherman of Lee-by-Wickham, to convey a similar message to the House of Commons. Within a few hours Thanet and Sherman were sent back into the county with an offer of indemnity, and permission for a small body of Kentish gentry to present the petition, on condition that the present "tumultuary gathering" was immediately dispersed and the petitioners departed to their dwellings. At the same time copies of these terms were dispatched into every lathe of the county. In the earl of Thanet's region and in the north-west of the county the terms were accepted without delay, and most of the petitioners laid down their arms and returned home.[1]

The defection of Thanet, whether or not his motives were sincere, brought to a head the crisis between the Cavaliers and the moderates of the county. Many of the latter were inclined to sympathize with Thanet, but they still hoped for a favourable hearing of their grievances in parliament. They endeavoured to negotiate with the "wavering city of London" for permission to march through the city and present their petition to the two Houses. "Seeing the city a little . . . inclining to favour, if not to assist the Kentishmen," however, parliament promised to take the Londoners' own grievances into consideration, and the desired permission was refused by the corporation. The moderates of the county were thus left at a stand, since it was impossible within the time allowed by parliament to call a "meeting of the gentry of the [whole] county, being now so far distant in several places. . . ."[2]

[1] E. 446. 1; *L'Estrange his Vindication*; CSPD, 1648–9, pp. 75–6; E. 445. 13; E. 445. 18; LJ, x, pp. 282, 286; CJ, v, pp. 572–3.

[2] BL, Tanner MS 57, f. 135; Clarendon MS 31, ff. 105, 110; LJ, x, p. 287; E. 445. 40 (2); E. 446. 16; E. 446. 28. A "great combustion" in

The initiative was seized, for the moment, by the Cavaliers. They had for some time been in touch with their countryman, Lord Culpeper, at St Germain, offering their lives and fortunes to restore his Majesty, and demanding "all possible assistance to be ready when we call for it. . . ." Their desire for commissions, directions, and supplies had been favourably received at the prince's court, and the duke of York, amid much rejoicing, had been declared admiral of the revolted ships. With these promises behind them, the Cavaliers could not countenance the moderates' compromising attitude. At the instigation of the irrepressible Roger L'Estrange, they returned an answer to parliament's offer of indemnity which purported to represent the sense of the whole county. Utterly spurning the accusations of "tumultuary proceedings," they declared that the county could not consider disarming while the "enraged Committee"—if only a rump of it—remained in being. "Tumults indeed there have been," they admitted,

"but not on our part. Horrid, unheard of violences complotted, menaced, nay in measure executed, by troops of furious precipitate persons upon us, and all this for but intending to desire not to be for ever miserable. At last, the county makes head, and as informed with one soul, rises to the redemption of their expiring liberties, which with much ado they had imperfectly recovered. . . . As to the petition, it shall not be presented by above twenty persons; but to deliver up our strengths and disband our forces, in this juncture of affairs, we humbly conceive neither secure nor honourable; and to conditions either unsafe or unhandsome we stand utterly disinclined."[1]

---

the Common Council, between Philip Skippon, who was "totally bent to engage against" Kent, and the "generality of the freemen," who were "wholly for an association" with the county, was said to have been avoided only by parliament's "great condescension" in acceding to the city's desires.

[1] BL, Clarendon MS 31, ff. 96–7, 108; *L'Estrange his Vindication*. From its style, this answer of the Cavaliers was clearly penned by L'Estrange himself. The gentry of East Kent, led by Sir Thomas Peyton, expressed themselves more mildly, but being "linked to the service by the golden chain of religion and loyalty," they were equally firm: "saving to ourselves," they said, "always the liberty of preserving the most ancient and inviolate freedoms of

This high-flying attitude of the Cavaliers for the moment silenced the moderates; but it only papered over the cracks in the petitioners' ranks. When parliament retaliated by ordering Fairfax to advance into the county on 26th May, the rebel gentry of Kent were left with only four days to mould their enthusiastic but undisciplined followers into an organized army. The gathering at Blackheath "could not be altered nor disappointed on a sudden because of the extent of the county." Yet everyone who came to the rendezvous near Rochester still considered his followers as entirely at his own disposal, and subject to his own discipline, and not to the petitioners' Committee. Within the Committee, or Council as it was now called, Roger L'Estrange had pleaded in vain for the inclusion of more royalists from other counties; for the reduction of the membership of the Council to a manageable size; for strict secrecy in its debates; and for the formation of a separate "cabinet council." He had also moved "that it might be published at the head of every troop and company . . . that we were no longer petitioners, but soldiers," and that countrymen who deserted to attend to "greater business at home" should give up their weapons to necessitous outsiders. No doubt aware that these proposals were an attempt to wrest the leadership from their own hands, the moderates of the county instantly retaliated by declaring L'Estrange "a traitor, and to be excluded from the Council" altogether.[1]

The foreigners thereupon declared, probably at L'Estrange's instigation, "that if the country will not stand to them, they will immediately possess themselves of all the castles and strongholds" in order to secure a landing-place for the troops from overseas. They also sent to France and Holland for

this county, we must desire your lordships to put a fair interpretation upon our . . . continuing within the safeguard of our arms."—BM, Add. MS 44846, f. 44 v; E. 446. 1, p. 9. The signatories to this letter to the Derby House Committee included Sir Thomas Peyton (of Knowlton), Anthony Hamond (St Albans Court), Sir Thomas Palmer (Wingham), Sir James Hales (The Dongeon), Sir Thomas Godfrey (Heppington), Sir John and James Darell (Calehill), Thomas Hardres (Upper Hardres), and six former committeemen.

[1] E. 449. 34, pp. 6, 11; Carter, pp. 79–80, and cf. pp. 82, 86 *et passim*; *L'Estrange his Vindication.*

10,000 arms and a "great proportion of ammunition of all sorts." Meanwhile, the country gentry "were then considering, and but then, how to form their forces into an army," lacking "all order, and form, and directions; everyone bidding and forbidding as they thought best. . . ." Some marched with the petition as far as Dartford, while the infantry of East Kent were only able to reach Rochester, and the horse got no further than Sittingbourne. When Matthew Carter took the county muster at Rochester, he found no fewer than 3,000 men were absent, strung out across the county from place to place, at Canterbury, Maidstone, Sittingbourne, Sandwich, and Dover. At Rochester itself, the headquarters, the horse were foolishly quartered at large in adjacent villages, instead of being gathered in camp. And in their very bosoms, said L'Estrange, were spies of both Fairfax and Sir Anthony Weldon, "whose infusions were eminently significant in all your consults: still some trick or other to spill more time even then, when every remaining moment was worth a kingdom."[1] Poor L'Estrange! The people of Kent were enough to make him despair.

Immediate disaster was only staved off by the unexpected appearance in Kent of the royalist earl of Norwich. Effective leadership was the rebels' essential problem, and for various reasons none of the men who had hitherto attempted to lead the county had proved acceptable. The earl of Thanet had deserted; the duke of Richmond had been over-cautious; young Edward Hales was inexperienced; and Roger L'Estrange, as a Norfolkman, was unacceptable to the local community. Whether Norwich was specifically sent to seize command by

[1] *Ibid.*; *Clarke Papers*, II, p. 22; Carter, pp. 55, 75–9, 86; E. 449. 34, pp. 11, 12. The total force of which Carter was quarter-master general comprised nominally about 7,000 foot and an unspecified number of horse. In all probability there were about a further 2,000 men at Dartford and 4,000 at Canterbury. These, of course, were *nominal* figures: one cannot regard all these men as fully armed and trained or properly clad and quartered. They had only been enrolled at most for a few weeks, apart from those who had formerly belonged to the parliamentarian regiments of the county. Regarded in this light, and considering the confusion of the times and brevity of time allowed them, it is remarkable, not that the rebels were disunited, but that there was any effective opposition to the New Model Army. In fact a parliamentarian source (E. 446. 11) confessed that Fairfax's army found the "Kentishmen better prepared than they had expected."

the royalists in London, as L'Estrange and Clarendon supposed, or whether his arrival "was as absolute an accident as could be, . . . being in his journey to Sussex," as his friend Matthew Carter asserted, it is now difficult to say. Possibly he was staking all in a desperate gamble to retrieve his shattered family fortunes. The foreigners at any rate welcomed him; and as the son-in-law of Lord Abergavenny of Birling Manor and the father-in-law of Edward Scott of Scots' Hall, he was also well known in the county. Though "he had no experience or knowledge of the war, nor knew how to exercise the office . . . of general," his "frolic and pleasant humour" proved "most apt to reconcile factions," and he listened without partiality to the suggestions and complaints of all parties. At the main rendezvous on Burham Heath, between Rochester and Maidstone, Norwich was appointed general on 29th May, "with mutual and equal satisfaction," amid a crowd, it was said, of 10,000 rebels. The foreigners, along with the Kentish gentry, were admitted to the new general's Council of War; commissioners were at last admitted into the county from the rebels in Essex; and, according to the optimistic Roger L'Estrange, the earl of Norwich "wanted not 48 hours of giving the king his crown again."[1]

(iii) *The Fight for the County*

Those forty-eight hours, however, were not given him. The county had refused the overtures of parliament and must reap the fruit of its refusal. When the Houses heard that the rebellious petitioners were forming an army under the earl of Norwich, and "that by the said party some maritime forts were seized, others beleaguered, and divers ships . . . withdrawn from their obedience," they voted "that they do leave the whole managing of the business of Kent" to the general. Warwick was dispatched to regain the ships along the coast; Captain Bethell was "desired to rally what ships he can and

[1] *L'Estrange his Vindication*; Carter, pp. 81–5; Clarendon, *History of the Rebellion*, ed. Macray, 1888, IV, pp. 343, 355–6. According to Clarendon, Edward Hales's leadership was opposed by his grandfather; but this seems to have been merely a political ruse of the cynical old Sir Edward Hales.

keep them firm" at Portsmouth; and Colonel Robert Hammond was ordered to prevent any danger in the Isle of Wight. On the day appointed for the petitioners' meeting Fairfax occupied Blackheath, and on the next morning began his famous march into Kent.[1] The rebels at Rochester received parliament's order at midnight on 30th May, and "this grain of paper quite turned the balance and absolutely altered the constitution of the general interest" of the county. The momentary agreement in which Norwich had been elected general vanished. Factious parties who "had not yet so clearly laid down their powers," and supposed that nothing must be done without them, beset the new general. The Cavaliers, led by L'Estrange, sent a futile letter of defiance to Fairfax and foolishly tried to seduce his soldiers by offering to pay their arrears.[2] The county gentry, "whose relations and habitudes with the people gives them the greatest interest amongst them," did not like "the peremptory declared engagement into a war, as disagreeing from the first principles of the country's motion, and in altering the interest of the cause. . . ." Angry at moves which only exacerbated Fairfax and parliament, and declaring that they had not "taken arms to affront others, but to defend ourselves," the moderates therefore again sought permission for ten gentlemen to present the petition, and desired Fairfax to mediate with parliament. When these terms were refused, the moderates themselves divided into two parties. About one thousand, met by Fairfax marching to Blackheath, refused, as mere petitioners, to engage in bloodshed, and laid down their arms. The rest, retreating east of the Medway, reluctantly threw in their lot with the earl of Norwich.[3]

Meanwhile, Fairfax sent a regiment under Colonel Gibbon through the Weald towards Dover and advanced with his main

[1] E. 446. 1; CSPD, 1648–9, pp. 84–7, 90; E. 449. 34, p. 6.

[2] Carter, pp. 77, 92; *L'Estrange his Vindication*; E. 445. 43; *The joint Declaration of the several Counties of Kent, Essex, Middlesex, Surrey, unto the Soldiers of the Army* . . ., 1648. It was, of course, a piece of bravado to call this last document a 'joint' declaration of the four counties. From the style, it was almost certainly drafted by l'Estrange himself, and Essex, Middlesex, and Surrey had little or no part in it.

[3] E. 449. 34, p. 11; HMC, xii, ix, p. 21; BL, Tanner MS 57, f. 130; Clarendon MS 31, f. 105; E. 446. 1; E. 453. 37; E. 445. 32.

force of about 7,000 men against Rochester. All the way along the route he was beset by sharp skirmishing. At Stone Bridge, a hundred rebels were taken prisoner following a stout fight in defence of the pass. Trees and branches were cut down by the rebels to block the roads, and the bridge at Rochester was barricaded.[1] Before reaching Gravesend, however, Fairfax changed his tactics. Sending only a small force to dispute Rochester, he turned southwards with his main body, and threading his way through the maze of wooded lanes in the hills north of Wrotham, came down the steep escarpment into Holmesdale near Ryarsh. As he marched through the quiet downland about Meopham and Luddesdown, he found the terrified countryfolk had fled; for some of their friends and neighbours had been shot by the parliamentarian troops, and none of them had ever seen warfare until that day. Between the deep folds in the downs Fairfax's scouts had observed through their glasses the enemy encampment on Burham Heath, eight miles eastward beyond the Medway. But the general and his army were themselves hidden by thick woods of hazel, yew, and whitebeam, and the rebels knew nothing of his movements until, late in the evening of the 31st May, the people of Maidstone discovered that the parliamentarians were encamped four miles to the west of the town, on East Malling Heath. During the night, the townsmen threw up hasty earthworks and barricades in the streets. Thinking that Fairfax was bound to cross the river either by the town bridge or at Aylesford, four miles downstream, they set a strong guard on the river. Once again, however, Fairfax changed his tactics and deceived them. Sending a small party as a feint towards Aylesford, he still continued southward, under cover of woodland, crossed the Medway by the next bridge upstream at East Farleigh, turned eastward towards Maidstone, and overwhelmed the rebels' guard by the bridge over the River Loose, one mile from the town. About seven o'clock in the evening of the 1st June, the

[1] BL, Clarendon MS 31, ff. 99, 105; Tanner MS 57, ff. 119, 130, 132; E. 446. 11; CCAM, p. 1229. Some sources put Fairfax's force as low as 4,000; a neutral letter (E. 445. 35) reckons it as high as 8,000 foot alone, but as this same author estimates the Kentish forces at 14,000, he may be suspected of exaggeration.

townsmen of Maidstone suddenly found Fairfax on their flank, by the barricades they had hastily thrown up, at the bottom of Stone Street.[1]

There were but two regiments in the town: that of Sir William Brockman, Dering's brother-in-law, and that of Sir John Mayney, his cousin. Hurriedly, the two colonels sent out messengers to Rochester and Aylesford for reinforcements, and from the latter village a large contingent swelled their numbers to about 2,000 men.[2] Troops were placed in all the shops and houses, and in each door and window of the streets, while ordnance were set pointing down the cross-roads in the centre of the town. As the lowering clouds began to break in torrential rain, the townsmen shouted "For God, King Charles, and Kent," and the storm of Maidstone began. Every street, house, and turning, said a parliamentarian, was disputed. Every inch was gained with difficulty: a defence extremely violent, an eye-witness observed, none more resolutely maintained since the war began.[3]

The storm continued till midnight; but eventually the superior numbers of the parliamentarians began to tell, and the

[1] SP. 23: G: 158, ff. 91, 92, 227–9; E. 445. 26; Carter, p. 87; Whitelock, II, p. 323.

[2] Some parliamentarian sources put the figure as high as 3,000.

[3] Carter pp. 87–91; E. 446. 11; E. 445. 42; Whitelock, II, p. 323. For other accounts of the storming of Maidstone, which Fairfax himself confessed was one of the most violent battles he had ever experienced, see J. M. Russell, *The History of Maidstone*, 1881, pp. 260 sqq.; Robert Furley, *A History of the Weald of Kent*, 1874, II, ii, pp. 545–9; H. F. Abell, *Kent and the Great Civil War*, 1901, pp. 213–19. According to E.445.42 the force of over 2,000 men in the town included few countrymen, but principally seamen, watermen, and Londoners, "chosen out as the only fighting men they had amongst them;" but this is not generally confirmed by other sources, and certainly Mayney's and Brockman's regiments would have been composed principally of countrymen. Neither is S. R. Gardiner's remark (*Civil War*, IV, 1901, pp. 140–1) that at Maidstone "Fairfax, it seemed, had to contend against the majority of the landowners and a great part of the middle class in the towns, not against the bulk of the country population" borne out by the evidence as a whole. The above account of the storming of Maidstone differs in some details from Gardiner's reconstruction of the event (which, however, is in general sound: *ibid.*, pp. 137–42); but I have utilized many references in contemporary newspapers which Gardiner does not seem to have consulted.

delays and follies in Norwich's camp on Burham Heath rendered any possibility of succour out of the question. First the frolic earl ordered advance, then he ordered retreat, and finally he called a council. At the council

"Colonel Culpeper propounded to draw out horse and foot to a man, incontinently, and fight them; some cried, 'Twas too late; others that their men were weary, and could not march; some had not their regiments within call; others not their resolutions; . . . some were of opinion 'twas best for them to do as well as they could."

Then, about midnight, the rebels at Rochester received news "that the town [of Maidstone] was forced." Three hundred rebels had been killed. Many fled away into the country under cover of rain and darkness and hid in the woods, hopyards, and fields. Several hundred, with 500 horse and 3,000 arms, were recaptured and locked up in the great town church of All Saints; for Leeds Castle and Westenhanger House were already overcrowded with rebel gentry. Sir John Mayney was reported slain—wrongly, as it turned out—and Sir William Brockman and 160 other officers and gentlemen were taken prisoner, including Norwich's own son-in-law, Edward Scott. The next day news came into Kent that other shires were now rising to their aid; that the county of Essex was sending troops at last; and that the king had attempted to escape from Carisbrooke Castle and join them. The news, of course, even if it was correct, came too late. In London the puritan ministers gave thanks in the churches for the providential destruction of the rebels at Maidstone.[1]

The remaining rebels under the earl of Norwich were left entirely without plans, and great fear fell on "the hearts of the whole county." By a "silent and sudden counsel of their own breasts, every man began to think of his particular safety;"

[1] *L'Estrange his Vindication*; E. 445. 40; BL, Clarendon MS 31, ff. 100, 109; E. 446. 11; E. 445. 30; E. 446. 10. Some sources put the Kentish losses higher: E. 446. 10 says 1,500 were taken prisoner, 160 officers and gentlemen, and 500 horse, together with 4,000 arms, 40 barrels of gunpowder, and papers of instructions, lists, and "papers of correspondency." Some of the latter are printed in E. 445. 40 (2).

"the generality, utterly repenting of the enterprise," crept home to their wives and children, and the country people did "exceedingly cry *peccavi*." As in former insurrections, it proved impossible to hold the connexions of the county gentry together when the immediate occasion of revolt was removed and the excitement of the county abated. Three thousand rebels, remembering their neglected fields and sodden hay-crops, quietly returned home. Young Edward Hales and his family, with Sir Anthony Aucher of Bishopsbourne and Roger L'Estrange, fled to Sandwich and took ship for Holland. At Rochester, to the old disputes of moderates and Cavaliers, were now added the recriminations of defeat. An attempt to seize the ships in the Medway was thwarted by Peter Pett, and Norwich was compelled to abandon the town. When Fairfax entered, he found the famous bridge over the river broken down, the rebels fled, the people very full of discontent, and the women "with curses in their mouths against Goring [Norwich], Hales, and Compton, who had engaged their husbands, and now betrayed them, cursing them for bringing in a company of strange officers that were not known to the country [*sc.*, county]. . . ."[1]

Nominally, there were still about 6,000 rebels under arms, and these now divided into two groups. Unwilling to be shut up in East Kent with the forces under Sir Richard Hardres, a minority followed Norwich and decided to join the insurrection now gathering strength in Essex. At Gravesend, they found the ferry boats in the hands of parliament and the fort at Tilbury garrisoned by Captain Temple. Upstream, wide marshes hemmed in the river and rendered a crossing impossible. When they reached Dartford, therefore, still hoping to benefit from the divisions in the Common Council of the city, some of the rebels once more appealed to the lord mayor for permission to pass through London. Marching the whole of the next night and day, without any refreshment or repose at all, they reached Greenwich and encamped in the royal Park. While Norwich, under cover of darkness, crossed the river

[1] E. 446. 9; E. 446. 11; E. 449. 34, p. 12; E. 446. 10; *L'Estrange his Vindication*; Carter, pp. 98–9; E. 447. 15; E. 447. 28; E. 446. 18, pp. 4–5.

alone to sound the ominous silence of Essex, news came that the lord mayor of London had sent their letter unopened to the Speaker of the House of Commons. The gates of the city had been shut against them, and a body of Fairfax's horse was in pursuit.[1] Troubled at the prospect of leaving their native county, and "discontented that they might not march to the rescue of their friends" in East Kent, a further group of Kentish gentry now seceded, "crying out they were betrayed." Just as the men of Kent had refused to leave their homeland at the order of parliament during the war, and the men of Cornwall had refused to cross the Tamar at the command of the king, so now these local people refused to follow the Cavaliers across the Thames. Soon after they left Greenwich, "one riding into the Park in the dark of the night, told the soldiers that they were in very great danger, and that their officers wished them to shift for themselves. . . ." Suddenly the whole encampment was stricken with panic. Some "timorous spirits" stole away; some seized on the boats by the shore and got over the river; others jumped into the water and swam across or were drowned; whilst the horse, half swimming, half riding, followed them. By dawn, fifteen hundred men had reached the opposite shore—only to find themselves, not amongst their friends in Essex, as they supposed, but facing a body of Tower Hamleteers at Bow. Hastily rallying his men, the able Sir William Compton managed to beat his way through the ranks of the enemy and form some sort of order among his bedraggled troops. Met by Norwich as he returned from "agitat[ing] the business with the gentlemen of Essex," and fired at by parliamentarian soldiers nearly all the way, the little force of rebels then began its march to Chelmsford and Colchester.[2]

The famous siege of Colchester lies outside the scope of this study. It has been so graphically depicted by the pen of Matthew Carter, who was himself one of the rebels in the town, as to require no recapitulation here. The Essex insurrection was less

[1] BL, Clarendon MS 31, ff. 109, 110; Carter, pp. 98–101; E. 445. 42; E. 446. 9; E. 446. 11; LJ, x, p. 300; CJ, v, p. 583.

[2] E. 453. 37; Carter, pp. 101–4; BL, Clarendon MS 31, ff. 109, 110.

widespread than that of Kent, since discontent was less prevalent and the county as a whole was more loyal to parliament. Under the command of Sir Charles Lucas, however, it was better led.[1] The Essex rebels were also less insular than those of Kent, and were encouraged by a number of small parties from Norfolk, Suffolk, Bedfordshire, Hertfordshire, and London. Of the thirty-six senior officers known to have been present in the siege, as many as one third came from Kent; the proportion of Kentishmen in the ranks was probably not so high. At first, the earl of Norwich seems to have turned his thoughts towards Sir Marmaduke Langdale in the North or to the parties of rebels which were said to be rising in East Anglia and the Midlands. On 9th June, however, his advance party, under Sir Thomas Peyton and his stepson William Swan, was taken captive at Bury St Edmunds, and on the 12th Norwich's harassed forces took refuge in Colchester. A few days later, Sir Thomas Fairfax arrived, and the town was invested. After ten weeks of unbelievable hardships, it surrendered on 28th August.[2]

While the rebels under Norwich were crossing into Essex and marching to their doom at Colchester, the remainder were dealt with by Sir Thomas Fairfax within the county. After the fall of Maidstone, the division between the Kentish moderates and the local Cavaliers was patent to everyone, and eventually they split into two distinct parties. Of the Cavalier group, some escaped towards Tonbridge, and the rest either joined the garrisons in the coastal castles of Walmer, Deal, and Sandown, or embarked on the rebel ships in the Downs, with a view to facilitating the landing of foreign troops.[3]

Amongst the moderates, lack of pay and victuals, the proximity of the victorious Fairfax, and the call of their farms and

[1] E. 449. 30; Carter, pp. 119 sqq. The more important sources for the Essex Rebellion, in addition to Carter, comprise more than 100 tracts in E. 448–E. 462.

[2] E. 461. 24; E. 461. 35; E. 446. 11; E. 448. 8; E. 447. 1; E. 447. 10; E. 461. 18; Carter, pp. 168 sqq. Peyton's second wife was Lady Cecilia Swan. According to John Clopton's Diary (Essex Record Office, B/7 B, 38. 1502, f. 39 r.), Peyton was captured on the 8th. Prisoners taken on the surrender of Colchester are said to have totalled 3,531.—E. 461. 35.

[3] *L'Estrange his Vindication*; E. 453. 37.

families led to widespread demoralization and desertion. When Colonels Gibbon and Rich arrived at Dover on 5th June, after their march through the Weald, the siege of the castle was hastily raised in great confusion, and the bulk of the rebel forces either dispersed home or crossed the Downs towards Canterbury.[1] There they were joined by those who had refused to follow Norwich and had marched eastward under Sir Richard Hardres. The city of Canterbury thus became "the seat of the whole action" in Kent. Colonels Rich and Hewson approached it from the south, and Fairfax himself from the west. Within the town, there was time neither to replace the gates removed and burnt in the previous December, following the Christmas Rising, nor to repair the breaches then made in the city walls. Money and provisions were scarce; there were "not above 1,300 fighting men" within the city, and those were perforce spread out "by reason of its compass, requiring so many to guard it."[2] Neither garrison nor townsmen were anxious to face a siege, for they were entirely isolated from any Cavalier forces in the rest of the kingdom, and, as one royalist observed, "by this time a man might read the fate of Kent without an oracle." Fairfax himself was aware that most of them were aggrieved petitioners rather than thoroughgoing royalists, and was willing to treat. The commanders within the town sent two commissioners to the parliamentarian general, and after brief negotiations articles of surrender were drawn up at Faversham on the 8th June. Only *bona fide* men of Kent were included within the terms; royalists from other counties were specifically excluded. All arms were to be delivered to Fairfax, and the rebels were to return to their homes, conform to all ordinances of parliament, give security never to take up arms again, and submit to such "fines or other punishments as might be imposed." These terms may have seemed harsh; but the rebels wisely trusted to Fairfax's word that no one should be plundered, no one executed, and that only moderate and reasonable fines should be levied. The general's promise to mediate with parliament was their surest guarantee

[1] E. 446. 23; E. 447. 10; E. 447. 15.

[2] E. 449. 30; E. 453. 37. Fairfax asserted there were more than 2,000 men in Canterbury.—E. 449. 30.

of fair treatment. Next day, 3,000 arms were laid down in the close and on the floor of Canterbury Cathedral.[1]

Very different was the treatment meted out to the Cavaliers and strangers in the county. After the capitulation of Canterbury, and despite the widespread passive resistance to parliament still prevalent in Kent, these royalists had determined to ignore local discontent and to act on their own initiative alone. Even although the village people were reluctant to sell food to the parliamentarians, who according to a royalist would find Kent "but a scurvy country for the saints to go on pilgrimage to the shrines of bag-puddings and powdered beef," the Cavaliers now rejected their assistance. Those who had escaped towards Tonbridge lent their support to the proposed rising in Sussex and Surrey. They also arranged meetings in the wild heathland south of Tonbridge itself, where the wells discovered in James I's reign were already becoming well known as a rustic rendezvous for jaded gentry, gamblers, and spendthrifts. There they were joined by another group of Cavaliers, who had come into the county from London and had agreed to raise horse "under an oath of secrecy" in the city. No one who was not a thoroughgoing royalist was now admitted to the Cavaliers' circle. Every soldier was hand-picked and personally sworn to "endeavour the freedom and restoration of my sovereign Lord King Charles to all his full and just rights."[2]

Meanwhile, in East Kent, the Cavaliers encouraged themselves, as Sir Anthony Weldon told the House of Commons, with "great hopes of succour by a foreign invasion, and the advantages thereto by the revolted ships and castles in the Downs, together with the declared countenance of the Prince . . . and . . . the dissolution of the whole frame of the [county] militia." Six of them—St Leger, Bosvile, Hamond, Bargrave, Palmer, and Harfleete—had boarded the ships, and flatly rejected all parliament's overtures of peace. About the 10th June, they crossed the Channel to Holland to secure the

[1] E. 453. 37; *L'Estrange his Vindication*; E. 449. 30; E. 447. 15; E. 447. 21; E. 447. 24. According to E. 447. 21, 300 horse were also delivered to Fairfax, and 32 prisoners, to whose lot it fell to die, were sent to Leeds Castle.

[2] E. 450. 13; E. 446. 34; E. 451. 13; E. 453. 14.

addition of fourteen sail of Dutch, and returned at the beginning of July with the duke of York. As they landed in Kent, at St John's-in-Thanet—according to one report with 1,500 Dutchmen—the long-awaited revolt of Sussex broke out with the capture of the magazine at Horsham. While one party of the Tonbridge Cavaliers marched into Surrey, others seized the magazine at Tonbridge and laid "the persons of the most eminent factionists . . . in lavender . . ."[1]

For once, the elaborate schemes of the Cavaliers had been successfully co-ordinated; but they had now lost the support of the community of Kent. Those Kentish petitioners who had submitted to Fairfax were frightened at this further provocation of parliament, and the countryfolk were panic-stricken—as they had been in 1640—at the introduction of a body of foreign soldiers into the county. "The tide is now turned," a Kentish observer of parliamentarian sympathies remarked;

"our countrymen begins to thwart the sands; for upon. . . . the duke of York's landing with an army from Holland . . . they resolved to adhere to their late principles and to stand for the defence of the liberties of their unconquered nation, and have declared their joint resolution to oppose all forces whatsoever that shall endeavour to make an inroad within the bowels of this county, to disturb the peace thereof, being resolved to display their banners in opposition to the ban of the new-raised royalists."

Many Kentishmen who had "lately appeared against [parliament] seem to be much . . . enraged against those that land; crying out (with much sense and apprehension of the danger) that foreigners are brought thither to surprise them." Sir Michael Livesey, said a parliamentarian, was likely to find "a great deal more ready compliance to join with him in this design against this invasion and the outlandish brought over than he did in the late commotion about the petition."[2] The counties of Sussex and Surrey were not able to gather strength before their forces were overwhelmed by Livesey, who then covered the 75 miles between the Surrey border and Thanet

[1] HMC, XIII, i, p. 472; E. 449. 30; E. 461. 3; E. 453. 14; E. 450. 13; E. 451. 13; E. 451. 46; E. 453. 8.

[2] E. 453. 34; E. 453. 14.

with extraordinary speed, joined forces with Colonel Rich at Sandown, and defeated the party of foreigners.[1]

Only the Kentish Cavaliers still aboard the ships in the Downs, with the prince, now remained at large. After fruitless attempts to disembark at Yarmouth, raise Norfolk, and relieve Colchester, the prince and their leader, Sir John Boys of Bonnington, brought them back to the Downs and made one last desperate effort to rouse rebellion in Kent on 14th August. The task was hopeless. Walmer Castle, reduced to desperate straits, had already been taken; Deal and Sandown were on the verge of surrender; the Kentish Cavaliers were finally defeated by Sir Michael Livesey; and Sir John Boys himself was taken prisoner. "Poor prince!" exclaimed Boys, as he was captured, "what will he now do? All is lost, all is lost!"[2]

Quite clearly, the collapse of the Kentish Rising of 1648 was due not only to the superior strength of parliament and the New Model Army, but to the disunity amongst the rebels themselves. The community of Kent as a whole was scarcely more ready to sink its provincial outlook in loyalty to Charles I than in loyalty to parliament. The rebellion had begun with a petition against the County Committee, and few of the rebels ever thought of themselves as other than petitioners. Only the Cavaliers saw the need of co-ordinating county grievances with the political requirements of the state. Unable to secure the support of those galaxies of county families in whose hands the power of the local community resided, these Cavaliers were eventually forced to try and raise the county without their assistance. The collapse of their attempt only showed that some kind of working agreement between Cavaliers and moderates was essential, so far as Kent was concerned, if the Stuarts were to regain the throne, and if stable government was to be restored. It took both parties eleven years of disillusionment, however, either in exile or in eclipse, before they learned that bitter but salutary lesson.

[1] CSPD, 1648–9, pp. 163–96, *passim*.

[2] E. 459. 19; E. 462. 29; E. 459. 1–3. The prince of Wales himself seems to have remained with the ships, though he is said (E. 459. 2) to have landed 500 of the land forces, who were joined by 250 seamen and 50 from Sandown Castle.

VIII

THE COMMUNITY IN ECLIPSE, 1649–59

(i) *The Cleavage between Moderates and Cavaliers*

THE CROMWELLIAN INTERREGNUM was a period unique in English history. For eleven years Cromwell and his successors tried in vain to establish a firm government. The reasons for this lack of success are as subtle, complex, and obscure as the reasons for Charles I's failure to establish his personal rule upon a permanent basis during the 'thirties. Possibly, indeed, they are even less understood. The present study makes no claim to elucidate those causes in the kingdom as a whole, because the story of Kent was no more typical of that of the rest of England during this period than during the Civil War itself. By fixing the microscope on a single county, however, it is possible to understand some of the intractable problems which faced both Cromwell and the royalists in endeavouring to realize their ambitions.

On the royalist side, so far as Kent was concerned, the salient factor in the inability to establish secure government was the continuing cleavage between the moderates and the Cavaliers. This factor, however, itself requires explanation, and is by no means easy to account for. Why did the cleavage which emerged in 1648 take eleven years to heal when both parties were equally unsympathetic, by temperament, to the autocracy of the protectorate? The problem is only accentuated when we take into account the execution of Charles I six months after the collapse of the Kentish Rebellion. The execution is usually credited with driving moderates and neutrals into the royalist camp, and in Kent it undoubtedly sent a thrill of horror through the community. Quite certainly, only a small body of Republicans in the county supported it, and those were headed by Sir Michael Livesey, John Dixwell, and Augustine Garland, none of whom can be said to have represented Kentish opinion in general. These Republicans did indeed organize a county petition in favour of the execution; but it is doubtful if the lengthy lists of signatures appended to it are genuine.[1] In fact, many of the kinsmen of the Republicans were themselves shocked by the deed, including the family of Philip and Algernon Sidney at Penshurst Place. Former parliamentarian officers, moreover, like Henry Oxinden of Great Maydeacon, now turned to composing royalist poems. Former committeemen subscribed their letters with pious mottoes like "Venit Carolus Rex." William Somner, the Kentish antiquary, devoted himself to writing *The Insecurity of Princes, considered in an Occasional Meditation upon the King's late Sufferings and Death*. Cavaliers like Matthew Carter described the execution as "the martyrdom of the most saint-like man that ever swayed an earthly sceptre." The earl of Dorset is said to have made a vow that he would never stir out of his house again until he should be carried out in his coffin. The halls and chambers of Kentish manor-houses were adorned with copies of Van Dyck's portraits or with busts of the king. In fact, the loyalty of the county to Charles II was regarded at the exiled Court as quite exceptional.[2]

Underlying this sudden revulsion of feeling, however, deeper causes were at work to perpetuate the cleavage between the Cavaliers and the moderates. Except in a few select bosoms, sentimental attachment to the late king was soon apt to weaken under the pressure of more immediate burdens. One important element in the division between the two groups was undoubtedly the legacy of bitter recrimination bequeathed to the county by the collapse of the Rebellion, and the violence of the ensuing pamphlet warfare. What began with such fair prospects had ended in such ignominious failure that all parties were anxious to find a scapegoat. Some blamed the failure of the rising upon the yeomanry and poor labourers of the county, who had deserted the Cavaliers to attend to their farms and families. Some blamed the shires of Essex and Surrey for neglecting to rise in time to support the Kentishmen. Some blamed "the prince's counsels and those commanders in France"

[1] Lenthall's notes to his own copy of the petition seem to suggest this.—BL, Tanner MS 57, ff. 476–87; Rawlinson MS A. 298.

[2] *DNB*, s.v. William Somner; Carter, p. 205; Victoria Sackville-West, *Knole and the Sackvilles*, 1958 edn, p. 114; Mordaunt LB, p. 160.

for lying so long idle and wasting "all these fair opportunities of appearing in England." Some blamed the Cavaliers for bringing strangers and foreign troops into the county. Others criticized the Kentish gentry for objecting to having "any strangers to come among them," until it was too late, "which hath been no small prejudice to their affairs." As for the unfortunate Roger L'Estrange, "you have not left one atom of my reputation without a wound," he complained of the people of Kent; "you have murthered me . . . as an apostate."[1]

Another factor perpetuating the division between Cavaliers and moderates arose from the economic circumstances of the period. There can be no doubt that by 1650 a great many gentry in Kent, as in other parts, had become involved in a terrifying web of debt, although the causes of their misfortunes are often hard to define. At first sight, their entanglements seem to be due to heavy composition fines; but in fact these fines rarely crippled a healthy state. There had indeed been "such a general and public unanimity" in the Rebellion of 1648, such a "concurrence as was never yet seen or heard of in one county," that parliament found it both impolitic and impracticable to inflict too severe a punishment upon the county. Sir Anthony Weldon, the chief architect of extreme measures in Kent, had died in October 1648. Sir Thomas Fairfax had promised to plead the cause of the Kentish petitioners in parliament, and agreed with the new County Committee's opinion that moderation "towards those who have been misled by others" would "be a winning mercy upon ingenious spirits. . . ." Though insisting that the rebel gentry should pay for the maintenance of the county forces by composition fines, parliament therefore expressed itself

"desirous to use all possible lenity towards those who are in any measure capable thereof. And do, therefore, hereby

[1] E. 448. 24; *L'Estrange his Vindication*; E. 453. 37; BL, Clarendon MS 31, f. 109. The recriminations stung L'Estrange, who shared the obloquy heaped both upon Kent by the Cavaliers and upon himself by some people in Kent, to write his *Vindication to Kent. And the Justification of Kent to the World . . .*, in 1649. Matthew Carter's more temperate and careful *Most True and Exact Relation of that as Honourable as unfortunate Expedition of Kent* was published in 1650 from similar motives.

declare, that although we see a necessity that some capital examples be made, yet shall our principal aim therein be, that all may be warned by the punishment of few."[1]

Under the Canterbury Articles, in fact, no capital examples could honourably be made, and in the end there were no enforced sales of rebels' estates. Leaders like Sir John Boys of Bonnington and Sir Richard Hardres of Upper Hardres escaped with composition fines at one-tenth or one-sixth. Those who could pretend any real force upon them—provided they engaged themselves not to bear arms and had their names inscribed by the churchwardens in the "register or book wherein the said engagement is to be written"—escaped with smaller fines or without punishment. Under the mild chancellorship of Sir Cheney Culpeper, many minor rebels with relatives or friends to plead their cause avoided punishment altogether at the hands of the new Committee of Kent for Compositions, as it was called. Sir Thomas Peyton, who cannot have expected much mercy, declared that he had

"this happiness to trust to, that I fall into the hands, not only of my countrymen and neighbours, but of fellow-Christians, the crown of whose profession is charity, which infuses benignity and the law of kindness . . . I beseech you to let me rest wholly upon yourselves."

It was hardly surprising, then, that the fines set upon the 280 families who eventually suffered—hastily calculated, without the lengthy particulars of estates upon which the old Committee had insisted—fell short of the sum spent in suppressing the rebellion by as much as £6,958, and totalled a mere £32,748: an average fine of only £117 upon each family.[2]

[1] E. 449. 34, p. 12; Dean and Chapter Library, Canterbury, Hales MSS; HMC, XIII, i, pp. 459, 472; CJ, v, p. 628. The ministers were ordered to read this declaration "before the dismissing of the congregation from the morning's exercise; and at the same time to give the people some seasonable instructions and exhortations."

[2] Whitelock, II, p. 358; HMC, XIII, i, p. 472; SP. 23: G: 100, ff. 525–8. A further £1,112 was levied in fines by the Committee for Advance of Money.—CCAM, *passim*. In 1654 £1,539 of the £6,958 was still owing to Sir Michael Livesey and four of his officers who had been in charge of main-

Though widely spread, the composition fines were all paid up by the autumn; the royalists regained their property and no one had been ruined.

Nevertheless, in Kent as elsewhere, the 'fifties were for many families a period of economic stringency. No doubt it was a hard basis of financial reality that compelled royalists in many counties to lead, like the Fanshawes when in Yorkshire, "a harmless country life, minding only the country sports and country affairs." The truth was that the mismanagement of delinquents' estates under sequestration and the ruthless exploitation of their farms and woodlands bequeathed a far heavier burden than mere composition fines. Sir George Sondes of Lees Court, who compounded for his estates at £3,450, reckoned his total losses from sequestration at more than £20,000.[1] Many other families, such as the Twysdens of Roydon Hall, found themselves saddled with similar burdens. If their estates had been well managed during the generation before the Civil War, they were usually able, with the assistance of kinsmen and forbearance of tenants, to weather the storm. But a whole nexus of royalist families—Peytons, Fludds, Stedes, Swans, Harfleetes, Culpepers, Tuftons, Heaths, Menneses, and others—seem to have become entangled in a vast web of debt at the hands of the purse-proud Haleses of Tunstall. Sir Thomas Peyton claimed to have lost £600 a year by the sharp practice of the Hales family: "such was the effect of a two years' difference, . . . contracting great debts, and paying great interest, and driven upon great changes, and losing all the profits. That affair," he concluded, ". . . weighed me down more than all the seizures, sequestrations, and pressures I ever received. . . ." Quite possibly, there was a

taining the peace of the county following the Rebellion: one example of many that parliamentarian families were by no means always well rewarded for their sacrifices for the cause (cf. SP. 23: G: 100, ff. 528–30; SP. 23: G: 16, ff. 32, 127; SP. 23: G: 27, f. 46). No doubt such conditions help to explain the vindictive treatment Livesey and his supporters later meted out to royalists like Sir Thomas Peyton: see pp. 276–7, below.

[1] *Memoirs of Lady Fanshawe*, ed. B. Marshall, 1905, p. 110; P. H. Hardacre, *The Royalists during the Puritan Revolution*, 1956, p. 120; Harleian Miscellany, x, *Sir George Sondes his Plain Narrative*, p. 42; cf. SP. 23: G: 178, f. 249.

connexion between these burdens and the dominant part played by the Hales family in the finances of the 1648 Rebellion.[1]

What rendered these economic pressures doubly burdensome was the intense sense of family loyalty amongst the Kentish gentry. The manorial household in Kent often comprised brothers, sisters, nephews, nieces, and cousins as well as the children and servants of the family itself. Whatever the financial stringency of the time, these kinsmen had to be provided for. The household of Sir Thomas Peyton of Knowlton Court was probably typical of many others in Kent at this time. In addition to seven children left to his care by his deceased sister, and nine more of another sister "who expects every day to be a widow," Peyton and his wife had eight children of their own "to employ our most dear and natural care about," besides "a brother unfortunately married, who together with his wife and 6 small children are supported almost totally by myself, and whose callings and livelihood I must inevitably provide for." He also had sisters and brothers dependent on him, and nephews and nieces "who, together with their children, have all their support and maintenance from my direction. . . ." No wonder if, during the 1650's, people like Sir Thomas Peyton and his wife found themselves "almost fainting under the multiplicity of our mutual sufferings."[2]

The nervous strain and tension of the period were further exacerbated by the lawless condition of the shire and the inability of the new County Committee to control it. Under the Republican régime, indeed, the Committee was not only incompetent but often quite unscrupulous. Men like Sir Thomas Peyton found the law stretched and strained against them with remorseless rigour by Republicans like Sir Michael Livesey. If Livesey was in the chair at the Committee, the law afforded no defence to a royalist like Peyton when his local minister demanded exorbitant tithes of him. On one occasion Livesey and his legal adviser, Thomas St Nicholas, compelled a

[1] BM, Add. MS 44846, f. 70 *et passim*; KCA, U. 55, Heath Letters, *passim*. See p. 238, n. 1. The evidence, however, for a connexion between the Haleses' dominance in 1648 and their financial activities in Kent is not conclusive.

[2] BM, Add. MS 44846, ff. 68 v., 69 v.

Kentish jury to find Peyton's innocent manservant guilty of murder. At another time, when John Stodder of Canterbury laid claim, without any ground of right, to one of Peyton's farms, the law was powerless to condemn him. Or a malicious neighbour might make innocent words like the lines scrawled on the glass of a window at Knowlton Court seem "quite another thing, according to the various inclinations of men's minds." Both the earl of Leicester and the Haleses of Tunstall were illegally plundered by the ill-disciplined soldiers of Sir Michael Livesey; and the outrages, "murders, and other foul acts" of Captain Swan's company became notorious.[1]

Such were the burdensome circumstances which, despite the execution of Charles I, still kept the moderates and Cavaliers apart and prevented any rapprochement between them till after the death of Oliver Cromwell. For the moderates, the social insecurity and economic stress of the times rendered a decade of retrenchment and retirement imperative if society, as they knew it, was to survive. As Sir Thomas Peyton observed, most people, "however dissatisfied with the present government, were not willing to incur any danger. . . ." Many of the moderates gradually came to fix their hopes on Oliver Cromwell, not because they believed in his principles, but because they needed first and foremost stable government. Under his rule, moreover, most of them, in Kent at least, eventually managed to regain a measure of prosperity. Those prepared to have "all [their] time taken up with the business of farming" invariably survived the economic stringency of the period. The unremitting care of Sir Roger Twysden of Roydon Hall enabled him to purchase new property in Great Chart, when the lands of the Dean and Chapter of Canterbury were sold in the 'fifties. By much patient husbandry, Sir George Sondes was at last able to complete the reconstruction of his beautiful house, Lees Court, at a cost that must have been very considerable. Minor gentry, like the Elyses of Stoneacre, though often declaring themselves ruined, usually managed to restore their fortunes under the Protectorate, and to enjoy

[1] BM, Add. MS 44846, ff. 51 v., 64 v., 70 v.; Add. MS 28003, f. 332; Dean and Chapter Library, Canterbury, Hales MSS; CSPD, 1648–9, p. 292, 1649–50, p. 174, 1651, *passim*.

another century or more of prosperous life in their medieval or Tudor manor-houses. Even recusants, like the Darells of Scotney Castle, with two-thirds of their estate sequestrated for a period of twelve years, yet managed by ingenious conveyances, uses, and redemptions to retain their lands from year to year and finally emerge unvanquished.[1]

For the genuine Cavaliers, however, there could be no compromise with the usurper. Rigid attention to the management of their estates offered them few attractions. Families like the Sondeses and Twsydens they ridiculed as "the female gentry of the smock."[2] Their own property was often either leased out to strangers, heavily mortgaged to finance futile conspiracies, or squandered in senseless extravagance. The high-flying notions of men like Richard Lovelace, the poet, and Sir John Mayney of Linton Place, too often landed themselves or their descendants in bankruptcy.[3] Cavaliers of this type, however, were not very numerous in Kent. A list of the leading royalists in the county about 1655 includes sixty-five names, of which perhaps half were genuine Cavaliers.[4] They were headed by Richard Thornhill of Olantighe; by the earl of Winchilsea and

[1] CCSP, III, p. 222; Twysden, *Certain Considerations*, pp. xxiii–xxiv n.; CCAM, p. 1393; SP. 23: G: 158, ff. 321, 323; CCC, p. 245. Recusants often conveyed estates to protestant kinsmen, professing to retain only a life interest. Sondes's expenditure on Lees Court, which was begun before the Civil War and is regarded as one of the few buildings genuinely attributable to Inigo Jones, is not known; but possibly his £7,000 debts alluded to in SP. 23: G: 178, f. 249, relate to his building operations at this time. He was unquestionably one of the wealthiest men in the county, and was later created earl of Feversham.

[2] The phrase occurs in BM, Harleian MS 6918, f. 34.

[3] According to Aubrey (*Brief Lives*, ed. A. Clark, 1898, II, pp. 37–8) Lovelace died in a cellar in Long Acre. It was apparently Sir John Mayney himself and Charles Cotton who afforded Lovelace his sole relief from absolute indigence, though Aubrey's account is ambiguous. Clark is incorrect in tentatively identifying Aubrey's "Sir . . . Many" with "Sir John Mennis" (i.e., Mennes), another Kentish Cavalier, often confused with Mayney, though the two families were unrelated. Mayney and Lovelace had been neighbours as well as brothers-in-arms: Lovelace Place and Linton Place are both in mid-Kent, about fifteen miles apart.

[4] BL, Rawlinson MS A. 27, f. 383. The list includes two peers, seven baronets, three knights, ten other major gentry, and about forty parochial gentry.

two other members of the Finch family; by two of the Tuftons, two of the Filmers, and two of the Crispes; and by the important East Kent connexion of Auchers, Boyses, Palmers, Menneses, Hamonds, and Kingsleys, which had been so prominent in 1648. Among them was a high proportion of relative newcomers to the shire, like the Thornhills of Olantighe and the Braemeses of Blackmansbury, and a handful of adventurers with no roots in the county at all. Nearly all of these men had once been officers in the king's army, and most of them were still young men: some with the winsome gaiety of a Thomas Walsingham, heir-apparent of old Sir Thomas of Scadbury, and son-in-law of the earl of Suffolk; others with the drunken debauchery of a Richard Thornhill. One of them, Arthur Hascott, possibly the Major Ascott who was a client of the duke of Buckingham's, was described as having "been a major always for the king; he is about thirty years, hath brown hair, and hath had a great hurt on his face; he wears thereon always a round black patch. . . ." Another, one Mr Stone, was a "tall black man, with a long visage, about thirty years of age . . . in a grey suit trimmed with black ribbons, and a large dark stuff coat. . . ."[1] Frustrated and restless, these Cavaliers now led a strange and discontented life: sometimes attending crowded house-parties at Olantighe, Knowlton, or Tunstall Place; sometimes devising conspiracies in lonely inns by the seashore; sometimes paying a fleeting visit to the exiled Court of Charles II; and sometimes spending weary years of imprisonment in Leeds Castle or in London.[2]

The leader of these Cavaliers of the county was that complex, ambivalent figure, Sir Thomas Peyton of Knowlton Court. The curious fact about Sir Thomas was that he was himself in many respects quite untypical of these Cavaliers. He had begun his political life as a firm opponent of Charles I, and had been driven to support him principally by the violence and injustice of the Weldonians. As a consequence, beneath his Cavalier exterior, he was at heart still a moderate. Though a member of the royalist 'Action Party's' central organization, Peyton felt

[1] Thurloe, VII, p. 221, III, p. 348; for Buckingham's client or servant cf. CCSP, III, p. 374; *Nicholas Papers*, I, 301.

[2] BM, Add. MS 44846, *passim*.

unhappy when circumstances drove him to accept the leadership of the county. His sister-in-law, Dorothy Osborne, to whom he was much attached, could not understand how a man so high-minded could endure the drunken orgies of the Cavaliers at Knowlton Court. Himself temperate almost to a fault, he used to sit among them at table sipping nothing but cold water. When they sang their bacchanalian songs, he betook himself to the Bible, and Greek and Hebrew authors, "whose company I only enjoy." While they wasted their substance in riotous living, he quietly devoted himself to the necessary "business of farming."[1] And yet there was a strain of uncertainty, gallantry, and ambition in Sir Thomas Peyton, too. He was one of the few moderates of the county whose personal devotion to the king was more than a passing sentiment. As the natural leader, moreover, of the galaxy of East Kent families which comprised the Auchers, Boyses, Palmers, and Hamonds, he could not permanently remain aloof from the Cavalier circle of the county. Just as, in 1640, the puritans of the shire had been compelled to realize their ambitions through the moderate Sir Edward Dering, so in the 'fifties the Cavaliers were compelled to realize theirs through the moderate Sir Thomas Peyton. Their reliance upon him was a curious comment upon both the social structure and the political sentiments of the community as a whole.

In consequence of Peyton's leadership of the Cavaliers, his quiet manor-house in the downland of East Kent became the centre of royalist conspiracy. With the cleavage between the moderates and Cavaliers, conspiracy rather than outright rebellion was the only means of action left to the royalists in England. With the exile of the Court, moreover, Kent was brought from the rear of royalist strategy into the forefront, since the county was the kingdom's bridgehead with Europe.[2] Situated as it was within fifteen miles of both Dover and Sand-

[1] BM, Add. MS 28003, f. 332; Add. MS 44846, *passim*; cf. G. C. Moore Smith, ed., *The Letters of Dorothy Osborne to William Temple*, 1928, pp. 90, 169, 171, 174–5. For the 'Action Party' and the activities of Peyton and other Kentish Cavaliers in connexion with it see David Underdown, *Royalist Conspiracy in England, 1649–1660*, 1960, pp. 109–10 *et passim*.

[2] CSPD, 1649–50, p. 140.

wich, and yet in a remote country district, Knowlton Court provided the Cavaliers with an ideal centre to hatch their conspiracies.

(ii) *The Conspiracies of the Cavaliers*

The earliest plots of the Cavaliers were devised amongst the exiles who fled overseas after the Rebellion of 1648. It is practically certain that Walter Braemes and other Kentish gentry were involved in the assassination of Dr Dorislaus in May 1649. When these same men landed at Dover a few weeks later, they were arrested as suspected accomplices, and the "meetings and preparations of disaffected persons," which their friends were promoting in Kent, were scotched by parliamentary troops.[1]

In July of the following year the Cavaliers planned a second conspiracy. Dover Castle was to be taken by stratagem, and risings were to be organized in Kent, Surrey, and Sussex. Richard Thornhill drew up plans for a "perfect list of the model of an army in Kent," visited the Court, and propounded his schemes to the king. He and John Heath suggested as commander the duke of Richmond, at Cobham Hall, "as the fittest person and [one] whom they thought the country people did well affect." The duke himself, however, when approached, professed, as in 1648, a desire "but to live quietly" and avoid all "country affairs." Shortly afterwards Dover Castle was secured for parliament by the Republican Algernon Sidney, and the second plot of the Cavaliers also came to nothing.[2]

For the royalists in England, the next spring was brightened by the prospect of the king's invasion from Scotland, and at Richard Thornhill's prompting John Gerard was now suggested as one who might lead a rising. Gerard himself had no connexion with the county, but his officers, so far as Kent was concerned, were to be drawn from the circle of Peyton's relatives in the east of the county, including Sir Anthony Aucher, Anthony Hamond, Thomas Harfleete, Sir Henry

[1] CSPD, 1649–50, pp. 133, 141, 1650, pp. 419–20, 516, 1651–2, p. 250.

[2] HMC, XIII, i, pp. 582, 597; CSPD, 1650, pp. 228, 233–4, 279–80; *Nicholas Papers*, I, pp. 238–40.

Palmer, and Sir John Boys. In order to draw a crowd of people together, horse-races and similar meetings were organized in March, apparently as a "beginning of insurrections." But the plans of the royalists had barely matured when Thomas Coke, the king's emissary, was arrested and induced to divulge the names of his accomplices. In Kent the County Committee was ordered by the Council of State to secure Dover Castle and seize malignants, and for a few weeks Leeds Castle and other prisons were crowded with suspects. The evidence against most of these men was nebulous and they were soon released upon bonds. But when the king advanced from Scotland in the summer, they were in no position to wake a response in their native county.[1] The summer passed uneventfully away, and for the next three years, while the moderates were attending to their estates, the Kentish Cavaliers remained quiescent.

The next occurrence was Gerard's Plot in 1654. In this wild conspiracy, several of the young Kentish Cavaliers who were to have been John Gerard's officers in 1651 were involved, including Francis Lovelace, Walter Braemes, Sidney Fotherby, and Charles and John Finch. The plot itself had little connexion with Kent, but it set off a train of events leading to the most serious insurrection of the Interregnum, the Rising of 1655, usually known by the name of its Wiltshire leader, Penruddock. On this occasion, rebellion was to be raised in several counties at once. Such towns as Plymouth, Portsmouth, and Carlisle were to be seized, and the plans in Kent formed but a single part of a widespread organization.[2]

By 1655, however, Cromwell was too firmly fixed in the saddle to be easily dislodged. In Kent he placed implicit trust in his henchman Thomas Kelsey, not only as governor of Dover Castle, but as ruler, in fact if not in name, of the whole county. By means of his tireless journeys from town to town, Kelsey was enabled to devote minute attention to many of the by-ways of rural life which the County Committee of Sir

[1] CSPD, 1651, pp. 114–15, 193–245 *passim*; BM, Add. MS 44846, f. 56 v.

[2] BL, Clarendon MS 48, ff. 326–7; E. 813. 22, p. 10; CSPD, 1654, pp. 273–4; Thurloe, II, pp. 331–74 *passim*. For the plot as a whole, see Underdown, *op. cit.*, pp. 97 sqq. Lovelace was a kinsman of the poet Richard, but of a different branch of the family, at Hever Place in Kingsdown.

Anthony Weldon's day had suffered to remain in obscurity. Early in 1655 his lieutenant informed him that "the faces and carriages of the malignants" indicated that new storms were rising, and that the Cavaliers were "only waiting an opportunity to imbrue their hands in blood" once again. A rising was to take place on the 13th February; and there was no place in England, next to London, which "would be sooner attempted by them than this, considering the nearness to France and who they are."[1] Before long Kelsey had unearthed the details of the whole conspiracy. The Cavaliers' magazine was discovered, and Sir John Boys, Edward Hales the younger, Colonel Thomas Culpeper, and other leaders were arrested. In other counties their friends suffered a similar setback. Some argued that, since Cromwell had discovered so much, they should rise "incontinently" to prevent the arrest of those still at liberty. The Action Party as well as the Sealed Knot, however, realized the strength of the government, and in Kent Sir Thomas Peyton and his supporters advocated delay. The month of February 1655 therefore came and went without the expected signal to rise.[2]

Early in the spring, however, new meetings of royalists took place at Bruges, Ostend, and Dunkirk, and early in March, 150 men passed through to Calais and sat watching the coast of Kent. John Heath of Brasted and Sir John Mennes acted as intermediaries between the overseas Court and the Kentish Cavaliers. Richard Thornhill was described as the "chief agent" in Kent, and Sir Thomas Peyton met some of the chief agents of other counties in London. Arms and horse-furniture were purchased in the city and surreptitiously conveyed to various Kentish manor-houses. Neighbouring shires, it was agreed, would stage a rising to draw off Cromwell's troops from Kent, and, under the young earl of Winchilsea, the county would then be enabled to secure Rochester and Dover Castle and form a bridgehead with Essex. Joined by adventurers from the London suburbs, Sussex and Surrey were to send reinforcements, while the king was to land in Kent with foreign troops

[1] CSPD, 1655, p. 20.

[2] BL, Rawlinson MS A. 21, f. 449; CSPV, 1655–6, pp. 11–12; *Clarke Papers*, III, p. 18; BL, Clarendon MS 50, f. 4; cf. *Nicholas Papers*, II, p. 218.

and lead the South-East in its attack upon the capital. The new date fixed for the rising was the 8th March.[1]

All these elaborate schemes were, of course, little more than a dream. Nevertheless, a definite royalist organization was being patiently built up in Kent with a view to laying up arms and raising troops in the county. In East Kent this organization was in the hands of Sir Thomas Peyton, seconded by the Palmers of Wingham and Bekesbourne, the Braemeses of Blackmansbury, and the Fotherbys of Barham. In the valley of the Stour, the movement was led by the earl of Winchilsea and Richard Thornhill of Olantighe, supported by Lord Tufton, the earl of Thanet's heir, at Hothfield Place, and Zouche and Sir William Brockman of Beachborough. In the downland, conspiracy was planned by the Haleses of Tunstall Place, the Bunces of Otterden Place, and the Hugessens of Provender in Lynsted. In West Kent the organization was in the hands of Sir John Mayney of Linton Place, young Francis Clerke of Ford Place in Wrotham, Francis Lovelace of Hever Place in Kingsdown, Richard Lee the younger of Great Delce, and Colonel Newman, a former committeeman, at Rochester.[2] As was usual with the Kentish Cavaliers, nearly all the members of this group were near kinsmen of one another, and most of them were relatives of one or other of their leaders, Sir Thomas Peyton and Richard Thornhill. Richard Lee, for example, was Peyton's nephew and Newman's brother-in-law. Arnold Braemes was Sir Thomas Palmer's son-in-law. Sir John Boys had married the aunt of the earl of Winchilsea, was brother-in-law to Sidney Fotherby (Winchilsea's 'agent'), and nephew to John Fotherby and Sir Henry Palmer. Sir William Brockman was brother of Zouche Brockman, father-in-law of Sir William Hugessen, and cousin of James Bunce and of his son; and so on.

It was impossible, however, for plans so widespread to escape the vigilant eye of Cromwell's government. The move-

[1] BL, Clarendon MS 49, f. 390; Clarendon MS 50, f. 4; BL, Rawlinson MS A. 27, f. 383; CSPD, 1655, p. 225; Thurloe, III, pp. 211, 330, 355–6, 428, IV, pp. 10, 132–3.

[2] BL, Rawlinson MS A. 25, ff. 163–5; Thurloe, III, pp. 252–3, 300, 355–6, 428, IV, pp. 10, 132; *Nicholas Papers*, II, pp. 221, cf. III, pp. 160–1.

ments of well-known Cavaliers like Francis Lovelace, who were "privy to the intricacies of the whole design," were carefully observed by Thurloe in London. The Cavaliers had been forced to purchase their arms in the capital, and before long one of the tradesmen from whom they had obtained supplies took fright and divulged his patrons' names to the government. Warrants were immediately issued for their arrest, and, in the act of "taking horse and going down to raise the county," Lord Tufton was arrested and consigned to the Tower. On the road to Davington Priory, where he had been forming a magazine in the cloisters of the old nunnery, Tufton's chests and trunks of arms were secured by Major-General Thomas Kelsey. The major-general was also ordered to search the county for Tufton's accomplices, and most of the Cavaliers either were arrested or fled overseas. Rochester and Queenborough were carefully watched, and guards were set along the Kentish coast to arrest suspects arriving from the continent.[1] In other counties, the royalists were equally unfortunate. In some, the leaders were seized and committed to prison; in others, they failed to appear. The proposed rally at Marston Moor came to nothing, and Penruddock himself was defeated in Devon, at South Molton.[2]

Despite their failure in 1655, the same group of Cavaliers were involved in further conspiracies in Kent in almost every succeeding year of the Interregnum. On each occasion, their plans were linked with those of other shires; but, as in 1655, they were invariably hampered by inadequate co-ordination and local independence.[3] They stood no chance of success against the centralized and efficient government of the Protectorate. None of these plots, moreover, was of comparable importance with Penruddock's Rising, and there is no need to pursue them here in detail. Between his spells in prison, Sir Thomas Peyton was still regarded as the royalist leader in the

[1] Thurloe, III, pp. 211, 252–3; *Clarke Papers*, III, p. 28; *Nicholas Papers*, III, pp. 160–1; CSPD, 1655, p. 75.

[2] A. H. Woolrych, *Penruddock's Rising*, 1655 (Historical Association, Pamphlet G. 29), 1955, pp. 15–20.

[3] For this lack of regional co-ordination in 1655, see particularly Underdown, *op. cit.*, Chapter VII.

county, and Knowlton Court remained the focal point of the Cavaliers' activities. The moving spirits among them were still the earl of Winchilsea and his brother Charles Finch, Sir John and Thomas Boys, Walter and Arnold Braemes, Sidney Fotherby, and Lord Tufton of Hothfield. In spite of the futility of their schemes, it is arguable that, by constantly disturbing the peace of the county and forcing Cromwell into harsh repressive measures, the Cavaliers ultimately paved the way for the Restoration. If Cromwell could have stabilized his government and permitted rural life to return to normal, the moderates, in Kent, might have eventually accepted his dynasty as permanent.

Perhaps the most striking feature in the royalist conspiracies of the 'fifties, however, was the fact that none of them were spontaneous local rebellions: all owed their inspiration to the connexion of the Cavaliers with the exiled Court of Charles II. So far as the community of Kent in general was concerned, this rendered every one of them suspect from the outset. Each succeeding conspiracy only confirmed the moderates of the county in the conviction that the Cavaliers were prepared to sacrifice social order to restore the House of Stuart: and there was not the faintest possibility that the Kentish moderates would countenance such a restoration, if it necessitated the disruption of provincial life. Not until confidence was re-established between the moderates and Cavaliers was there any likelihood of the return of Charles II, despite the dissatisfaction which both groups felt with the government of the Cromwellian Protectorate.

(iii) *Government, Committee, and Major-General*

There was much in addition to military repression to render the government of the Interregnum unacceptable to the moderates. The salient feature of the successive régimes of the period, so far as domestic order was concerned, was the growth of centralization, and this tendency was anathema to the Kentish community as a whole. In consequence of the reconstruction of the County Committee after the 1648 Rebellion, moreover, followed by the change in the strategic position of the county after the exile of the Court, the growth in the power of the central government at the expense of the local community was yet more evident in Kent than elsewhere. As the chief bridgehead with the continent, the county could no longer be left to rule itself as it pleased. The various local jurisdictions which Sir Anthony Weldon had so painstakingly brought under the control of the County Committee were now taken over, one by one, by the Council of State. The series of nine garrisons around the coast of Kent, hitherto maintained by the county, were governed by the Council, whilst the forts were restored and the castles re-edified under its direction. The Lord Wardenship, which had been virtually taken over by the Committee, was resumed by the government and held by a succession of army officers. The powers of the Kentish vice-admiral, Sir Thomas Walsingham, were curtailed. The governorship of Dover Castle was transferred from the hands of local families to those of the Cromwellian major-general, Thomas Kelsey. The protection of coastal villages from the raids of pickeroons and pirates, the care of wounded sailors after battles at sea, even the ordering of the county's fisheries and oystershelves, was undertaken by the Admiralty Commissioners. In the two dockyards at Woolwich and Chatham, Committee influence was abruptly terminated. In the Cinque Ports a close watch was maintained upon the activities of searchers, postmasters, travellers, and members of the corporations. The sheriff and justices of the county were more minutely directed by the Council than ever before: they themselves sometimes went so far as to beg to be "informed of our duty that we may not get into trouble." Again and again the justices were instructed to keep "diligent watch," take "strict account of all strangers," dissolve "dangerous meetings" at the popular Wells near Tonbridge, disperse crowds at horse-races, attend to the posts along Watling Street, and examine persons who spoke "contemptuous words . . . against government." Such orders had not been unknown in Sir Anthony Weldon's day; but under that martinet the details of local government had in general been left to the discretion of the County Committee.[1]

[1] SP. 23: G: 100, ff. 525–6; BL, Tanner MS 57, f. 367; CSPD, 1648–56, *passim*; CJ, v, p. 623, vi, p. 573; *DNB*, s.v. Thomas Kelsey.

The attrition of the powers of local County Committees formed part of a systematic policy of the Commonwealth governments throughout the period. Committees had found little favour with Oliver Cromwell, who had endured much from their vexatious provincialism in the Eastern Association. In Kent, this policy of attrition began with the abolition of the local Accounts Committee at the end of 1648, and the transfer of its powers to the central Committee of Accounts in London. Since the members of the general County Committee had suffered much unjust accusation at the hands of the local Committee of Accounts, one might suppose they would have welcomed its abolition. In fact, they deeply resented the change, which they now declared was based upon "mere jealousies" and "general surmises . . . of abuses and miscarriages. And we hope your condition is not so universally sad," they told the government,

> "as neither the former Committees for Accounts nor any other persons within the county are or can be found fitting and of integrity to examine . . . an account upon the place, where in all probability the truth may be best sifted. . . . We never yet did nor shall decline the giving an account . . ., only we humbly crave that what is intended for satisfaction to yourselves . . . may not be turned to a mere matter of grievance and vexation to your servants. . . . It will be a very great vexation and charge to the country to travel to London and attend there with their several accounts, vouchers, and witnesses. . . ."

What the Committee of Kent feared was chiefly the fact of centralized control, together with their own loss of power, and the consequent possibility that the Committee of Accounts in London, "in case of any failing in themselves about their own accounts," would lay the blame at the door of the Committee of Kent.[1]

The abolition of the local Committee of Accounts was followed by an equally determined assault upon the powers of the county Sequestration Committee. Under the chancellorship of

[1] SP. 28: 234, papers of Nicholas Bix of Canterbury; SP. 28: 260, paper headed "Proposal" (for terms of reference for reformed central Committee of Accounts); BL, Tanner MS 57, f. 289.

Sir Cheney Culpeper, and in accordance with the spirit of the Canterbury Articles, the Committee set up after the Rebellion of 1648 had pursued a consistent policy of conciliation towards delinquents. Its moderation soon began to win the confidence of the milder royalists, but in the eyes of the Rump Sir Cheney Culpeper was probably too closely related to the leading rebels of the county—most of the Culpeper clan were royalists—to be trusted. When the yield of fines levied by his Committee was found to fall short of the extravagant Sir Michael Livesey's expenditure in maintaining peace by nearly £7,000, the fate of the Kentish Sequestration Committee, or Committee for Compounding as it was now called, was sealed.[1] Hugh Justice, the agent of the central Committee in London, was sent down to spy out the land, and a few weeks later he returned with an impressive dossier of its misdeeds. Sir Anthony Weldon's last act before his death, in demanding, it seems, a year's reprieve for the Committee, was for the moment successful; but such bodies were already being abolished elsewhere, and in February 1650 the Kentish Committee, with its elaborate structure of lathal subcommittees, was dissolved.[2] Its functions were taken over by the central Committee in London, and in place of the seventy members of the former body three local commissioners were appointed: Alexander Roberts of Maidstone, John Browne of Orpington, and Edward Peake of Sandwich. These commissioners were selected from the same stratum of parochial gentry as the former Compounding Committee; but they had hitherto acted merely as servants of the Committee, and in their new capacity they were little more than servants of the Committee in London. Their appointment was bitterly opposed by the old Committee for Compounding. Its chief official, Lambarde Godfrey, absolutely refused either to co-operate with them or to surrender the records of sequestrated estates in Kent, which in fact remained in his custody till after the Restoration.[3]

[1] SP. 23: G: 100, ff. 525–8; BM, Add. MS 5494, f. 281; Add. MS 44846, f. 48.

[2] BM, Add. MS 5494, ff. 285, 287–8; cf. BL, Tanner MS 57, f. 289.

[3] SP. 23: G: 158, *passim*; CCC, I, pp. 171, 186, 229–30, 239, 448; SP. 28: 258, Francklyn to CAC, 1 April 1650, Bowles to Ufflett and CAC.

That the new arrangement was fiscally more efficient than the old, though the main lines upon which sequestration business was carried out remained unaltered, is unquestionable. In 1654–5, for example, from the thirty-two Kentish estates still under sequestration (mainly those of recusants), the gross receipts totalled £6,863, and expenditure totalled £6,741.[1] Of the latter, 67 per cent was spent by the state, and nothing by the county, all disbursements being now centralized; 28 per cent was disbursed upon estate management and estate charges, and 5 per cent upon salaries and "incident charges" (travelling, posts, and the like).[2] Under the old régime, by contrast, the pattern of expenditure had been as follows: state 15 per cent, county 23 per cent, salaries, etc., 7 per cent, estate charges 55 per cent.[3] Equally striking was the decline in the power of the general County Committee which these figures illustrate: before 1650, 85 per cent of sequestration expenditure had been controlled *de facto* by the

---

Peake was succeeded, on his decease, by Thomas Morris, formerly treasurer to the Canterbury Committee. He possessed further qualifications as a local lawyer; so too probably did Roberts, and possibly Browne. The 1652 Act of Pardon, which might otherwise have terminated sequestration, was largely nullified by its provisos and exceptions: e.g., all delinquents were excluded from it who were sequestered before Dec. 1651 (CCC, I, p. xviii). The further attrition of the sequestration commissioners' powers consequent upon Cromwell's advent to supreme control in 1654, though described by Mrs A. E. Green (*ibid.*, p. xx) as a "death-blow," was not so far-reaching in Kent as the changes of 1650. A new commission was issued, but the same commissioners were continued (except Roberts, who was accused of embezzling £1,000). Compounding was formally terminated, but had in fact long since ceased; there were to be no 'new sequestrations,' but these also had already ceased. These changes marked a decline in the power of the central committee in London, and were carried a stage further by the appointment of receivers-general; but in Kent at least there was no actual breach of continuity in the system, merely a *de jure* confirmation of existing conditions.

[1] SP. 28: 210 B, Browne's and Monins's account books. Kent was seventh among English counties in the yield of its sequestered recusants' estates. Nearly all other delinquents had compounded on the Canterbury Articles, so that there was no yield from their estates to the sequestrators.

[2] SP. 28: 210 B, Browne's and Monins's account books.

[3] Based on sequestration account books for Sutton-at-Hone Upper and St Augustine's in SP. 28: 210. Cf. Chapter V, pp. 160–2, 168–70.

general Committee; after 1650, virtually all was paid into the hands of the central body in London. Moreover, the decisions of the new commissioners no longer originated in the county, but with the London Committee. Their orders required its seal to render their demands valid, and their activities were thence minutely observed. They were not permitted to let sequestrated estates for more than one year nor were they permitted to pay or appoint their own officers. They could not compel witnesses to attend and give evidence, neither could they punish those who opposed their proceedings or summon the county forces to secure the execution of their orders. Their premises comprised a single room in Alexander Roberts's house in Maidstone, and their agents "came sneaking to back doors" to collect rents, and were "received with many cross answers." They remained the most dutiful of servants, but their work was purely menial.[1]

The abolition of the Kentish Committee for Sequestration, or Compounding, was quickly followed by a complete reorganization of the general Committee of the County. In losing its power of sequestration, the general Committee had in fact lost its most powerful weapon, not only against royalists, but against the central government: for it had lost one of its principal sources of revenue. It was now powerless to withstand its own abolition, and this was effected by the creation of two separate bodies denominated the Militia Committee (or Commissioners) and the Committee of Assessment. Once, in 1649, a second time, in 1651, and a third time upon Cromwell's advent to power in 1653, the existence of these two bodies was suspended or called in question. But by and large the twofold pattern, and the lathal structure inherited from the old Committee, remained unimpaired until 1659. The headquarters of the two new Kentish Committees remained at Maidstone; an early suggestion for their removal to Rochester was rejected. In all probability the meetings of both bodies were still held in the premises of the old Committee in the town, belonging to the Swynokes, and if they obeyed the Council's order they met daily. How far the division of

[1] SP. 23: G: 158, *passim*; SP. 23: G: 30, f. 191; SP. 23: G: 158, ff. 35, 125, 163, 190–3; CCC, *passim*.

functions was practically maintained it is difficult to say, owing to the comparative paucity of Committee records during the Interregnum; but the membership of the two bodies was almost identical, and they evidently shared the same officials.[1]

From henceforth the new Committee of Kent was too impotent to withstand, as Sir Anthony Weldon had withstood, the increasing burden of taxation laid on the county, or to resist the minute and almost daily direction of its affairs by the Council of State. Its desires were no longer consulted when the county regiments were marched into other counties or to Ireland, and it was not permitted to appoint its own officials. The letters of the Council of State to the new Committee gave detailed instructions for the raising, arming, payment, and disbandment of troops and garrisons; for the securing or bailing of disaffected persons; the dispersal of "meetings for bowling, horse-racing, etc.;" the settlement or protection of ministers; and the disposal of the magazine, provisions, and prisoners in Leeds Castle—even for the swans and fish in the Castle lake.[2] In the time of Sir Anthony Weldon, such matters would rarely have been mentioned, but quietly left to the County Committee to settle as it pleased: indeed, Sir Anthony would never have tolerated such interference.

The final stage in the attrition of local authority and the process of centralization came in 1655, when, following the abortive rising of Penruddock, the whole country was divided into military districts, each under the command of one of Cromwell's major-generals. Thomas Kelsey had long been governor of Dover Castle and virtual governor of the county of Kent; but his appointment as major-general of Kent and Surrey was the final blow to county autonomy. Personally, Kelsey had no connexion with the Kentish community, and his circle of intimate supporters comprised his fellow-officers alone. His loyalties lay entirely with the Protector, not with the shire. Under his régime, the Committee became a mere cipher, a kind of local *parlement* existing merely to ratify his arbitrary decrees. Though the interference of the major-

[1] CSPD, 1651, p. 334; SP. 28: 340.

[2] Cf. BL, Tanner MS 57, f. 509; CSPD, 1649–50, pp. 264–5; 1650, *passim*; 1651, *passim*.

generals in private life may have been exaggerated by contemporaries, there can be little doubt that Kelsey's vigilant policing of the shire often desecrated the secrets of the family circle.[1] The decimation tax made the realities of a military state unpleasantly plain to many moderates who had taken part in the 1648 Rebellion, and who might otherwise have come to acquiesce in Cromwell's supremacy.

Designed for the maintenance of Kelsey's government of the two counties, as well as for the punishment of the rebels of 1655, the administration of the decimation tax engaged a good deal of the major-general's attention during the next two years. The orders and accounts of the Kentish Committee, relating to the tax, have survived almost intact, and render it possible to piece together a detailed story of this administration. The first meetings of the Committee were held in November and December 1655, when all those Kentish delinquents who had fallen foul of the government since the beginning of the war were summoned to furnish detailed 'particulars' of their estates and revenues. Families with property valued at under £100 per annum were not subject to the levy: it is significant that all but 91 of the county's 500-odd delinquents (if their 'particulars' are truthful, which may be doubted) came within this category—such was the preponderance of minor gentry in the shire. In fact, Kelsey complained to the Protector that, if he had been permitted to decimate estates worth £50–£100 per annum, the total yield of the tax would have been doubled.[2] In the case of the remaining 91 gentry, however, no pleas for exemption upon grounds of hardship or of subsequent service to the Commonwealth were of any avail. The earl of Thanet pleaded his good deeds in behalf of parliament in 1648,

[1] It was mainly the towns and a few Cavalier manor-houses like Knowlton Court that occupied Kelsey's attention; but the movements of more than one hundred Kentish families were also noted and regularly reported to Secretary Thurloe.—BM, Add. MS 34013–34014.

[2] Thurloe, IV, pp. 224–5, 293. The major-generals in Wales and East Anglia came to a similar conclusion: P. H. Hardacre, *The Royalists during the Puritan Revolution*, 1956, p. 127. I doubt whether Professor Hardacre's conclusion, that the royalists whom the major-generals most feared were not the "landed royalists," is correct. Those whom Kelsey referred to were not landless, but small gentry, often minor branches of county families.

and his appointment by Cromwell as sheriff of Kent in 1654; but he pleaded in vain. The administration of Thomas Kelsey was as severe as it was just; and this fact, coupled with the large number of delinquents in the county, rendered his 'precinct' the only one, it seems, in which the yield of the tax proved sufficient, with a small margin, to cover the pay of the militia for which it was intended.[1] In the eighteen months during which it was levied it totalled £3,936. Of this sum, Edward Hales of Tunstall, having recently succeeded to his grandfather's great estates, contributed nearly one quarter; his income was over £6,000 per annum, and he paid no less than £302 every six months. The earl of Thanet paid, upon his Kentish estates, £157 every six months; the Darells of Calehill, £68; Richard Thornhill of Olantighe, £63; and Sir Thomas Peyton of Knowlton, £27. That the expense of administering the tax was under 9 per cent of total receipts bears fair testimony to the efficiency of Kelsey's régime.[2]

In controlling the elections to the new Cromwellian parliament, Major-General Kelsey was less successful than in levying the decimation tax. The simple fact was that military rule could extract money from people's pockets, but it could not alter their political convictions or dispense with the age-old social structure of the county. The disfranchisement of Hythe and New Romney, and the reduction in the representation of Rochester, Maidstone, Dover, Sandwich, and Queenborough to one member apiece, may have been intended to forestall the election of Cavaliers: for it was in the towns, Kelsey believed, that royalist influence was most powerful. Nevertheless, the electoral structure of the shire was fundamentally the same in the 'fifties as that through which Sir Edward Dering and his

[1] According to CSPD, 1656–7, however, the pay of Kelsey's troops was £1,772 in arrear in Nov. 1656.

[2] SP. 23: G: 228, f. 26; BL, Rawlinson MS A. 33, f. 770; BM, Add. MS 44846, ff. 68 v., 70 v.; KCA, U. 455. 04; SP. 28: 159, Accompt Book of Decimation Tax for Kent; Thurloe, IV, p. 293. Numbers of delinquents mulcted (and their assessments) tended to decline: there were only 64 in the last assessment. Despite Kelsey's vigilance, many royalists escaped the levy, because the former local committee with whom they had compounded refused to part with its records to him. The expense in administering the tax totalled £353.

friends had secured their return to parliament in 1640. Precisely the same kind of gentry, moreover, were elected. In Kent, at least, it was still necessary to choose local men and to win support through the social hierarchy of county gentry, parochial gentry, clergy, and commonalty. Of the thirty-six members returned for the county and its boroughs to this and the following parliament, Kelsey himself was the sole outsider, and no fewer than nineteen men were members of the former County Committee which had turned traitor in 1648. Peter Pett reported that the major-general's influence was "too much undervalued," and Kelsey remarked that the spirit of the people was "generally bitter against swordsmen, decimators, courtiers, etc. . . ."[1] At Sandwich, the large electorate of several hundred voters was as opposed to Cromwellian interference in the 'fifties as it had been to that of Charles I in 1640. At Dover, despite the fact that the corporation were virtually nominees of Thomas Kelsey, "the rabble of the town" endeavoured to return George Cony, who had recently challenged at law the Protector's right to collect taxation under the Instrument of Government: "which will be hard to prevent," Kelsey commented to Cromwell, "if he be not secluded." Fearing "blood and confusion," Kelsey was ultimately forced to ask Cromwell for "commissions dormant" so that the honest party might know to whom to rally in event of emergency. There was "such perverseness in those chosen," he commented afterwards, "that without resolution in you and [the] Council to maintain the interest of God's people, . . . we shall return to our Egyptian taskmasters." In the end, Kelsey's suggestion was adopted for secluding from parliament those who would not accept the Instrument of Government as it stood. At least eight Kentish members were in consequence ejected: a higher number than in any county except Lincolnshire.[2]

Thomas Kelsey's failure to secure the return of suitable

[1] BM, Add. MS 28004, ff. 37–52 *passim*; CSPD, 1656–7, pp. 87, 416; Thurloe, v, p. 308.

[2] CSPD, 1656–7, pp. 87–8; BL, Tanner MS 52, f. 156; CJ, VII, p. 425. The eight secluded were: Sir Thomas Style, William James, John Boys, Lambarde Godfrey, Richard Beale, John Seyliard of Penshurst, Daniel Shetterden, James Thurbarne. Eight from Lincs. were also secluded.

members of parliament was symptomatic of a deeper problem: the lack of support for the Cromwellian régime amongst the Kentish gentry as a whole. This lack of support is strikingly illustrated in the history of Committee membership during the period.[1] The abdication or ejection of the greater gentry from the seats of local government was now virtually complete; and in Kent it was far more marked than in many counties—for example, Suffolk and Northamptonshire—where a number of knights and baronets remained on the Committee throughout the Interregnum. Whereas in February 1648 more than one third of the Kentish committeemen had been knights or baronets, at the end of that year only three of the committeemen were titled, and nearly sixty came of small parochial families like the Amhersts and Paramores, or were former officials like Peter Pett of Chatham Dockyard.

At first sight, it is tempting to attribute this change in Committee membership to a simple class cleavage in the county; but closer analysis shows that such a theory is untenable. In the first place, only a small proportion of the parochial gentry of the shire ever supported the Commonwealth and Protectorate: the vast majority were as antipathetic to the new régime as were the greater county gentry. Secondly, most of these parochial families were themselves so closely interrelated with the greater gentry of the shire as to preclude the likelihood of class rivalry. Finally, the group of parochial gentry who sat on the County Committee was itself in a constant state of flux. Of the 58 members of the Committee appointed after the Rebellion of 1648, 44 had never sat before. In that of April 1649, when numbers rose to 94, sixty-four members had not sat on the previous Committee, and all but six of the new members appointed immediately after the Rebellion were dropped. The same kaleidoscopic pattern continued throughout the Interregnum, and it is perfectly clear that among the minor gentry of the shire, as much as the major, it was difficult to find support for the new régime. Probably less than one-tenth of the minor gentry appointed to the Committee, moreover, were active Independents, whilst many, such as the

[1] The following account is based on the names of committeemen in F and R, and CJ, v–vii.

Paramores, were undoubtedly anglicans and monarchists.[1] Since they were little more than temporary, unpaid officials, their political and religious scruples were of less importance than their administrative abilities.[2] The mercurial character of their allegiance, however, does help to explain not only why the Cavaliers were able to stage so many conspiracies in the county, but why Cromwell was eventually compelled to resort to the military regimen of the major-generals. The truth was that once the greater county families, the normal leaders of the shire, had withdrawn their support in 1648, the parochial gentry were powerless to govern the county, and there was no other means of controlling its wayward propensities than by a centralized military despotism. A similar problem, in varying guises and degrees, faced the Protector in most counties. There is reason to think, however, that it was particularly acute in Kent, both because of the county's strategic importance, and because the revolt of its leading families in the second Civil War had been more sudden and complete than elsewhere.

[1] E. 449. 34, p. 13, says that at the time of the 1648 Rebellion there were "about six or seven, or a few more busy pragmatical committeemen . . . patronizing the separatists and sectaries of the country," who numbered "so many hundred perhaps" (i.e., 600 or 700), compared with 600 or 700 knights and gentlemen *plus* five times so many thousand yeomen opposed to these committeemen and separatists. This, however, is a hostile source and no doubt greatly underestimates the numerical strength of Independency. The correspondence of Charles Nichols, the highly individual and attractive separatist leader in Kent, does suggest, however, that Independents were relatively few and that they were scattered about in mainly small communities (BM, Add. MS 44847–44848, *passim*). In the Compton Census of 1676 (*A Seventeenth Century Miscellany*, Kent Arch. Soc. Records Publication Committee, XVII, 1960, pp. 153–74) nonconformists comprised only a very small fraction of the Kentish population, although more than in other dioceses if the large walloon congregations are included. In the late eighteenth century Hasted, in his *History* of *Kent*, sometimes remarked on the great number of nonconformists in the former Wealden wool villages, and occasionally estimates their numbers at about one third of the local population; but this was after the first impact of the Methodist revival, which strongly influenced these parishes.

[2] On several occasions during the Interregnum the office of sheriff was filled by well-known royalists in Kent, including the earl of Thanet, Thomas Fludd of Gore Court in Otham, and a member of the recusant Selby family of Ightham Mote.

(iv) *The Rapprochement of Moderates and Cavaliers, 1657–9*

It was the paradox of Cromwell's rule that its very measure of success helped to bring about its own downfall. It is true, as has often been remarked, that in its later years numbers of prominent 'presbyterians' came to support the Cromwellian régime; but in Kent, as elsewhere, this was certainly not true of the generality of the gentry. The habit of centralization, though forced upon Cromwell by the intractability of provincial life, was necessarily unwelcome to a community where the grass-roots of the gentry ran so deep as in Kent. Precisely because of its impersonal efficiency, the military rule of Thomas Kelsey could not be grafted into a society knit together by personal bonds of kinship and custom. In Sir Anthony Weldon's day, delinquents had been befriended by their kinsmen on the County Committee, and the rigour of the law had still been tempered by many deeds of kindness and courtesy. Under Thomas Kelsey's regimen, however, no such forbearance was tolerated. "Was I made a commissioner to do good or favour to my friends?" one of Kelsey's officials angrily replied to Henry Oxinden, when such forbearance was sought; "what justice had that been? . . . I never thought so, but to serve the state."[1] To serve the state: that was the essential principle of the new régime: whereas the unwritten code of Kentish life was rather the service of the county community, with all the personal influence, compromise, and modification which that code entailed.

Equally inimical to any lasting sympathy between the new régime and the community of Kent was the insecurity of the government, and the atmosphere of tension and suspicion it engendered. This sense of insecurity runs like a refrain through the family correspondence of the period. "Pray seal your letters well," wrote Henry Oxinden to his wife, upon one occasion,

"and write nothing but what if they be broke open may be seen . . . As for public news, men are afraid to speak one to another, though friends. Let none of my letters be seen, nor

[1] BM, Add. MS 28003, f. 278.

report any news against the present proceedings; times are now so as a man can hardly walk securely."

When the brother of Sir George Sondes of Lees Court sent to him from overseas for a loan, Sir George told him that he "neither would nor durst let him have it. . . ." The atmosphere of suspicion was such that he was obliged to instruct his brother's messenger "to return again as soon as he could. For I knew," he says,

"there would be jealousies upon me as long as he was here. I desired him not to come to me, or to speak to me in private. . . . Therefore I wished the messenger to return to my brother, and in a letter which I sent then to him, desired to be excused if I had some care of my own safety."[1]

As men like Sir George Sondes and Henry Oxinden doubtless knew, every detail of the domestic movements of more than one hundred Kentish families was regularly noted by Major-General Kelsey and reported to Secretary Thurloe, though the majority of these families were at this time entirely innocent of royalist activities.[2]

The sense of insecurity which haunted society in this period is also apparent in the life of the church. Though the influence of anglican prejudices and ideals was almost as powerful as ever in Kent, it was now rather in the realm of domestic pietism than in public worship that it was most apparent. Many of the clergy who had retained their benefices under the wing of the old County Committee had now been expelled under the more efficient regimen of the Protectorate, and became private chaplains to families like the Peytons of Knowlton Court and the Knatchbulls of Mersham-le-Hatch. Of approximately 450 Kentish benefices and canonries, 233 are known to have been sequestered or forcibly vacated, and the full number was certainly higher, perhaps as much as three-quarters.[3] These livings were now filled with a constantly

[1] BM, Add. MS 28003, f. 327; Harleian Miscellany, x, *Sir George Sondes his Plain Narrative*, p. 55.

[2] Based on BM, Add. MS 34013–34014 (movements of suspected persons).

[3] These figures are based on many references in Hasted, *passim*, and on A. G. Matthews, *Walker Revised*, 1948, pp. 209–28.

changing succession of ministers who rarely struck deep roots in their parishes. Under the old régime, an incumbency like that of Barnabas Knell, who was vicar of Reculver-cum-Hoath for 44 years, or of John Smith, rector of Wickhambreaux apparently for over 40 years, enabled a couple of generations to grow up to maturity under the familiar ways of a single pastor. The parishioners may or may not have welcomed such lack of variety, but it is indisputable that the influence of continuity and custom had been profound. During the Interregnum, by contrast, all possibility of continuity vanished. At Boughton Malberbe, Robert Barrell's incumbency of 32 years was now followed by a succession of at least five ministers before 1659; at Northbourne-cum-Sholden, Edward Nicholls's of 22 years was followed by five ministers within four years.[1] It is evident that such rapid changes, whether desirable in other ways or not, were not conducive to stability in the life of the church or the village community.

Despite the fact, therefore, that most of the Kentish gentry, in order to repair the ravages to their estates, acquiesced in an outward conformity to Cromwell's rule, the community as a whole was at heart opposed to him. The far-reaching power of the indigenous clans of the county still worked, if now in a hidden and half-conscious way, through countless secret channels against him. Such families had no special love for the Stuarts; but the ways of life to which they were accustomed could not survive without a more stable form of government than that of the Protectorate. They could not or would not support the public proscription of anglicanism, whose rites and ceremonies were still practised in secret in the chapels and prayer-closets of many Kentish manor-houses.[2] They longed to return to the old days before the war, which seemed in retrospect, however mistakenly, so placid and secure; days when there had been no army, no major-generals, no restless plotting, no sectarian experimentation, and no incessant spying upon those quiet homes whose unquestioned dominion

[1] *Ibid.*, pp. 210–11, 220, 223, 225.

[2] The children of Richard Fogge of Danescourt in Tilmanstone, for example, were still baptized "in the old way *cum signo crucis*."—AC, v, p. 113; cf. p. 115.

and ordered, tranquil life was, with all its faults, the only kind of existence they understood. They could not for ever remain excluded from their inherited place at the seat of county government without a far more drastic social revolution than Cromwell himself contemplated. They had failed to regain their ruling position by rebellion in 1648; but when the history of that rebellion came to be written in the 'fifties, by the graphic pen of Matthew Carter of Great Winchcombe, one of his fellow-countrymen apostrophized him:

"Then lead the way, and we will learn of thee
Anew to spell our misled loyalty . . .
No more shall Kent hang down her drooping head
And sadly tell the number of her dead,
But bless her overthrow, as proud that thou
Hast taught her thus the way to conquest now."[1]

Such poetic effusions, which were common at the time, may seem merely sentimental, but they were none the less both popular and influential.

By the time of the death of Oliver Cromwell, the Kentish moderates were more ready to join hands again with the Cavaliers than they had been at any time since the king's execution in 1649. The futility of the government of Richard Cromwell undoubtedly confirmed their willingness for a rapprochement; and by the time of Richard's abdication the same desire was becoming apparent in many other parts of the country. For if the success of the Cromwellian rule was based upon the victory of the nation-state over the county community, it also, in the end, created a nation-wide craving to return to the older forms of society and government whose genius was essentially provincial and local. In most counties, I believe, this craving was a far deeper factor in the restoration of the monarchy than sentimental attachment to the king. Much of the secret of the success of General Monck in restoring Charles II depended on the fact that in so many counties, severally and independently, the gentry united to present their own *local* petitions in favour of a restored parliament and a more stable form of government.

[1] Carter, pp. 213–14 [211–12].

IX

THE COMMUNITY OF KENT AND THE RESTORATION, 1659–60

IN THE MAZE of political events following Cromwell's death, it is essential to keep a firm hold on the end of the story, and relate events to the gradual rapprochement of parties whose union made the king's ultimate restoration inevitable. In Kent these parties comprised, on the one hand, the small group of Cavaliers, and the large group of moderate royalists (or former 'neuters'); and on the other hand, first, the old committeemen or members of the pre-1648 County Committee, who were for the most part now barely distinct from the moderate royalists; secondly, the small clique of republican committeemen, who had supported the king's execution but generally speaking opposed the Protectorate; and thirdly, the more moderate Cromwellian committeemen, composed of parochial gentry, whose sympathies were often equivocal but who came gradually to align themselves with General Monck. These groups were not 'parties' in the modern sense of the word, of course. None of them were held together by any formal party organization. Indeed, it was the looseness of their political and institutional ties that rendered their ultimate reunion possible. They were paralleled by similar parties in other counties, though the numbers and influence of each group varied greatly from shire to shire.

(i) *The Royalists, 1659–60*

The first link in the chain of events leading to the Restoration was Sir George Booth's Rising in August 1659. Though known by the name of its north-western leader, the rising of course had connexions in all parts of the country. Nominally, Kent was joined in an association with Sussex and Surrey; but in practice, as in former risings, there seems to have been little co-operation between the county and its neighbours.[1] The

[1] Underdown, *op. cit.*, pp. 241, 266–8.

Kentish moderates played no part in the rising at all, since they were still suspicious of such conspiracies, especially those inspired from overseas. The Cavaliers, however, were once again active participants. Their hopes had begun to revive in May, with the abdication of Richard Cromwell and the dissensions in the reinstated Rump. Their leader was still Sir Thomas Peyton, who had returned to Knowlton Court in March, after four years of more or less continuous imprisonment. Two other Kentishmen had challenged Peyton's right to lead the local royalists: the aging 'presbyterian,' Sir William Waller, and the amorous young peer, Heneage Finch, earl of Winchilsea.[1] Waller, however, though of Kentish origin, now had too slight a connexion with the county to influence its politics; whilst the Finch family had not yet attained the local ascendancy which they and three or four other magnates acquired in later generations. In Kent, in contrast with some shires, such as Leicestershire, it was still the gentry rather than the nobility who controlled the community and who must organize revolt. It was Sir Thomas Peyton who was favoured at Court, and he was supported in Kent by his neighbours Sir John Boys of Bonnington and Sir Anthony Aucher of Bishopsbourne.

These three colleagues were granted a royal commission "to treat with subjects formerly in rebellion," and spent the summer months in organizing a rising in the county. Through their friendship with Lord Mordaunt, the leader of the new royalist organization, the Great Trust, of which Peyton was a member, they maintained close contact with the exiled Court. Their activities were seconded by the same Cavalier group that had fomented the risings of 1648 and 1655: in the east of the county by the Haleses of Tunstall, the Braemeses of Blackmansbury, the Culpepers of Hackington, the Kingsleys of Ickham, the Wilsfords of Ileden, and the Bests and Robertses of Canterbury; in the west and south by Lord Tufton of Hothfield, Sir John Tufton of Le Mote, Viscount Strangford of Westenhanger,

[1] As ambassador to Turkey (1660–69), Winchilsea was reputed to have "had many women" and "built little houses for them." On his return Charles II remarked to him, "My Lord, you have not only built a town, but peopled it too"—with his illegitimate children.—G.E.C., *The Complete Peerage*, XII, ii, p. 778 n.

and the Courthopes and Bettenhams in the High Weald.[1] Several of these Cavaliers were recusants, and all were near kinsmen of one another. The Braemeses, Courthopes, Wilsfords, and Robertses were cousins; Strangford was half-brother to Thomas Culpeper and cousin of Sir John Tufton; and Sir John Tufton himself was brother-in-law of Sir Edward Hales and cousin of Lord Tufton.

At the new 'spaw' in the heathlands south of Tonbridge, this group of Cavaliers was joined by royalists from other counties and from London. Under pretence of taking the waters, secret meetings were held and plans co-ordinated for securing Sandwich and Dover Castle, in preparation for the arrival of Charles II and the duke of York with foreign forces. "Almost all the arms in the shops about London [were] bought up," and "notwithstanding all the pains that [were] taken for prevention," many horses were conveyed out of the capital, and numbers of apprentices left London for Tonbridge. Other supplies were acquired overseas and transported to Thanet or Dover, and in the confusion of the times many "dangerous persons" passed through the Kentish ports unobserved.[2] That the government allowed these activities to continue unchecked for nearly four months is evidence both of the weakness of an overcentralized state when bereft of its originator, and of a new spirit of self-confidence amongst the Cavaliers.

Two or three days before the rising was due to take place, however, on the 1st August, the plans of the Cavaliers were discovered through the interception of a packet of incriminating letters and the arrest of one of their agents, Lady Mary Howard. Faced with a restoration of the Stuarts, the Rump and the army leaders for once drew close together and acted with unwonted vigour. The day after their "Articles of High Crimes and Grand Misdemeanours" against Major-General Thomas

[1] CSPD, 1659–60, pp. 68, 223; CCSP, IV, p. 326; *Nicholas Papers*, IV, p. 180; E. 993. 7.

[2] *Ibid.*; CSPV, 1659–61, p. 53; CCSP, IV, pp. 348, 349, 367; *Clarke Papers*, IV, p. 31; CSPD, 1659–60, p. 61; Mordaunt LB, p. 34 and n.; HMC, X, vi, p. 206; E. 993. 1; Underdown, *op. cit.*, pp. 266, 267. At Tunbridge Wells certain "noble persons" had recently bestowed "great charge . . . to set a marble cistern in the well, and to pave it and rail it round."—HMC, VII, p. 84.

Kelsey had been promulgated, Kelsey was reinstated in his command and ordered to rejoin his Kentish adjutant, Colonel Gibbon. Within a few hours he and Gibbon dispersed the meeting at the wells near Tonbridge, and Colonels Blount and Rich a subsidiary gathering at Blackheath. The arms and horse of the rebels were confiscated and fifty or sixty Cavaliers were committed to custody.[1]

The Rump then unwisely proceeded to measures of uncalled-for severity, not only against the Cavaliers, but against the county as a whole. Additional troops were sent down to awe the county, and "scouting upon all roads and looking diligently to all ports" ensured that there should be "no going yet towards London. . . ." Travellers to and from Kent were refused passes, and an act was passed to compel householders to give an account of lodgers, horses, arms, and ammunition. Inhabitants suspected of disaffection and dangerous to the peace of the county were arrested, and the manor-houses of both Cavaliers and moderates were searched for horses and arms.[2] After a lapse of three years, the Kentish Committee of Sequestration was revived, along with those in other counties, and royalist estates again became a prey to the activities of informers. With the revival of these activities, the moderates at last came to realize that there could be no permanent prospect of security under the present régime. The Protector's tactics had at least kept them from actively joining the Cavaliers, but the political measures adopted by the Rump helped to reunite them.

In spite—or perhaps because—of the successful measures taken against them, the royalists' hopes rose steadily in Kent and other counties during the winter of 1659–60. Cavaliers arriving from Flanders "talked stoutly as if they were cocksure of the game. . . ." One optimistic emigré declared that the number of troops "now controlling in Kent is . . . not more than 250 horse and foot," and that "if 1,000 soldiers were transported to give leave to their friends to rise, the work

[1] CSPD, 1659–60, pp. 48–87 *passim*; CCSP, IV, pp. 308, 313, 326; CSPV, 1659–61, p. 53; E. 993. 7; E. 993. 8; E. 993. 11.

[2] BM, Add. MS 34167, f. 45; CSPD, 1659–60, *passim*; HMC, *Bath*, II, p. 137.

would succeed." Off the Kentish coast the newly knighted Arnold Braemes endeavoured to corrupt the Commonwealth navy, and Vice-Admiral Lawson, having yielded to his overtures, left the Downs in December, and resolved with General Monck and the city of London for a free parliament. At Gravesend five companies of Sir Brice Cockram's regiment besieged their colonel in his chamber, seized their colours, and marched out of their quarters to Crayford. Along the Thames, Thomas Culpeper of Hackington raised a body of 100 horse, fell upon "a congregational troop" there quartered—probably the militia—and killed or disarmed the soldiers.[1] Through the good offices of John Heath of Brasted Place, an eager supporter of Peyton and an agent of the Court, these local riots were co-ordinated with the plans of the overseas government. "I shall put my accounts in a method in Kent as well as I can," wrote Heath, under the guise of a London merchant, probably to Mordaunt, "where I find great readiness to do our friend [the king] service, but much want of order in adjusting the accounts. . . ." ". . . If your Majesty could have landed 3,000 men," commented Mordaunt to the king in January 1660, ". . . Kent itself would have raised an army [which] might for numbers have reasonably disputed your right both with Monck and Lambert, although united. Sir, I am fully satisfied with the inclination of that county," whose loyalty was proved, said Mordaunt, in the Rising of 1648.[2]

The time had come to unite these conspiracies of the Cavaliers with a genuine movement of the county itself. In other regions, the royalists were coming to the same conclusion, and organizing county petitions to General Monck for a full and free parliament. At the instigation of Sir John Boys of Bonnington, the Kentish Cavaliers decided to launch a Declaration in the name of the whole county of Kent, and to phrase it so as to encourage the moderates to support it. The group of Kentish gentry who met in Canterbury, in January 1660, to publish this Declaration, was thus markedly different in character from the group of royalist conspirators who had staged the Rising of 1655. Its members were mostly middle-

[1] E. 775. 3; CCSP, IV, pp. 321–2; E. 775. 1; Mordaunt LB, pp. 89, 90, 142, 144 (where Culpeper is incorrectly identified with Sir Thomas of Hollingbourne).

[2] Mordaunt LB, pp. 142, 160.

aged men, moderate representatives of old-established families. Sir John Boys and Sir Thomas Peyton were now well over fifty; Sir John's father, Edward Boys of Bonnington, was nearly eighty, and his cousin John Boys of Fredville was fifty-five; Thomas Engeham, his fellow-parishioner in Goodnestone next Wingham, was sixty-two; William Somner of Canterbury was also sixty-two; Sir William Mann of Canterbury was fifty-five; and his neighbours Mr Master and Mr Lovelace were respectively fifty-six and at least forty.[1] Of these men, perhaps only Sir John Boys could be called a true Cavalier. The ambiguous political position occupied by Sir Thomas Peyton has already been described. Lovelace was possibly the Cavalier Lovelace of Hever Place in Kingsdown, but more probably the somewhat equivocal Canterbury citizen who had been imprisoned in Leeds Castle after the Christmas Rising of 1647. Sir William Mann and John Boys of Fredville had both been prominent members of the pre-1648 County Committee. Mr Master was probably the son of old Sir Edward Master, the Canterbury member of parliament who had been secluded, along with John Boys of Fredville, in Pride's Purge in 1648. The aged Edward Boys and the antiquary William Somner were both moderate royalists. The attitude of William Somner was probably typical of most of the members of this group. In the "impetuous storm of Civil War" he had "murmured not but made a soft complaint," eschewing politics, and devoting his energies to the composition of a treatise *Of Gavelkind, both Name and Thing*. In the preface to this treatise, Somner now recorded that the chief subject of his daily devotions was "our county's peace . . . with an enlargement and establishment of that blessing throughout the three kingdoms. . . ."[2]

The terms of the Declaration published at Canterbury in January 1660 ran to much the same pattern as those of other counties. It lacked those specifically local touches which had lent significance to the famous Kentish Petitions of 1642 and 1648. Weighing

"with sadness . . . the multiplied calamities wherein we are at present involved, how friendless we are abroad, and how

[1] E. 773. 51; E. 773. 53; CJ, VII, p. 849; CSPD, 1659–60, pp. 330, 349.
[2] E. 1005. 1; *DNB*, s.v. Sir John Boys, William Somner.

divided at home; the loud and heart-piercing cries of the poor, and the disability of the better sort to relieve them; the total decay . . . of trade, together with the forfeiture and loss of the honour . . . of the nation, and . . . the apparent hazard of the gospel through the prodigious growth of blasphemies, heresies, and schism, all which own their birth to the instability of our governors and the unsettlement of our government,"

the Kentish leaders desired the restoration of the members of parliament secluded at Pride's Purge, and a free election, without any oath or engagement, to fill the vacant seats. They were not able to obtain the county's formal ratification of the Declaration by presenting it to the Grand Jury at the assizes, as in 1642 and 1648. Instead, they sent copies of it to the corporations of Canterbury, Rochester, Dover, and Sandwich, and secured as many subscriptions as possible by canvassing each lathe and parish in the county in turn. They planned to convey the Declaration both to the Speaker of the House of Commons and to "the present great arbitrator of the nation's peace and happiness," General Monck.[1]

These activities of the Kentish gentry did not, of course, proceed unobserved by the Rump. The uncompromising Kentish Republican John Dixwell had now been reappointed to the governorship of Dover Castle, and was ordered to "have a vigilant eye upon that county. . . ." The ringleaders were promptly arrested and imprisoned in the castles of Dover and Deal. An over-hasty group of their supporters, coming towards London to present their copy of the Declaration to the Rump, was brusquely "hastened back" by the Council of State. It was impossible, however, to stamp out the new movement. The quiet organization of the Declaration in lathe and parish continued without any real check. The political power of the Rump was rapidly declining. The document was printed and published, though with the subscribers' names carefully suppressed, and a copy was presented to General Monck along with similar declarations from other shires.

[1] E. 773. 51; *The Declaration of the Nobility, Gentry, Ministry, and Commonalty of the County of Kent*, 2 Feb. 1660; E. 775. 3.

When Monck reached London, he told the Rump that he found the people in all parts desirous of a full and free parliament. The excluded members he desired should be re-admitted without delay, and a date must be fixed for the dissolution of parliament. Along with their confrères from other counties, the surviving excluded members from Kent resumed their seats on 21 February 1660. Two days later, Sir John Boys and his fellow-promoters were released from Dover and Deal, and their arrest declared null and void. It only remained to elect the new House of Commons, recall the lords, and invite the king to cross the Straits of Dover.[1]

(ii) *The County Committee, 1659–60*

While much had been happening in Kent to reunite the Cavaliers and moderates, the County Committee had been powerless to organize any effective support for the Rump. Its failure to do so was ultimately due, not only to the weakening of the central government, but to the gradual attrition of its own powers under the Commonwealth, which had bereft it of the initiative to meet a crisis. During his rule as major-general, Thomas Kelsey had made few friends in the county, and when his commission as governor of Dover Castle was terminated early in 1659, the Committee was left without an effective leader. The Rump resorted to a variety of expedients to restore its authority; but none was successful. An early suggestion to abolish the Committee altogether and substitute for it a junto of seven members proved impracticable, and was soon abandoned.[2] Next, the six Kentish Republicans who had returned to power with the restored Rump in May 1659 were reappointed to the Committee, in order to form a controlling nucleus: Sir Henry Vane the younger, whose local family seat was at Fairlawne, near Tonbridge; his brother-in-law and friend Sir Robert Honywood of Petts in Charing; his neighbours Lord Lisle and Algernon Sidney at Penshurst; and his former colleagues Sir Michael Livesey of Eastchurch and John

[1] E. 773. 53; CSPD, 1659–60, pp. 329, 330, 340–1, 349; CSPV, 1659–61, p. 114; E. 775. 8; HMC, *Leyborne-Popham*, p. 144.

[2] BM, Add. MS 28004, f. 45.

Dixwell of Broome. These Republicans were all men of more than ordinary ability; but at a time when so many parties were contending for power, their interests centred on the state rather than the county. All were members of the Council of State; Algernon Sidney and Sir Robert Honywood were sent abroad on foreign missions; Lord Lisle's local influence was neutralized by his quarrel with his father, the earl of Leicester; whilst the cloudy political and religious theories of Sir Henry Vane roused little enthusiasm in Kent.[1]

Finally, the Rump was forced to try and govern the shire through the minor gentry, who still formed the backbone of the County Committee. Here again, however, it was beset by insuperable difficulties. Unable to find the necessary number of genuine Republicans, the Council of State unavoidably retained most of the members who had sat during Oliver Cromwell's time—in fact nearly 60 per cent of the total membership of about eighty—and for the remaining 40 per cent appointed a miscellaneous collection of republican lawyers, aldermen, doctors, and small gentry without any real influence in the community. Thus of the twenty-two new members appointed in July 1659 and January 1660, ten were of old but insignificant families like the Owres and Romneys, five had only recently settled in the county, one was an unimportant alderman of Canterbury, and two were complete outsiders: the only member of any political weight was Sir Thomas Walsingham of Scadbury, and he had recently sold his Kentish estates, whilst his family had migrated to Essex.[2]

Instead of forming an effective barrier to the rising tide of royalism, the County Committee thus became a centre of warring factions. The Republicans were led by John Dixwell and William Kenwricke, and the remaining two thirds of the Committee by the very moderate Oxindens of Deane. The

[1] *The Memoirs of Edmund Ludlow . . . 1625–1672*, ed. C. H. Firth, 1894, II, pp. 83–4; *DNB*, s.v. Sir Henry Vane, jr, John Dixwell, Sir Michael Livesey, Sir Robert Honywood, Algernon Sidney; *Papers of the New Haven Colony Historical Society*, VI, p. 341.

[2] E. A. Webb, G. W. Miller, J. Beckwith, *The History of Chislehurst*, 1899, pp. 145, 152. Sir Thomas himself went to live in Fulham apparently (*ibid.*, p. 151). The above analysis is based on names of committeemen in F and R, CJ, V, LJ, V–VI.

former, of course, countenanced nothing but outright support of the Rump; whilst the latter gradually came to fix their hopes upon General Monck. Some of the group led by the Oxindens had held office under the Protectorate at Dover or Chatham, and were embittered by the Rump's neglect in paying their arrears. Some, like the Skynners of East Farleigh, had become entangled in a web of financial difficulties. A few, like James Thurbarne and John Maudit, seem to have been mere time-servers.[1] The great majority, however—some 72 per cent—came of minor landed families whose opinions differed little from those of the moderate royalists, though they had placed greater reliance upon Cromwell's ability to form a stable government. This last group did not really wish to rule the county, but circumstances had forced them to take the reins during a time of emergency. Now, as soon as there was a prospect of the major gentry resuming control in Kent, they hastened to abdicate. When ordered by the Rump to revive the machinery of sequestration in the county, they refused to do so because "the work [was] one of time and trouble . . ." A fortnight later, when sent a commission constituting them sequestrators, they curtly replied: "we have already signified our unfreedom to act as commissioners for this county, and we return you the box with the commission and other papers just as we received them." Finally, on 17 February 1660, when ordered to levy a six months' assessment on the county, no more than fifteen of the eighty-seven committeemen (and those probably the republican clique) appear to have executed the order.[2] In all probability, many of the remaining seventy-two

[1] BL, Carte MS 73, f. 382; CSPD, 1659–60, pp. 3–4; 1660–1, p. 1; E. 1016. 12; HMC, XIII, i, p. 697.

[2] CCC, pp. 764, 766; E. 775. 6. The names of these fifteen are not known, but probably they included the fourteen members omitted from the Restoration County Committee of March 1660: namely, Philip Sidney (Lord Lisle), Algernon Sidney, Augustine Garland, Richard Parker, George Cadwell, Edward Owre, Thomas Romney, William Lancaster, Thomas Plumer, jr, Thomas Butcher of Canterbury, Farnham Aldersey, Viscount Monson, Nathaniel Rich, James Temple. The list illustrates the fact that the newer families tended to take extreme political positions: Garland, Parker, Lancaster, Plumer, Butcher, and Aldersey were all relative newcomers, and Monson, Rich, and Temple had no roots in the county.

members had already signed the county Declaration of the Cavaliers and moderates for a full and free parliament.

So far as Kent was concerned, one of the main factors in the Restoration of Charles II was thus the disintegration of the County Committee. When the Rump eventually dissolved itself in obedience to General Monck, all but a small clique of the committeemen had already declared for the king. In the royalist Committee appointed in March 1660, they comprised half the total membership. Their period of independent rule, however, was over. After nearly two decades, the leadership of the community was about to return to its original governors, the same group of major gentry who had controlled the county during the elections to the Long Parliament in 1640, and for several generations beforehand.

(iii) "*The King Comes Again*"

With the exception of the small group of diehard Republicans, the community of Kent was now virtually united in favour of a new parliament and a restored monarchy. The hated Rump had at last agreed to liquidate itself. As the new elections drew near, the Kentish Republicans made a last desperate bid for power by trying to "beget a pernicious jealousy" between the Cavaliers and moderates. They published a declaration that "those who adhered to the king do still retain a spirit of revenge against all that were of a contrary party;" but their efforts were unavailing. Cavaliers like the new Sir Edward Hales, older royalists like Sir John Boys and Sir Thomas Peyton, moderates like Sir Roger Twysden, and former committeemen like George Newman met together and issued a declaration refuting the charge. "We do therefore declare," they said,

"in the presence of God, that we utterly abhor all revengeful thoughts and actions against any party or persons whatsoever. And as we have great reason to wish those divisions had never been born, so we hope and will do our utmost they may never be remembered, and shall look on all persons as the worst and common enemies of this nation that shall offer to revive them. In pursuance whereof we further declare . . . that we will thankfully acquiesce in the resolutions of the next ensuing parliament for a due and just settlement of church and state."[1]

The enthusiasm of the county during the elections for the new parliament recalled the hectic days of 1640 and 1648. In the county the election was organized once again by those same galaxies of Kentish families who had then galvanized the community. On the eve of the election, under the chairmanship of the earl of Winchilsea, the gentry met once more in the County Chamber of the Star Inn at Maidstone, the chief hostelry of the town. On the following day the son and heir of old Sir Edward Dering of Surrenden Dering was returned as knight of the shire, along with his kinsman Sir John Tufton of Le Mote.[2] In the boroughs and Cinque Ports, as in towns in other shires, extraordinary pressure was exerted by government officials and outsiders to secure seats in the new parliament. Ultimately, however, all but three of the eighteen members returned to the House of Commons from Kent came of local families. In the Cinque Ports, Admiral Edward Mountagu endeavoured to revive the customary right of the Lord Warden to the nomination of at least one candidate; but his pleas were completely ignored. At New Romney, the townsmen revived their tradition of returning two members of the Knatchbull family of Mersham-le-Hatch, on this occasion Sir Norton and his son Thomas. At Hythe, the corporation politely assured Mountagu of their utmost endeavours in his behalf, "could they prevail with the freemen;" but the freemen preferred to return Viscount Strangford of neighbouring Westenhanger House and Phineas Andrews, squire of Denton Court. At Sandwich, where Mountagu pressed for the election of a kinsman, the corporation, after deeply "wading into the business," replied that they had already concluded upon Henry Oxinden of nearby Deane as their first man, and for the second place supported their own faithful townsman, James Thurbarne. Nowhere, except at Dover, where he himself stood, was Mountagu's influence successful. Even there, it was only by

[1] E. 183. 7; *The Declaration of the Gentry of the County of Kent who have adhered unto the King . . .*, 20 April 1660. Other counties issued similar declarations.

[2] BL, Carte MS 73, f. 393.

withholding the date of election from Mountagu's rivals, and advising him to remain with the fleet in the Downs and appear in person "in the hall with the other gentlemen who stand for this corporation," that the mayor and jurats secured his election.[1] Everywhere, indeed, the resurgence of county sentiment proved inimical to outside influence though favourable to the Restoration: just as local loyalties had gained the ascendancy in every previous crisis of the period—in 1640, in 1642, and in 1648.

Such was the temper of the county in which Charles II first set foot as sovereign instead of as exile. On the 4th April 1660 Charles had issued his Declaration from Breda, and three weeks later the members from Kent took their seats in the new House of Commons. On 11th May, whilst hundreds of people from counties all over the kingdom made their way into Kent, the town clerk of Dover recorded that

"the king's Most Excellent Majesty Charles the Second, by the grace of God King of England, Scotland, France, and Ireland, . . . was proclaimed in this town and port of Dover King . . . by the mayor and jurats . . . accompanied with the Right Honourable Heneage earl of Winchilsea, . . . Governor of the Castle and Town of Dover, and divers other knights, gentlemen, and others of his Lordship's troops, with their naked swords in their hands held up . . ., all persons present being bare and uncovered. And there was great acclamations of joy and rejoicing for his Majesty, and crying out, God save the king!"[2]

The same day the earl of Winchilsea wrote to Edward Mountagu in the Downs:

"You . . . have prosperously steered through the Dead Sea of our calamities and confusions into that blessed haven of peace and unity, and nothing is now wanting to make up all that can be wished (almost in this world) but what your Lordship is

[1] BL, Carte MS 73, ff. 242, 369, 374, 393, 386.

[2] Minutes of the Common Assembly of Dover, quoted in S. P. H. Statham, *The History of the Castle, Town, and Port of Dover*, 1899, pp. 118–19. The king was proclaimed in Canterbury on 14 May: E. 183. 16.

going about: to bring a most glorious prince unto his most dutiful subjects."[1]

It had always been the duty of Kent to welcome foreign ambassadors and crowned heads with a certain amount of pomp and circumstance. These visitors usually disembarked at Dover and spent their first night at Canterbury, where they were received by the mayor and aldermen, arrayed in their scarlet gowns, and attended with guards of honour and "bands of music."[2] Never before, however, had there been such elaborate preparations as those now made for the reception of Charles II. After twenty years of repression, confusion, and warfare, all the carefree delights of a Kentish May suddenly blossomed into life again. The new royalist County Committee instructed the gentry to provide men and arms to be sent to Dover for a military escort for the new king. The rusty family armour laid aside in 1648 was brought out and refurbished, or hurriedly sent to the braziers of Canterbury, Maidstone, and Tonbridge to be cleaned and repaired. With their neighbours, tenants, bailiffs, and the trained bands of the lathes, every man with the king's colours in his hat, the gentry made their way to the ancient rendezvous of the county on Barham Downs, between Canterbury and Dover. There the earl of Winchilsea and his faithful kinsmen Sir Thomas Peyton and Edward Wilsford marshalled the nobility and gentry of Kent to meet Charles II. Many "gallant troops of horse" arrived from other counties, headed by the duke of Buckingham, Lord Mordaunt, the earls of Oxford, Derby, Northampton, and Lichfield, and a host of "gentlemen and persons of quality." As one observer remarked, it would be "endless to reckon the numbers of those that are gone" down into Kent, wending their way seventy miles and more from London to Dover. In Canterbury there was "so great a confluence of people, that hardly any lodging is to be had," and the justices had difficulty in "making of provisions for the great train which is coming along with the Lord General . . ." In London itself the city was

[1] BL, Carte MS 73, f. 447.

[2] Cf. CSPD, 1619–23, pp. 599, 609, 614 for the reception of the Spanish ambassador in 1623.

"... empti'd, all towards Dover strive,
And like starv'd bees for sunshine leave their hive."[1]

On Friday, 25 May 1660, at about three o'clock in the morning, twenty sail of his Majesty's ships and frigates came in sight of Dover. The following afternoon, with "all the people making joyful shouts, and the great guns from the ships and castle telling aloud the happy news," his Majesty landed at the beach near the pier, with the duke of York, duke of Gloucester, and many of the nobility. "Now did all put themselves into a posture," said an eye-witness,

"for to observe the meeting of the best of kings and most deserving of subjects. The admirers of Majesty were jealous on the king's behalf of too low a condescension, and the lovers of duty fearful on the other side of an ostentation of merit. But such an humble prostration was made by his Excellency [Monck] kneeling, and so fitting a reception by his Majesty kissing and embracing him, that all parties were satisfied, ... His Majesty walked up with the Lord General, a canopy being carried over his head ... In this passage the mayor and aldermen of Dover, with Mr Reading the minister met his Majesty, and after a short speech, Mr Reading presented his Majesty with a large Bible with gold clasps ..."[2]

Accompanied by General Monck and the nobility, and with "his life-guard all most richly attired," the king then made his way by coach to Barham Downs, where "multitudes of the country people stood, making loud shouts," and the troops "bowing to him kissed the hilts of their swords, and then flourished them above their heads, with no less acclamations; the trumpets in the meantime also echoing the like to them." The same evening, the mayor and corporation of Canterbury received the king at the entrance to the city with loud music,

[1] BM, Add. MS 34167, f. 45; Harleian Miscellany, III, p. 373; E. 183. 19; 'A Poem to his Majesty [Charles II], on his Landing,' printed in J. H. L. de Vaynes, *The Kentish Garland*, 1881, I, p. 77.

[2] Harleian Miscellany, III, p. 373; E. 183. 21; Statham, *op. cit.*, p. 119; cf. *The Diary of Samuel Pepys*, ed. H. B. Wheatley, I, 1904, p. 150, for additional details of the king's landing at Dover.

and presented him with a golden tankard "of two hundred and fifty pounds value: whence after a speech made to him by the recorder he passed to the Lord Campden's house, the mayor carrying the sword before him."[1] On Sunday the king "went to his devotions to the Cathedral, which was very much dilapidated and out of repair, yet the people seemed glad to hear the Common Prayer again." Afterwards Charles II held his first English court, and "at personal inconvenience he remained standing many hours to receive the respect and submission of the great numbers who came on purpose to kneel and kiss his hand."[2]

Next day the king and his entourage left Canterbury by the Westgate, and traversed the Forest of Blean and the cherry orchards of Teynham. As the Restoration traveller, Thomas Baskerville, described it, the route was a "way leisurely descending through the midst of pleasant woods, made sociable by several booths where the good-wives stand ready to invite you [to] taste a cup of their good liquor."[3] As the king passed the villages of Harbledown and Boughton-under-Blean, the road was "so full of people and exclamations as if the whole kingdom had been gathered." At Rochester

"the people had hung up over the midst of the streets, as he rode, many beautiful garlands, curiously made up with costly scarfs and ribbands, decked with spoons and bodkins of silver, and small plate of several sorts; and some with gold chains, in like sort as at Canterbury; each striving to outdo others in all expressions of joy."

During the afternoon the king "went to Chatham to see the Royal Sovereign, and the rest of his ships, where he gave Commissioner Pett so much honour as to receive the entertainment of a banquet from him." When he returned to Rochester, he

[1] Statham, *loc. cit.*; Harleian Miscellany, III, pp. 373–4; E. 183. 21. Lord Campden had married a coheiress of the Wottons of Boughton Malherbe, and inherited a house in Canterbury on what is now known as Lady Wotton's Green.

[2] Clarendon, *History of the Rebellion*, ed. Macray, 1888, VI, p. 233; CSPV, 1659–61, p. 155.

[3] HMC, XIII, ii, p. 278.

lodged at Colonel Gibbon's house on the Vines, where he received the loyal address of the Kentish regiments.[1]

Early on the following morning the mayor and corporation "presented his Majesty with a bason and ewer of silver gilt." After knighting Francis Clerk and William Swan, "his Majesty took the journey from Rochester betwixt four and five in the morning, the militia forces of Kent lining the ways, . . . the several towns hanging out white sheets," and the country maids standing—

> ". . . all in white by the high-way,
> Their loyalty to Charles to show,
> They with sweet flowers his way to strow;
> Each wore a ribbon blue,
> They were of comely hue;
> With joy they did him entertain
> With acclamations to the sky,
> As the king passed by,
> For joy that he receives his own again."

Bonfires were made as his Majesty came along, and "one more remarkable than the rest for its bigness," where the Arms of the Republic were burnt. At Dartford the loyal address of Monck's horse was received, and on the spacious plain of Blackheath the king reviewed

"divers great and eminent troops of horse in a most splendid and glorious equipage; and a kind of rural triumph, expressed by the country swains in a morris-dance, with the old music of tabor and pipe; which was performed with all agility and cheerfulness imaginable."

On the 29th May, which was the king's birthday, the royal procession left the Heath, and as the maids of Kent from "flaskets . . . full of flowers and sweet herbs strewed the way before him," Charles II entered London amid "great pomp and triumph."[2]

[1] Harleian Miscellany, III, p. 374; E. 183. 21. The house, built in 1587, still survives, now known as Restoration House.

[2] E. 183. 21; 'The Glory of these Nations', de Vaynes, *op. cit.*, I, p. 82; Harleian Miscellany, III, p. 374; CSPV, 1659–61, p. 155.

(iv) *The Community and the Restoration Settlement, 1660–88*

After nearly twenty years of strife, the dreams of the royalists had come true. Yet one cannot but wonder what were the inner feelings of the Kentish gentry, especially of the moderates, as the king's procession crossed London Bridge, and they returned to their homes in quiet downland valleys and the isolated dens of the Weald. The excitement had been as brief as it was intense, and the realities of life faced them once again. What did the two main political groups in the county—Cavaliers and moderates—actually gain by the Restoration Settlement?

In the months immediately following the Restoration, the Cavaliers seemed to gain most. The moderates confined their interests to county administration and resigned their share in the national political life to the Cavaliers. Both in parliament and at Court the latter played the principal rôle. The Kentish elections of 1661 presented a marked contrast to those of 1640. In the earlier year more than three-quarters of the Kentish members of parliament came of moderate and ancient county gentry. In 1661, three-quarters were thoroughbred Cavaliers and no less than half were strangers to the county. The influence of the Lord Warden was no longer repulsed, and that of the Lord Chancellor was welcomed. At Hythe, one of the local candidates stood down on hearing that the Lord Chancellor sought a seat for Sir Henry Wood, and actively canvassed for Wood himself merely "to gratify my Lord." Even the notoriously recalcitrant electors of Sandwich returned one courtier and outsider to the Cavalier parliament.[1]

At Court, the Cavaliers were as prominent as in parliament. The old county gentry were too set in their ways to adapt themselves to the new régime. When the earl of Leicester was recalled to Court, he seems to have felt himself strangely old-fashioned, and returned to Penshurst to spend his old age amongst his scientific instruments and books of devotion.[2] The

[1] KCA, U. 47. 3. F3/7; Sandwich Muniments, Letter Book, 1295–1753, f. 108; S/N. 14, letters of Sir Edward Partheriche and Sir John Mennes.

[2] R. W. Blencowe, ed., *Sydney Papers*, 1825, pp. 158–60 *et passim*. His excuse was ill-health, but it is clear the Court had no attraction for him.

Cavaliers, however, had no desire to bury themselves in the country, and enthusiastically joined in the universal scramble for places at Court. Some of them had been among the suppliants whose shameless begging disgusted Charles II on his arrival in Canterbury.[1] Scores now renewed their demands in petitions pleading their sufferings for the late king and their part in the Restoration. Many had done little enough to earn royal favour. Squire Beverton of Canterbury, for instance, had merely signed the Kentish Declaration of January 1660 and received Charles II at the city gates; yet he petitioned for the captaincy of Deal Castle, the captaincy of Archcliffe Fort, the auditorship and receivership of Christ Church, the customer's place at Dover, the receivership at Sutton's Hospital, and in fine any fitting office which might fall vacant.[2] It would be unfair to regard this egregious character as a typical Cavalier, however. Men like Hatton Aucher of Bishopsbourne had been devoted royalists since 1648, and Hatton's petition for office was justly granted "on account of his deservings and the great sufferings of his father," Sir Anthony. Similarly, the claim of Francis Lovelace of Hever Place was made in respect of his loss of office under the Commonwealth; that of Arnold Braemes for his important services in securing the fleet in 1659; and of the earl of Dorset for his mother's care of Charles I's children during a period of twelve years.[3]

If these petitions showed how the Cavaliers were orienting their ambitions, the sycophantic language in which they were couched illustrates the manners of the new Court. Two examples will suffice. A minor gentleman of East Kent, John Gookin of Ripple Court, addressed the king's admiral, the earl of Sandwich, in the following terms:

"The notes of your nobleness, as they have engaged the world to your honour, so it is the height of my ambition to be registered in the number of the meanest of your servants; the generous demonstration of those late undeserved favours re-

[1] *The Continuation of the Life of Edward, earl of Clarendon*, 3rd edn, 1761, II, pp. 8–9.

[2] CSPD, 1660–1, pp. 14, 88, 155, 348. 'Squire' was his Christian name, not his rank.

[3] CSPD, 1660–1, pp. 139, 143, 152, 155, 341, 575.

ceived from your Lordship in my late entertainment abroad gave me a complete evidence, as of your worth, so of those imbrued principles of honour, which abundantly flow from you, wherein . . . God . . . hath selected you as a vessel of honour . . . Ride on triumphantly, . . . ride on, and the God of peace . . . remunerate your exemplar [*sic*] virtues. . . ."

The purport of these phrases and a dozen further lines in the same vein was a simple request for the captaincy of a garrison.[1] The second example comes from West Kent. In a declaration of loyalty to Charles II, thirty-five royalist clergy professed that their sole desire was that God might

"bless you with length of days, and crown you with His lovingkindness and tender mercies and be a wall of fire round about you, to scare away all foreign invaders, and preserve you in safety from domestic conspiracies, and so fasten you as a nail in a sure place that your throne being established in righteousness, your crown may never be shaken till you change it for that immarcessible crown of glory which is prepared in the highest heavens . . ."[2]

No doubt extravagant language is the prerogative of courtiers in any age; but hitherto country gentry and clergy had usually —though certainly not always—spoken in more sensible terms. The times, however, were changed. Eleven years of exile had wrought a transformation in Court society, and aspirants to favour must trick their sails to the new breeze.

Meanwhile, the Kentish moderates were devoting their energies to the humdrum task of local administration. If the Great Rebellion had proved anything, it was the necessity of employing country gentry in country affairs. It was not for nothing that Sir Robert Filmer discoursed on their influence in

[1] BL, Carte MS 73, f. 433.

[2] *The Humble Address of your Majesty's most loyal Subjects of the Clergy in the County of Kent*, 23 Aug. 1660. Such declarations were frequently addressed to the king at this time by the gentry, and by gentry and clergy etc., but rarely by the clergy alone. Twenty-five of these ministers were of Sutton-at-Hone Lathe, that is the western extremity of the county, and many of them from the villages that had supported the 1643 and 1645 rebellions (see pp. 189 sqq., 215 sq., *supra*).

Patriarcha. As many as two thirds of Charles II's new deputy-lieutenants were selected from the older gentry of the shire, such as the Twysdens, Derings, and Knatchbulls, whilst most of the remainder had been seated in Kent for at least a century. Of the Commissioners for Corporations in Kent, four-fifths came of families settled in the shire for more than a hundred years.[1] Such men were not appointed to local office because they were specially agreeable to the new government: quite the contrary. They had supported the Restoration because they wanted stable government; but they had little sympathy with the Cavalier Court. They were appointed to office because they alone had power to govern the community. Ultimately, they proved as recalcitrant to the government of Charles II as to that of Cromwell and Charles I.

The leader of these moderates was that redoubtable provincial, Sir Roger Twysden. Despite his supposed royalism, Twysden had refused to attend the king at Dover in May 1660. He had sent his servant Richard Sutor "to meet the king coming out of Holland;" but he himself remained at home, recording in his account book, sadly and almost bitterly, each item in the £3 5s. spent in fitting out his servant with "armour, back, breast, and headpiece." With such a man as chairman of the Assessment Commissioners, it is not surprising that the levy of £70,000 laid on Kent under the Militia Act of 1662 dragged on for years, because the assessors could not agree upon the method of assessment. They apparently deemed it illegal to base it, as was the obvious solution, upon the fiscal experience of the Interregnum. On another occasion, when it was proposed to tax a man in each lathe of the county who held property in various parts of the shire, Sir Roger Twysden objected that it was contrary to the law and custom of assessment in Kent, and the commissioners allowed the unpopular proposal to drop. In 1668 Twysden was stigmatized by the Lord Lieutenant, the young duke of Richmond, as troublesome, unreliable, and disaffected to the royal service. Eventually, rather

[1] SP. 29: 4, f. 34; SP. 29: 7, f. 144; BM, Egerton MS 2985, f. 66. The numbers involved are too small for much weight to be placed on these proportions, but they show how the original group of families who led the county in 1640 re-emerged as its rulers in 1660.

than concur in the levy of coat money, Sir Roger resigned his deputy lieutenancy.[1] In fact, his position had not moved one inch from that he had taken up thirty years earlier in opposing Ship Money. In his eyes, however, such constancy was not a matter of disgrace, or even intransigence, but of dedication to principle. In the world in which men like Twysden moved, everything was governed by a cherished *corpus* of established law and local precedent: a *corpus* which in certain circumstances might be added to, but could never be fundamentally altered.

Although the Cavaliers seemed to be the immediate beneficiaries of the Restoration, their long-term fortunes proved far more unstable than those of the moderates. In endeavouring to replenish their empty coffers by obtaining royal grants and places at Court, they often neglected to care for their family property. In a community where values were still based on land, however, it was impossible to retain one's political influence for long without rigorous attention to one's estate. Of the 179 families whose history has formed the basis of this book, 76 per cent retained their ancestral lands and their position in the county until the Revolution of 1688.[2] The proportion of 19 per cent[3] who disappeared from Kent between 1640 and 1688 was probably but little higher than that which died out in the half-century preceding 1640. The 'mortality rate' among Kentish families was practically identical in both periods: the effects of sequestration and composition produced no sudden landslide in county society as a whole. As between moderates and Cavaliers, however, a dramatic difference comes to light in their ability to survive. Of the former,

[1] BM, Add. MS 34167, f. 45; Twysden, *Certain Considerations*, pp. lxxxii–lxxxiii; Sir J. R. Twisden, *The Family of Twysden and Twisden*, 1939, pp. 178–80.

[2] See Appendix, Table VI. The figure of 179 differs slightly from earlier totals, because two or three new families had been established and a few old ones had set up new branches. For sources, see p. 33, n. 3, *supra*.

[3] The remaining 5 per cent either did not found Kentish families or else cannot be traced with certainty beyond 1660: namely, Thomas Kelsey, John Browne of Orpington, Thomas Dyke, the Bothbys of Westerham, Andrew Broughton of Maidstone, Captain Joseph, Alexander Roberts of Maidstone, the Wyvilles of Wye. None seem to have set up local dynasties, however.

94 per cent retained their family position until 1688; of the latter only 30 per cent. Of the small group of former parliamentarians and Republicans, no more than 24 per cent retained their standing in the county. Thus of the 47 Kentish families who adopted extreme political positions, to right or left, between 1640 and 1660, barely one-quarter survived until 1688. Of this small remnant, moreover, the Dennes sold their estates in 1694, the Bowleses also had severed their connexion with Kent by that date or soon after, the Weldons and Sedleys died out in the early eighteenth century, the Thornhills and Braemeses were ruined by debt and sold out in Queen Anne's reign, and the Peytons, Mayneys, Richauts, Skynners, Liveseys, and Lovelaces of Lovelace also disappeared from the county.[1] Nor were these striking differences due to heavier fines inflicted on more devoted partisans during the Civil War: there is abundant evidence that moderates had been penalized by the state quite as severely as Cavaliers.

The history of Kentish families between 1660 and 1688 thus contradicts Dr H. E. Chesney's statement that "the actual land settlement at the Restoration was a triumph for the 'new men' . . . businessmen who had thriven under the Commonwealth."[2] In Kent at least the truth was the opposite. The older gentry who formed the backbone of the moderate party proved far more capable of weathering the economic storms of the period than the new. Not a single family of importance was established in the county as a result of the Restoration settlement. Of the families who had established themselves in Kent since 1603, only 29 per cent retained their hold till 1688; whereas 87 per cent of the gentry of medieval stock survived into the eighteenth century. More than two thirds of the properties sold by the newer families, moreover, were now purchased by those who had been established in the county since before the Tudor period. There is nothing surprising in

[1] Hasted, IV, p. 367, V, pp. 39–40, 142, VI, p. 256, VII, pp. 349–50, IX, pp. 288, 344–6, 594, X, pp. 80, 81, 91; G.E.C., *Complete Baronetage*, I, pp. 173–4; W. H. Bowles, *Records of the Bowles Family*, 1918, pp. 60–3; D. C. Coleman, 'London Scriveners and the Estate Market', EcHR, 2nd Ser., IV, 1951, pp. 223–5; Goodsall, *op. cit.*, pp. 108–12.

[2] 'The Transference of Lands in England, 1640–1660', TRHS, 4th Ser., XV, 1932, p. 210.

this fact. The older families not only had a longer tradition of careful estate management, but also many kinsmen who, if but for the sake of family pride, would prefer to see *their* influence maintained rather than that of newcomers, and would often come to the aid of their relatives in event of misfortune.

With the gradual restoration of their prosperity following 1660, these native families indulged once more in their favourite pastime of rebuilding or adorning their manor-houses. When they rebuilt, they now adopted the classical style favoured elsewhere. To the disgust of sophisticated observers like John Evelyn, they still usually clung to their old, unhealthy, moated sites, or rebuilt their homes round the core of the original hall or farm. Today, in visiting houses so deep in romance as Lullingstone Castle or Groombridge Place, one may be grateful for their conservatism.[1] There are still scores of such houses in Kent, scattered in all parts of the county: none of them palatial or outlandish, but all evincing that intense conservatism, shot through with vivid threads of change, which had characterized the community of Kent for generations.

The theme of this book has been the conflict between loyalty to the state and loyalty to the county which underlay so many political problems during the Great Rebellion. This conflict neither began nor ended during the period under review; but perhaps at no time before the nineteenth century was it more acute. The creation of the New Model Army in 1645, followed by the defeat of the Kentish Rebellion in 1648, seemed to herald the final victory of the state over the shire. The history of the Protectorate, however, proved that this apparent triumph was premature. Oliver Cromwell could neither dispense with the support of the county gentry nor subdue the independent spirit of provincial life. Ultimately, the very success of his policy of centralization created a craving to return to older forms of government whose genius was essentially local: just as the autocratic rule of Laud and Strafford had ultimately forced Charles I to summon that parliament of

[1] Tradition frequently modified the new style, moreover: Tudor woodwork and Jacobean panelling were re-employed in rebuilding Groombridge Place, whose plan also is typically conservative in retaining a 'great hall' as its principal feature.—Arthur Oswald, *Country Houses of Kent*, 1933, p. 51.

angry countrymen which overthrew his régime between 1640 and 1642.

The Great Rebellion was not simply an interlude, however, in English or in Kentish history. The community of 1660 was not identical in character with that of 1640. The hidden forces of social and economic change which underlay the triumph of the revolutionary party in 1649 were neither reversed nor halted by its defeat in 1660. The transformation of local life which the edicts of Charles I and Cromwell had been powerless to produce was gradually brought about by more subtle and irresistible influences. The dominant desire of the community of Kent, in 1660 as much as in 1640, had been to live a life of its own apart from the mainstream of national development. But despite its long and independent history, the county was linked by too many ties of geography, economics, and religion to remain apart. The Civil War had for a time torn many of its inhabitants from their roots. It had given them a glimpse of the habits of other counties, and bred a certain restless temperament amongst them. The increase of travel after the Restoration, and the growing popularity of watering-places, such as Tunbridge Wells, in some ways tended to weaken the links of the gentry with the local community, and create an artificial society divorced from the land. The widespread habit of strengthening family fortunes by marrying local heiresses ultimately set the gentry apart as an exclusive caste, since it concentrated land in an ever-narrowing circle of proprietors, and thinned the ranks of the minor families through whom yeomen had hitherto worked their way up into gentility. By the end of the seventeenth century, the grandsons of many of the old Kentish squires of Charles I's reign, like Nicholas Toke, had ceased to farm their demesnes themselves, and lived at home as mere *rentiers*, or spent part of the year in London or at Bath. The lovely home of Nicholas Toke at Godinton, with its strange carved friezes depicting the exercising of the militia, of which he had been captain for a whole generation, was by then no longer a manor and farmhouse, but a gentleman's seat: in the countryside but not truly of it. With the continued expansion of London, moreover, the threads of local life, both social and economic, became more and more drawn towards the metropolis. Though with the decline of the cloth trade there was now little industry in Kent, much of the county's agricultural output went to feed the milling throngs of the city. Here and there rich London businessmen, like the Bankses and Furneses, bought country estates in Kent and married into the original families of the shire.[1] At St James's the restored Court set the standard of manners and morality, and in the countryside the outward fashions and habits of society gradually changed with the changing fashions of the nation at large. In many ways it was inevitable that the deep diversities in provincial life should become assimilated to a national pattern of existence. Certainly that pattern came increasingly to be expressed in the kind of social and political activity that centred round Westminster.

Yet it would be a mistake to suppose that these developments were peculiar to Kent, or that there was any rapid or radical change in the genius of the Kentish community after the Restoration. The local power of the gentry had not been diminished but rather increased by the Great Rebellion. As the fortunes of the court-families declined, the old ruling families of the shire returned once more to the national, as well as the local, political scene. At the time of the Revolution of 1688 they again represented the county in parliament,[2] and many of them continued to do so until the first Reform Bill in 1832. The variety, the cohesion, and the obstinacy of that local life which formed the basis of their power, and which had defeated first the king, then parliament, and finally Cromwell, was not fundamentally altered until the nineteenth century. Each subsequent chapter in the history of the county community proved the truth of the old observation of 1642: "the Kentishmen are a people that are sooner drawn by gentle means than any way enforced; their affection must flow uncompelled."[3]

[1] For the Banks family in this period, see D. C. Coleman, *Sir John Banks: Baronet and Businessman*, 1963, and cf. p. 18, n. 1, *supra*.

[2] Besides the 18 members who sat for Kent, its boroughs, and Cinque Ports, twelve other Kentish families were represented in the Convention Parliament of 1689, and in all nearly four-fifths of the Kentishmen in the House came of the older county gentry.

[3] E. 128. 27.

APPENDIX

Table I

Marriage Connexions of Kentish Gentry about 1640 (Percentages)

	With Kent	With Sussex	With Surrey	With Essex	With Middx.	With Other S.E. Counties	With Other Counties
Whole County	67	6	1	3	7	5	10
East Kent	85	6	0	1	4	2	2
Upper Stour	72	7	4	4	8	2	3
N.E. Kent	61	0	0	6	0	11	22[1]
Weald	48	18[2]	4[2]	0	20[3]	0	9
Mid-Kent	58	11	0	1	3	7	20
Holmesdale	72	0	0	7	0	10	12
N.W. Kent	16	0	0	10	29	18	26

1 Mainly recusant families, such as the Ropers.

2 Mainly with neighbouring families in parishes in Sussex and Surrey.

3 The smallness of the Wealden sample impairs the significance of this figure.

Table II

Marriage Connexions of Different Social Classes in Kent about 1640 (Percentages)

	With Kent	With Sussex	With Surrey	With Essex	With London	With Other Counties
Peers	27	14	0	4	0	55
Baronets	55	4	3	4	11	23
Knights	63	4	0	3	11	19
Untitled Gentry	82	9	1	1	3	4

TABLE III

Income of Kentish Gentry about 1640–60[1]

	Aggregate Income	Number of Gentry in Sample					Average Income
		Peers	Baronets	Knights	Untitled	Total	
Pre-Tudor Families	63,972	4	9	18	58	89	719
Tudor Families	12,043	1	4	2	13	20	602
Stuart Families	10,239	1	0	4	10	15	683[2]
Origin Uncertain	2,324	0	0	0	11	11	211
	£88,578	6	13	24	92	135	£656

[1] Sources: PRO, SP. 28: 159, Decimation Tax Account Book; SP. 23: G: 6, f. 77; SP. 23: G: 34, f. 119; BM, Add. Ch. 66,169; Add. MS 28006, f. 277; KCA, Darell MSS; CCC, *passim*; CCAM, pp. 182, 1221; Proc. in K., p. 76; AC, xv, pp. 155, 389; Hasted, I, p. 229; *DNB*, s.v. Sir Henry Vane, sr and jr; M. F. Keeler, *The Long Parliament, 1640–1641*, 1954, *passim*.

[2] £438 if, as is probable, the 11 families of uncertain origin were newcomers.

TABLE IV

The Committeemen

Date of Committee	Number of Committeemen	Peers %	Baronets %	Knights %	Esquires %	Gentlemen %
1643 March	24	–	22	33	45	–
1643 Nov.	59	–	16	24	56	4
1648 Feb.	63	–	16	18	63	3
1649 May	94	2	7	7	74	10
1652 Dec.	96	2	5	6	77	10
1657 June	99	–	5	4	69	22
1660 Jan.	87	2	4	2	75	17

TABLE V

Assessments, 1647–9. Abstract of Charles Bowles's Receipts from the Lathes as Receiver General of the County Committee of Kent[1]

(The figures are rounded to nearest £1)

Assessment	1647 June 3rd. 20d.	1648 Mar. 2nd 15d.	1648 Oct. 3rd 15d.	1649 Apr. 1s. 10d.	1649 Aug. 9d.	Total
Shepway	9,748	6,452	5,623	8,196	2,845	32,864
St Augustine	8,219	6,607	6,188	6,912	2,969	30,895
Sutton-at-Hone Upper	3,922	1,946	2,781	3,357	1,571	13,577
Scraye Lower	3,505	2,360	2,700	3,111	970	12,646
Aylesford South	3,566	2,147	2,610	3,012	1,294	12,629
Aylesford North	2,542	1,873	1,809	2,469	895	9,588
Scraye Upper	2,566	1,930	1,811	2,240	1,000	9,547
Aylesford East	2,625	1,445	1,628	2,172	841	8,711
Sutton-at-Hone Nether	1,924	1,123	1,463	1,679	710	6,899
Thanet	2,040	1,220	1,150	1,414	661	6,485
Canterbury	720	515	458	528	168	2,389
Total	41,377	27,618	28,221	35,090	13,924	146,230

[1] SP. 28: 130, Bowles's account books as Receiver General.

TABLE VI

Estates of Kentish Gentry, 1660–88 (Percentages)

	Pre-Tudor Families	Tudor Families	Stuart Families	All Families[1]
Estates retained until 1688	87	69	29	76
Estates alienated by 1688	13	31	71	19
Purchasers of alienated estates[2]	46	12	12	–

[1] The history of the estates of the remaining 5 per cent have not been traced. See p. 323, n. 3, *supra*.

[2] The origins of the remaining 30 per cent of these purchasers are not known, but they were probably mostly small local landowners.

INDEX

[*In indexing place-names, the county is given only in the case of small places outside Kent.*]